The World of Benjamin Cardozo

The World of
Benjamin Cardozo

PERSONAL VALUES AND THE
JUDICIAL PROCESS

Richard Polenberg

HARVARD UNIVERSITY PRESS

Cambridge, Massachusetts

London, England

1997

Library of Congress Cataloging-in-Publication Data

Polenberg, Richard.
The world of Benjamin Cardozo : personal values and the judicial
process / Richard Polenberg.
p.   cm.
Includes bibliographical references and index.
ISBN 0-674-96051-3 (alk. paper)
1. Cardozo, Benjamin N. (Benjamin Nathan), 1870–1938—Ethics.
2. Judges—United States—Biography.   3. Judicial process—United
States.   I. Title.
KF8745.C3P59   1997   97-2053

To the memory
of my father,
Morris Polenberg

CONTENTS

ILLUSTRATIONS

Anna Aumuller. New York State Archives.

Hans Schmidt. New York State Archives.

Professor Oliver LeRoy McCaskill. Division of Rare & Manuscript Collections, Cornell University Library.

Louise M. Hamburger. Division of Rare & Manuscript Collections, Cornell University Library.

Cardozo and Chief Justice Charles Evans Hughes, May 6, 1937. Underwood & Underwood, Collection of the Supreme Court of the United States.

Louis D. Brandeis and Stephen S. Wise, ca. 1920. Courtesy American Jewish Historical Society, Waltham, Massachusetts.

Cardozo in the fall of 1937. Harris & Ewing, Collection of the Supreme Court of the United States.

Frank Palka and his mother in January 1936. Historical Collections, Bridgeport Public Library.

The jury in the first Palka trial. Historical Collections, Bridgeport Public Library.

Portrait of Cardozo by Augustus Vincent Tack. Collection of the Supreme Court of the United States.

PREFACE

I began the research for this book during the academic year 1988–89, which I spent in Jerusalem teaching at the Hebrew University. In the library of the Law School there is a particularly tranquil, inviting room in which is housed the personal library once belonging to Felix Frankfurter. Among the friends who presented him with inscribed copies of their books was Benjamin Nathan Cardozo. The words Cardozo wrote (or sometimes pasted) on the flyleaves were, to me, as intriguing as the books themselves. It was in this setting that I first came across *The Nature of the Judicial Process* and his other writings, and decided to find out more about him.

In most respects, it turns out, Cardozo led a rather unexciting life. He experienced no marital conflicts because he never married or even had a love affair. He had no thrilling, dangerous adventures because he disliked traveling and hardly ever went anywhere. He had no enemies (well, hardly any) because his personal style was conciliatory, not adversarial. His gentleness, integrity, and generous nature are legendary, and in these respects, at least, the legend is accurate. It is difficult to imagine a more erudite, conscientious, or dedicated jurist. Yet this most refined of men, greatly prizing civility and genteel culture, found himself dealing with most known forms of disreputable conduct: injury, infidelity, rape, robbery, and murder. "The sordid controversies of litigants," he once said, are "the stuff from which great and shining truths will ultimately be shaped."

As an historian interested in social aspects of the law, I wished to explore the context in which those controversies arose, to understand, that is, the relationship between the individuals, issues, and interests involved in the cases and the ways Cardozo resolved them. In drafting opinions Cardozo naturally emphasized certain aspects of a case and played down or even ignored others. His choices become understandable only when viewed as an expression of a deeply rooted system of personal values.

Cardozo is not the only judge, in his era or our own, whose rulings have been shaped by underlying convictions. But in his case, because of his self-consciousness about "judge-made law," his unusually revealing use of language, and the nature of the cases that came his way, the process was both more subtle and pronounced. To understand his decisions, then, it became necessary to locate the wellspring of his beliefs, a task complicated by his passion for privacy and the destruction of most of his personal papers.

In a judicial career spanning twenty-five years, Cardozo wrote the opinions in nearly seven hundred cases, some of which are still taught in law schools as models of judicial reasoning. I have omitted his decisions in such areas as torts and contracts, partnerships and real property, wills and estates, and insurance and workmen's compensation. Instead, I have focused on cases involving morality, scholarship, sexuality, religion, and criminality. My choice is necessarily eclectic, based on what I believe will reveal centrally important themes in his own life as well as in the broader development of American law.

ACKNOWLEDGMENTS

In the course of writing this book I have had many opportunities to present my findings to scholars in the fields of law and history. I received valuable suggestions from faculty members at the University of Michigan Law School, Indiana University School of Law, Cornell Law School, Boston University School of Law, the Nova Southern University Shepard Broad Law Center, Binghamton University, the University of Illinois, and the University of Wisconsin.

I am also profoundly indebted to my friends who read the manuscript and offered detailed comments. I alone am responsible for the book, but for their sound advice I wish to thank Howard Feinstein, Don Herzog, Michael Kammen, William E. Leuchtenburg, R. Laurence Moore, Steven H. Shiffrin, S. Cushing Strout, and Melvin I. Urofsky. Aida Donald of Harvard University Press offered encouragement at every stage. I had the good fortune to work with Camille Smith, a superb editor.

Many other people helped as well. Gerald Gunther generously made available to me copies of Cardozo's extensive correspondence with Learned Hand. Jeanette Lambert sent me copies of all the letters Cardozo wrote to her parents, who were his next-door summer neighbors, over a thirteen-year period. The late Michael H. Cardozo graciously answered several questions. For helping me obtain library materials, I am deeply grateful to Laurel Spindel, Steven Rosenblatt, David Goldston, and my son Michael Polenberg.

I wish to thank Jonathan Hand Churchill for permission to quote from the Learned Hand Papers; the New York State Court of Appeals for permission to quote from its Internal Reports; and the Board of Regents of the University of California for permission to quote from its Executive Session Minutes. I am grateful to Jonathan Marshall for granting me access to the Louis Marshall Papers, and to Hugo L. Black Jr. for permission to use the Hugo L. Black Papers.

Many librarians and archivists proved helpful, but I received particularly valuable assistance in locating hard-to-find documents from John J. Hasko and Gould P. Colman of Cornell, James D. Folts of the New York State Archives, Susan Tobin of Congregation Shearith Israel, and Judith W. Mellins of the Harvard Law School Library. My research was supported, in part, by the Colonel Return Jonathan Meigs First (1740–1823) Fund.

During the last few years I have offered an undergraduate seminar on Cardozo and the Judicial Process. My students have taught me as much as I have taught them. Their interest and enthusiasm sustained my belief that Benjamin Cardozo is, in truth, as fascinating a figure as I thought when, in Jerusalem, I first came across his penned inscriptions.

The World of Benjamin Cardozo

A Man of Fastidious Reticence

On February 15, 1932, President Herbert Hoover nominated Benjamin Nathan Cardozo to fill the Supreme Court vacancy created a month earlier by the resignation of Oliver Wendell Holmes Jr. Prominent lawyers, judges, and politicians of both parties applauded the choice. By virtue of his attainments, outlook, and professional stature, the sixty-one-year-old Cardozo was commonly regarded as the most suitable successor to the venerable Holmes. Hailed as "a profound scholar, a lucid and courageous thinker and a saintly character,"[1] the newly designated associate justice quickly won unanimous Senate confirmation.

Newspaper reports at the time provided little biographical information about Cardozo. Born in New York City in May 1870 and raised by parents who were devout Jews, members of the Spanish-Portuguese Synagogue, he had been privately tutored by Horatio Alger Jr., the author of popular books for young readers. Cardozo attended Columbia College, compiling a brilliant undergraduate record and graduating at the age of nineteen. He then studied law at Columbia for two years and was admitted to the bar in 1891. In 1913, following a successful career as a lawyer, he was elected to the New York State Supreme Court. But in February 1914, barely a month after he was seated, the governor offered him an interim appointment to the Court of Appeals, the state's highest court. Elected in his own right in

November 1917, Cardozo became Chief Judge in 1926, the position he held when designated by Hoover for the United States Supreme Court.

His writings, lectures, and professional activities had brought Cardozo considerable renown. In his most influential work, *The Nature of the Judicial Process* (1921), he posed the intriguing question: "What is it that I do when I decide a case?" His answer struck many in the legal profession as "an electric flash from the high heavens, clearing away the murk." Cardozo was also the author of *The Growth of the Law* (1924), *The Paradoxes of Legal Science* (1928), and a collection of essays and addresses, *Law and Literature* (1931). He was a founder and vice president of the American Law Institute, an organization dedicated to codifying legal principles. He served on the Board of Governors of the American Friends of Hebrew University in Palestine and, since 1929, had sat on the board of the American Jewish Committee. The recipient of honorary degrees from many universities, including Columbia, Yale, and Harvard, he had declined other distinctions, including, for example, an invitation to represent the United States on the Permanent Court of Arbitration at The Hague.

Cardozo had handed down pathbreaking decisions which demonstrated the law's adaptability to modern needs. That was the underlying message of *MacPherson* v. *Buick Motor Company* (1916), the ruling cited most frequently at the time of his elevation to the high court. Writing for the Court of Appeals, Cardozo held that automobile manufacturers' responsibility for the safety of their product extended not only to the dealers to whom, technically speaking, they sold the cars but also to the customers who eventually bought them from the dealers. The opinion rejected "precedents drawn from the days of travel by stage-coach" and insisted that legal principles should harmonize with "the needs of life in a developing civilization."

To friends and relatives, Cardozo expressed some misgivings about moving to the Supreme Court, but none serious enough to give him any real pause. "I find that I am rapidly developing into a myth. If I were not a Jew, I should expect to be transformed pretty soon into a Greek God," he told one acquaintance.[2] To another, he wrote: "Of course I like the applause, but it has been so dreadfully overdone that I can hardly look the knowing ones in the face . . . Such a fuss and bother, and see the ordinary creature who stirred it all up! . . . It is going to be a fearful wrench for me to pull up stakes. The excitement dulls my sense of it for the moment."[3] When his friend Judge Learned Hand warned that the Supreme Court was so bitterly divided as to resemble "a hell of a bear garden," Cardozo replied confidently, "It takes two to make a fight."[4]

Photographs of Cardozo usually showed him in formal poses, clothed in dark robes, sitting before shelves of leather-bound legal tomes. He was variously described as a "small thin man, with the pallor of a student and the eager eyes of a searcher for truth, under a shock of white hair," or "a picturesque figure, of Portuguese Jewish origin, with a thin face, lofty forehead, big-bridged nose, blue eyes and unruly white hair." "Monkish in his habits," he worked from early in the morning until late at night. He resided in an "old-fashioned mansion" on West 75th Street in New York City, but stayed at the Ten Eyck, an Albany hotel, while court was in session. He had few diversions, avoided exercise except for short walks, and took delight in his books. "He reads Greek and Latin for pleasure," noted one account. Cardozo was unmarried, another stated, adding: "The bachelor judge has led an almost hermitlike existence." To a reporter who interviewed him, Cardozo said, "There is not anything very interesting about me."[5]

In truth, most of what was interesting about him went unreported, either because the personal details were not known or because the press tacitly agreed not to print them in deference to Cardozo's sensibilities. Throughout his career Cardozo had politely but firmly discouraged aspiring biographers. After his appointment to the Supreme Court, when accounts of his life and work appeared more frequently, he was invariably displeased no matter how complimentary they were. In 1935 he tried unsuccessfully to persuade a publisher to suppress a book that discussed (in a highly flattering way, it may be added) the opinions he had written. He privately denounced the book as a "crime against good taste."[6] In 1937, discovering that some of his undergraduate lecture notes had mistakenly been included with books he wished to donate to the Spanish-Portuguese Synagogue, Cardozo urgently asked the rabbi to return the material, which he considered "so intimate and personal."[7]

"He never quite wanted anybody to penetrate into his inner life," Hand recalled.[8] Irving Lehman, Cardozo's closest friend and colleague on the Court of Appeals since 1923, phrased it somewhat differently. Shortly after Cardozo's death in July 1938 Lehman eulogized him as follows: "A man of fastidious reticence, he guarded jealously his personal privacy . . . Always he selected the field to which he would admit even his chosen friends, when he would disclose to them his thoughts and feelings; always he would reserve for himself fields from which he would gently exclude even his friends. He would be distressed if what he reserved for a friend were exhibited to the world."[9]

For the last few months of Cardozo's life, Lehman managed most of his affairs. In April 1938 the justice, who had suffered a heart attack and stroke in Washington some months before, was brought to Lehman's home in Port Chester, New York, to recuperate. Lehman supervised Cardozo's medical arrangements and kept members of the Supreme Court informed as to his condition.[10] It was at Lehman's home, eventually, that the funeral service was held. In his will, Cardozo left his residuary estate to Columbia University, but he expressly bequeathed to Lehman "any books in my library that he may care to own."[11] Lehman and Cardozo's executor construed this language to include all letters and personal papers.

In August 1938, when Cardozo's first biographer, George S. Hellman, requested access to the correspondence, Lehman turned him down: "I feel strongly that no account of Ben's personal life should be written and published and I am sure that he would feel the same way."[12] In September Hellman tried again to elicit Lehman's cooperation, promising "to consult you and to be advised by you in many respects," only to be rebuffed again.[13] Lehman conceded that Hellman, a friend of his as well as the justice's, would undoubtedly treat his subject "with affectionate reverence," but he reiterated the theme of his eulogy: Cardozo "chose what he wished to disclose to his friends and what he wished to hold in the solitude of his own self. I cannot change my opinion that neither what he disclosed to his chosen friends nor what he held back from them should be published for all to read."[14] Hellman made a final attempt in April 1939, indicating this time that Lehman's wife, Sissie, had "candidly told me that she felt more strongly than you did against such a biography," but was again refused.[15]

Turning next to Columbia University, the residuary legatee, Hellman learned to his horror that, in the interim, Lehman had destroyed Cardozo's correspondence. In October 1939 a university official explained that "Judge Lehman indicates that Judge Cardozo felt the personal letters should be destroyed"; only such material as related to public matters would be deposited at Columbia.[16] Responding to another inquiry about the papers, the provost reported that Lehman had told Columbia president Nicholas Murray Butler "that he is so clear as to Judge Cardozo's attitude on the matter of private correspondence that they would not suggest the release of anything of a private nature. We have not been able to make the point, apparently, that the papers and letters are a part of the residuary estate and might, therefore, appropriately come to the University."[17]

So his desire to protect his friend's privacy—not to mention his reputation, memory, and posthumous fame—had led Lehman to set fire to Cardozo's personal letters. This calculated act of destruction naturally excited the indignation of scholars who later learned of it. The reaction, many years afterward, of the Columbia law professor Harry Willmer Jones was typical. A librarian at the Supreme Court had told Jones that Cardozo's last clerk, Joseph Rauh, "says that the papers were left to the late Judge Lehman and he believed that they were destroyed by the Judge because they were so exceedingly personal in nature. This coincides with a notation in the MS Division of the Library of Congress, which says 'The main group of papers were destroyed by Judge Lehman' . . . it is clear enough that the papers left to Columbia were burned by that vigilant censor, Irving Lehman." The whole matter, Jones said, "was 'handled' all right—the way Warwick handled Jeanne d'Arc."[18]

Among the letters consigned to the flames were those Cardozo had written to his older sister, Ellen Ida ("Nell"). Cardozo had lived with Nell and had cared for her during many long years of invalidism until her death in 1929. One friend, who had seen some of the letters, described them as "very, very intimate and personal."[19] But Lehman's attempt to erase the written record did not fully succeed. The letters Cardozo wrote to friends and other relatives were, fortunately, beyond Lehman's reach. A substantial portion of Cardozo's correspondence has survived, as have the reports he drafted for the internal use of the Court of Appeals. Taken together, they allow a portrait of the man, however incomplete, to emerge.

The portrait can be enhanced by examination of some of his rulings. In eighteen years on the Court of Appeals, Cardozo wrote more than 500 opinions; and in six years on the Supreme Court, more than 170. Many of them dealt with technical, even arcane, aspects of the law. But certain cases raised crucially significant questions, and in answering them Cardozo revealed his innermost sentiments on subjects ranging from sexuality to religion, from insanity to criminality. Once, describing his indirect manner of expressing himself, Cardozo alluded to his use of "the veiled phrase and the uncertain line."[20] Drawing the veil and removing some of the uncertainties should help us to understand the man, the judge, and the legal world in which he dwelt.

1

Such a Delicate Youth

The Cardozos

On May 24, 1870, Rebecca Washington Nathan Cardozo gave birth to twins, to be named Benjamin and Emily. Nearly forty-two years of age at the time, Rebecca was the mother of four other children: twelve-year-old Albert Jr.; ten-year-old Ellen; nine-year-old Grace; and two-and-one-half-year-old Elizabeth. Rebecca, of course, did not have to manage this household all by herself. Her husband, Albert Cardozo, was a successful lawyer with excellent political connections. He had recently been elected a justice of the New York State Supreme Court, and the family was able to afford spacious Manhattan homes, first on West 47th Street just off Fifth Avenue, and later on Madison Avenue and 68th Street. Live-in help did most of the work: a coachman, and five young women, mostly in their twenties, who cooked, cleaned, and cared for the children. All the "servants," as the census-taker described them, were recent immigrants from Ireland.[1]

Shortly before the twins' eighth birthday Rebecca suffered a stroke and came under the care of Dr. William Polk, who would attend her until the end. The stroke eventually left her paralyzed. She succumbed to her illness on October 28, 1879, at the age of fifty-one. Her physician listed "cerebral apoplexy" as the immediate cause of death.[2] But even before the onset of her infirmity, when Benjamin and Emily were still babies, Rebecca looked worn beyond her years. In a surviving photograph she is hugging Benjamin, perhaps fifteen months old, who is sitting in a pram opposite Emily, and she is smiling faintly at the camera: a handsome woman, but with her graying hair and shrunken figure she might easily be mistaken for the children's grandmother.

Although cradled protectively by his mother, her arm resting securely on his shoulder, Benjamin, unlike Emily, makes no effort to smile. To the contrary, he seemingly recoils from the photographer, remote, withdrawn, even suspicious. Despite his guarded appearance, one can easily see why Benjamin, with his delicate, finely sculpted features and expressive eyes, was considered an unusually lovely child. "Ben was very beautiful as a youth, greatly resembling the poet Shelley," one of his cousins recalled, adding that she was always impressed by the "gentle, shy poetic quality in his face."[3]

His mother's death when he was only nine and one-half years old had a traumatic effect on him, as it also did on Emily and the older children. In a poem Elizabeth later wrote, "To My Sister Ellen," she recalled "the tears we shed together" when she, then aged twelve, along with her older sisters Ellen and Grace "wept our newly dead."

> Oh, joy and pain may fade throughout the years
> But not the tie was forged of those shed tears![4]

While Benjamin seems never to have committed his thoughts about his mother to paper, his feelings of loss are clearly evident in letters of condolence he wrote over the years. In 1921, writing to a friend his own age whose mother had just died, Cardozo expressed his sympathies and added: "To have had her so long, so far into your own life, is, indeed, a high and rare privilege, but I can well believe that the sense of separation, of the loss of the necessary and indispensable, is the more acute and poignant."[5]

Cardozo's phrase, "the necessary and indispensable," suggests his acute awareness of the lingering effect of his mother's death. Childhood bereavement has drawn considerable attention from psychoanalytic writers and theoreticians. Some analysts maintain that children who lose parents are predisposed later in life to experience depression, anxiety, and other emotional difficulties, while others insist that childhood loss has no discernible pathogenic effects. Yet all writers agree that the loss of a parent potentially disrupts the integrity of a child's personality, that children need to sever their emotional attachment to the deceased parent, and that the process is facilitated if an emotional bond can be transferred to another adult, "a new parental love object."[6]

"A young bereaved child needs an adult to serve as a focus for his reactions to loss," one psychiatrist who has studied childhood mourning concludes: "Without a continuous tie to a living adult, the child may not be able to maintain ego functions, to react affectively to the death, or to relinquish the narcissistic satisfactions found in the tie to the dead one."[7] For Benjamin Cardozo the painful void was filled by his nineteen-year-old sister, Ellen ("Nell" as she was always called), who seemingly accepted the maternal mantle for the other children as well. In her poem to her sister, Elizabeth spoke of the "soul-tie" she felt with Nell, who comforted her in times of pain:

> . . . and as I look again,
> Lo, the old play-name now comes back to me,
> Fraught with new readings of love's mystery,—
> My "mother-sister," runs the old refrain.

Becoming the "mother-sister" gave Nell considerable satisfaction. Kate Tracy, the family's loyal nurse and housekeeper for nearly half a century, remembered that "Nellie took care of her family beautifully." In fact, Tracy added, she "was absorbed in her own family, and was never happier than at a family dinner. 'I love you' and 'I love you' she would say, turning to each of her brothers and sisters, and finally: 'I love you, too, Kate.'" (Tracy's usual reply: "Yes, after a little hesitation.")[8]

Intrigued by the lifelong bond between Nell and Benjamin—who always lived together, at first with their siblings and later by themselves—relatives and acquaintances were uncertain how to understand it. Some saw it as mutually protective and others thought it a mutual entrapment. To Aline Goldstone, a great-niece, it was a case of "two people shut in through natural hypersensitivity . . . self-deprived of normal outlet[s] for affection—giving each other devotion and tenderness." Nell had "a heart entirely given over in a mother-sister devotion—a sublimated love—a family bond such as might belong to life in heaven—they lived in ideal companionship—above all things a *pure* life—a crystal purity."[9] To others, such as Adeline Cardozo, a first cousin, it seemed that Nell was imperious and domineering, Benjamin unduly submissive and indulgent. Nell, she remembered, "monopolized his later life. She was always regretful on the few occasions when he could not spend the evening with her in their [75th] Street home. There he played [piano] duets with her, and stayed reading with her or to her until she went to bed . . . So devoted was Ben to his sister that he called himself Nellie's doggie, and was amused when other members of the family teasingly and affectionately used this phrase."[10]

Among those who knew Nell and Benjamin best were Rabbi Stephen S. Wise and his wife, Louise Waterman Wise. Nell and Louise had a long-standing friendship, and the Wises were among the few who actually saw the letters Benjamin wrote to Nell before they were destroyed. According to Wise: "If the letters of Cardozo to his sister could be published (some of them were in my wife's possession), it would be found that they equal in loving tenderness and beauty the famous letters of Ernest Renan [the nine-teenth-century French historian and philologist] to his sister Henriette. I once asked him, with such delicacy as I could muster, why he had never married, and he answered quietly and sadly, 'I never could give Nellie the second place in my life.'"[11] Wise was referring to *Brother and Sister: A Memoir and the Letters of Ernest and Henriette Renan,* published in 1896. Like Cardozo, Renan cherished his sister, wanting nothing so much as to merit her good opinion. Renan, however, did get married, but only after Henriette had given her consent. At first, when she stormily objected, Renan told his fiancee that he "could never see her again until my sister's heart ceased to bleed at the thought of our meetings."[12]

While Benjamin's letters to Nell are not available, many of the letters he wrote about her are, most of them dating from the last ten years of her life, when her failing health was a constant source of concern to him. At once tender and solicitous, the letters express a growing sense of helplessness as her condition worsened. "I have been so upset and worried that I have had time and mind and heart for little beyond the sick room," he informed one relative.[13] He found it hard to be away from her, he explained: "My sister has no one here except a nurse; and if I were to leave them all alone, your philosopher friends, who would probably scorn to speak of so old-fashioned a thing as conscience, would none the less get at me . . . I should fancy things were going wrong as soon as my back was turned."[14] More than a year before she suffered her fatal heart attack and stroke Cardozo wrote: "She is silent nearly all the time, saying little more than 'yes' and 'no.' I am grateful that she has been spared to me at all, for she does not suffer; yet the ravages of illness are cruel and inexorable. I shall be glad when I am back at my work."[15]

When Nell died on November 22, 1929, Cardozo's initial reaction was one of sorrowful resignation. As he told a friend:

When the end comes, we generally reproach ourselves for this failing or that, saying to ourselves that we might have done a little better here or shown ourselves a little kinder there. It is simple truth to say that I have no such reproach now. I could not do it any better if I were to do it again. The credit is not mine. My sister's nature was so beautiful that to be good and kind to her was to be good and kind to myself, and praise would be no more due for the one than for the other. Often during her life she said to me that if anything befell her, I was to remember of our life together that it had been perfect. So I think it was.

His idealization of their relationship, however, did not cause Cardozo to deny his feelings of relief at being freed from the daily worry, anxiety, and responsibility of caregiving: "I feel very strange. I do not owe a duty to any one in the world. I think perhaps great criminals who have broken with society must have something of the same feeling."[16]

Writing to Melville Cane a month after Nell's death, Cardozo voiced his heartache more affectively if less self-analytically. Cane, a friend who was a poet as well as a lawyer, had sent Cardozo a new volume of his verse which included "Tree in December":

> Above the field, beneath a sky
> Heavy with snow stirring to fly,
> A tree stands alone,
> Bare of fruit, leaves gone,
> Bleak as stone.[17]

An anguished Cardozo replied: "The tree of my life is feeling the December blasts. Four weeks ago today I lost my dearly loved sister. I am indeed forlorn and desolate."[18] Nell had died after suffering a heart attack, followed by a stroke, as had their mother fifty years before. How could the twice-bereaved man that he had become not wince at Cane's final image? "The man trembled with cold, with dread," the poem concluded:

> Thinking of all things dead
> And his own earthen bed.

Cardozo's grief-stricken response to Nell's death differed from his more composed reaction when his twin sister Emily had died in 1922. "I lost my twin sister," he wrote to a friend on April 5: "I am one of a pair. She was married, but we remained companions as in youth. Her death is a hard blow."[19] To another acquaintance he apologized for a slight delay in replying to a letter: "A great misfortune overtook me, however, in the loss of my married sister. She and I were twins, and her death is a heavy blow to me."[20] Emily was the only one of the six Cardozo children to marry, and her husband, Frank R. Bent, was a Christian. Not only had Emily married, which may have been a violation of the family's tacit understanding that members would have a primary allegiance to one another, but she had also severed her ties to the larger Jewish community by intermarriage. Consequently, no Orthodox rabbi would officiate at her funeral. She could not be buried in the family plot in the section of Cypress Hills Cemetery reserved for members of Congregation Shearith Israel but was interred at Woodlawn Cemetery. Cardozo asked Stephen Wise, a Reform rabbi, to conduct the funeral service, and he wrote an essay describing his sister to assist Wise in preparing the eulogy.

In the essay he unintentionally described himself and Nell even more accurately than he did Emily. His twin sister, Cardozo began, had beautiful traits of character, among them "a warmth and cheerfulness and cordiality of disposition which made her love everyone, and which in turn made everyone love her." Many friends truly loved her, he said, and she returned their affection: "They were all precious to her. People who seemed tiresome or flat or commonplace or even a bit vulgar to Nellie and me were all dear to her. She saw the essential human traits, and what we often thought her blindness was truer than our wisdom." He and Emily were the biological twins, but Cardozo acknowledged that he and Nell were psychologically more alike. Another of Emily's distinctive traits, Cardozo continued, was her generosity. "She did not have many worldly goods. She saw others about her—her brother and sister—who had much more. Never in all her life did I note even a passing shadow of jealousy or envy, never did she seem to wish that they might have a little less and she a little more." Again, a telling contrast: between Emily, content with the little she had, and Benjamin and Nell, by nature somewhat more possessive.

In his tribute Cardozo implicitly recognized the distance that had developed between himself and Emily. During her last illness, he noted, she was comforted by her husband's "loving care, and by that of his brother who made his home with them, and who tended her with a devotion which has won my gratitude and affection."[21] Her brother-in-law, then, not her twin brother, was closest to Emily in her final days. True enough, Cardozo felt his chief obligation was to Nell, already a very sick woman, while Emily had a husband and brother-in-law to help care for her. Even though male-female fraternal twins are the least likely pair to be on close terms as adults, Benjamin and Emily appear to have had unusually little in common.

As fraternal twins they were no more genetically alike than any two siblings. Perhaps, as children, they developed their own secret or autonomous language and enjoyed a close relationship. But a common problem faced by identical or same-sex fraternal twins—developing a unique personality—does not affect opposite-sex twins.[22] The differences between brother and sister are therefore not surprising. They emerged clearly in Cardozo's glowing remarks about Emily, and in the reminiscences of those who had known her. Kate Tracy recalled that Emily was "very warm hearted and liked to help people."[23] Another acquaintance described her as "the one high-spirited member of the family."[24] And a cousin recalled that she and Emily had tried, as young women, to get Benjamin "to forgo his studies in the evening and go out with them, but with little success"; they finally told him: "You've got all the brains and we've got all the fun."[25]

In a formally posed photograph of the twins taken when they were about five years old, some of the differences that later manifested themselves were already evident. Although he has a short, boyish haircut, Benjamin, after the fashion of the day, is wearing a skirt, a matching jacket, a blouse, and leggings, and is holding a hat with a fancy ribbon at his side; Emily, the shorter by an inch or two, is wearing an ankle-length dress, with leggings that appear to match her brother's, and is holding a hat with an even frillier ribbon. Benjamin exhibits a stiffness and reserve, however, in contrast to Emily's more relaxed posture and open countenance.

Benjamin's relationships with his sisters Emily and Nell and the death of his mother, Rebecca, were among the crucial shaping experiences of his childhood. Aside from faded photographs, one of the few surviving documents from his early years is a poem he wrote for an aunt when he was about ten years old. Since the poem is about the New Year, it might have been written in late 1879 or early 1880, shortly after his mother's death. Entitled "The Dream," it tells how "a little black spirit" appeared to Benjamin while he was asleep, urged him to write a poem, promised to help, and handed him a pen:

> Seizing hold of the pen, for I never knew fear
> The subject said he Sir said I the New Year,
> Begin Sir—
> Each coming year brings new delight
> —What now is that, twas Aunty said goodnight.

Aunty I wish you had not said goodnight
You have arroused me from a worlds delight
Both spirits & dreams have flown away
Perhaps to come some other day
And when they do I promise truly then
You shall heare more from
Master Ben[26]

The confident use of language is striking in one so young, as is the self-assurance implicit in using not only his name but also the title by which he was usually addressed. The insecurity lies below the surface: only when sleeping and dreaming can he imagine a future filled with "delight"; the somber reality is represented by "Aunty" saying "goodnight"—a child's way, possibly, of referring to "Mother" saying "goodbye."

The World of the Sephardic Jews

Within a year or two after writing this poem, young Benjamin Cardozo began to prepare for his bar mitzvah, which took place on June 2, 1883. The family belonged to Congregation Shearith Israel (Remnant of Israel), the oldest continuous Jewish community in the United States, and played an active part in its governance: Rebecca Cardozo's brother, Benjamin Nathan (for whom her son was named), had served as president, and Albert Cardozo as vice president. The Spanish-Portuguese Synagogue, as it was known, was located on West 19th Street near Fifth Avenue. By the early 1880s, however, to accommodate the many congregants who had already moved into more fashionable uptown neighborhoods, the religious school for children was meeting in a rented facility at West 42nd Street and Sixth Avenue. Cardozo either attended class there or was tutored at home. The Congregation's spiritual leader, Rev. Henry Pereira Mendes, prepared Cardozo for his bar mitzvah.

Shearith Israel had been founded by Sephardic Jews, descendants of those who had been expelled from Spain in 1492. While most of the Jews had fled to neighboring North Africa, some of the wealthiest went to Holland. In 1630, when the Dutch captured Brazil from Portugal, hundreds of Sephardic families moved to that colony, where the Dutch West India Company permitted free Jewish settlement. Residing chiefly in Recife, an eastern seaport, they established themselves in business and commerce. In 1654, when the Portuguese retook Brazil, the Jews were again forced to leave. Most returned to Holland, but one ship, numbering twenty-three Jews among its passengers, was caught in a storm and sought shelter in New Amsterdam. Ten years later the English captured the city and renamed it for the Duke of York. By 1730 the Sephardic Jewish community in New York had grown to the point where it was able to build a synagogue. It remained the only one in the city for nearly a century.

The Sephardic Jews of New York took great pride in their heritage. As one scholar explained, the Sephardim "considered themselves a superior class, the nobility of Jewry, and for a long time their coreligionists, on whom they looked down, regarded them as such."[27] The influence of the leading Sephardic families probably reached its apogee some time in the 1870s or 1880s. By then, a congregant could boast, "the Portuguese Synagogue represented a very prominent share of the wealth, culture, social standing, business enterprise, of the Jews of New York. Its leading members were household names, and the assemblages that attended services at the Nineteenth Street Synagogue, had a charm and interest of their own which was unique in its day." As late as 1897, when the congregation moved into a newly built synagogue on Central Park West and 70th Street, it was remarked that "Rarely has come into one hall a gathering more representative of the intellect, culture, and social leadership of our community."[28]

Many of the families associated with the Synagogue had deep roots in the American past. Benjamin Cardozo's own great-great-grandfather, Aaron Nunez Cardozo, had emigrated to America from London in 1752; his great-grandfather, Isaac Nunez Cardozo, had fought in the Revolutionary war. Shearith Israel's "patriot rabbi," Gershom Mendes Seixas, had temporarily moved to Stratford, Connecticut, taking the congregation's Torah scrolls with him, rather than remain in New York City under British rule. Members of the congregation seldom missed a chance either to commemorate their ancestors' part in the nation's history or to emphasize the continuity between past and present. Once, for example, they mounted a historical pageant described as "a series of unusually beautiful and stirring tableaux representing the influence of Jews on the early history of America. As far as possible the characters were represented by descendants of the original characters themselves which added to the interest." Reenacting the important role Sephardic Jews had played in American history, congregants dressed themselves where possible in authentic costumes which their families had treasured for generations.[29]

Notwithstanding its members' identification with things American, the congregation adhered strictly to Orthodox Jewish traditions. Only men and boys were allowed to sit in the main auditorium where the services were conducted; women and girls occupied a balcony which was reached by a separate staircase. Services were conducted in Hebrew, pronounced with a distinctively Sephardic accent: To-*rah,* for example, or Shab-*bat* (rather than the Ashkenazic form, *To*-rah and *Shab*-bos). Prayers were chanted to ancient Sephardic melodies which differed from those favored by the Ashkenazim. Certain Spanish and Portuguese phrases remained in use: the congregant who lifted the Torah scroll after it was read was the "levantador," and the seats of honor reserved for the officers of the congregation were the "banca." But perhaps the most obvious contrast concerned the atmosphere at Sephardic services. For Ashkenazic Jews the synagogue often served a social function and the setting could be at once noisy and relaxed. At Shearith Israel services were austere and decorous.[30]

The structure was certainly conducive to services of this sort. The Nineteenth Street Synagogue, built in 1860, was widely considered a triumph of architectural design, for "without being extravagant, it is still rich and chaste." According to one description: "The ark is formed by a portico of four Corinthian rouge antique columns, with gilded capitals, and standing on pedestals of verde antique scagliola, having bronze mouldings, while the whole is covered by a rich entablature and pediment." The ark which held the Torah scrolls was enclosed by panels and doors of rosewood, over which there was "a projecting canopy holding the Ten Commandments, chiselled upon marble and standing from the wall." There were stained-glass windows, and gas jets which provided "a beautiful mellow light."[31]

The individual who presided over religious services in Benjamin Cardozo's formative years felt quite at home in such surroundings. Henry Pereira Mendes came to Shearith Israel in 1877 and remained its guiding spirit for more than forty years. Born in Birmingham, England, in 1852, he was educated at University College, London, received most of his instruction in Judaism and Hebrew from his father, and was a religious teacher in Manchester when the call came from Shearith Israel. An aristocratic-looking man, he had a precisely trimmed beard and moustache, and was partial to using a pince-nez. He had "a clear ringing voice of unusually sympathetic quality, precision of diction, and a rich and poetic vocabulary," an associate recalled: "Small of stature, he was yet possessed of a benign dignity which emanated from within. Soft-spoken, courteous, fatherly, and tender, he won all hearts."[32]

Shortly after assuming his post at Shearith Israel, Mendes entered New York University medical school. He was graduated in 1884 but decided to devote himself exclusively to the rabbinate and never practiced medicine. He threw himself into Jewish charitable and benevolent causes, helping, for example, to organize the Hebrew Congregation of the Deaf, and founding a school for handicapped Jewish children. He lobbied aggressively for Jewish interests, protesting against Christian exercises in the public schools, discriminatory immigration policies, and Sunday laws which penalized observant Jews who would not work on Saturdays. He was an early advocate of Zionism. He was also a founder of the New York Board of Jewish Ministers, its first secretary, and later its president. If all this were not enough, Mendes played an active role in the wider community, representing the Jewish faith on important civic occasions. Once he delivered the prayer at the opening session of the United States Senate.

Conscientious to a fault, Mendes abided by an austere moral code. He disapproved of such secular temptations as "low 'movies' and suspicious dance-halls." To combat their appeal, he suggested that religious groups of all denominations cooperate to provide healthy alternatives for young people as a means of encouraging the "re-creation of the good that is in everybody and its evolution into higher realms. Those were the days of saloons at street-corners, billiards and dance-halls in the rear of the saloon."[33] Like all Orthodox Jews he deplored intermarriage, and early in his ministry he wrote a play, based on the story of Esther, condemning the practice. Nothing better illustrated his unique way of combining religion and ethics than the sermon Mendes preached at the dedication of the Central Park West synagogue in 1897: "'How far is God a power in shaping your life or character?'—that is the main question. Have you ever stopped the unkind word on your tongue? Have you ever removed the impure thought from your heart? Have you ever abstained from gain through another's loss? Have you ever conquered yourself? Do you do anything for God's sake, remembering that He does so much for you? Then is He our banner, leading you to victory over those most insidious Amaleks—our own passions, greed, and selfishness."[34]

Benjamin Cardozo had surely heard a similar message when studying for his bar mitzvah. In preparation for the service formally marking his entry into manhood, Benjamin, like all boys in the congregation, had to demonstrate a knowledge of the synagogue service, the principal Hebrew prayers, the major Jewish Holy Days, biblical history, and the Ten Commandments.

But Mendes also laid great stress on living a moral life, as he explained in his little volume *Bar Mitzvah for Boyhood, Youth and Manhood,* which, while written many years later, reflected the views of a lifetime. He instructed each of his pupils to resolve: "I will, to the best of my ability, all my life live according to the spirit and word of God. I'll do my best to set the right example by making my personal life and my home life loving, and my business life, when by and by I enter business, honorable." The thirteen-year-old who was about to assume new responsibilities must also accept new obligations: "therefore you never will be a sneak at school, or a moral coward in business; you will never be ashamed of your religion and try to hide it." Religion had to be a force in everyday life, Mendes continued: "We consecrate ourselves and our lives when we have the moral courage to speak out for what is right and pure, to speak out against what is wrong and impure." The three R's of Judaism, the rabbi said, were Reverence, Righteousness, and Responsibility.[35]

These were the strictures that a youthful Benjamin Cardozo took with him on Saturday morning, June 2, 1883, as he set out with his father and sisters for his bar mitzvah in the Spanish-Portuguese Synagogue. The reading from the Torah that day consisted of Numbers 1–4:17, following which Benjamin was called to the Torah, recited the introductory prayers, and then chanted the prophetic reading, or Haf-torah. He intoned the verses in Hebrew, according to the carefully prescribed cantillation. A musically gifted child, who had been taking piano lessons from an early age, Benjamin may well have sung in an especially clear voice. Taken from Hosea 2:1–22, the selection opened with God's promise: "Yet the number of the children of Israel shall be as the sand of the sea, which cannot be measured nor numbered." There followed an account of the retribution that a wrathful God would visit upon a disobedient people, concluding with a vision of the Messianic age when a covenant would be made with all living creatures, great and small, when peace would reign, and when all Israel would place its trust in God:

> And I will betroth thee unto Me for ever;
> Yea, I will betroth thee unto Me in
> righteousness and in justice,
> And in lovingkindness, and in compassion.
> And I will betroth thee unto Me in faithfulness;
> And thou shalt know the LORD.

Cardozo, however, did not become the observant Jew that Henry Pereira Mendes undoubtedly hoped he would. Within a year or two after his bar mitzvah, a rabbi who knew him recalled, he "had swung away from all interest in ceremonial religion, and during his later life did not attend religious exercises at the Synagogue."[36] Cardozo always remained a member of Shearith Israel, and he felt a continuing debt of gratitude to Mendes, presiding, for example, many years later, at a reception marking his seventy-fifth birthday and his fiftieth year with the congregation.[37] But any lasting influence Mendes exerted over his former pupil derived more from his teachings about universal principles of morality than from his instruction in the precepts of Judaism.

The Tutor: Horatio Alger Jr.

Soon after celebrating Benjamin's bar mitzvah, the Cardozos went on holiday. The servants packed them all off to Long Branch, where the family had a summer home. Located on the north shore of New Jersey, just south of Monmouth Park race track and a few miles north of Asbury Park, Long Branch in the 1880s was one of the most fashionable resorts in the country. According to one account, "it aimed at exclusiveness, and endeavored to attract people of wealth. It offered brass bands on the lawns of the hotels, tents where pop and gingerbread were sold, hundreds of red, white and blue flags and pennons waving from hotels, carriages swirling in the dust along Ocean Avenue, and shooting galleries."[38] Its summer visitors, in the years the Cardozos vacationed there, included four Presidents of the United States. Ulysses S. Grant owned a home in the village, while his successor, Rutherford B. Hayes, stayed at one of the better hotels.[39] After James A. Garfield was shot by an assassin in July 1881, he was taken from Washington to Long Branch, where he died in September. Vice President Chester A. Arthur got the news quickly, for he was also spending that summer in Long Branch.

Among the prominent seasonal residents were Joseph Seligman and his family. A German Jew who had started out in America as a pack-peddler, Seligman had gone on to found a successful international banking house. He had five sons—David Joseph, Isaac Newton, George Washington, Edwin Robert Anderson, and Alfred Lincoln—all of whom were tutored privately by Horatio Alger Jr.[40] From 1869 to 1877 Alger lived in the

Seligmans' brownstone mansion on West 34th Street, and he also visited occasionally at Long Branch, since he was not only the boys' tutor but also their escort and travel companion and a family friend. The Seligmans and Cardozos were neighbors in Long Branch, and that is probably how Albert Cardozo met Alger and learned of his effectiveness in preparing the Seligman boys for admission to college (four of them attended Columbia). In 1883 he decided to hire Alger as a tutor for his son Benjamin and daughter Elizabeth.

Horatio Alger Jr. was a most improbable tutor for the children of Orthodox Jewish parents. The son of a Unitarian minister, he was born in Massachusetts in 1832, entered Harvard at the age of sixteen, and was graduated at twenty unsure of what career to pursue. After trying his hand at writing and then teaching in a private boarding school for boys, he entered the Harvard Divinity School in 1857, graduating three years later. In the fall of 1864, after spending a few years traveling abroad, offering private tutorials, and writing poetry and fiction, Alger applied for a position with the First Unitarian Church and Society of Brewster, Massachusetts. In November he was invited to become minister. At his installation in December— described as "a very pleasant occasion, not soon to be forgotten by those who were privileged to participate"—Edward Everett Hale, the well-known author, delivered a speech, and the Reverend Horatio Alger Sr. offered the ordaining prayer.[41]

On the surface the first year of Alger's ministry was a popular and successful one. But early in 1866 a boy in the congregation reported the unthinkable: that Alger had sexually molested him. With rumors spreading like wildfire, the congregation created a three-member investigating committee. It took only a few days to discover the truth, or at least enough of it to take action.[42] On March 19 the committee reported that it had met with two boys, one fifteen and one thirteen, both members of the congregation. "We learn from John Clark and Thomas S. Crocker, that Horatio Alger Jr. has been practicing on them at different times deeds that are too revolting to relate." The committee also said it had "good reason to think" that other boys had been molested. Describing the incident to the American Unitarian Association in Boston, the congregation explained that Alger had been charged "with gross immorality and a most heinous crime, a crime of no less magnitude than the abominable and revolting crime of unnatural familiarity with *boys,* which is too revolting to think of in the most brutal of our race—the commission of which under any circumstances, is to a refined or christian mind to be utterly incomprehensible."[43]

The language used by the committee—elsewhere its members referred to the "unnatural crime," "this diabolical transaction," and "the depth of depravity"—barely conveys the congregants' rage and sense of betrayal. Equally galling was Alger's unruffled response when informed of the allegations, "which he neither denied or attempted to extenuate but received with the apparent calmness of an old offender." Admitting only that he had been "imprudent," he "hastily left town on the next train."[44] Even more infuriating was Alger's request that the affair not be made public because of the effect it would have on his parents. Alger's letter, according to one parishioner, was "full of compunction of feeling for the disgrace he has bro[ugh]t on himself and the consequent grief of his parents and family, but not one feeling properly expressed of that remorse and penitence which ought to be consequent on the commission of such crime against God and the injury he has done to the cause of religion, to our society, and youth in particular. It is all too selfish to be sincere,—it is all in consequence of detection, and not in consequence of guilt."[45]

Worst of all, from the standpoint of the congregation and the aggrieved parents, the American Unitarian Association decided to cover up the incident. Alger's father urged the Association not to give the matter any "unnecessary publicity," promising in return that his son would never again seek employment in the ministry, and adding: "His future, at the best, will be darkly shaded. He will probably seek literary or other employment at a distance from here." So although the Brewster congregation requested action to "prevent his imposing on others" and sought advice "as to what further duties devolve on us as a Christian Society," the Association's general secretary responded evenly: "It is a serious injury to the church & to the ministry that such a thing should occur"; but "the injury is greater the wider it is known. Consequently I think that since Mr. Alger has absolutely taken himself from the ministry, & is never to bear its name or try to exercise its functions, it will not be necessary for us as an Association to take any action." It would be sufficient for the parish to pass a resolution of condemnation for the record, "not to be published, but only to stand as assurance of your own clear views of the case."[46]

Whatever measure of guilt or remorse Alger experienced was evidently expressed in a poem he wrote only days after leaving Brewster. Entitled "Friar Anselmo's Sin," it began:

Friar Anselmo (God's grace may he win!)
Committed one sad day a deadly sin
Which being done he drew back, self-abhorred,
From the rebuking presence of the Lord.
And, kneeling down, besought, with bitter cry,
Since life was worthless grown, that he might die.

The poem went on to tell how the friar aided a weary traveler and was visited by an angel who offered him reassurance:

"Courage, Anselmo, though thy sin be great,
God grants thee life that thou may'st expiate.
Thy guilty stains shall be washed white again,
By noble service done thy fellow-man.
His soul draws nearest unto God above,
Who to his brother ministers in love."[47]

The poem, it has been suggested, shows that Alger "resolved to expiate his own sin through a literary ministry."[48] The tone of the poem, however, conveys less a sense of contrition than of an absorbing self-pity.

Moving to New York City in 1866, Alger soon established himself in his chosen calling. A writer of boys' stories, he declared, "should remember his responsibility and exert a wholesome influence on his young readers. Honesty, industry, frugality, and a worthy ambition he can preach through the medium of a story much more effectively than a lecturer or a preacher."[49] His first effort, *Ragged Dick* (1868), told of one Dick Hunter, a poor, homeless, grimy bootblack who nevertheless "was above doing anything mean or dishonorable. He would not steal, or cheat, or impose upon younger boys." He also had the knack of being in the right place at the right time: he rescued a child who was about to drown and was rewarded by the grateful father with a job in his counting house. Gradually acquiring respectability by dint of hard work, he became Richard Hunter, Esq., "a young gentleman on the way to fame and fortune." The novel was an instant success, and the formula, once found, proved infinitely adaptable.[50] Over the next thirty years, Alger published more than one hundred juvenile novels. Despite a literary style so stilted that it occasionally bordered on self-parody, the books sold well, and won praise for their "clear insight into boy-nature."[51]

The heroes of Alger's novels were nearly always boys in their early teens, often from an underprivileged background; his exploration of their lifestyles provided an outlet for his obsession with boys nearing puberty. He spent a good deal of time befriending the indigent children who roamed the streets of New York, and he often slipped them some candy or a little money. He haunted the piers and docks where, in his words, "the friendless urchins could be found."[52] He liked to visit the Newsboys' Lodging House, and his own boarding-house room "became a veritable salon for street boys." As his sister recalled, he loved to sit at his desk writing while surrounded by youngsters: "Nothing delighted him more than to get a lot of boys between the ages of 12 and 16 years in the room with him."[53] Horatio Alger even informally adopted three adolescent boys who roomed with him, and whom he put through school or set up in business. In May 1883 one of those wards, fifteen-year-old John Downie, moved into his flat, where he remained for the next two years.

The fifty-one-year-old man who appeared at the Cardozo home on Madison Avenue to meet Benjamin in the fall of 1883 did not cut an imposing figure: only five feet, two inches tall, with a round face, balding pate, and heavy moustache, Alger was described by an acquaintance as a "little, unassertive tutor, with his complex of inferiority."[54] But he had impeccable credentials as a tutor. A Phi Beta Kappa graduate of Harvard, a man who knew both Greek and Latin, a widely read author, an experienced teacher— all of these qualifications surely commended him to parents who wanted the best for their children and who were, of course, unaware of his hidden past. In his own way, Alger was an erudite man. His novels, however slight their literary merit, were studded with quotations from Cicero, Horace, Shakespeare, Milton, and Pope, not to mention the Bible.

Far from glorifying the self-made man, Alger was a critic of cutthroat capitalist competition. Maintaining that "we all ought to help each other," he advocated "an endless round of charitable reciprocation." His heroes rose not to riches but rather to positions of respectability as a result of their innate virtue, and they always took the side of the weak against the strong. They cultivated good habits, such as studying and saving their money, and turned their backs on drinking, smoking, and "the seductive lures of the gaming table."[55] The boys in his stories craved, above all, the protection of an older man. The plots, based on the absence of a father, revolved around the boy's search for a substitute, usually in the person of a wealthy male benefactor. As Michael Zuckerman has shown: "Alger's every novel was a novel of nurturance, a novel whose dearest ideal was to be cared for and indulged, not to be self-sufficient and self-reliant."[56]

These themes and others appear in the novels Alger wrote during the two years he tutored Benjamin Cardozo. *Frank Hunter's Peril* (1885) and *Bob Burton* (1886) have similar plots. Frank and Bob are fifteen-year-old boys whose doting fathers have died (either before the story begins or early on), and whose inheritances are threatened by unscrupulous men who seek to wed their widowed mothers and who conspire to kidnap or even murder them. Frank and Bob, of course, foil the conspirators with the help of newly found father figures. Both books contain villains whose description fits the stereotype of Jewish moneylenders: Job Green, who lives on New York City's Lower East Side and lends money at usurious rates, plays only a minor part in trying to undo Frank; but Aaron Wolverton—"a meager and wrinkled man" who eyes rolls of bills "with eager cupidity" and has "yellow fangs which served for teeth"—is Bob Burton's chief nemesis.[57] The only romantic interest Frank is allowed (Bob is permitted none) centers on his benefactor's daughter, Beatrice, "a lovely girl of twelve" who treats him "in a frank, sisterly way, which Frank found agreeable."[58]

Some of the characters in *Frank Hunter's Peril* may have been patterned after members of the Cardozo household. Frank's trustworthy friend is named Ben Cameron, which is about as close as Alger could come to Ben Cardozo without appearing obvious. "Ben's" loyalty is rewarded—the novel ends as so many of Alger's do with a brief glimpse into the future—when Frank becomes "a junior partner in a prosperous New York firm," and "Ben Cameron is a trusted clerk in Frank's employ, and our hero will take care that his old school friend prospers."[59] There is also a maid named Katy O'Grady, a feisty, down-to-earth woman with a thick brogue who could have been modeled on one of the servants whom the Cardozos employed. (Kate Tracy had not yet joined the household, but in 1880 one Lizzie Murphy worked as a full-time nurse.)

Many years later Benjamin Cardozo was asked about his boyhood tutor. He replied that Alger "did not do as successful a job for me as he did with the careers of his newsboy heroes,"[60] by which he meant that he had not acquired the riches popularly associated with those heroes. He had, however, surely acquired the work ethic so close to his teacher's heart. Moreover, Cardozo may have absorbed elements of Alger's distinctive view of personal relationships, in which sexuality tended to be equated with unscrupulous men preying, feral-like, on trusting widows, and in which security was found only in idealized, nonsexual forms of affection: between a boy and his mother, or a boy and a girl who was like a sister to him, or a boy and an older, protective male or father-surrogate. To all outward appearances, however, as a tutor for Benjamin Cardozo, Alger did precisely what he had been hired to do. "I have finished teaching at the Cardozos," Alger wrote on July 1, 1885, "Bennie . . . has been admitted to college."[61]

Albert Cardozo and the Tweed Ring

Cardozo entered Columbia that fall, but premature death cast its shadow once again across his path. In less than ten months he lost his father and his older sister Grace. In January she had come down with the measles. The illness contributed to a case of acute lobar pneumonia which, despite the efforts of Dr. William Polk (who had attended her mother, Rebecca, six years earlier) proved fatal. Grace died in February at the age of twenty-four.[62] Then, in November, Benjamin's father died of complications resulting from kidney failure. For some years Albert Cardozo had quietly been practicing law. In 1872 he had resigned as a justice of the New York State Supreme Court in order to avoid probable impeachment for malfeasance in office. This was an event of seismic significance in his life and that of his family, ending a brilliant public career and, according to some accounts, shaping the career of his son Benjamin.

Born in Philadelphia in 1828 but raised in New York City, Albert Cardozo read law with a prominent attorney and was admitted to the bar at the age of twenty-one. Working steadily to build a successful practice, he also entered Democratic party politics, joining forces with Mayor Fernando Wood and the Tammany Hall stalwart William M. Tweed. In 1863 he was rewarded with a nomination to the Court of Common Pleas and was easily elected. One of his more notable decisions came in a case involving a conflict over a child's religious upbringing: the father, a Catholic, favored a parochial school education, while the court-appointed guardian, a Protestant welfare organization, wished to enroll the child in public school. Cardozo ruled that the father had a right to determine the child's religious creed and restored custody to him. The decision was consistent with the Sephardic community's emphasis on the primacy of the family's religious teachings, but it also strengthened Cardozo's position with Catholic voters. As one account put it, "the fact that, although a Hebrew, he had thus intervened in behalf of a Catholic gave him popularity among people of that religious faith."[63] The popularity may have paid off in 1867 when, running on the Democratic ticket for justice of the Supreme Court, Albert Cardozo won handily.

For the next four years Cardozo was a figure to be reckoned with in political as well as legal circles. As a Tammany regular with a voice in its general committee, he was regularly consulted by party officials on appointments and patronage. A man of mark in the Sephardic community, an officer and trustee of Congregation Shearith Israel, and president of the Board of Delegates of American Israelites, he worked assiduously in behalf of Jewish charitable causes. In 1870, at the laying of the cornerstone for Mt. Sinai hospital, he made a speech which the *Jewish Messenger* labeled "truly a gem of oratory." He also helped obtain a major legislative appropriation for construction of the Institution for the Improved Education of Deaf Mutes. St. John's College awarded him an honorary Doctor of Laws degree, a distinction widely commented on since it was "the only instance in which a purely Catholic institution had so honored a Hebrew."[64]

"Judge Cardozo was a good-looking man," the *New York Times* reported, "with dark complexion, bright black eyes, and black hair. He was a marvel of neatness in his attire, and yet he affected peculiarities in the matters of collars and trousers that attracted attention to him."[65] A fuller description, more vivid but perhaps less reliable, comes from one of his political enemies, whose number was legion. "Cardozo's personal appearance was peculiar and striking," wrote one critic: "He had a slender lithe figure, an active springing step, and the bearing of a gentleman. His features had a slight Hebrew cast; his face was beardless and his complexion almost livid; he wore long, thick curly hair; but his eye was his most marked feature. It was black, piercing, and ever alert. A bitter opponent once said that he had the eyes of a serpent looking from the face of a corpse, and the description was not unhappy. He dressed simply. His manner was courteous but inflexible. He never lost his self-possession, but beneath his calm exterior was a heart the resentments of which were implacable. He lived quietly, going but little into society, and his domestic relations were free from taint."[66]

Even his critics, however, conceded his impressive ability as a Supreme Court justice. The picture that emerges is of an able and talented man whose sole defect—fatal, of course, in a judge—was a willingness to permit considerations of both personal gain and political loyalty to influence his rulings. "He had undoubted talent," one writer said: "he was a sedulous student, and well versed in the theory of his profession. Such of his opinions as were not influenced by partisanship were usually sound, and were expressed in clear and forcible language."[67] In the words of another observer: "Hard working, learned in the law, perfect in his demeanor on the bench and controlling his temper with wonderful equanimity, he seemed a model of a judge and of a gentleman; yet his career was marked by an utter disregard of law and equity. He is said to have sold justice 'as a grocer might have sold sugar.'"[68] The judgment of Albert Cardozo's contemporaries is therefore remarkably consistent.

His Supreme Court rulings that did not involve matters of personal interest, and most did not, provide evidence of a fine legal mind. Typically, Cardozo presented the facts of a case in plain language, referred to British as well as American precedents, and offered trenchant justifications for his conclusions. There are, indeed, striking similarities, rhetorical and substantive, between a number of his opinions and those written more than fifty years later by Benjamin. To cite only one instance: in 1869 Albert upheld a statute whose wisdom he doubted on the grounds that judges ought to defer to legislative prerogative. His words could well have been written by his son and would, in fact, be echoed by him: "The responsibility of the legislation does not rest with me; but I am responsible for the construction I give to that legislation; and I am bound to give it a fair and just one, and not to resort to ingenious and refined theories and unusual interpretations of words which are of common use, and of sentences which are of ordinary import, for the purpose of evading or defeating what congress may have, perhaps unwisely, attempted."[69] Without unduly pressing the point, for Benjamin was more learned, talented, and creative than his father, the resemblances are still suggestive of a shared quality of mind.

Albert Cardozo's public career was intertwined with that of his patron, William M. Tweed, and so was his subsequent undoing. By the fall of 1870 newspapers were branding the Tweed Ring "the most licentious government ever known," and its Boss "the incarnation of all the vice in the City government."[70] The following summer, when Thomas Nast's famous anti-Tweed cartoons were appearing in *Harper's,* the press was full of talk of swindles and "Gigantic Frauds." Anti-Tammany forces banded together to form a Committee of Seventy to investigate the allegations against Tweed—then serving as commissioner of public works—his ally Mayor A. Oakey Hall ("The Elegant One"), and their associates. By the end of 1871 grand jury proceedings had been instituted against the Ring's leaders and some bench warrants issued for arrests. Tweed was charged with signing vouchers without examining their validity. By February 1872, facing five separate indictments for conspiracy, perjury, and grand larceny, he was well on the way to political oblivion.

The reform forces then turned their attention to the three judges who were widely regarded as Tweed's front men: Superior Court Justice John H. McCunn and Supreme Court Justices George G. Barnard and Albert Cardozo. Spearheading the attack was the newly formed Association of the Bar of the City of New York. It petitioned the state legislature, which in turn authorized the Judiciary Committee of the state Assembly to investigate "alleged abuses in the administration of justice."[71] From February 19 to April 11, 1872, the nine-member committee, made up of seven Republicans and two Democrats, conducted a closed-door inquiry at the Fifth Avenue Hotel in New York City. Three lawyers represented the Bar Association: Joshua M. Van Cott, John E. Parsons, and Albert Stickney. Each of the accused judges was permitted to have two lawyers. Cardozo selected William Fullerton, a former judge of the Court of Appeals, and Edward H. Owens. The sessions often ran from early in the morning to late at night. Each side called its own witnesses, and cross-examination was allowed, although the stringent courtroom rules governing admissibility of evidence were not followed. In Cardozo's case, 64 witnesses were examined; their testimony covered nearly 500 printed pages.

The Bar Association charged that Cardozo was "guilty of mal and corrupt conduct" on five counts. First: on September 29, 1869, he had granted an injunction without adequate cause which sharply restricted the operations of the New York Gold Exchange Bank, his intent being to benefit Jay Gould and James Fisk Jr., who otherwise stood to lose "many millions of dollars." Second: on the application of a noted law firm, Howe and Hummel, he had over a period of four years discharged without sufficient legal basis some 140 criminals imprisoned in the penitentiary, thereby enabling the firm "to coerce large sums of money from such persons, in consideration of procuring such discharge, to the perversion and obstruction of justice and the due administration of the law." Third: in May 1869 he had illegally imprisoned two women against whom no complaint had been made "on the pretence that they were charged with keeping a bawdy-house," had kept them behind bars for two weeks, and had attempted to browbeat their lawyer. Fourth: in September 1868 he had unjustly refused to vacate an order denying alimony to a woman who had won a divorce because her husband had committed adultery. Fifth: in appointing referees to handle foreclosure and real estate transactions, Cardozo had acted on the basis of favoritism and nepotism, awarding an unreasonable share to William Tweed Jr. and to Gratz Nathan—his wife, Rebecca's, nephew—and had then ensured that Nathan received "grossly extravagant and exorbitant sums."[72]

Several of the charges—the second, third, and fourth—were never substantiated. As to the second, Cardozo did not deny that he had released many of Howe and Hummel's clients (who had been convicted in the Court of Special Sessions of petit larceny, assault, impersonating an officer, and other such crimes) but insisted that there was a solid procedural basis for discharging them. Howe testified without contradiction that many convictions in the Court of Special Sessions were invalid because the cases had been heard before only one judge, not the required minimum of two. In April 1870 the New York State Court of Appeals had even ruled that such convictions were unconstitutional. Noting that he also obtained discharges from other judges, Howe explained that he preferred to deal with Cardozo because he was always in the courthouse early and so was readily accessible. "My business being principally criminal, in fact wholly so," the attorney said proudly, "I have obtained the sobriquet of 'Habeas Corpus Howe.'"[73]

The third and fourth allegations against Cardozo were so dated and so meagerly supported that their inclusion seems capricious. The two women who were supposedly imprisoned without cause were sisters, Mary Pearsall and Joanna Conner. A third sister, Julia McGraw, had been involved in a divorce proceeding before Cardozo. Fearing she would lose custody of her five-year-old daughter, she had evidently hidden the girl with her sisters, who were said to be running a house of prostitution. Cardozo's counsel simply argued that the judge had attempted "to rescue the child from degradation" by extricating her "from the association of these women." Cardozo's threat to the sisters' attorney consisted of the remark, as the lawyer recalled it: "Do not touch that case, if you do you will displease me; if you take this case, you need never expect any favors from me while I am on the bench."[74] Cardozo's behavior can be faulted but it hardly provided a basis for impeachment, especially in view of his unselfish motive. The next charge was no more substantive. Cardozo had merely upheld an order of Judge Barnard's denying alimony in a divorce case. The Bar Association called only one witness, whose testimony took a scant eight pages.

By contrast, twenty-five witnesses were heard on the first allegation, the most sensational, regarding Cardozo's motives in granting an injunction against the Gold Exchange Bank. In the fall of 1869 Jay Gould and James Fisk Jr., both railroad magnates and friends of Boss Tweed, were in the process of making a fortune by conspiring to drive up the price of gold. But on "Black

Friday," September 24, the bottom dropped out of the gold market, the price plunging from 163 to 133 dollars an ounce in the space of fifteen minutes. To avert financial disaster, Gould and Fisk hatched a plot to prevent the clearance of transactions through the Gold Exchange Bank. They sought to enjoin the Bank from acting as a clearinghouse for the Gold Exchange, and to place its assets in the hands of a receiver "on the pretense, known to be false, that the bank was insolvent." Albert Cardozo not only cooperated by granting the injunction but also went a step further, directing the receiver to pay huge sums to Gould, Fisk, and other "favored parties."[75]

As sensational as the Gold Exchange Bank disclosures were, the evidence relating to the charge of nepotism ultimately proved more damaging. Originally the Bar Association thought it had merely uncovered a case of favoritism: in four years Cardozo had assigned a total of 511 receiverships, some of them quite lucrative: 63 went to William M. Tweed Jr., and no fewer than 335 went to Gratz Nathan. In 1868, when his uncle began sending business his way, Nathan was a twenty-five-year-old lawyer who was busily making the most of his family's political connections. By gaining an appointment as an assistant to the city's corporation attorney, for example, he managed to work out of a municipal office and pay no rent. Testifying before the inquiry at the Fifth Avenue Hotel, Nathan did his best to stonewall. Asked if had received 335 references from his uncle, he countered: "I have not the slightest idea." Would he, then, permit an examination of his checkbooks? "I have already answered that. For no purpose would I permit strangers to examine my check-books."[76]

As the inquiry proceeded, however, the lawyers for the Bar Association realized they had uncovered something even juicier than nepotism. In their words: "We had not been given to suppose that it was expected that a case of pecuniary corruption could be established."[77] To all appearances, however, that is exactly what was established. Even without access to Gratz Nathan's checkbooks, a comparison of cash withdrawals from his bank account with cash deposits in Albert Cardozo's revealed a pattern that could not be coincidental. On more than a dozen occasions, Nathan had withdrawn a large amount and Cardozo had deposited the same sum, down to the last dollar. Once Nathan had withdrawn $1,017 in cash and Cardozo had deposited exactly the same amount on the very same day. The existence of slight discrepancies only made matters look worse: a Nathan withdrawal of $8,707.50, for example, was collated with a Cardozo deposit that day of $8,700. Confronted with this evidence, and asked if any money transactions had taken place between him and his uncle, Nathan replied lamely: "That depends on what you call money transactions."[78]

In all, $30,000 had changed hands in this manner, and while the Bar Association could not prove that this was Nathan's way of paying off Cardozo for assigning him receiverships, no other explanation made as much sense. Certainly Cardozo's lawyers could offer none. According to one commentator (whose likely source was one of the Bar Association attorneys), when it was revealed at the hearing that the bank records had been subpoenaed and the two accounts compared, Cardozo, "who was intently listening, grew deadly pale. He realized that he was lost."[79]

By April 9, 1872, as the hearings wound down, the members of the Bar Association were given a preliminary report on the findings regarding Cardozo, Barnard, and McCunn, whom the *New York Times* now branded "OUR CORRUPT JUDGES." Speaking for the three attorneys who managed the Association's cases, Van Cott said the hearing had found "a state of things in the Courts not to be endured" and that the legislature now had to decide "whether the kind of Judges we have exposed, who have befouled the ermine, are the kind of Judges we wish to have as descendants of the honored Judiciary of New York."[80] Acting on the Association's recommendations, the state Assembly's Judiciary Committee unanimously approved a resolution of impeachment against Albert Cardozo (and Barnard and McCunn) for "mal and corrupt" conduct in office; eight of the nine members also wished to see Cardozo impeached "for high crimes and misdemeanors." By a vote of 33 to 16 the Assembly accepted the resolution concerning all three judges.

But Albert Cardozo, unlike Barnard and McCunn, never stood trial. On April 30 he suddenly resigned, submitting his letter only two hours after the Assembly received the report of its Judiciary Committee. "Wisely recognizing the completeness of the ruin," one observer wrote, Cardozo had decided to "tak[e] refuge from impeachment in voluntary resignation." There was considerable speculation to the effect that he had struck the best deal possible, agreeing to resign in return for a promise that the Bar Association would not seek his disbarment. Some even thought he had escaped expulsion "only by a piteous appeal to the mercy of the Bar Association, accompanied by the assurance of his intention to immediately leave New York and settle in the extreme West," a promise on which he later reneged.[81] Whatever the details, an editorial in the *Argus* succinctly expressed the general feeling: "Resignation is confession."[82]

Cardozo's letter of resignation, however, said nothing of the sort. Rather, he represented himself as a victim of mudslinging by the Bar Association and the press. He was leaving office not because he had done anything wrong, he said, but because a judge must command the confidence of the public, and even if he were to be acquitted of all charges, "I would have my usefulness so far impaired as to render it questionable whether consistently with self-respect and due regard for the station I occupy, I should retain office." Offering a blanket defense of his behavior on the bench, he insisted: "No man can truly say that I ever gave an unjust or corrupt judgment, or that knowingly I ever did a wrong to any one in my office." But exoneration, he added, was unlikely because "a political majority opposed to my party faith, intend to force me at all hazard out of office . . . I have not the time, means nor health to consume in vainly resisting a preordained partisan decision."[83]

Cardozo then returned to private practice, forming a partnership with a younger man, Richard Newcombe. They were not only partners but next-door neighbors on Madison Avenue. Outwardly successful, Cardozo, according to one of his opponents, never lived down his humiliation: "his haggard, anxious face testified to the suffering which his disgrace had caused him, and those who knew him best spoke of him as a broken-hearted man."[84] Forty-four years old at the time of his resignation, Cardozo had only thirteen years left to him, time enough to grieve the death of his wife, Rebecca, and daughter Grace. He ultimately contracted nephritis, Bright's disease as it was then known, an infectious disease of the kidneys. He showed up at his office a week before his death but seemed so "dull and dispirited" that his partner "asked him to go with him to the Superior Court, remarking that it would enliven him to see him engaged in a legal battle."[85] Cardozo soon took to his bed and fell into a coma. He died on November 8, 1885, surrounded by his children and family.

Two hundred friends and relatives gathered for the funeral services at his home on Madison Avenue. "The body lay under the arch between the parlors. It was wrapped in a shroud of white satin. Laurel and roses covered the breast. High candles at the head and feet lighted up the heavy pall and the face of the dead." The Reverend Dr. Frederick De Sola Mendes, the older brother of Henry Pereira Mendes, delivered the eulogy, speaking on the lessons of death. "All heads were covered, after the Jewish custom, during the services, which ended with a prayer in Hebrew. Then all were allowed to see the body." Finally, "the pall was removed from the rosewood coffin, which was carried to the hearse between lines of friends extending the width of several houses on each side of the stoop." The mourners included prominent judges, aldermen, senators, assemblymen, and city commissioners. Tammany Hall sent a thirty-five-member delegation and flew its flag at half-mast.[86]

Among the mourners, of course, was fifteen-year-old Benjamin, then a freshman at Columbia College. Virtually nothing is known either about his relationship with his father or about when, and from whom, he learned of Albert's disgrace. It is possible that Albert spoke to Benjamin about the circumstances surrounding his resignation, or that his older brother or sisters told him. Or perhaps it was a taboo subject, too painful to discuss within the family. In later years Benjamin's acquaintances generally avoided mentioning Albert's resignation on the supposition that it was too delicate a subject to broach. One of the few friends who did mention it, Charles C. Burlingham, reported only: "I once asked BNC about his father. His reply was he was a good dad." Burlingham added that Cardozo's best friend, Irving Lehman, thought "Albert was cold and not sympathetic with Ben. But [Lehman] says Albert had the same charm."[87]

If it is uncertain how Cardozo learned of his father's resignation, we are on firmer ground in speculating about what he learned. Since relatives and friends accepted Albert Cardozo's own explanation of his decision to resign, it is likely that his son did, too. The family's version was given by his niece Annie Nathan Meyer. She remembered "how annoyed my father was that [Albert] had not stood trial, but had been persuaded by his wife, my father's sister, to resign office rather than go through the trial. We all felt it was bad policy and undoubtedly it led people to think he must have been guilty, but my Aunt was not a well woman (though it was before she was paralyzed) and the judge was a devoted husband—whatever else he *might* have been." By placing his wife's well-being ahead of his own vindication, he had, in this view, behaved with characteristic selflessness. Meyer added that Albert Cardozo had left a relatively small estate, amounting, in all, to about $100,000, and many therefore concluded that tales of his corruption had been exaggerated. "Some people after that felt that he had been merely weak and leaned towards favoritism especially towards Tammanyites but took no bribes."[88]

Meyer also believed that Benjamin shared her view, a reasonable supposition in light of his refusal, throughout his career, to join the Association of the Bar of the City of New York. If Benjamin regarded his father as a fundamentally good if flawed man who fell victim to his political enemies, then the effect of Albert's resignation on his son should be reconsidered. Many writers have asserted, although without supporting evidence, that Benjamin devoted his life to clearing the family name. The language varies only slightly: he "set out upon a life plan designed to exonerate, or at least vindicate, his father, and bring back honor to the Cardozo name";[89] or "his sensitive soul took on the resolve to restore the name of Cardozo to its former honor";[90] or "it was the ambition of his life to wipe out his father's shame."[91] These assertions, however, depend on a series of unlikely propositions: that Benjamin believed that his father had dishonored the family name, that his own behavior could somehow redeem it, and that it made sense to devote his life to such a purpose.

His father's tarnished honor, however, may have had a more modest effect on Benjamin's outlook. Justified or not, the successful attack on Albert Cardozo taught an unforgettable lesson: to remain above suspicion, a judge must remain above politics, even above strong partisan sentiment. Throughout his long career on the bench, Benjamin Cardozo observed a code of judicial conduct far exceeding the standards of the day. "One has to be so terribly circumspect when one holds judicial office," he once explained to a relative who had asked him to make a public statement praising a mutual acquaintance.[92] When Annie Nathan Meyer urged him to contribute to a fund to help enact an anti-lynching bill, assuring him that his contribution could be anonymous, Cardozo begged off. A judge could not support a measure that might one day come before him for decision, he insisted, since litigants "may challenge his impartial judgment in a suit to set the law aside. It doesn't help to make the contribution anonymously. A judge mustn't have any secrets of that kind."[93]

In the end, however, Albert Cardozo's influence on his son may have had less to do with the circumstances of his resignation, which occurred when Benjamin was two years old, than with the kind of person he was. Gratz Nathan, in his testimony before the Judiciary Committee, provided fascinating insights into his uncle's character: "His life is what most people call a very slow one; he devotes himself almost entirely to his judicial duties. I never knew him to attend any public amusements, and don't remember to have seen him out of an evening more than once or twice in my life. You can always find him at his house at night engaged looking over cases, or with his family."[94] A stay-at-home, sober, responsible, devoted to his work and family—the description could have applied as well to Benjamin, in later years, as to his father.

At Columbia: "A Clean-cut Modest Stripling"

It was only a short trip from the Cardozo residence on Madison Avenue and 68th Street to Columbia College, then located on Madison between 49th and 50th Streets, an easy walk when the weather was fair. Classes met at ten, eleven, and twelve o'clock, five days a week. Professor John W. Burgess, who taught political science and constitutional law, remembered the reaction when he suggested adding additional hours of instruction: "I was regarded as a barbarian . . . Civilized men did not rise before eight or breakfast before nine, and the afternoons and evenings were for society and recreation." In the mid-1880s about 250 students were enrolled in the School of Arts. Burgess viewed most of them as "rich loafers." With a few "rare and honorable exceptions," he noted, the typical student made no preparation for class "but chanced it every time, depending upon his wit for guessing and the help and indulgence of his teacher." Faculty members seemed reconciled to this lackadaisical approach; as a colleague told Burgess, "I do as little as I can for these dunderheads and save my time for research."[95]

If any student belied this description it was Benjamin Cardozo, Class of '89. Columbia College may never have enrolled a more diligent or conscientious scholar. In his freshman year he achieved perfect grades of 100 percent in Greek, Latin, and German, 99.6 percent in mathematics, and 98.1 percent in rhetoric. As a sophomore, he again attained perfect scores in the three languages, and received a 97.6 percent in mathematics and a 98.7 percent in rhetoric. Columbia then changed to a letter-grade system. In his junior and senior years Cardozo received an A in every course he took: physics, logic, literature, philosophy, ethics, political economy, psychology, and history. He graduated with honors in four subjects: Greek, Latin, political economy, and philosophy.

Cardozo's lecture notes were not so much notes as near-verbatim transcripts, marvelously accurate and precise, written in a flowing hand, sentences and paragraphs alike meticulously well-ordered. Doubtless he took rough notes during class, perhaps using a form of shorthand, and later spent hours transcribing them. Running to some two thousand pages, the notes contain the lectures in many of his undergraduate- and graduate-level courses, including Archibald Alexander's "History of Philosophy," Richmond Mayo-Smith's "Political Economy," Edmund Munroe Smith's "History of English Jurisprudence," John W. Burgess's "Political Science and Comparative Constitutional Law," and Nicholas Murray Butler's "History of Philosophy" and "Ethics."

Here, for example, is a rendering of Butler's discussion of Spinoza's Sephardic Jewish background, a topic in which Cardozo may have had a special interest:

> Spinoza is known in English as Benedict Spinoza. He was born at Amsterdam of Jewish parents, 1632, and he belonged to those Spanish Jews who left Spain for Holland in order to avoid the persecution of the Inquisition; and his was a very learned and cultivated family of a very remarkable branch of the Hebrew race. Spinoza was educated by the rabbis at the synagogue at Amsterdam, and in early life was a very promising student of Jewish literature and the orthodox Jewish theology. He also studied physics, and paid considerable attention to mathematics. He came in contact also with the philosophy of Descartes. In consequence of having given utterance to heretical opinions concerning the Scriptures, he was expelled from the Synagogue and obliged to leave Amsterdam. His life from then on is remarkable for its secluded character and the privations which he suffered.[96]

Cardozo referred to these notebooks for years after his graduation, periodically updating those dealing with political and economic issues by inserting current newspaper clippings.

Butler later described Cardozo as a "desperately serious" student,[97] and his solemnity, as well as his solid learning, is certainly evident in three lengthy essays he wrote during his senior year: "The Moral Element in Matthew Arnold," "Some Notes on George Eliot," and his sixty-five-page senior thesis, "Communism."[98] Although one could not claim true originality for any of them, the essays are marked by a grace and sophistication all the more remarkable when it is remembered that they were written by an eighteen-year-old.

Cardozo may have been drawn to Matthew Arnold precisely because Arnold was, in the Columbia senior's words, "primarily an ethical writer" whose "conception of the importance of conduct" could be clearly traced in his poetry, prose, and criticism. Arnold's moral theory, Cardozo thought, could be stated simply: "Perfection, that is, the full and free development of man's being,—this, if I correctly follow Arnold, is in his eyes the supreme good." Defending Arnold's belief in the importance of ethics, Cardozo criticized those who emphasized, instead, the primacy of imagination in poetic composition: "Mere imagination is the sport, the revelry, the madness of the brain; it gives us dreams, pictures, phantasms; but it does not give us poetry. Not till the criticism of life has lent meaning, soberness, coherence to the play of the imagination, has toned and subdued it, not till then have we a really poetic creation." Yet Cardozo was by no means an uncritical admirer of Arnold. He detected a lack of "rugged manliness" in him, "a certain primness and precision and daintiness that almost reached the point of affectation . . . Arnold's personality is a forcible reminder of how narrow is the line between culture and foppishness, between a 'sweet mild reasonableness' and a sort of effeminate sentimentalism." Having ventured these reservations, Cardozo concluded with praise for a writer who understood that what an individual needs most is "a clear vision and a lofty soul."

Similarly, Cardozo's interest in George Eliot centered on the "reverence for the teachings of morality which was part and parcel of her being." Maintaining that Eliot's strength as a novelist lay chiefly in her analysis of motives, Cardozo wrote: "Of her it may be said in truth that she takes us into the workshop of the mind; and all the hidden springs of action, all the mental processes and involutions, with the thousand gradations from doubt to decision and from decision back again to doubt, are laid bare before us, and we are left to observe their slow and stern and remorseless workings." Granted, Eliot was at times overly didactic, Cardozo conceded, and "too anxious to *tell* the story rather than to let the story tell itself." Yet that did not detract from her overall stature: "Her books are precious to the moralist, not for any coherent and consistent doctrine they present, but simply from that high and generous and exalted spirit which they themselves breathe and which they cannot fail to stimulate in others."

Cardozo's reading of Eliot was based on familiarity with her best-known novels: *Adam Bede* (1859), *Silas Marner* (1861), and *Middlemarch* (1872). But he also devoted considerable attention to *Romola* (1863), one of her less acclaimed works, which, he thought, clearly laid out "the warring claims of pleasure and gratitude." The novel is set in fifteenth-century Florence. A youth named Tito has gained fortune and his heart's desire, Romola, by selling jewels which properly belong to his foster father, Baldasarre, who is being held as a slave by the Turks. Should Tito abide by the teachings of conventional morality and seek Baldasarre's release, thereby jeopardizing his own privileged way of life? Or should he just enjoy what he has? Convincing himself that social rules are, at best, contrivances and that one's aim in life should be to maximize pleasure, Tito, as Cardozo saw it, "denies his father and leaves him to misery, betrays every trust that is reposed in him, comes in short to commit some of the basest deeds—such deeds as make men infamous." Eliot thereby exposed the "dreadful vitality of wrongdoing." Cardozo approvingly quoted Romola's declamation: "We can only have the highest happiness . . . by having wide thoughts and much feeling for the rest of the world as well as ourselves."

In Arnold and Eliot Cardozo found authors with whom he felt a common bond; for his senior thesis, however, he wrote on communism, a system which deeply offended him. Conceding that such utopian theorists as Etienne Cabet and Robert Owen were moved by a laudable desire to eradicate capitalism's evils, Cardozo nevertheless rejected their solution as both impractical and pernicious. No scheme of "untempered altruism" could possibly work, he argued, because it "radically contravenes the essential impulses of our human constitution." Since enforced economic equality was "directly opposed to the instincts of our nature," it followed that such a system would stunt individualism, produce a grinding poverty, and engender "one common type of man, passive, heartless, and mechanical." Communism, he concluded, "marks the dawn of a new serfdom in which all men will be the serfs and government the master." Cardozo made it clear that his objections to communism applied with equal force to socialism: both "would make each man the image of his neighbor."

The student who produced these essays was the youngest member of his class, the smallest, the slightest, and the least physically mature. The impression Cardozo made on his classmates and professors—aside from sheer brilliance—was chiefly one of delicacy and frailness. Trying to remember him as a student after a half-century had passed, they came up with similar phrases: "a clean-cut, modest stripling"; "small of stature and looking like a mere boy"; "his frail physique"; "very slight in build"; "a small, slender boy, almost delicate in appearance"; "he did not seem to be very strong physically"; "such a delicate youth."[99] A teaching assistant in Cardozo's freshman mathematics class recalled the time the professor posed a difficult question: "One after another the boys failed to answer, until it was the turn of a frail lad—fourteen or fifteen years old. I can still see him rising quietly, hardly more than a child. I remember his voice—a soprano voice like that of a choir boy. It was Bennie Cardozo, giving the correct answer."[100]

His boyishness helps explain his failure to participate in undergraduate social life. While other students liked Cardozo well enough and respected his ability, they considered him remote, reclusive, and standoffish. There was as much agreement on this point as on his appearance: "We were all very fond of him, but he was too young to enjoy our social activities"; "he seemed to be of a retiring disposition and quietly disappeared when the lectures were over"; "he mingled very little with the rest of the students."[101] The *Columbiad* for 1889, Cardozo's senior year, published doggerel to the same effect:

'Tis he, 'tis Nathan! Thanks to the Almighty!
Women and men he strove alike to shun,
And hurried homeward, when his tasks were done.[102]

Although he participated in the college's debating society, according to one member "he would never take part in one of the joint debates with the other societies or in any way force himself into the limelight."[103]

On June 12, 1889, Cardozo was graduated from Columbia in ceremonies held at the Metropolitan Opera House.[104] He was one of four seniors selected to give orations, and his speech, entitled "The Altruist in Politics," must surely have impressed his audience. Summarizing the argument of his senior thesis, he also threw in quotations from Tolstoy, Emerson, and George Eliot, and, for good measure, cited Matthew Arnold: "The reader of Mr. Arnold's works must have noticed the emphasis with which he dwells on the instinct of expansion as a factor in human progress. It is the refutation alike of communism and socialism that they thwart the instinct of expansion; that they substitute for individual energy the energy of government; that they substitute for human personality the blind, mechanical power of the State." As in his thesis, Cardozo portrayed communism as the doctrine of "an all-reaching and all-controlling altruism" whose effect would be to "thwart," "dwarf," and "stunt" individualism.[105]

Cardozo had already decided to enter the law school at Columbia, and given his brilliant record it was assumed that he would now have new intellectual fields to conquer. The Class of '89 yearbook prophesied his future in verse:

Cardozo's scholarly fervor and zeal
Will hurry him on towards the legal ideal,
Where he'll snatch all the buns from the Bar he can freeze on
Thus proving his size is no gauge for his reason.[106]

(The word "buns" was slang for "honors" or "rewards.") For two years, starting in the fall of 1889, Cardozo attended courses in the School of Law.

Rebecca Cardozo with Benjamin and Emily at Long Branch, New Jersey, 1871.
The twins are about fifteen months of age.

Benjamin and Emily, about five years old.

Albert Cardozo.

Horatio Alger Jr. around 1890.

Rev. H. Pereira Mendes.

Cardozo at the age of twelve.

Cardozo at the age of twenty-seven.

Chief Judge Cardozo and New York Governor Alfred E. Smith,
January 1927.

Cardozo walking to work at the Supreme Court.

He also studied in the recently established School of Political Science, which awarded him a Master's degree in 1890. But he never received a law degree. Cardozo's class was one of the first to be required by Columbia to take a three-year course of study for the degree. Along with most of the students who had entered with him, Cardozo chose not to remain for the third year. Instead, he simply took the Bar examination and entered practice.

Cardozo later offered a disingenuous and defensive explanation for his decision.

> After graduating from the School of Arts in '89, I went to the law school which had then a two year course. Just about the middle of the second year, when the men had received the same instruction that had led to an LL. B. in the past, the trustees tacked on a third year. I was anxious to go out into the world and make my living, so I never came back for the third year. It wasn't of much value, for it had not yet been coordinated with other courses of instruction, but represented a lot of extras. Of course, later on it became an integrated part of the law school scheme. A good many of my classmates did as I did. So I never received an LL. B., though I left in good standing, and have no reason to doubt that I could have had it if I had been willing to stay.[107]

This version of events blurs the actual chronology and omits a crucial consideration which affected Cardozo and many of his classmates: Columbia's decision in 1891 to replace Theodore William Dwight, who had headed the law school for more than thirty years, with a new Dean, William A. Keener, whose pedagogical philosophy and style were exactly the opposite of Dwight's.

For many years after his appointment as Warden and Professor of Municipal Law in 1858, "the Law School of Columbia College was distinctly Theodore Dwight's school. It is no exaggeration to say that the School was Dwight." He taught all the classes and did all the necessary administrative work. He controlled the school's finances, enjoying a comfortable arrangement which permitted him to pocket the tuition fees to supplement his salary. He lobbied successfully for a bill providing that graduates would automatically be admitted to the Bar without having to pass an outside examination, a system that remained in force from 1860 to 1881. He was an impressive figure, "a man of robust health, of considerably more than ordinary stature, erect, and well built. His head was made venerable by a plentiful growth of hair almost white. His eye needed no glass, was bright, and his ruddy face lighted up easily with a smile, altogether giving an impression of benignity and abiding youthfulness."[108]

His system of teaching depended on several elements, the first a reliance on authoritative textbooks rather than the cases themselves to teach essential legal principles. "The great object aimed at," he declared, "is to store the mind of the student with the fundamental principles of law." To help novices master the textbooks, Dwight employed the Socratic method in class, but ever so gently. His pedagogical technique was described as "oral colloquy adapted by the teacher to the mental necessities and varying stages of progress of each individual learner." His students reported: "He knew his men, not by name merely, but by calibre, and put just strain on each student's faculties as he deemed might be safely borne . . . He never mortified a student; if an answer were manifestly wrong, he would say: 'Would you not rather say it is so and so.'" Finally, Dwight believed that law must be founded on ethics. "It is not law that he has taught, so much as justice," one student related, while another added: "He taught us not only law, but law morals. He impressed us with a belief that the law is the most honorable of all callings in life."[109]

Despite the apparent success of Dwight's method, a movement eventually developed among Columbia's Trustees to modernize the school and its curriculum. In 1878 several additional professorships were created, but Dwight managed to fill most of them with hand-picked appointees, such as George Chase, his former student. The effort to add a required third year to the law program sparked considerably more controversy. In May 1888, after years of discussion, the Trustees finally adopted the three-year plan, and decided that it would apply to the class entering in the fall. Dwight urged a postponement on the grounds that students who had accepted admission assumed that they were making only a two-year commitment. When the Trustees insisted on implementation, Dwight stalled. Refusing to propose an acceptable three-year curriculum, he "wished simply to tack on to his old course a third year of odds and ends."[110] Of the 205 students who entered in the fall of 1888 and completed their second year in 1889–90, only 77 returned for the now-obligatory third year (63 of them actually graduated). So while Benjamin Cardozo and his fellow students who entered in the fall of 1889 may have doubted the value of a third year of study, they knew that it would be required for a degree.

But the uproar among students in the School of Law during Cardozo's second year was caused less by uncertainties over the new curriculum than by Dwight's announcement that he would retire at the end of the academic year, and by the simultaneous resignations of two of the other three law professors, George Chase and Robert D. Petty. Recognizing that the new president of Columbia, Seth Low, had decided to overhaul the system of legal education, Dwight simply surrendered control of the school, and his allies departed with him. As Dwight noted in a memorandum he drafted in defense of his outlook, "Everything points to view that P. has lost confidence in me, wants my scalp."[111]

With Dwight on the way out, President Low selected William Albert Keener, the remaining faculty member, as the new dean. Only thirty-five years of age, Keener had been recruited from Harvard Law School the year before. A more striking contrast than that between Dwight and Keener can hardly be imagined. Dwight taught from textbooks, while Keener leaned to the case-method system pioneered at Harvard by Christopher Columbus Langdell and James Barr Ames: students were given the original sources and the decisions in key cases, and were expected to discover their underlying principles inductively. Dwight emphasized ethics, but Keener regarded his enterprise as essentially scientific in nature. And where Dwight was sensitive to his students' feelings, Keener was not. As one account puts it:

> With his bulky and bearlike figure, his great red beard, and his piercing, almost predaceous eyes, Keener's physical appearance was most impressive and his personal manner in the classroom was brutally aggressive. He would assault a student with a rapid fire of searching provocative questions that soon drove the unwary legal neophyte into a ridiculous and untenable position. He seemed determined to prove to each student called up for interrogation that he was completely unqualified to discuss intelligently any legal point. The students thought him almost sadistic in his ruthless disregard for their personal dignity.[112]

Keener's first year at Columbia, 1890–91, was Cardozo's second year as a law student. For a month Keener taught the second-year class in equity jurisprudence. Cardozo recalled that he reacted to the new professor's classroom manner as unfavorably as his classmates:

> I went to Columbia Law School in the transition days when it was passing from the old method of instruction by textbook . . . to the case method now in vogue. I had been there more than a year under Dwight and Chase and their associates when Prof. Keener, fresh from Harvard, descended on

41

a bewildered class. The course was so nearly over that he had little time to do more than endeavor to convince us that we had learned nothing in the past, were learning nothing in the present, and were not likely, unless we improved a good deal, to learn anything in the future, which truth he proceeded to expound with great variety of illustration, with much satisfaction to himself, and with effects upon the class varying from rage to incredulity, and from incredulity to despair.[113]

Most Columbia law students resented the changes that were taking place all around them. Early in 1891 when Dwight announced his retirement and Chase and Petty their resignations, "the students were thrown into a turmoil of excitement." In a show of support for their professors, they held a mass meeting on March 9, 1891. They expressed their regret at the loss of the three professors and requested the Trustees to permit them to receive their degrees at the conclusion of their second year, a request that was denied. That June Professors Dwight and Chase posed for a photograph on the steps of the School of Law with members of what would have been the graduating class had the request been granted. One of the students held a blackboard with the chalked words: "THE CLASS OF 91 AND THE OLD ADMINISTRATION GO OUT TOGETHER." There were 202 students in that class; Benjamin Cardozo and 133 others did not return for the disputed third year.[114]

To Cardozo's own explanation for leaving law school without a degree—his desire to get going on his career—we should, therefore, add another: his allegiance to his mentor, Dwight, and his lack of rapport with Keener. Cardozo has provided yet a further clue to his motivation. Once, speaking to a law school graduating class, he remarked:

> I remember the sense of relief, of an incubus cast aside, with which I took my last examination after the years that I had passed in college and in law school. There, I said to myself, was a chapter closed. I might make mistakes in the future, but I should no longer make them under the eye of examiners charged with the special duty of exposing my failings and giving them a quantitative value in comparison with my virtues. Exposure thereafter would be, so to speak, a matter of chance. A class of professional detectives would be no longer on my tracks.[115]

Even for so able and precocious a student, the unrelenting pressure to prove himself had become overly burdensome.

As he left law school and prepared to enter practice, the lineaments of Cardozo's personality were, at the age of twenty-one, already well defined.

He was scholarly, fastidious, and shy. Aside from members of his immediate family he had no close friends, a consequence possibly of being tutored privately at home and then entering college when he was younger and physically less mature than his classmates. He was uncomfortable in social situations, acutely so where young women were involved. Whether out of insecurity, disinclination, or lack of opportunity, he had never had an intimate relationship with any young woman. Devoted to his studies and brilliantly successful at them, he nevertheless felt insecure about his own abilities. The loss of his parents when he was still quite young, the two years with a tutor intent on hiding a furtive past, the atmosphere in a household scarred by scandal—all may have contributed to some of the more striking aspects of his personality: his strongly moralistic outlook and his unusual sense of reserve.

His dutiful nature was certainly worlds removed from the unscrupulous Tito, the dishonorable son in George Eliot's *Romola* whose behavior he condemned in his senior essay. But one aspect of Cardozo's character was strikingly similar to that of Eliot's fictional figure. As she described him: "Tito had an innate love of reticence—let us say a talent for it—which acted as other impulses do, without any conscious motive, and like all people to whom concealment is easy, he would now and then conceal something which had as little the nature of a secret as the fact that he had seen a flight of crows."[116]

2

The Insanity Defense

Lawyers' Lawyer, Judges' Judge

On June 26, 1891, Benjamin Cardozo was admitted to the New York State Bar. He joined the law firm founded by his father and Richard S. Newcombe, in which his older brother, Albert Jr., was by now a partner. Newcombe died shortly thereafter, and the firm became known simply as Cardozo Brothers. There matters stood until 1903, when the brothers entered into a partnership with two older attorneys, Angel J. Simpson and Louis Werner. After Albert Cardozo's death in 1909 and Werner's retirement in 1911, George H. Engelhard joined the office, and when Simpson retired in 1913 the firm became Cardozo and Engelhard. Cardozo's election to the New York State Supreme Court in November 1913 ended his career in private practice.

During this time Cardozo lived with his brother and sisters, first in the family home on Madison Avenue, later in a brownstone at 16 West 75th Street, just off Central Park West and only a few blocks from the newly erected Spanish-Portuguese Synagogue. His twin sister, Emily, "the sweetest thing that ever breathed" according to one relative, left to marry Frank R. Bent, who worked in a bank.[1] His sister Elizabeth devoted herself to drawing and poetry. She eventually purchased a small cottage at Shippan Point, in Stamford, Connecticut. An invalid who required a full-time nurse, she was supported by Benjamin but cared for by Kate Tracy. Very little is known about the oldest brother, Albert Jr. He passed away on January 24, 1909, at the age of fifty-one, a victim of heart disease, his death receiving only a brief notice in the *New York Times.* After that, Benjamin and Nell resided together, attended, according to the 1910 census listing, by two young women, Elizabeth Callanan and Katherine Durnell, recently arrived from Ireland, who did the cooking and other chores.[2]

At some point Cardozo gave up the family's summer home in Long Branch, New Jersey, which had become less fashionable and genteel with the passing years, and arranged to lease a cottage in Allenhurst, a quiet coastal village a few miles to the south. According to one account, Allenhurst "was but a tract of farm land until 1896, when the Coast Land Company was organized under the presidency of Mr. Edwin P. Benjamin, which attracted to the place many men of wealth and position, and it was soon transformed into a pleasant village." Before long, hotels were built, "provided with all modern conveniences, including amusement halls for both children and adults . . . A fine esplanade extends along the entire ocean front of the village, and its center is a spacious pavilion which is the meeting point for all summer sojourners."[3] Benjamin and Nell went to Allenhurst every summer. Cardozo allowed himself the luxury of only one extended vacation: in 1907 he and Angel Simpson spent several months in Europe, visiting, among other places, London, Paris, Venice, and Berlin.

Otherwise Cardozo devoted himself exclusively to his work. An observer noted that he "lived almost the life of a hermit, spending all his spare time in the library," that his years as an attorney constituted "a period of toil devoid of almost all the usual pastimes of youth."[4] Working day and night, he gradually established himself as a highly successful practitioner. He seemed to know more about the law than other attorneys, even those more experienced than himself, and the facts were invariably at his fingertips. His powers of recall astonished associates who wondered at his ability to cite from memory the volume, sometimes the page, on which pertinent precedents, English as well as American, would be found. One of his clerks later called him "a walking encyclopedia of the law."[5] So well researched and elegantly written were his briefs that other lawyers sought his assistance in preparing their appeals, thus earning him the sobriquet "the lawyers' lawyer."

After he had practiced law for only a few years, Cardozo's reputation had advanced to the point where he was invited to contribute an essay to *A System of Legal Medicine,* a handsome two-volume work edited by Dr. Allan McLane Hamilton and Lawrence Godkin. Published in 1897, it contained articles by more than two dozen distinguished lawyers, physicians, judges, and scholars. Cardozo's essay, "Identity and Survivorship," treated two puzzling questions: how did courts determine a person's identity when it was contested, and how did they decide the order in which two or more individuals had died when the deaths were apparently simultaneous? He took as his point of departure Oliver Wendell Holmes Jr.'s famous aphorism in *The Common Law* (1881): "The life of the law has not been logic; it has been experience." Cardozo contended that in the areas under consideration the law derived "from the life, the emotions, and the history of men," and consequently resisted "our efforts to formulate it as a rule of orderly, coherent thought."

Where identity was at issue, Cardozo maintained, because an individual either claimed a certain persona for reasons of financial gain or had allegedly committed a crime, courts could properly consider facts pertaining to general appearance, mental and physical peculiarities (such as tattoos), or coincidences of history or past experience. But courts were not restricted to these areas. They could also admit circumstantial evidence: "any fact that in the ordinary course of events renders it probable that the person before the court is the person by whom an act in issue has been perpetrated." Even so, there was no guarantee that identity could always be correctly established, certainly not on the basis of appearance. To illustrate this Cardozo ranged across a broad legal terrain, referring to more than twenty cases, from sixteenth-century Toulouse when Arnaud du Tilh, an impostor, claimed to be Martin Guerre, to nineteenth-century England when a man falsely represented himself as Sir Roger Tichborne, heir to the Tichborne estate.

Cardozo believed that mental traits were a more reliable indication of identity than physical characteristics. For example, in the Tichborne case, despite "the most striking similarities of feature and of form," the fraud was exposed because of "the disparity in the intellectual acquirements of the two men" and the claimant's "want of those instinctive tendencies of mind which a man of Sir Roger's birth and breeding could never, it was felt, have lost." The body could undergo radical changes over the years, Cardozo asserted, but the mind, while it might atrophy, would remain recognizable. "Some faint and feeble echo, some elusive, mocking memory of what was once its own, would haunt it with a sense of latent force, and stir it sometimes with resurgent powers."

Drawing on recent developments in epistemology, Cardozo noted that relatively little knowledge is acquired directly through the senses but that knowledge is rather the product of associations and comparisons working upon raw materials supplied by the senses. Even the simplest assertion, such as "I see my brother," is not merely a perception but an inference. So, "from a philosophical standpoint almost all evidence is the evidence of a fact, not directly, but indirectly perceived" and is therefore a conclusion: "the difference between the proof we call circumstantial and the proof we call direct is one not so much of kind as of degree." But Cardozo acknowledged that courts could not permit such subtleties to disturb the execution of justice. Like it or not, the law was made "for a work-a-day world" and so "it must often rest satisfied with external standards, and govern itself by rules which it knows are but provisionally true."

When it came to survivorship, Cardozo asserted that the law had moved away from formal, artificial doctrines—under which, for example, an older person was always presumed to have predeceased a younger one, or a wife her husband—and toward rules based on the available evidence, however slight. Arbitrary presumptions as to survivorship, he thought, were always suspect; property rights should not be determined by any such "fixed and arbitrary standard." Cardozo's argument is compelling, but his language is even more striking. Although he was still in his twenties, his prose already had an unmistakably authoritative ring. He did not state his conclusions so much as pronounce them: "I can never believe that it is wise to place the doctrines of the law out of relation either to the teachings of experience or to the promptings of reason; and it seems to me that courts of justice, by frankly admitting their inability to solve a problem which in its nature is insoluble, will better promote the ends of their existence than by the forced assumption of a knowledge which it is not given them to have."[6]

The publisher of *A System of Legal Medicine,* E. B. Treat of New York City, distributed a publicity brochure which declared: "Mr. Cardozo's large experience in our courts as a prominent member of the New York bar entitles his opinions in the expositions of the law bearing on this question to be regarded as conclusive."[7] The accompanying photograph made the youthful author appear as mature and dignified as possible. Fastidiously well dressed and well groomed, refined-looking and detached, he gazes off into the distance, avoiding eye contact with the camera, his slightness of stature merely suggested by the narrow, sloping shoulders. In all, the photograph instills confidence in the viewer while revealing little about the youthful attorney.

The "large experience in our courts" to which the brochure referred derived not from Cardozo's activity as a trial lawyer but primarily from his work in preparing appeals, both for the New York State Supreme Court and for the Court of Appeals. His personal style was not well suited to the adversarial, often fractious atmosphere of the courtroom. As one writer put it, "the comparative quiet and dignity of appellate courts gave him his greatest confidence."[8] His briefs usually exhibited careful scholarship and, no matter how disputatious the case, "a certain sense of detachment, or refinement."[9] In twenty-three years as a lawyer, he submitted briefs in 197 cases on appeal, 128 of them at the intermediate-court level (he prevailed 89 times) and 69 of them to the Court of Appeals (he prevailed 44 times).

Nearly all of his suits dealt with either real property or aspects of civil law. The bulk of his practice centered on technical disputes over foreclosures and sales, the interpretation of wills, the construction of leases, the recovery of goods and chattels, the behavior of court-appointed referees, and the marketability of titles. Of his 197 appeals cases, only four dealt with negligence. Only two dealt with the criminal law—one involving an appeal from a conviction for grand larceny[10] and the other an attempt to move a trial from the Supreme Court to the Court of General Sessions[11]—and Cardozo lost both of them. Cardozo was not above characterizing opposing attorneys' arguments as a mixture of "vain hypocrisy and bald pretense." Nor were opposing attorneys above characterizing his as "disingenuous" or remarking that his reasoning "is based on false premises and is dishonest."[12]

His style in writing briefs was, on occasion, strikingly similar to the style he later employed in writing opinions. In 1905, for example, he submitted a brief on behalf of the Waldorf Astoria Segar Company, which had rented a store on the corner of Fifth Avenue and 42nd Street and had signed a lease in which the owner agreed not to rent any other part of the building to a competing business which also sold cigars and tobacco. The owner, however, then rented the property to a grocery store which sold a great many items, among them cigars and tobacco. Cardozo wrote, in part: "We are not to fritter away a covenant which was plainly intended to accomplish something by assigning to it a meaning which will render it ineffective to accomplish anything." In this instance the Court of Appeals unanimously upheld Cardozo's position.[13]

In 1903 Cardozo published *The Jurisdiction of the Court of Appeals of the State of New York,* a work chiefly of interest to attorneys who would be arguing cases before that court. In 222 pages of text and appendices, Cardozo cited no fewer than 900 cases. His view that "the constitutional theory of the function of the court" was to interpret the meaning of the law was unexceptional, but he described that function in remarkably abstract, impersonal language: "It is, briefly stated, the function, not of declaring justice between man and man, but of settling the law. The court exists, not for the individual litigant, but for the indefinite body of litigants, whose causes are potentially involved in the specific cause at issue. The wrongs of aggrieved suitors are only the algebraic symbols from which the court is to work out the formula of justice." The only exception occurred in cases involving the death penalty; then the court was free to review the facts and order a new trial "whenever the court is satisfied from the record that a new trial will promote the interests of justice."[14] However specialized its audience, the volume added to Cardozo's professional stature, especially when the judges themselves took to citing it as the definitive work.

Cardozo's reputation in legal circles eventually reached the point where his name arose in connection with the New York State Supreme Court. A justiceship, however, was an elected position which required nomination by a political party. Although Cardozo was a Democrat, he was a conservative who had bolted his party in 1896 to support the Republican William McKinley over William Jennings Bryan (whose victory, he feared, would have meant "the crack of doom")[15] and an independent who had no ties to Tammany Hall. In 1913 these qualities translated into decided advantages when a newly formed, broadly based Fusion movement, sparked by revelations of corruption in Tammany-controlled City Hall, made a bid for control of municipal government.

Directed by a blue-ribbon "Committee of 107," Fusion faced the unenviable task of uniting three diverse, headstrong groups: local anti-Tammany Democrats, who were being encouraged by several high-ranking officials in the Woodrow Wilson administration; Progressives, supporters of Theodore Roosevelt's third-party presidential candidacy in 1912, who sought to advance their own agenda; and Republicans who wanted to smash Tammany Hall. On July 31, 1913, by the narrowest of margins, the Committee of 107 selected the youthful John Purroy Mitchel, a Wilsonian Democrat, over District Attorney Charles S. Whitman, a Republican, as its mayoral candidate. Disgruntled Republicans then had no choice but to support Mitchel, who faced Tammany's uninspiring nominee, Judge Edward E. McCall, in the general election.

To draft Fusion's slate of judicial nominees its leaders created a five-member committee headed by Charles C. Burlingham, a prominent attorney and civic reformer. On August 14 the committee voted to nominate two independent Democrats, Cardozo and Eugene A. Philbin, for the two existing Supreme Court vacancies. Philbin was approved easily (and later ran unopposed), but Republicans on the committee had favored one of their own, William H. Wadhams, for the other seat. According to the *New York Times*, the final committee meeting was marked by "wrangling and protracted delays,"[16] but Cardozo finally emerged the winner, perhaps because of the high regard in which he was held, but perhaps, too, as one of Cardozo's friends later suggested, because Fusion was "looking for a very high class Jew to nominate to the Supreme Court."[17]

The Progressives enthusiastically endorsed the slate, but the Republicans balked. Still seeking to replace Cardozo with Wadhams, party chieftains sent a seven-member delegation to argue the point with the Fusionists. As Burlingham recalled: "We informed the Republican leaders that having persuaded Mr. Cardozo to accept a nomination, obviously it would be improper for us to withdraw his name."[18] On August 26, realizing they lacked the leverage to force a change, the Republicans finally acceded to the nomination after listening to a perfunctory speech in his behalf. As a reporter noted, "it was a bitter dose for the Republicans to swallow, and they did not disguise their true feelings."[19]

Cardozo's Democratic opponent, Bartow Sumter Weeks, already held an interim appointment to the state Supreme Court. Weeks had also attended law school at Columbia, but was best known for his unswerving allegiance to Tammany Hall. The city's legal elite quickly closed ranks behind Cardozo. One hundred and thirty eminent attorneys endorsed his candidacy. The list included Joseph H. Choate, Henry W. De Forest, Henry L. Stimson, Charles S. Whitman, Harlan Fiske Stone, Charles Evans Hughes Jr., and Louis Marshall, all of whom signed a letter testifying to Cardozo's "great learning, ability, and devotion to the highest ideals of his profession."[20] A young associate, Walter H. Pollak, arranged many of the details of the campaign, which consisted chiefly of obtaining the needed signatures and then making sure that the testimonial was privately circulated among lawyers. Cardozo did not think it seemly to publish the list of signatories, and he may have felt that the names would carry little weight outside the legal community.

In November 1913 Fusion won a victory of landslide proportions. Mitchel carried every borough and won by a margin of 121,000 votes. But in the First Judicial District, encompassing Manhattan and the Bronx, Cardozo managed only a narrow victory. He received 152,594 votes and Weeks 149,798. His plurality—2,796 votes—represented less than one percent of the total. Weeks carried the 31 assembly districts in Manhattan, Tammany's former stronghold, by 1,945 votes; but Cardozo carried the 4 assembly districts in the Bronx by 4,741 votes. Cardozo later maintained that he owed his election to Italian-American voters in the Bronx "who voted for me on the supposition that since my name ended in 'o' I was one of their race." In fact the 32nd and 34th Bronx assembly districts, which gave Cardozo his largest pluralities, 2,437 and 2,080 votes respectively, and assured his victory, were more heavily Jewish than Italian.[21]

Cardozo would now be seated on the same court on which his father had served more than forty years before. But where Albert Cardozo, a Tammany regular, had been elected by a large margin, Benjamin had won a slim victory on an anti-Tammany ticket; where Albert had been swept out of office on a wave of civic reform, Benjamin owed his position to a later manifestation of the same reform impulse; and where Albert had been pilloried by the city Bar Association, Benjamin's candidacy had been endorsed by the state Bar Association. On January 5, 1914, when Cardozo took his seat at a special term of the New York State Supreme Court, a spokesman for the Association offered welcoming remarks and predicted a bright future for him, one that "will measure up to your professional reputation, your personal integrity, and probity." Responding to applause from the spectators, Cardozo replied that the tasks facing him would appear overwhelming "if I could not count upon the aid and loyalty of the members of the bar."[22]

Even as he was settling into his new position, negotiations were under way which would take Cardozo to the state's highest court. The Court of Appeals consisted of seven judges who were elected to serve fourteen-year terms. But the governor had authority to appoint up to four additional judges, chosen from the Supreme Court, to help the appeals court relieve a congested calendar, and such an opening existed in January 1914. Governor Martin Glynn was an Albany Democrat who had been elevated from the lieutenant governorship the previous October following the impeachment of Governor William Sulzer for various kinds of financial misconduct. Glynn originally favored another candidate for the vacancy, Justice Samuel Seabury, who had run unsuccessfully for a seat on the Court of Appeals in 1913. Glynn, however, turned to Cardozo at the urging of the newly elected Chief Judge, Willard Bartlett, and his associates.

Cardozo may also have been the unwitting beneficiary of a campaign by prominent Jewish social reformers to have the governor appoint a forward-looking Jew to the vacancy. Ironically, this campaign was not undertaken in behalf of Cardozo but of Abram I. Elkus, a prominent attorney whose reform credentials included service as counsel to the New York State Factory Investigating Committee. As late as January 28, Rabbi Stephen S. Wise told Glynn that Jews "would be sensible of the honor conferred upon them through [Elkus] if you should appoint him now." But Elkus was, in fact, ineligible because he was not a Supreme Court justice, as the law required. On February 2, 1914, Glynn designated Cardozo as a judge of the Court of Appeals for a term of three years with the possibility of redesignation or election in his own right when the term expired.[23]

So at the age of forty-three, Benjamin Cardozo joined the court on which he would serve for the next eighteen years. He would hand down one of his most significant early decisions in a sensational, macabre murder case that was then very much in the news. In September 1913, just as the Fusion campaign was getting under way, the corpse of a young woman, horribly dismembered, was found floating in the Hudson River; and on February 5, 1914, three days after Cardozo was named to the Court of Appeals, a jury brought in its verdict in the case of Father Hans Schmidt, a Catholic priest who had confessed to the murder but who, his attorneys claimed on his behalf, was insane.

The Death of Anna Aumuller

On the morning of September 5, 1913, eighteen-year-old Mary Bann and her eleven-year-old brother, Albert, who lived in a ramshackle house alongside the Hudson River in Woodcliff, New Jersey, noticed a large brown bundle floating in the water. By noon it had become entangled in driftwood, and Albert dragged it ashore with a long stick. Wrapped in thick brown paper tied with coarse twine, the bundle contained a pillowcase with a flower design on red and blue stripes, also fastened with twine and wire. Inside was "the trunk of a young woman severed at the waist and wrapped in an undergarment. The head and arms had been cut off."[24]

Over the next few days further grisly discoveries were made. The lower torso, wrapped in a pillowcase on which there was a hand-embroidered white silk A, was found three miles further downriver at Weehawken by some boys who were out hunting crabs. It was weighted down with a piece of schist, a greenish-gray rock peculiar to Manhattan but rarely found in New Jersey, and was wrapped in pages of the August 31 edition of the *New York Times*. Part of a leg, from the thigh to just below the knee, turned up on the beach at Keansburg, some twenty miles south of Woodcliff. The county physician who performed an autopsy conjectured that the victim was in her twenties, about five feet, four inches tall, weighing 120 to 130 pounds. His examination of her remains "gave every evidence of recent pregnancy." The dismemberment had been done so skillfully, he said, "that it might be the work of a surgeon."[25]

The vital clue turned out to be the manufacturer's tag affixed to the pillowcase, which enabled the police to trace the order to a small retail shop in Manhattan, located on Eighth Avenue and 147th Street. The owner had purchased twelve of the pillows but had sold only two. One had been delivered, along with a bed and other furniture, to an apartment at 68 Bradhurst Avenue, a street just off Eighth Avenue between 145th and 146th Streets. The apartment, on the third floor in the rear, had been rented to one "H. Schmidt." Detectives staked out the apartment for five days, and by Saturday evening, September 13, when no one had appeared, they climbed up a fire escape, jimmied a window, and barged in. What they saw confirmed their worst expectations: bloodstains on the walls and floor, a fifteen-inch butcher knife, a large handsaw, and several handkerchiefs on which the letter A had been hand-embroidered. There was also a trunk with letters and cards addressed to "Anna Aumuller."

The woman, it was quickly determined, had resided most recently in the parish house of St. Boniface's Church, on 47th Street and Second Avenue, where she was employed as a servant. The pastor, Father John S. Braun, confirmed that she had worked there, adding that a priest named Hans Schmidt had been connected with the rectory during that time but was now attached to St. Joseph's Church at 405 West 125th Street, at St. Nicholas Avenue. The detectives, led by Inspector Joseph Faurot, raced uptown, not imagining that Schmidt was implicated but hoping to obtain further leads from him. Arriving at St. Joseph's shortly before midnight, they found Schmidt and identified themselves.

According to newspaper accounts, "the nervous shock Schmidt experienced convinced the detectives that they were at the end of their search for the murderer." Alternately throwing his hands over his face and pressing them against his chest, trembling with fear, he first denied even knowing Anna Aumuller. Faurot then thrust her photograph under his eyes, exclaiming: "What? You didn't know that woman?" Schmidt recoiled, covered his eyes with his hands, then "sank into a chair and began to weep." Faurot placed his hand on the priest's shoulder: "Don't lose your nerve. Brace up and tell us the truth. You murdered Anna Aumuller. We know all about it. Now control yourself and tell us the truth." Three times the detectives asked, "Did you kill her?" Twice Schmidt did not reply but then he answered: "Yes. I loved her."[26]

The curate was taken to police headquarters, where the grilling continued through the early morning hours. When Assistant District Attorney Deacon Murphy asked him how he had killed Aumuller, "he drew his left forefinger across his throat." "You cut her throat," Murphy inquired, and Schmidt answered, "Yes."[27] The only explanations he offered for his action were, "I had to kill her. She had to go to heaven," or, "I loved her. Sacrifices should be consummated in blood."[28] He described dismembering the body, even drawing dotted lines on a sketch of a figure to show how he had done it. He described how he had wrapped various parts of the body and dumped them from the Fort Lee ferry. He described the vacant lot where he had burned the blood-soaked mattress and had gotten the rocks to weigh down the bundles.

Newspapers carried the story of Schmidt's arrest and confession on Monday morning, September 15. The headlines read "RIVER MURDER TRACED TO PRIEST WHO CONFESSES," and "PRIEST CUT BODY OF GIRL INTO BITS."[29] The accounts, detailing "a butchery of a most revolting nature," were illustrated with photographs of Schmidt, Aumuller, and the Bradhurst Avenue apartment. Before long 3,000 gaping bystanders had congregated outside the apartment, and police reserves were summoned to disperse them. The *New York Times* dispatched a special correspondent to Aschaffenburg, Schmidt's home town in Germany, where everyone was "talking and thinking of little else." The reporter interviewed members of Schmidt's family, his boyhood teacher who remembered him fondly as "an intelligent and ambitious lad," and others who had heard talk that while at the seminary he had "led a notoriously dissolute life."[30]

Born in 1881, the sixth of ten children, Hans Schmidt had apparently been influenced to enter the priesthood by his mother, a devout Catholic (his father was a Protestant). After attending college he enrolled in St. Augustine's Seminary in Mainz and was ordained in December 1906. He then served in a number of parishes, never staying long at any one place, always arousing suspicion because of his idiosyncratic ways. Late in 1908 he turned up in Munich. Calling himself "Doctor Zantor," he wrote to several hundred university students claiming he would, for a price, prepare them for their examinations by a form of telepathy. He was found in illegal possession of forged seals of the Royal University and pads of faked Regents' certificates. He was arrested, ordered to undergo a mental examination, found to be suffering from a "diseased mental condition," and discharged in his father's custody. In January 1909 the ecclesiastical court of the Bishop of Munich suspended him from all priestly functions. His father sent him to an asylum but later explained that Schmidt "fled from the insane asylum where I put him and wandered to America."[31]

He sailed from Bremen to the United States in June 1909. Armed with impressive-looking ecclesiastical credentials, some authentic and others forged, he began his travels, which took him first to Louisville, Kentucky, where he remained for a time as a visitor at the home of Father Henry B. Westerman. There Schmidt rapidly perfected his English although he never lost his German accent. In March 1910 he left Louisville for Trenton, New Jersey, where he was taken on as an assistant pastor at St. Francis's. In December 1910 he moved to a similar position under Father Braun at St. Boniface's, where Anna Aumuller was employed. Schmidt never got along very well either with Braun or his sister, Magdalen, who ran the rectory. Finally, in November 1912, he moved to St. Joseph's as an assistant to Father Gerard H. Huntmann.

The picture that emerges of Hans Schmidt is that of a charismatic but unscrupulous man, charming, devious, and unstable. Father Braun and his sister mistrusted him because they noticed certain oddities: that in distributing communion, for example, he held the Host with his thumb and second finger instead of his thumb and first finger, as was proper; and that he once baptized a child without donning cassock, surplice, or stole. Yet even the Brauns admitted that he was generous to a fault: "He was very good to the poor; anyone came in there and gave a good story he was ready to give to them."[32] Many parishioners at St. Joseph's refused, at first, to believe the charges against him. As one woman said, "Father Schmidt was idolized by most of his parishioners. By many he was considered almost a saint."[33] The police obtained a letter Schmidt had written to his brother, in Germany, explaining his resumption of clerical duties: "American bishops do not bother much about Bureaukratie (red tape). The gentlemen here simply look to what a man is, not what a man has been."[34]

Within days of Schmidt's arrest the police discovered he was also involved in a counterfeiting scheme. Rent receipts found in his room at St. Joseph's led investigators to still another four-room flat, this one on West 134th Street, where they found everything needed to manufacture ten- and twenty-dollar bills—a printing press, high-quality paper, chemicals, copper plates, engraving tools, and a specially constructed camera. Schmidt had purchased the equipment and rented the apartment under a pseudonym, but he also had an associate: an unlicensed dentist, Ernest Arthur Muret (whose real name was Arthur Heibing). Muret had studied dentistry in Germany for two years and like Schmidt had often passed himself off as someone he was not. Both men were indicted for counterfeiting, but only Muret stood trial since Schmidt faced the murder charge. In October, testifying at Muret's trial, Schmidt claimed lone responsibility for the operation, but Muret was convicted of possessing counterfeiting equipment and sentenced to seven and one-half years in the penitentiary.

At his own trial Schmidt was represented by Alphonse Koelble, an active member of the German Catholic community. Forty-five years old at the time, Koelble was president of the German-American Citizen's League, and he later headed the Catholic Federation of the State of New York. Koelble acknowledged more than a passing acquaintanceship with the accused man: "I used to know Schmidt fairly well, having met him several times when I lectured at gatherings of German Catholics." Once, in the spring of 1913, when Koelble was unable to appear at such a meeting, Schmidt substituted for him and "delivered an extempore lecture in which he outlined the position the Catholic Church took against Socialism and descanted on some of his own theories of social reform." Explaining his engagement as Schmidt's counsel, Koelble said: "I am a German Catholic, and I interested myself in Schmidt at the request of a number of German Catholic laymen who had been friendly to the prisoner."[35]

"I have talked with the man," Koelble continued, "and am certain that he is insane. I do not see how any one hearing him talk could escape that conclusion." Schmidt had been acting "in a wholly irrational manner," insisting that "the Almighty God inspired and directed the act."[36] The lawyer claimed: "I will not have the least difficulty in convincing a jury that this man is insane."[37] The team of prosecutors—District Attorney Charles S. Whitman and two of his top assistants, Deacon Murphy and James A. Delehanty—realizing that the trial would hinge on expert testimony, accepted Koelble's request that Schmidt undergo further psychological testing. The prosecution recruited a team of experts, who examined Schmidt at some length and then pronounced him sane. Undeterred, Koelble arranged for Schmidt to be seen by a different group of physicians, who arrived just as firmly at the opposite conclusion.

As the trial approached, therefore, the issue seemed clearly drawn. Since Schmidt had confessed to the murder, his fate depended on which set of experts the jury believed. The case, however, turned out to be infinitely more complex than it seemed. Over the course of two years it found its way to the New York State Court of Appeals, where it occasioned a decision by Judge Benjamin N. Cardozo that he considered one of the most important he ever wrote. In it, he recalled years later, he "expounded the statute defining mental irresponsibility in the criminal law."[38]

The Trials: Psychiatry and Law

The trial of Hans Schmidt took place before Judge Warren W. Foster in the Court of General Sessions. Jury selection began on December 8, 1913, and was completed the next day. In deciding whether or not to challenge potential jurors, Schmidt's lawyers, Alphonse Koelble and his senior colleagues, William M. K. Olcott and Terence J. McManus, were not interested in whether the talesmen had formed an opinion as to the defendant's guilt but only in their view of the insanity defense. In his examination Olcott even characterized his client's behavior as "brutal," "monstrous," and "inhuman."[39] The jury numbered among its members a machinist, a clerk, a soap manufacturer, a real estate broker, a cashier, a construction engineer, and several retirees. The foreman was a lumber merchant.

Schmidt sat at a separate table, apart from his counsel, during the selection process. He had not shaved or had a haircut since his arrest nearly three months before, and so, as one account had it, "he presented anything but a priestly appearance in court. His pale face was framed in a shaggy brown beard over which hung wisps of his long brown hair. He wore a black suit and had a handkerchief knotted about his neck. A derby hat and a fur coat bore evidence of some hazy notion that he might be discharged at any moment." His head swayed unsteadily, his eyes roaming about the room. The authorities took special precautions to prevent any outbursts. An inkwell was moved from Schmidt's reach lest he hurl it at someone. Moreover, "the attendant sat behind him instead of beside him in order to be in a better position to frustrate any possible violence on the part of the prisoner."[40]

Throughout the trial the courtroom was packed, and some of the proceedings were marked by high drama. When Inspector Faurot took the stand, Assistant District Attorney James Delehanty asked him to demonstrate Schmidt's reaction when first confronted at St. Boniface's, and so the witness "went through the motions of showing the man, first with bowed head and clasped hands; then, with his elbows on the table, he covered his whole face; next he covered his eyes with one hand and then the other and at last folded his arms in front of him, and, resting them on the table, buried his head in them, his whole body shaking with convulsive sobs."[41] The defendant's confession at police headquarters was read aloud, "save for the depraved passages in which Schmidt confessed to [the] most revolting practices."[42]

Those practices, however, would be fully described during the testimony of the rival "alienists," the term applied to psychiatrists or neurologists who appeared in court to testify regarding a defendant's sanity. The District Attorney called in four physicians, all highly respected in the field and known for the skepticism with which they regarded defendants who pleaded insanity. They interviewed Schmidt on five occasions in September and October. The defense also recruited four specialists of equal repute but known for their tendency to credit such pleas. They saw Schmidt ten times in November and December. As the *New York Times* editorialized: "We are in for a battle between experts as to whether or not the man is 'insane,' but it will be largely a conflict between the supporters of different definitions for the same word. Disputes of that kind are beyond settlement."[43]

Hans Schmidt told essentially the same story to both groups of forensic psychiatrists, and a shocking story it was. All his life, he claimed, he had been fascinated with blood and always associated it with sexual arousal. As a child he frequented the slaughterhouse and played with the heads of freshly killed geese; once he had taken a rooster's head and had "put it while still bleeding on the end of his penis and had walked around strutting about."[44] At the age of fourteen, he continued, he had slept in his older sister's bed and had become sexually aroused because she was menstruating. Schmidt also reported several homosexual experiences, the first at the age of seven with a friend, another when he was thirteen with his brother, and more recently with young boys in his parish. While making love to Anna Aumuller, he said, "I used to bite her sometimes, I liked to taste the blood. I would bite her on the arm, I would bite her on the breast. There would be teeth marks and it always made me feel better."[45]

To discover what God thought of his intimacy with Anna, Schmidt declared, he decided to seek a sign from on high. Taking Anna into a church, "I brought her to the altar, and I had intercourse with her before the altar. To this she objected, as she did not like it. I was very much excited, I was more worried about it than she. I kept looking at the host all the time, there was no change."[46] One day, however, looking into the chalice as he was saying Mass, he heard God's voice saying, "Anna should be a sacrifice of love and atonement." On the night of the murder, he went on, "I heard the voice again insistently. I got the knife which I had bought two weeks before . . . I knew that God had spoken to me to do it." He described himself as experiencing a religious reverie: "I had spoken to God directly. I felt in a state of elation that I had been in communication with God."[47]

On that fateful night, Schmidt concluded, he approached the sleeping Anna, kissed her, cut her throat, drank some of her blood, decapitated her, and drank some more. But that was not all, for "as the blood ran all over, it excited me greatly. I attempted intercourse with her while the blood was flowing. I was pressing her against me." He then "committed sexual pervert acts on the body." When asked if he did not consider his behavior wrong, he replied that he knew he had acted against the law but was "not guilty in the eye of God."[48] He proceeded to cut Anna's body into seven parts because "seven was the number of candles on the altar, and seven was the number of the secrets of Christ."[49]

If Schmidt's story was only half-true he had surely set a record for violating taboos. But the alienists who testified for the defense were convinced he was telling the whole truth. All were noted experts in the field. Smith Ely Jelliffe was president of the New York Neurological Society; William Alanson White was head of St. Elizabeth's Hospital for the Insane in Washington, D.C.; Menas Gregory was chief of Bellevue Hospital's Psychopathic Ward; and Henry A. Cotton was medical director for the New Jersey State Hospital. Jelliffe and White were old friends who had founded the *Psychoanalytic Review* in 1913 and collaborated on a leading work, *Diseases of the Nervous System: A Text-Book of Neurology and Psychiatry* (1915).[50] They had testified at other trials, always for the defense. In thirty hours of interviews with Schmidt they found no sign of shamming. To Jelliffe "he was as convincing as anybody with whom I have ever talked."[51] To Gregory "he seemed to be as sincere and as honest and as genuine as I have ever seen a man do or say things, and relate things."[52] The doctors indignantly rejected the suggestion that Schmidt was faking: "Absolutely not; absolutely impossible . . . A man cannot sham insanity such as he has any more than I can make an apple or an orange; it is a product of nature, not a product of artifice."[53]

To dispel any lingering doubts, however, the alienists had performed a test the results of which they considered conclusive. At one of their meetings Schmidt kept staring at Menas Gregory's fingernail, under which there was a blister, the result of a bruise suffered in changing an automobile tire. Recognizing the serendipitous nature of his injury, Gregory positioned himself behind the priest, pricked the blister with a pin, raising a large drop of blood, and then thrust his finger in front of Schmidt's face. "And then a very definite transformation took place in Father Schmidt," Jelliffe recounted: "He immediately got red, he flushed, his pupils dilated, he grabbed at the hand, he stood up, Dr. Gregory retreated, he followed him around the room, he grabbed at his hand." Gregory evaded the priest's clutches, "but a drop of blood fell on his lip, which he licked with his tongue and said, . . . 'allus blut ist mein.'"[54] The dilated pupils, the flushed appearance, the cold sweat the doctors felt on his forehead—Schmidt, they thought, could not possibly have faked these physical symptoms.

From their observations the doctors concluded that they could "draw a valid scientific deduction" that Schmidt was suffering from "the paranoid type of dementia praecox," a chronic, progressive, and incurable disease. Asked to describe the symptoms, Jelliffe said that most sufferers had "a bad heredity," were "hard children to get along with," and were given to "various forms of sexual perversities, excessive sexual furiousity, oftentimes acts of cruelty." By adolescence they were subject to "an overweening conceit" and began to have hallucinations that convinced them that they were different from other people, that they had "been set apart by somebody to do some special work." In some ways, the doctors believed, the priesthood had offered Schmidt a protected environment in which his fantasies could flourish. The paranoid form of the illness could be discerned "because of the peculiarities of the individual[s], their suspiciousness, their watchfulness, their ideas that they are the centre of almost everything, that they have special powers that others have not, and as a rule their mental deterioration take[s] place very slowly."[55]

Having extracted these opinions from the defense's physicians—opinions which remained unshaken even during a pointed cross-examination—Schmidt's lawyers then asked the witnesses the crucial question, the answer to which would determine whether the insanity plea would succeed: Did

Hans Schmidt understand that it was wrong for him to murder Anna Au-muller? Jelliffe: "In my opinion he did not understand the nature and qual-ity of the act . . . In my opinion he believed that he was right and was not in the condition of mind to know that he was wrong."[56] Gregory: "He thought he was doing the proper thing, that he was obeying the order, the command-ment of God; he thought it was the right thing to do."[57] Once, dispensing with all highfalutin' language, Jelliffe used the vernacular: "I have seen enough evidence to show me . . . that the man was a crazy man, now, and then and before."[58]

The alienists who testified for the prosecution had credentials no less im-posing than those of Jelliffe and his colleagues: William Mabon was a pro-fessor of Mental Disease at New York University; Carlos F. MacDonald, a professor emeritus at Bellevue Hospital Medical College, had headed the New York State Commission on Lunacy; George Kirby was director of the insanity clinic at Manhattan State Hospital; Alan Ross Diefendorf, of New Haven, was also a noted authority. But they reached the opposite conclu-sion: that Schmidt fully understood the nature of his actions and was now shamming insanity to escape punishment.

They too had administered what they considered a foolproof test. In talking to Schmidt they concocted "symptoms" and asked if he had expe-rienced any of them: shooting pains, numbness, tingling sensations in his head and body, balls of fire appearing before his eyes. When Schmidt said that he had, in fact, experienced all of them, the psychiatrists triumphantly concluded that he had fallen into their trap. The very claim that he had these "absurd and ridiculous symptoms," Mabon asserted, was itself "marked evidence of shamming."[59] MacDonald placed even greater reli-ance on this test: "When he admitted that he had the symptoms which I knew did not exist I assumed naturally that he was shamming."[60] The doc-tors added that when they berated Schmidt his pulse rate jumped from 75 to nearly 100.

And berate him they did, in harsh, uncompromising terms. Where Jel-liffe and his colleagues had been deferential in their dealings with the ac-cused man, addressing him as "Father Schmidt," Mabon's group took a dif-ferent approach. Usually calling him "Schmidt," more rarely, "Mr. Schmidt," they denounced him to his face: "Your history shows that you have been a criminal man all your life, that you have been using religion as a mask to cover up criminal acts all your life . . . You have been lying about the voice of God." They told Schmidt that he did not know enough about the symptoms of insanity to hoodwink them, and that he might as well "drop that role of shamming insanity, because you can't deceive us, not for a moment."[61] Although a transcript cannot convey the doctors' tone of voice, it is easily surmised, as is their moral outrage: "Now, Schmidt, you have lied straight through about this thing . . . Now see here, Schmidt, do you suppose there is any woman, a Catholic, a Protestant, or a heathen, that would have intercourse with a priest of the church on the altar of the church?"[62]

The techniques employed by Mabon and his associates followed the prescriptions for detecting spurious claims of insanity found in the psychiatric literature. According to a leading work, E. C. Spitzka's *Insanity, Its Classification, Diagnosis and Treatment,* published in 1883 but still widely used, defendants who claimed to have experienced bogus "symptoms" suggested by the physician gave themselves away. An experienced doctor, by "impressing the impostor with the hopelessness of his attempt to succeed in gaining his object," might well succeed in putting an end to the shamming.[63] The prosecution's alienists may also have been influenced by another early treatise which recommended: "In all such investigations the physician must never show the most trifling sign of doubt or hesitation; he must, on the contrary, appear to know everything, in order to discover everything, and must present a firm and imposing front in all his intercourse with the accused."[64]

Both teams of specialists placed great emphasis on observable physical characteristics, such as Schmidt's dilated pupils at the sight of blood or his elevated pulse rate when being reviled, for these clinical reactions, it was thought, provided the strongest empirical evidence for their conclusions. Leading works in the field of forensic medicine argued that mental illness could usually be diagnosed entirely from a person's outward appearance. In *The Unsound Mind and the Law* (1918), George Jacoby held that melancholia, mania, and paranoia had such distinctive physiognomies that "it is almost possible to read the diagnosis from the patient's face." But Schmidt's case presented a difficulty: dementia praecox did not manifest itself so obviously. As Jacoby wrote, "a specific demented expression, one that could be utilized for purposes of differential diagnosis, does not exist."[65] Although the illness was said to be accompanied by a lack of energy, an unsteady gait, and a sagging head, the inability to make a positive diagnosis from such concededly general traits led the rival sides to seize on any concrete evidence that would support their claims.

The two groups of psychiatrists offered radically different diagnoses, but both sides may well have been correct. Cast by the courts as gatekeepers, physicians were supposed to decide who was "sane" and therefore legally responsible, and who was "insane" and therefore exempt from the normal penalties of the law. But the legal definition of insanity—not knowing the nature of an act or knowing that it was wrong—was not an accurate medical definition. As an editorial writer for the *New York Times* noted, Schmidt's trial "starts with the legal, but fallacious, assumption that insanity and irresponsibility are interchangeable terms."[66] While Jelliffe's group wanted to say that Schmidt should not be punished because he was mentally ill, it had to say he did not understand the nature of his act. While Mabon's group wanted to say that Schmidt should be punished because he knew what he was doing, it had to say he was feigning insanity. The possibility that Schmidt was psychopathic and also engaged in shamming—the concept of "the simulation of insanity by the insane" was well understood at the time—was never mentioned, for it would not have served the purposes of either side.

The trial lasted for three weeks. It concluded on December 29, 1913, with emotional appeals to the jurors. The defense attorney, William M. K. Olcott, affirmed that Schmidt was "a half educated, half ignorant, poor German philosopher, a man cursed with hereditary insanity," whose "only possible motive for the killing of the unfortunate woman was an insane, morbid love, which was a result of a disease of the mind."[67] Summing up for the prosecution, Assistant District Attorney Delehanty declared: "This Schmidt is the twentieth century Judas Iscariot. He is no more a priest than a tramp in the gutter . . . He is not a priest! He is a thief! thief! thief! . . . I and every other believer in the doctrines of the Roman Catholic church are ashamed that this man was ever connected with our faith."[68] The jurors retired early in the afternoon only to find themselves hopelessly deadlocked. After wrangling for thirty-three hours and taking fifteen ballots, all of which resulted in identical 10-to-2 votes for conviction, they were discharged. One of the holdouts explained he voted for acquittal "because I was convinced he was insane when he did this act, both by the testimony of the medical experts and the man's past history."[69]

So Hans Schmidt had to stand trial again, this time before Justice Vernon N. Davis in the criminal term of the Supreme Court. Women seeking admittance were stopped at the door, informed of the shockingly explicit nature of the testimony, and "although they were not ordered to stay outside, the doorkeeper told them that Justice Davis warned them that the testimony was such that no woman should hear."[70] Virtually the same evidence was presented as at the first trial, although to expedite matters each side called only two alienists, Jelliffe and Gregory for the defense, Mabon and MacDonald for the prosecution. The trial began on January 19, 1914, and ended on February 5. This time it took the jury only two and one-half hours to find Schmidt guilty of murder in the first degree. District Attorney Charles S. Whitman was present, seated next to Delehanty, when the verdict was read. "Schmidt broke the silence with a laugh," a reporter wrote, "and then turned as if to leave the courtroom."[71] On February 11 Justice Davis imposed the death sentence and Schmidt was taken to Sing Sing to await execution.

Even before sentence was pronounced Alphonse Koelble said that he would appeal. He explained that Justice Davis's charge to the jury—which asserted that the definition of "wrong" in the insanity defense meant knowing an act was "against the law" rather than knowing it was morally wrong—had incorrectly stated the law. But Koelble also hinted at another, more dramatic basis for the appeal. As yet revealing no details, he suggested that Schmidt had been shielding someone else. Anna Aumuller, he said, had "died from the effects of a criminal operation."[72]

"A Criminal Operation"

Within days of his arrival at Sing Sing, Hans Schmidt came up with an entirely new story. He told it to James Delehanty, with Koelble and a stenographer present, in three marathon sessions on February 15 and 19 and March 13. Schmidt now said that Anna Aumuller had died as the result of a botched abortion. He admitted that he had helped procure the abortion, which had been performed by Ernest Muret with the assistance of Bertha Zech and with the knowledge of a third friend, Dr. Arnold Leo. In September Leo and Zech were brought to Sing Sing to confront Schmidt and denied his allegations. In October Schmidt submitted an affidavit setting forth the new version and asking for a retrial. In December Koelble filed his own affidavit, which revealed many facts that had not been known. The District Attorney's office then presented counter-arguments, and on January 28, 1915, nearly a year after Schmidt's conviction, Justice Davis denied the request for a new trial.

Schmidt's revised account offers a credible picture of his relationship with Anna Aumuller, refracted, to be sure, through the lens of self-interest. Born in Hungary, Anna emigrated to the United States as a child and as a teenager became a cook and cleaning woman at St. Boniface's Church. In December 1910, shortly after she took this position, Schmidt appeared on the scene. He was twenty-nine, she was nineteen, and almost immediately they began an affair. In December 1911 she had her first abortion, illegally performed, somewhere in the Bronx. In 1912 she had another abortion, this time going to Vienna, at Schmidt's expense. She spent six months in Europe, finally leaving Hamburg on October 27 and arriving in the United States on November 10. On board ship she formed a friendship with Anna Huttner, a somewhat older woman who resided in Cincinnati, and to whom she continued to write. Five of the letters and postcards she sent to Huttner, some written in English and some in German, were entered in the trial record.

Here Anna Aumuller's own voice finally emerges, and what a melancholy voice it is. Alone and frightened, she is profoundly grateful for Huttner's friendship: "I almost cried when I read that I could trust in you so happy was I over it. It must have been designed by God that we should meet in Hamburg." She desperately needs to hide her on-again, off-again affair with Schmidt from her superiors at St. Boniface's, Father Braun and his sister, Magdalen, and so begs Huttner not to mention his name on any postcards. She feels, slaving away in the kitchen, as if she is in jail: "At times I feel very lonesome and sick of living out because you are never your own boss. It seems to me when you are living out—the same as being in prison. The other girl here is a New York girl. She says we look like prisoners because the kitchen windows have iron bars in front, and we call the kitchen Sing Sing." She dreams of freedom: "Dear Miss Anna, I am longing for traveling. I would like to go on a ship as stewardess and travel all over the world. I hope that we can make that trip to the old country again together." She finds what joy she can in more mundane outings, visiting Palisades Amusement Park with Schmidt and reporting: "It is there the same as Coney Island, and I enjoyed myself fine." On August 23, 1913, in her last letter, she informs Huttner tersely: "Do not know as yet my new address. I leave the rectory September 1."[73]

She actually left a few days earlier because Father Braun's sister recognized that she was pregnant and turned her out. In April, when she had first suspected her condition, Schmidt had taken her to his friend Dr. Arnold Leo for an examination, but it was too early to confirm the pregnancy. As the months went by Schmidt promised he would leave the priesthood and marry her, so he claimed. But she objected, saying that if he gave up the priesthood on her account "it was only a question of time when I would abandon her." Illegitimate herself, Anna "often and keenly felt the shame of it" and decided, instead, that she wanted another abortion. When she had to leave St. Boniface's, Schmidt rented the Bradhurst Avenue flat, bought several items of furniture, and she moved in. On August 30, however, "she again brought up strongly the question of her pregnancy and urged me to secure some one to perform an operation."

Monday, September 1, 1913, was Labor Day. That morning, Schmidt reported, "I found her in bed complaining of pain; she said that she had tried something on herself after the manner of Hungarian women and that she was in pain." She had, he added, attempted to induce an abortion with "a crude imitation of a doctor's instrument," and she now pleaded with him to complete the operation. At ten in the morning, Schmidt fetched both Leo and Muret, who accompanied him to the apartment, examined Aumuller, and left saying she would be all right. Schmidt stayed until noon, left, then returned an hour later only to find "her pains had greatly increased." Again he went to see Muret, who, with his assistant Bertha Zech, returned to the apartment at about three o'clock. Muret brought some surgical instruments with him. While Schmidt waited in the kitchen, they performed or completed the abortion and disposed of the fetus. Returning to the bedroom, Schmidt found that Aumuller had fainted and was bleeding heavily. Muret was frantically attempting to staunch the flow with cotton balls. "All three of us were panic stricken," Schmidt recalled, and as Anna lost strength, "I put my hand on her forehead and talked in her ear to wake up and everything would be all right and so forth."

Anna Aumuller died some time that afternoon. Muret and Zech left the apartment, Schmidt continued, and he went in search of Leo. They returned that evening between nine and ten o'clock. Confirming that Aumuller was dead, Leo refused Schmidt's request to issue a death certificate "to save what was an awful situation." "Why should I want to help out when somebody else was responsible?" Leo asked, and cautioned Schmidt not to tell anyone that he, Leo, had been in the flat. Schmidt then went to Muret's home and returned with him to the apartment about midnight. Muret suggested dismembering the body in order to avoid detection. In a room "swimming with blood," Muret undertook the ghastly chore, using a knife and a saw that Schmidt had obtained for the counterfeiting operation. Muret handed Schmidt the body parts "which I took and carried into the kitchen and wrapped up." The next day Schmidt returned with Bertha Zech to complete the process, and they proceeded to drop the packages over the side of a ferry boat.

According to Schmidt, they also decided on a strategy in case the death was discovered: Muret suggested that the priest pretend to be insane. "With the insanity plea, it will not come to any trial at all, but you will be sent to an asylum where they will dismiss you after some time as cured." If their involvement in the abortion was discovered, Muret said, they both faced twenty-year sentences for manslaughter. To clinch his argument, Muret referred to the notorious case of Harry Thaw, who had murdered the architect Stanford White, had successfully pleaded insanity, and had been sent to the Matteawan Asylum for the Criminally Insane at Fishkill, New York: "Thaw was never half as crazy as you are now." (The case was then much in the news because on August 17 Thaw had escaped from Matteawan, though he was eventually captured.) Schmidt claimed he felt responsible for Aumuller's death, believed he would get off on the insanity plea anyway, and so promised Muret, Zech, and Leo that he would shoulder all the blame.[74]

Schmidt's revised account was abundantly supported by new evidence. While the second trial was in progress, Alphonse Koelble had accidentally discovered in Schmidt's cell a letter written by Muret, which the priest had tried to conceal, stating that Schmidt had said "that the Girl never was killed but died from an illegal operation." Koelble had also located a witness who had seen a man and woman fitting Muret's and Zech's description at the Bradhurst Avenue apartment on the day Aumuller died. Moreover, several of Schmidt's fellow prisoners reported that he had told them Aumuller had died following an abortion. The reason he had made a fraudulent confession, Schmidt told one inmate, was because he feared Muret, "and I think as a priest and with the co-operation of the church I can get off with a light sentence, or be sent to Matteawan and get out in a few years, whereas if I give up the whole thing on Dr. Muret, he will give up a number of things on me and I will get a good deal more for other things that I have done than I would on this." He also said that the prosecutor, James Delehanty, was a Catholic, and "if there were one or two Catholics on the jury he would certainly be sent to Matteawan," and as a German citizen, he could be repatriated and eventually go free. "As it is," Schmidt declared, "all roads lead to Matteawan."[75]

The most telling new evidence, however, was provided by two physicians, Henry W. Cattell and Justin Herold. In November 1914 both of them were taken to the New York City morgue where they examined the dead woman's remains, and they also viewed slides prepared from her uterus. They found no indication that death had resulted from a wound inflicted on the neck but much to show, in Cattell's words, that Anna Aumuller "came to her death from bleeding and shock due to an abortion." Herold's affidavit stated that death was caused "by shock and hemorrhage following an incomplete abortion." Both men were highly regarded pathologists. Herold, a professor of medical jurisprudence at Fordham University and author of "Herold's Legal Medicine," had performed thousands of autopsies. But Cattell had the more relevant, if appalling, specialization: performing autopsies on women who had died as a result of "criminal" abortions. As senior coroner's physician in Philadelphia, he reported, he had "made thirty-three autopsies on those dying from the effects of an abortion," and he had headed an investigation of several hundred such cases.[76]

At Schmidt's trials the prosecution had called two pathologists who testified that Anna Aumuller had been pregnant, probably in her sixth month, as of a few days or possibly even a few hours before she died, but that death had resulted from bleeding from the neck, not the uterus. They had testified briefly and had not been seriously challenged by the defense, which at the time was conceding Schmidt's guilt and attempting to prove him insane. Reading the physicians' trial testimony, Cattell and Herold dismissed it out of hand. They noted that the blood found in the victim's lungs could not have resulted from a stab wound to the neck, as had been testified, for such a wound would not have opened the chest cavity. Moreover, the state's physicians were mistaken in believing that the absence of any clot in the uterus proved that bleeding had not taken place there. Herold explained: "It is claimed that if hemorrhage from the uterus had caused death a clot of blood must of necessity be found in the uterine cavity. My reason for differing in this opinion is that the clot of blood is an evidence of arrested hemorrhage and not evidence of a hemorrhage having caused the death."[77]

If Anna Aumuller indeed died in this manner, she was a victim of New York State's Draconian abortion law. The state's penal law, passed in 1909, embodied provisions of the Penal Code of 1881, which was in turn based on a measure adopted in 1872 during a nationwide trend toward more restrictive abortion laws. As things stood in 1913, therefore, "the willful killing of an unborn quick child, by any injury committed upon the person of the mother of such child, is manslaughter in the first degree" unless necessary to preserve the woman's life. So if Muret indeed told Schmidt that they both risked twenty-year prison sentences for first-degree manslaughter if they were found out, he was exactly right. Anna Aumuller herself, in the event a legitimate doctor had been summoned to complete the self-induced abortion, would have faced a long prison term. She was in her sixth month and "quickening"—the ability to detect fetal movement—usually occurs late in the fourth month. The law provided that a woman quick with child, "who takes or uses, or submits to the use of any drug, medicine, or substance, or any instrument or other means with intent to procure her own miscarriage, unless the same is necessary to preserve her own life, or that of the child whereof she is pregnant, if the death of such child is thereby produced, is guilty of manslaughter in the second degree."[78]

Dr. Arnold Leo's wish not to be implicated in the case also made good sense from a purely legal standpoint. When a woman died as the result of an abortion, any physician known to have treated her at the time became subject to criminal abortion proceedings. In 1910 a New York attorney, Almuth C. Vandiver, wrote in the *American Journal of Obstetrics* that doctors might be arrested "simply because they were the last physician attending the patient and they had not made their report to the coroner." According to the historian Leslie Reagan: "If a woman died despite a doctor's efforts, he became a likely suspect in the criminal abortion case . . . Physicians learned that if they failed to report criminal abortion cases, the investigative process could be turned against them." Doctors who failed to cooperate with the authorities might actually be indicted or might be expelled by their state medical societies and lose their licenses.[79]

A number of law enforcement officials were apparently anxious to believe Schmidt's second story, for it described actions by a priest which, however disgraceful, were less morally reprehensible than the long list of excesses to which he had originally confessed. One of the detectives—himself a Roman Catholic—who arrested Schmidt suspected from the outset that Aumuller had died as the result of an abortion; according to Schmidt, "after taking off his hat," he said, "Father, please tell me the truth, because you know you have not told the truth. Remember the church."[80] Later, after Schmidt changed his story, he was interviewed at Sing Sing by Assistant District Attorney Delehanty, whose line of questioning suggested a similar desire to have the priest recant: "Of course what you told the doctors about drinking her blood wasn't true, was it? . . . You didn't have intercourse with her, of course. You wouldn't do such a thing after death." And as for having sexual intercourse on a church altar: "That wasn't true, was it? . . . She never went out on the altar with you and submitted to intercourse, did she? When you think it over now, she didn't do it, did she." He was seemingly relieved when Schmidt replied, "No."[81]

Given the prosecutors' own inclination to credit the veracity of Schmidt's second version, the question arises: Why did they oppose Koelble's request for a new trial? There are several possibilities. They may not have believed all that Schmidt now told them, perhaps accepting his account of his own role in the abortion but not that of his three confederates. The District Attorney's office continued to insist that it would not trust anything Schmidt said because he was a "colossal liar."[82] Or the prosecutors may, in fact, have believed his whole story but wished to spare themselves the embarrassment of relying on Schmidt's testimony to convict the others, since there was no certainty a conviction could be won on his say-so alone.

Ernest Muret, Bertha Zech, and Arnold Leo consistently denied any role in the affair and branded Schmidt's claims "wholly false."[83] On different occasions in September 1914 Leo and Zech were taken to Sing Sing to see Schmidt in the presence of Delehanty and Koelble. Leo and Schmidt sparred the entire time. Leo: "I saw this woman's dead body, did I?" Schmidt: "Don't ask me; you know it." Leo: "I know nothing about it and you know I know nothing about it." Schmidt: "You can say that to the District Attorney, but don't say it to me."[84] Zech and Schmidt traded insults. Zech: "But why do you tell such a lie now?" Schmidt: "You're a snake with the face of a dove." Delehanty also joined in, telling Zech: "Now listen, the key to the death house is in your hands; . . . This man should not die if he is not guilty of murder." Zech: "Don't you believe me? You can't believe this man. You can't. He's a liar." Koelble also interceded: "Miss Zech, you are a woman. I can't call you what I would like to call you, but if you were a man I would do it in a minute, but you are the nearest approach to a constitutional liar that I have ever seen." Zech: "I am a liar?" Koelble: "Why, you have lied until you are black in the face." Zech had the last word: "Oh, I just hate him. I don't hardly know what to think. He's a liar . . . He's a liar. He has to die for that; he's responsible for it."[85]

For some reason Muret was not taken from the federal penitentiary at Atlanta where he was serving his counterfeiting sentence to confront

Schmidt. Instead, in November 1914, Deacon Murphy, an assistant district attorney in Whitman's office, went to Atlanta to obtain a statement from Muret denying Schmidt's allegations. Department of Justice officials in New York City expedited Murphy's task, alerting the attorney general to the importance of his mission ("You may recall that Muret was mixed up with the Priest, Hans Schmidt, who was afterwards convicted of the murder of a young woman and who is now under sentence of death"), and seeing that Murphy was provided with a letter of introduction to the warden at Atlanta.[86] Muret's affidavit asserted that he had never met Anna Aumuller, knew nothing about her death, and had never been in the flat on Bradhurst Avenue.

In view of these denials it may have seemed simpler for the prosecutors to stand by Schmidt's original story, which at least had led to a conviction of the right man, even if for the wrong crime. Given Koelble's appeal on behalf of Schmidt, however, the legal system was going to have to disentangle a situation that seemed hopelessly snarled, involving, as it did, the proper definition of what constituted legal insanity, the evidential basis upon which a new trial should be granted, and the role of the courts in seeing that justice is done. The task of disentanglement was left to the New York State Court of Appeals or, more precisely, to Benjamin Cardozo, the judge to whom the case of *People* v. *Hans Schmidt* was assigned.

The Insanity Plea: People v. Hans Schmidt, 1915

Unlike the United States Supreme Court and the appellate courts of most states, where the chief justice or chief judge typically assigns the writing of opinions, cases in the New York State Court of Appeals were assigned on a basis of rotation (at present they are randomly chosen by the drawing of lots.) This eliminated any possibility that judges might think they were being given a disproportionate share of unimportant cases, and it created a setting in which judges viewed themselves as generalists rather than specialists.[87] Purely by chance, then, the Schmidt case fell to Cardozo, who was, indeed, eminently well qualified to treat the historical development of the law regarding the insanity plea. But the case also forced Cardozo to confront shockingly aberrant forms of behavior which elicited a decidedly moralistic response.

The brief Alphonse Koelble submitted on Schmidt's behalf endeavored to show that he was not a murderer but was rather guilty of manslaughter "in aiding and abetting and procuring the abortion of Anna Aumuller." He pointed out internal inconsistencies in the affidavits submitted by Muret, Leo, and Zech. He explained why the pathologists who concluded that hemorrhaging following an abortion was the cause of death had much the better medical argument. He noted that if Schmidt had been capable of committing cold-blooded murder and dismembering his lover's body, he would have been "a man of iron nerves" who would not have presented the "pitiable picture he did at the time of his arrest," shaking and quaking before the police. Finally, while Schmidt had often used an alias, he rented the Bradhurst Avenue flat in his own name, hardly, Koelble reasoned, the act of a man with murder on his mind.

Koelble also made three crucial legal arguments. First, he asserted, the Court of Appeals was authorized to set aside a conviction for first-degree murder "where it appeared that injustice has been done to a defendant." Article 528 of the Code of Criminal Procedure allowed the Court to order a new trial in cases involving the death penalty "if it be satisfied that the verdict was against the weight of evidence or against the law or that justice requires a new trial." The evidence to be introduced at a new trial was supposed to have been "discovered since the trial." Conceding that the evidence concerning the abortion had always been known to Schmidt and so was "not newly discovered in the strict sense," Koelble nevertheless maintained that the claims of justice could be satisfied only if the court, in its discretion, ordered a retrial.

Second, Koelble maintained that the judge's charge to the jury had incorrectly stated the conditions under which a defendant could be found legally insane. Judge Davis had begun properly enough by quoting the penal law: a person might be considered insane only upon proof that at the time of the act "he was laboring under such a defect of reason as not to know the nature and quality of the act he was doing, or . . . not to know that the act was wrong." This was a commonsense definition, Davis said, adding: "'Wrong' there means, 'criminal'—contrary to the laws of the State." Koelble insisted that the jury should have been asked to decide whether Schmidt knew his act was morally wrong, not merely legally wrong. If he believed he was acting in obedience to a divine command, he could not have known he was acting immorally even if he knew he was violating the law. Although Schmidt was now disclaiming the insanity plea, that did not "shut the court's door to him" because due process depended on the jury's being properly instructed.

Finally, Koelble appealed to a provision of the Code of Criminal Procedure which was designed to prevent an individual from falsely confessing to a capital crime, being convicted, and then executed in the absence of corroborating evidence. Article 332 held that "a conviction shall not be had upon a plea of guilty where the crime charged is or may be punishable by death." If the rule prevented such a conviction, Koelble asked, "does not public policy require that when a man has been convicted on his own statement the conviction should not be upheld when he retracts the statement upon which he was convicted?"[88]

Koelble conceded that his client was a wicked man: "It is not denied that he has had criminal tendencies, that he was an unworthy priest, that he was a party to three abortions, that he committed fraud, that he deceived and that he counterfeited." But this characterization did not begin to satisfy the assistant district attorney, Robert C. Taylor, who prepared the brief opposing a new trial. He reviled Schmidt as "an unmitigated scoundrel masquerading as a priest." He could not bring himself to write about "the nauseating details of def[endan]t's sexual history," Taylor said, but promptly wrote at least a little about every one of them. Even if Schmidt had invented these details, Taylor said, "the fact that a man could tell such stories about himself . . . shows that he was a monster," in fact, "a gross monster, delighting in bestial lust, but incapable of anything like true affection."

Taylor then attempted to refute Koelble's three arguments. He denied the existence of any "newly discovered" evidence: the law could not allow a defendant to tell a false story, "speculate upon deluding the jury; and, if he fails, then be permitted to fall back upon a defense which he knew all about from the beginning, but knowingly chose to suppress." As to the meaning of the word "wrong" in the law concerning insanity, Taylor contended that the judge's instructions accorded well with precedent. Moreover, Schmidt was not convicted on his confession alone since the cause of Aumuller's death had been corroborated by the physicians who testified at the trial. Had the more recent findings of pathologists been available to the jury, Taylor admitted, the verdict might have been different. But the decision should stand "where the evidence before the jurors rendered it impossible for them to bring in any other verdict."

The prosecutor's brief affected a tone of high moral indignation: Schmidt's sexual history was a "mass of filth"; his behavior was "iniquitous"; his request for a new trial was "unholy and outrageous." To grant a new trial would make a "farce" of the judicial process. The fundamental point to be upheld was that "Courts never permit a man to profit by his own wrong." The only available recourse, Taylor asserted, was the pardoning power. "If there is any merit in def[endan]t's assertion that Anna died as the result of a criminal operation in which def[endan]t participated, this Court cannot relieve him; but the matter should be left to the Executive, who can be safely trusted to take such action as the circumstances warrant."[89]

The judges of the Court of Appeals were presented with a trial record and supporting materials in excess of 1,800 pages. Koelble's briefs amounted to an additional 300 pages and Taylor's to nearly 100. The documentation included photographs of Hans Schmidt, Anna Aumuller, and the bedroom in the Bradhurst Avenue apartment, and even one horrifying photograph of the nude torso. The case was argued before the court on October 27, 1915, and the decision was handed down on November 23 without dissent. Five other judges who took part in the decision agreed with Cardozo; the sixth, Chief Judge Willard Bartlett, concurred in the result but not in the way it was reached. Cardozo ruled that Schmidt had not had a fair trial, but, nevertheless, did not deserve a new one.

At the outset Cardozo stated that the evidence regarding Aumuller's death as the result of an abortion did not qualify as "new." Adopting Taylor's interpretation, Cardozo also paraphrased the prosecutor's language: "A criminal may not experiment with one defense, and then when it fails him invoke the aid of the law which he has flouted, to experiment with another defense, held in reserve for that emergency." To permit such a ruse would be to invite contempt of the court's authority. Even if Schmidt's second story was true, courts were powerless to intervene. Cardozo put the matter even more strongly than Taylor: "There is no power in any court to grant a new trial upon that ground." The proper remedy, Cardozo said, "is by appeal to the clemency of the Governor."

Having barred further judicial intervention, Cardozo could have stopped but went on instead to consider the meaning of the word "wrong" in the law regarding insanity. Here he sided squarely with defense attorney Koelble. To determine whether the word referred only to what was legally wrong, as opposed to what was morally wrong, Cardozo turned to the origins of the doctrine in mid-nineteenth-century England. In 1843 one Daniel McNaughtan had attempted to assassinate the prime minister, Sir Robert Peel, but instead had killed Peel's secretary, Edward Drummond.[90] The jury's verdict—not guilty by reason of insanity—produced such an uproar that the House of Lords summoned fifteen judges and proposed five questions designed to elicit the common law definition of insanity. The judges' reply—that to establish insanity the defense must prove that "the accused was laboring under such a defect of reason, from disease of the mind, as not to know the nature and quality of the act he was doing, or, if he did know it, that he did not know he was doing what was wrong"—quickly found its way into the laws and jurisprudence of New York State. Although the judges did not further define the word "wrong," Cardozo's reading of their replies in the McNaughtan case, which he cited at length, convinced him that "it is the knowledge of wrong, conceived of as moral wrong, that seems to have been established by that decision as the controlling test." In the absence of conclusive proof that the judges did not mean legal wrong, however, he merely asserted that he could not agree that the word "is to receive so narrow a construction."

Why not? To answer that question, he drew less on history than on "reason and justice." Insisting that the two possible definitions of "wrong" should be tested by their consequences, Cardozo offered an emotionally charged hypothetical case: "A mother kills her infant child to whom she has been devotedly attached. She knows the nature and quality of the act; she knows that the law condemns it; but she is inspired by an insane delusion that God has appeared to her and ordained the sacrifice." It would be a mockery to say she knew her act was wrong, Cardozo concluded, although according to the judge's instructions to the jury in the Schmidt case, she would have to be found sane and legally responsible, a verdict that Cardozo thought would be "abhorrent."

Having shown that the judge in Schmidt's trial had not gotten the law right, Cardozo had now only to explain why it made no difference. To do this, he circled back to where he had begun. Even though there was error in the judge's charge, a new trial was not required because Schmidt now conceded he was sane. His attempt to effect a "fraud" upon the court had backfired and the jury, as he now conceded, had reached the right decision concerning his sanity. The law, Cardozo said, does not require ministers of justice to "abet a criminal project to set the law at naught." Again paraphrasing Taylor, he added: "The principle is fundamental that no man shall be permitted to profit by his own wrong." Schmidt had effectively forfeited any right to avail himself of error in the judge's instructions to the jury.

In the final paragraph of his opinion Cardozo dealt briefly and unconvincingly with Koelble's argument that no one should be convicted of a capital crime solely on the basis of a confession. "The defendant has not been convicted upon a plea of guilty," Cardozo declared: "He has been tried before a duly organized court . . . and even though there may have been error, there has been no denial in any fundamental sense of due process of law." After a few lame attempts to explain why he had reached this conclusion, Cardozo frankly acknowledged that the central issue, to him, was that the court not appear to sanction Schmidt's duplicity: "We cannot extend the statute to the situation now before us, and we will not aid the defendant in his effort to gain the benefit of a fraudulent defense."[91]

Cardozo's decision did not mention that Hans Schmidt was a priest or that he was having an affair with Anna Aumuller. In fact, it never even mentioned Hans Schmidt by name. Cardozo usually called him "the defendant" but twice referred to him as "the criminal" and once spoke of his "criminal project." Cardozo provided no details regarding Schmidt's original story, noting only that the defendant had confessed to "unspeakable excesses and hideous crimes" and a life governed by "monstrous perversions and delusions."

Cardozo's ruling elevated the importance of moral considerations in making a legal distinction between sanity and insanity. For a man whose early training and outlook on life disposed him to emphasize those considerations, the resulting clarification of the law was undoubtedly satisfying. Yet at the same time the ruling was based on a narrow, legalistic reading of Schmidt's rights. It is true that Schmidt had been a bald-faced liar and had not told the truth until he thought it could benefit him. But having once committed perjury, what alternative was then left to him? Suppose Schmidt had maintained his pretense of insanity: Was Cardozo implying that he then would have been deprived of due process by the judge's inaccurate charge to the jury and would have deserved a new trial? If no man should profit by his own wrong, should he profit, so to speak, by perpetuating the wrong?

There is no way to know how Cardozo would have ruled on the meaning of the word "wrong" in the insanity plea if Schmidt had maintained his fraudulent plea. Perhaps he would have reached the same conclusion even if in so doing he would have aided Schmidt. Or, to avoid such a result, he might not have chosen the case as a vehicle for deciding the issue. Or, to uphold the jury's verdict, he might have taken the opposite view. Cardozo's construction of the judges' answers in McNaughton was plausible, but, as he conceded, it was not the only one possible. As late as 1952 an English court interpreted McNaughtan differently, asserting: "the word 'wrong' means contrary to law and not 'wrong' according to the opinion of one man or a number of people on the question of whether a particular act might or might not be justified."[92] Neither Schmidt nor his counsel could have predicted how the Court of Appeals would rule.

In the end Cardozo accepted Assistant District Attorney Taylor's proposal: since the courts were unable to help Schmidt, the only recourse was executive clemency. Schmidt's story about the abortion "supplies a plausible explanation of some of the mysteries of this tragedy," Cardozo stated, and added that "in an appropriate proceeding it would merit earnest scrutiny." That proceeding would have to take place in the Governor's chambers, not the Judges'. But among all the things Cardozo did not mention in his decision, perhaps the most significant was the name of the governor, recently elected in November 1914: Charles S. Whitman. As Alphonse Koelble had noted despairingly in his reply to the prosecution's brief: "The Governor of the State was the District Attorney in this case."[93]

The Death Penalty

As district attorney, Whitman had taken more than an ordinary interest in the Schmidt case. He saw to it that a detailed diagram of the Bradhurst Avenue flat was prepared for the trial. He recruited the alienists who would appear for the prosecution. He wrote to Ernest Muret in the federal penitentiary at a time when it appeared his testimony would be helpful. He made sure that his witnesses obtained suitable travel arrangements and hotel accommodations.[94] He appeared in the courtroom on February 5, 1914, the day the second jury pronounced its verdict. He mentioned the case in an article he wrote for the June issue of the *American Review of Reviews*. Boasting that he ran the "world's greatest prosecuting office," he described his successful prosecution of notorious underworld figures, all of whom had been executed, and added: "Still another case in which a murder was committed was that of Hans Schmidt, a pseudo-priest, who murdered the girl Anna Aumueller, and attempted to hide his crime by submerging parts of her dismembered body in the Hudson River. So much for the murderers who have been brought to justice in New York County in recent years."[95]

His reputation as a dogged, hard-hitting district attorney gained Whitman the Republican gubernatorial nomination in 1914 and helped him defeat Governor Martin Glynn in the election. The press hailed him as a "peerless prosecutor" who displayed "the old-time virtues of courage, honesty, ability, and public devotion."[96] He was described as "a quick, tense, nervous man, with a sort of perpetual scowl which conveys not ill-humor but merely mental concentration."[97] In his first inaugural address he warned that the "spirit of lawlessness and of contempt for legal authority" threatened "moral decadence and ultimate decay."[98]

As governor, Whitman took a hard line when it came to granting executive clemency. He ordinarily commuted a sentence only when the trial judge, the district attorney, or even the jurors, believing a mistake had been made, petitioned him, when he had received, as he put it, "numerous recommendations made by every official connected with the trial."[99] Yet on January 11, 1916, a few days after the Court of Appeals denied a motion for reargument and set a date for Schmidt's execution, Whitman granted him a thirty-day reprieve. The delay would allow the defense attorneys to ask the United States Supreme Court to rule on whether Schmidt had been convicted without due process of law.[100] Moreover, Whitman said, "in light of the opinion of the Court of Appeals, it seems but fair" that he should weigh the new evidence that had been produced since the trial.[101]

Any chance that the Supreme Court would consider the case was doomed from the start. At the same time that it refused to hear reargument, the Court of Appeals rejected Koelble's efforts to transfer the case to federal jurisdiction. "The request of counsel for a certificate that a Federal question was involved in the appeal cannot be complied with, for it is not the fact," said the court in an opinion, which, while unsigned, was probably written by Cardozo.[102] Koelble nevertheless traveled to Washington, where he appeared before Associate Justice Charles Evans Hughes, a former governor of New York, and asked him to grant a writ of error so that the case could be reviewed by the high court. Hughes turned down the request.

Any chance that the governor would find in Schmidt's favor was similarly remote. Noting that he was "thoroughly familiar with every detail of this case," since he had been the prosecutor, Whitman admitted that Schmidt's revised story, "improbable as it is," needed to be investigated "in all its hideous details." So he appointed two well-known pathologists, Dr. W. G. MacCallum and Dr. Francis Carter Wood, to make an independent determination, based partly on the trial record and information in the new affidavits but chiefly on an examination of the body organs which were, after all this time, still preserved at the Cornell Medical College. According to Whitman, the physicians reported that "there is no evidence in support of the defendant's assertion that Anna Aumuller died from a post partum hemorrhage from the uterus."[103]

But this was not quite what the physicians had reported. MacCallum only said that while there was no proof that death had resulted from uterine hemorrhaging, such a possibility could not be excluded: "I do not feel that I can offer a definite opinion as to the cause of death of the deceased." Wood went somewhat further. He began by making the irrelevant point that hospital statistics showed virtually no cases of death from post-partum hemorrhaging in full-term or even premature births. Then, he said, his examination of the uterus revealed "no indication of unskilled instrumentation." So if an abortion had taken place, it must have been performed, as Schmidt said, by a skillful person. Since such cases are "practically free" of rapid hemorrhaging, Wood concluded that Anna Aumuller had not died from such a cause.[104]

With one pathologist unable to offer an opinion and the other able to support his finding only with inapt statistical evidence, the governor could have reached any conclusion he wanted to. His statement suggests which conclusion that was: "This defendant has been fairly tried. He has attempted and once nearly succeeded in foisting upon the court a story which he himself now admits was false. He has demonstrated beyond the [sic] question his capacity and skill in shamming and falsifying, and all the proof before me compels me to believe that his assertion now as to the manner of the decedent's death is utterly false. In fact, I do not see that the falsity of his story could be more clearly established than it has been." Without a recommendation for mercy from the trial judge, "I should be recreant to my duty should I interfere with the judgment of the Court."[105] On February 9, Whitman turned down the appeal for clemency.

Schmidt had been awaiting the decision on Sing Sing's death row along with twenty other condemned men. The small green door leading to the execution chamber was but a few feet from the cells, a "barbarous" arrangement, the prison doctor later wrote, because the men "could not only hear with terrible distinctness everything that went on in the execution chamber . . . but also what went on later in the adjacent autopsy room." The law required that a physician saw open the dead prisoner's skull in order to examine the brain, and to the others "the most horrible thing on earth was the sound of that saw."[106] On February 18, 1916, at daybreak, Schmidt was led to the electric chair. As the straps were being fastened, he said: "Gentlemen. I ask forgiveness of those whom I have offended or scandalized. I forgive all who have injured me." He was reciting prayers when the executioner threw the switch. "When three shocks had been given Schmidt was pronounced dead."[107]

In later years Benjamin Cardozo remarked on the Schmidt case several times. In 1925 he listed it as among his most significant decisions in response to a query from the editor of a Columbia alumni magazine.[108] In 1927 he alluded to it in order to explain his view of what qualified as newly discovered evidence. Writing to Felix Frankfurter, he said: "The defendant claimed on a motion for a new trial that he had wilfully lied on the first trial, and he sought an opportunity to retry the issue of his guilt. The opinion pointed out that the motion did not comply with the requirements as to newly discovered evidence." Cardozo then quoted that portion of his opinion which held out an appeal for executive clemency as the proper remedy. He added: "The Governor (Whitman) conducted an inquiry (whether personally or by a representative I do not recall), but the man was executed."[109]

By far his most extended comment came in an address Cardozo delivered to the New York Academy of Medicine on November 1, 1928, entitled, "What Medicine Can Do for Law." In describing the problems connected with the insanity plea, especially the "narrow and inadequate" test of mental irresponsibility written into the law, Cardozo mentioned McNaughtan's inherent ambiguity with regard to the meaning of the word "wrong" and then described the Schmidt case and his decision. This is what he said:

One Schmidt, a priest, was charged with the murder of a woman with whom he had been intimate. Upon the trial his defense was insanity. He said he had heard the voice of God calling upon him by day and night to sacrifice and slay. He yielded to the call in the belief that slaughter was a moral duty. The trial judge held that this belief was no defense if he knew the nature of the act and knew it to be wrong in the sense of being prohibited by law. On appeal this ruling was reversed. We held that the word "wrong" in the statutory definition had reference in such circumstances to the moral quality of the act, and not merely to the legal prohibition. Any other reading would charge a mother with the crime of murder if she were to slay a dearly loved child in the belief that a divine command had summoned to the gruesome act. Let me say by way of parenthesis that Schmidt did not profit by the error in the charge, since he admitted under oath that the whole defense of insanity was an imposture and a sham.[110]

Cardozo's retrospective account, unlike his decision, mentioned Schmidt by name, noted that he was a priest, and acknowledged that he had been having an affair with Anna Aumuller. Once again, Cardozo conjured up the fearful vision of a deluded mother murdering her child. And it was certainly true that Schmidt had admitted the insanity plea was a sham. Yet Cardozo's listeners that evening could have been forgiven had they come away with an erroneous view of what had actually happened. Cardozo failed to mention that Schmidt had also stated under oath that he had not committed the murder, that his own opinion had suggested that the cause of death was a botched abortion, that the governor who rejected the appeal for clemency had prosecuted the case, or that a man who was guilty of many crimes but in all likelihood not murder had been executed.

Perhaps the key phrase in the account is that Schmidt "did not profit" by the judge's charge, or, rather, by the Court of Appeals' decision holding it to be erroneous. That echoed the language—"we will not aid the defendant"—of Cardozo's original decision. It was the language of a man whose deeply ingrained moral sensibilities were outraged by everything about Hans Schmidt. In his 1903 book on the jurisdiction of the Court of Appeals, Cardozo had said that the court existed not for the "individual litigant" who appeared before it but rather for the "indefinite body of litigants" whose causes are potentially involved in the specific dispute. The case of Hans Schmidt provided Cardozo and his fellow judges with an ideal opportunity to clarify the legal meaning of insanity for nameless litigants in the future, whatever the implications for the individual litigant whose fate they in fact decided.

3

Scholars and Universities

Law and Philosophy

On the morning of November 13, 1922, Benjamin Cardozo arrived by overnight train in Ithaca, New York, where he was to lecture at Cornell University. The dean of the College of Law, George G. Bogert, had orchestrated a year-long campaign to lure the busy judge to the campus. Enlisting the help of two of Cardozo's colleagues on the Court of Appeals, Frank H. Hiscock, the chief judge, and Cuthbert W. Pound, the dean also arranged for Cornell's president, Livingston Farrand, to extend a personal invitation, and promised Cardozo that his spare time "could be devoted to motoring through the picturesque Finger Lakes region hereabout, or to . . . playing golf, or engaging in some other diversion."[1] Cardozo was initially reluctant to accept, claiming he had nothing worthwhile to say. But after putting pen to paper during the summer of 1922, he informed Bogert: "I started out to write one lecture, but evil grows apace, and behold! I had before long not a single monster, but twins with even a faint menace of triplets. I may drown one of the puppies—I haven't made up my mind—but they are pleading pitifully to be allowed to stay, and I find it hard to slay them."

Still protesting that what he had written was "wretched trash," Cardozo nevertheless agreed to give two lectures on the philosophy of law: "I thought I might develop this field a little further and preach a little sermon on the value of such inquiries for lawyer, judge and student." Besides, he added, a visit would provide "an excuse for becoming acquainted with Cornell, its faculty and students."[2] In the lectures, Cardozo declared himself "the self-appointed spokesman and defender of the philosopher in the field of law." The philosophy of law, he said, dealt with "how law comes into being, how it grows, and whither it tends." A judge's philosophy was frequently decisive in shaping a decision. Judicial interpretations of the law "should be a means of obtaining an end," he told an enthusiastic audience, not of seeking "a set rule of regularity."[3]

Following the first lecture a luncheon was held in the speaker's honor attended by Dean Bogert, the law faculty and selected students, President Farrand, Mynderse Van Cleef, an Ithaca attorney, and other notables. Cardozo charmed them all with a humorous talk on changes in the methods of teaching law since his own days as a student. That evening, Cardozo was Bogert's guest at a recital by Ignace Jan Paderewski.[4] Nearly three thousand students, faculty, and Ithaca townsfolk crowded into the concert hall to hear the renowned pianist, composer, and Polish patriot perform works by Bach, Beethoven, Schumann, Schubert, and Chopin—and then play five encores. The next morning Cardozo gave his second lecture and departed on the noon train for New York City.

Some months later Cardozo told the Cornell philosophy professor Frank Thilly: "I felt a good deal of pride when I visited Cornell in establishing an *entente* between jurisprudence and philosophy. I am glad that where so many other *ententes* in the world are crumbling, this one seems likely to persist."[5] In truth, during his first decade on the Court of Appeals, Cardozo emerged as a leading advocate of an alliance between law and the wider world of scholarship. Judges, he never tired of saying, needed to listen to "scholars in the universities," not only to those teaching in law schools but also to historians, sociologists, and philosophers. In his rosy view, universities were places where the life of the mind was nurtured, where new ideas were encouraged, and where principles governing the social as well as the physical sciences were being discovered.

In all his dealings with academics Cardozo was unduly deferential, praising their work effusively while discounting the value of his own. One of his friends was Morris R. Cohen, who taught philosophy at the City College of New York. Cardozo often addressed him simply as "Philosopher," and told him "how greatly I admire your superb abilities and achievements."[6] After reading some of Cohen's work and praising it to the skies, Cardozo remarked: "I am left a little depressed, none the less, by the range of your learning and accomplishments. It seems as if a mere amateur like myself might as well hold his peace and be silent."[7] To Dean Roscoe Pound of Harvard Law School, Cardozo wrote: "I do not know where else to look for so extraordinary a fusion of learning at the service of wisdom, and of wisdom illumined by learning."[8] When Karl Llewellyn, a law professor at Columbia, asked Cardozo whether he wished to continue receiving reprints of essays, he replied: "For mercy sake, don't strike me off your mailing list. Where should I get my original ideas?"[9]

His self-deprecating comments may have been a form of affectation, a way, perhaps, of fishing for compliments, but Cardozo expressed his doubts so vividly that it is unlikely they were merely contrived. Not only did he warn Dean Bogert that "the talks which I am about to inflict on you are very slight and commonplace things," but he even told his sister Nell "that they didn't seem to me to be worth delivering."[10] A few years earlier, preparing a series of lectures for Yale, he reported, "They are without value or importance as a contribution to jurisprudence."[11] Later, working on yet another series for Columbia, he reproached himself: "They are wretched stuff, the worse I have done yet."[12] When the lectures were published, he inscribed a copy to Felix Frankfurter: "I ought not to let you see these pages. You will see too quickly how thin this stuff is. But they are sure to reach you in one way or another. So I cannot deny myself the pleasure of writing your name upon one of the unworthy volumes."[13]

Cardozo's insecurities about his published efforts led him to speak of his many "imperfections," and to complain, "the plain truth is that my equipment is woefully defective."[14] Once, when a reprint of one of his addresses arrived, he was so unhappy with it that, he said, "I banished it to a closet without a glance."[15] His friends, who had a more accurate appreciation of his ability, did not quite know what to make of his deep-seated uncertainties. As Cuthbert Pound commented, "The strange thing to me is that he seems unconscious of his own greatness, although he must know how good he is."[16] Cardozo once provided his own analysis: "Nature made me distrustful of myself."[17]

His election as a trustee of Columbia University in 1928—he was only the second Jew to serve on the board; the first was his great granduncle, Rabbi Gershom Mendes Seixas, in the eighteenth century—provided an opportunity for similar protestations. "I can't feel that I shall be able to do anything worth while as trustee," he told one friend, and to another added, "I am as ignorant as anyone can be of matters pedagogical."[18] These liabilities, he added quickly, might actually be virtues, since he believed trustees should merely rubber-stamp the decisions of professors, to whom important decisions were properly left. "Perhaps the consciousness of such ignorance is not a bad qualification for a university trustee," he commented: "He is the more likely to keep his hands off, and submit to the judgment of the faculty."[19]

Cardozo's opinions for the Court of Appeals drew more heavily on academic expertise than did those of his judicial colleagues. Scanning the pages of the leading journals as avidly as any prospector panning for gold, he often struck it rich. In an era when judges rarely cited scholarly works to support their conclusions, Cardozo prided himself on digging up "the treasures buried in the law reviews."[20] In his decisions Cardozo cited legal treatises three times as frequently as other members of the Court, and law reviews six times as frequently. In fact, he referred to law reviews more often than all the other judges combined.[21] He intentionally sought to give scholars "the feeling that their work is appreciated in the courts."[22]

Cardozo's extra-judicial efforts during the early 1920s exhibited a similar regard for scholarship. In February 1921 he delivered the Storrs Lectures at Yale Law School, which were published as *The Nature of the Judicial Process.* In 1921 he also made a much-remarked-on speech, later published in the *Harvard Law Review,* proposing the creation of a ministry of justice. He played a pivotal role in the creation of the American Law Institute in February 1923 and served as its vice president. Returning to Yale in December 1923, he gave another series of lectures, which appeared the following year as *The Growth of the Law.* In the space of three years Cardozo went from being a judge, highly respected to be sure, but known chiefly to members of the New York State bar, to having a national reputation as a disciple of legal scholarship and a contributor to it.

A Yale law professor, Arthur L. Corbin, who attended the Storrs Lectures, could recall, even after forty years, Cardozo's appearance and the impression he made. The first of the four lectures began at five o'clock in the afternoon. Corbin reminisced: "Standing on the platform at the lectern, his mobile countenance, his dark eyes, his white hair, and his brilliant smile, all well lighted before us, he read the lecture, winding it up at 6 o'clock. He bowed and sat down. The entire audience rose to their feet, with a burst of applause that would not cease. Cardozo rose and bowed, with a smile at once pleased and deprecatory, and again sat down." Cardozo finally exited to continued applause, followed by the law faculty. So many people showed up the next afternoon that the series was moved to a larger auditorium, seating five hundred people. After the final lecture Cardozo was asked to give the manuscript to the Yale University Press. "In his smiling but deprecatory way, he said that he did not 'dare to have it published.' Half seriously, he added: 'If it were published, I would be impeached.'"[23]

The manuscript was published, of course, and its author, far from being impeached, found his professional stature instantly enhanced. In *The Nature of the Judicial Process* Cardozo presented a strikingly modern interpretation of judicial decisionmaking that radically subverted the conventional understanding. Yet his presentation was so adroit, balanced, and elegantly fashioned that potential critics were generally disarmed. Moreover, he ranged confidently over the landscape of legal philosophy, citing French, German, and English as well as American writers, thereby making it appear that his interpretation reflected modern currents of thought that were sweeping triumphantly through the broader transatlantic legal community.

"I take judge-made law as one of the existing realities of life," Cardozo said early in the first lecture. He thereby disposed of the view that a judge's function was merely to find a preexisting law and apply it to the case at hand. That view of the judge as "oracle" was still widely held and just as widely used to justify a rock-ribbed conservative jurisprudence. To Cardozo, however, judging involved a process not of discovery but of creation. A judge's decision required the making of choices, "not a submission to the decree of Fate." The choices, in turn, reflected a judge's life experiences: "There is in each of us a stream of tendency . . . which gives coherence and direction to thought and action. Judges cannot escape that current any more than other mortals. All their lives, forces which they do not recognize and cannot name, have been tugging at them—inherited instincts, traditional beliefs, acquired convictions; the resultant is an outlook on life, a conception of social needs . . . which, when reasons are nicely balanced, must determine where choice shall fall."[24]

In making choices, Cardozo held, judges relied on four methods: "philosophy" involved drawing logical analogies from prior decisions; "evolution" required examining the historical development of relevant legal doctrines; "tradition" meant studying the prevailing customs of the community in the pertinent area. It was the fourth and most controversial of the "directive forces," however, to which he devoted most of his attention. This was the method of "sociology," which reflected a judge's outlook on "justice, morals, and social welfare, the *mores* of the day." These were legitimate areas of concern, Cardozo stated, because "The final cause of law is the welfare of society." To drive his point home, Cardozo invoked a Talmudic tale, although without identifying it as such: "There is an old legend that on one occasion God prayed, and his prayer was 'Be it my will that my justice be ruled by my mercy.' That is a prayer which we all need to utter at times when the demon of formalism tempts the intellect with the lure of scientific order."[25]

Just when it appeared that Cardozo had endorsed "the power of social justice" as a basis of judicial interpretation, his tendency to seek a stable equilibrium quickly asserted itself. Judges were not free, he insisted, to set aside existing rules at their pleasure. They had discretion only where gaps existed in those rules, for—and here he quoted Oliver Wendell Holmes Jr.—"judges must and do legislate, but they do so only interstitially." Moreover, even when judges were free to take social welfare into account, they should not rely on their own concept of welfare but on that of the larger community. Rather than writing into law their own "idiosyncrasies of conduct or belief," they should conform to "the accepted standards of the community, the *mores* of the times." Cardozo concluded: "The judge, even when he is free, is not wholly free. He is not to innovate at pleasure. He is not a knight-errant roaming at will in pursuit of his own ideal of beauty or of goodness . . . He is not to yield to spasmodic sentiment, to vague and unregulated benevolence."[26]

Cardozo's discussion did not answer every question or satisfy every objection. How, for example, could judges be certain that their presumably objective assessment of community standards was anything more than a way of rationalizing their own subjective preferences? Cardozo knew that some such distortion was inevitable: "The spirit of the age, as it is revealed to each of us, is too often only the spirit of the group in which the accidents of birth or education or occupation or fellowship have given us a place. No effort or revolution of the mind will overthrow utterly and at all times the empire of these subconscious loyalties."[27] But he imagined that these biases would eventually balance out. Privately, Cardozo conceded that judges might be deluding themselves when they claimed to be guided by a common will; but he insisted that in his own work as a judge, "somehow or other there are times when I do feel that I am expressing thoughts and convictions not found in the books and yet not totally my own."[28]

If *The Nature of the Judicial Process* had something to please everyone, those who wished law to be "plastic and malleable" as well as those who favored "adherence to precedent," it also had something to convince everyone. The work's strength rested, in large part, on its impressive grounding in the philosophy of law. To support his assertions Cardozo cited more than seventy-five authors. Some of them—Holmes, Roscoe Pound, Learned Hand, John Chipman Gray—were undoubtedly familiar to faculty members and students at every American law school. Others probably were not. Cardozo relied heavily on such continental theorists as Léon Duguit, Rudolf von Jhering, Eugen Ehrlich, Josef Kohler, and especially François Gény, the author of *Science et technique en droit privé positif*. Cardozo once said of Gény that "what he writes is so delightful in its literary form as to make it worth while for that, if for nothing more."[29] At times Cardozo cited French and German works in translation; where no translation existed he provided his own. By drawing on the work of these scholars, he effectively paid them tribute and, in the process, buttressed his own authority as a writer.

Cardozo exhibited a similar faith in academic expertise in calling for the creation of a ministry of justice, as he did in October 1921 in an address to the Bar Association of the City of New York, later published in the *Harvard Law Review*. By eliminating antiquated rules, he held, such an agency could "save our law from sterility and atrophy." Judges, legislators, attorneys general, bar associations, and practicing lawyers did not have the time, ability, or knowledge to modernize the law and bring it into harmony with modern social conditions. The task, he said, required "a scholarship and a habit of research not often to be found in those immersed in varied duties." As Cardozo saw it: "We must look to our redemption, not to practising lawyers, nor even to judges, but to the student and philosopher in faculties of law and Institutes of Jurisprudence."

He envisioned a ministry consisting of one judge, one or two attorneys, and two or even three professors of law or political science. The body, he continued, would "enlighten itself constantly through all available sources of guidance and instruction; through consultation with scholars; through study of the law reviews, the journals of social science, the publications of the learned generally; and through investigation of remedies and methods in other jurisdictions, foreign and domestic." Recommendations would require legislative enactment, but at least a start would have been made in the right direction. The esteem in which Cardozo held "the learned" was gratefully reciprocated. Harlan Fiske Stone, dean of the Columbia Law School, told him that "it was a novel situation to have a judge of the highest court in the state telling the membership of an important bar association that to an important extent the necessary scholarship and philosophy for this work was to be found in institutions of learning."[30]

Two months after his Bar Association address, Cardozo attended a meeting of the American Association of Law Schools in Chicago. He went at the urging of Joseph Beale, a Harvard law professor, one of a group of several legal scholars, including Corbin of Yale and William Draper Lewis of the University of Pennsylvania, who wanted the association to back the creation of an American Law Institute. As N. E. H. Hull has shown, the origins of the Institute "lay in the vision of a group of 'progressive-pragmatic' legal academics, who wished to reform law and promote the influence of law professors in the wider world of legal practice."[31] The reformers wanted to set up a coordinating committee of professors, lawyers, and judges with a view toward creating an ongoing body to propose improvements in the law. They understood that Cardozo was ideally suited to overcome old guard resistance, led, in this instance, by James Parker Hall of the University of Chicago, the association's newly elected president.

Cardozo's speech on December 30, 1921, exemplified his talent for making reform seem the only sane and prudent course. He began by explaining why, as a judge, he would find such a project helpful: "More and more, the need develops with the years, of giving to Judges, through some external agency, the things that organized and systematic and continuous research and study can alone supply." Many cases involved questions of such complexity that judges had to rely on scholars, for it could not be expected that "overnight and at the call of a single case we shall do the work which these men have been doing in lifetimes of devoted and intensive effort."[32] Cardozo even managed to co-opt Hall by praising his participation in an existing group which brought together scholars and practitioners. The law professors warmly applauded Cardozo's address and unanimously passed a resolution appointing a committee to establish the institute.

In February 1923, the groundwork having been completed, five hundred legal luminaries—lawyers, judges, and law professors—met in Washington, D.C., to found the American Law Institute. It was, the *New York Times* declared, "probably the most distinguished gathering of the legal profession in the history of the country."[33] William Draper Lewis became director, while Elihu Root was made honorary president and George W. Wickersham was chosen president. Cardozo was elected vice president. Prominent scholars were then assigned the ambitious task of preparing restatements of the law—that is, of identifying the principles of the common law—in all major fields, such as contracts, torts, agency, and property. Maintaining an active involvement in these deliberations, Cardozo also addressed the annual meetings in 1924 and 1925, using the occasions to defend the institute from critics who complained either that the restatements would stultify the law or, conversely, that they were a waste of time.

By December 1923, when Cardozo returned to Yale for a second lecture series, his theoretical writings, advocacy of a ministry of justice, and role in the ALI had confirmed his standing as a promoter of legal scholarship. The lectures provided a convenient platform from which to salute the scholars who had undertaken the project of restatement. After listing their names and impressive academic affiliations, Cardozo said: "If these men cannot restate the law, then the law is incapable of being restated by anyone." Paying homage to "the scholar in his study," the lonely seeker after truth, Cardozo spoke of the increasing reliance judges were placing on "this new organ of expression . . . the university law review."[34]

In the lectures Cardozo again commended a middle course that would avoid, at one extreme, the notion that law is "fixed and immutable, that the conclusion which the judge declares, instead of being itself a more or less tentative hypothesis, . . . has a genuine preexistence, that judgment is a process of discovery, and not in any degree a process of creation," and, at the other, a conception of law as "a series of isolated dooms, the general merged in the particular, the principle dethroned and the instance exalted as supreme." Between those extremes, he said, "we have the conception of law as a body of rules and principles and standards which in their extension to new combinations of events are to be sorted, selected, moulded and adapted in subordination to an end."[35]

The Growth of the Law, published in the summer of 1924, advanced familiar themes, but Cardozo's message was beginning to wear thin. Views which had once been fresh and insightful were, with repetition, starting to seem stale and obvious. Cardozo was the first to realize the problem. Preparing an earlier version of the second set of Yale lectures, he noted with characteristic and, in this case, justifiable modesty that they were "a sort of diluted broth made out of the stock of the lectures" which he had delivered the first time around. As he told Dean Bogert of Cornell: "I recall a story that Lowell relates of Agassiz. The great naturalist said that on the occasion of his first lecture, he gave his students during the opening half hour the real fruits of his thought. 'Then,' he said, 'I began to repeat myself, and I have done the same thing ever since.' We haven't many ideas in our minds. When we get a few, we ring the changes on them."[36]

One of those ideas he attributed to Roscoe Pound, dean of Harvard Law School: "Law must be stable, and yet it cannot stand still."[37] A case that provided a test of Cardozo's ability to navigate the shoals of continuity and change was then working its way to the Court of Appeals. It was of more than ordinary interest precisely because it challenged Cardozo's concept of the nature of the university and the role of the faculty, and at a place with which Cardozo was familiar. The case originated when a young woman attending Cornell University suffered severe eye injuries in an explosion in a chemistry laboratory and sued for damages.

An Explosion in a Chemistry Laboratory

Louise Margaret Hamburger entered the New York State College of Agriculture at Cornell University in the fall of 1915. She was twenty years old, a graduate of Manual Training High School in Brooklyn. As a state resident, she paid no tuition but only nominal fees for matriculation, laboratory materials, and use of the infirmary. She was a student in the Department of Home Economics and was therefore required to take an introductory course in chemistry. The course, taught in Morse Hall, numbered about one hundred students, among them five or six women. The lectures were given by Professor Louis Munroe Dennis, the department chairman. Dr. Thomas W. B. Welsh, an instructor in the department, supervised the laboratory sections which met three times a week. A doctoral candidate, Dyer B. Lake, tutored Hamburger's section. Students worked from *The Laboratory Manual to Elementary Chemistry,* of which Professor Dennis was a coauthor.[38]

Dennis had come to Cornell as an instructor in 1887 when he was only eighteen. He had then spent two years in further study at Dresden, Munich, and Wiesbaden, returning to Cornell as an ardent Germanophile. In the words of a colleague, Emile M. Chamot: "He was a great admirer of German chemists, German artists, German industry, German architecture, German methods, and German beer." Appointed chairman in 1903, he governed the chemistry department autocratically, as if by divine right. As Chamot explained: "He was generally known—behind his back—as 'King Dennis' or 'The King.' He was king, and the Department was his kingdom, to be ruled with an iron hand. Most of the other professors deferred to him and paid him homage, either because they agreed with him, or, perhaps, from other reasons." Dennis would admit a mistake when convinced he was wrong, Chamot added, "but in my long association with him . . . I rarely knew him to be convinced that he was wrong."[39]

Dennis constituted himself a one-man purchasing agency for the chemistry department. He believed that the best bargains were to be had in Germany, and he convinced the Cornell administration, according to Chamot, "that it was necessary for him to go to Europe about every alternate summer—largely or entirely at University expense—to talk with manufacturers of chemical supplies and equipment and to acquaint himself with new instruments and types of apparatus, as well as to meet the chemists in the European universities. He was assumed to conduct this purchasing with unusual astuteness and economy." To question his decisions—for example, the purchasing of hand-blown German glassware rather than the more shock-resistant American-made pyrex—was to invite his withering scorn. When, toward the end of Dennis's reign, Chamot tried to bring some order to the inventory of chemicals in the basement, he found only chaos: "Apparently the chemical stores had been operated on a 'last in, first out' basis; the shelves were loaded with full or partly full bottles of ancient vintage, with labels brown with age and indecipherable, and thick with dust."[40]

By 1916 the chemistry department had developed certain routine procedures for its introductory course. Supplies were brought from the storeroom to the first-floor laboratory for each day's experiments, a procedure supervised by a four-member departmental committee. In the laboratory, students stood behind long tables, each equipped with mortars, pestles, and glassware. Instructions were written on the blackboard to direct students to the necessary supplies: inexpensive chemicals were stored in containers on side shelves while more expensive ones were dispensed from the stockroom. One Andrew Hagin was in charge of the stockroom. His fifteen-year-old son, Max, often assisted him.

Arriving in the laboratory on the afternoon of Wednesday, January 12, 1916, Louise Hamburger saw that two experiments in the *Manual*, numbers 84 and 88, were to be performed. Experiment 84 required the student to mix 1 gram of potassium chlorate with 9 grams of strontium nitrate; then, after washing the mortar, the student was instructed to grind 3 grams of shellac and add it to the mixture "with as little friction as possible." Then came a warning: *"Do not grind the shellac in the mortar with the other ingredients. An explosion would result."* The entire mixture, when placed on a brick or tile and ignited, "should burn with a brilliant red flame."[41] But

Hamburger did not obtain the required chemicals or do the experiment. Instead, she recalled, she copied the results from a nearby student. "It was a short experiment and I saw her results and I took my conclusions from hers," she said, adding that this was a common practice in the course.[42]

She did begin Experiment 88. The instructions were: "Mix 2 g. of mercuric sulphide with an equal weight of powdered lime [calcium oxide] and heat the mixture in a hard-glass tube until the residue assumes a dark yellow color. What collects in the upper part of the tube? What is left in the lower part?"[43] According to her account, she went to one of the side shelves to obtain the calcium oxide. She waited while another student weighed his amount, and then she measured out 2 grams of a white powder from the same jar, labeled Calcium Oxide, and carried it back to her desk on a piece of paper. Then she went to the stockroom window and waited on line, directly behind another student, Edward Feuerstein. When she got to the window, she found Max Hagin, "a small boy handing out materials," but no trace of his father. She asked for mercuric sulphide and received the same "reddish-black powder" that Feuerstein had. Returning to her table, her account went on, she mixed the two powders in a clean mortar. She cut off a six-inch length of glass tubing and attempted to seal one end over a Bunsen burner. Dyer Lake then appeared at her side, suggested she use a hotter flame, and sealed the glass for her. She started to pour the mixture into the tube but Lake told her she only needed to use about one-inch's worth and walked off. Wrapping the top of the tube in some paper, she held the mixture over the Bunsen burner.[44]

Even as she was doing the experiment, she heard an explosion at the other end of the laboratory. But it was not very loud and so she and the other students went on with their work. Only later would she realize that Feuerstein's test tube had exploded. A minute or two later, Louise Hamburger's did, too, only more violently, sending shards of glass flying in every direction: "And the next thing I knew, I had just barely had it over the flame, when I heard this noise, and felt something strike my face and something got in my eye, and I saw blood streaming down, so my first inclination was to get a handkerchief and wipe my face off, and then I was led out to the sick room, to a sink that was in the sick room, and as I remember Mr. Feuerstein was standing there wiping his ear off, there was blood on his ear." Washing her face at the sink, she reported: "I felt something in my eye, and I tried to wash that out . . . And I was then taken to the women's rest room where they had me lie down on a couch."[45]

Vilma Viegert, a fellow student, confirmed the essentials of Hamburger's account. Hearing an explosion and that a "girl" had been injured, she rushed over to find that "some man" was leading Hamburger to a sink and she was surrounded "by a group of people, mostly boys. I don't believe there was more than two girls around her. I went to assist her and led her from the sink into the women's rest room. Her face was covered with blood, and her eyes, well she could hardly keep them open. One eye it must have hurt it terrible, the other seemed to be filled with pins so she could hardly open it." Escorting Hamburger to the rest room, and assisting her onto a lounge, she attempted to wipe away the blood covering her face. Then she helped her into her coat and downstairs to a waiting car, and accompanied her to the office of Dr. John S. Kirkendall.[46]

"Upon examination of the eye," Kirkendall later testified, "I found a lacerated wound, perhaps, oh, an eighth of an inch in the lower part of the cornea, or more . . . It was a punctured wound . . . and the injury had extended into the anterior chamber of the eye . . . when the puncture took place there is always a force upwards in the eye, such that it drew the iris, which should float freely within the eyeball, it sucked it into the wound, from the pressure from within outwards."[47] He telephoned the president of the university. After cleaning and dressing the eye, he sent Hamburger to the infirmary. "The first night," she recalled, "I hope I may never see another such night. It was extremely painful."[48]

She remained there in a darkened room for a month, attended by a nurse, and then spent two additional weeks under the nurse's care at her aunt's home in Ithaca. In the meantime she consulted two specialists recommended by Kirkendall, to no avail. The injury, it was found, produced a "traumatic cataract" in her left eye which left the lens opaque. She could make out lights and shadows, but not distinct forms. Test results showed that before the accident the vision in her left eye was 20/20; afterward it was 0/0. Moreover, as Kirkendall explained, "there is always a humiliation and anxiety attached to the loss of an eye."[49]

Shortly after Louise Hamburger's test tube exploded, Dyer Lake began collecting the mixture that remained in her mortar as well as samples from the containers in the storeroom and on the side shelves. He evidently acted quickly, because when a concerned, somewhat older student in the course ventured into the stockroom to examine the ingredient that had been dispensed, he found it had already been removed. Lake also obtained the remainder of the mixture Feuerstein had used. He delivered all the evidence to his supervisor, Thomas Welsh, who in turn gave it to Professor Chamot for analysis. That analysis would become the basis for Cornell's response to Hamburger's allegation that the university had acted negligently.

Working with perhaps a thimbleful of Hamburger's mixture, Chamot reported on January 14 that it indeed contained mercuric sulphide, but instead of lime it also contained potassium chlorate, one of the ingredients put out for the previous experiment. Feuerstein's mixture was similar, Chamot reported. The containers, he added, were correctly labeled. He concluded that the two students had carelessly failed to follow instructions. To Hamburger's claim that the explosion resulted because she either had been given something other than mercuric sulphide at the stockroom or had obtained something other than lime from the jar labeled calcium oxide on the side shelf, the department countered that the fault was entirely hers. Dennis asserted that she had "disregarded the repeated warnings . . . and that she further made the deplorable mistake of taking for the experiment in question the substance potassium chlorate instead of the powdered lime."[50]

Any chance of independently verifying the department's analysis was irretrievably lost a month later. In the early morning hours of February 13, 1916, a fire of undetermined origin broke out on the third floor of Morse Hall and raged through the building. Five Ithaca fire companies battled the blaze, only to find their efforts hampered by inadequate water pressure and freezing conditions. Some professors and students risked serious injury to remove valuable items from the burning building, including five thousand books from the library on the first floor. Everything else was destroyed, including the evidence removed from the laboratory after the explosion. It was the most destructive fire Cornell University or Ithaca had ever seen. "For over three hours," the papers reported, "until only the brick walls remained standing, the flames or smoke could be seen for miles around."[51]

Not until a few months later, on June 30, did University officials learn that Louise Hamburger had contacted a lawyer and lodged a complaint charging negligence. Her attorney, Nash Rockwood, sent two investigators to Ithaca to look things over. Then he filed a suit on her behalf asking for $100,000 in damages on the grounds that "a bottle which was labeled as containing lime was in fact permitted to contain a highly explosive powder." This negligence led to a "terrific explosion," the affidavit continued, in which she suffered burns, permanently impaired eyesight, and "a terrible nervous shock and great pain, agony and sickness."[52]

Cornell quickly obtained a statement from Dennis which set forth the

THE WORLD OF BENJAMIN CARDOZO

department's version of the incident and noted that thousands of students had performed Experiment 88 over many years with only one previous mishap. The university, having as yet no counsel's office, entrusted its defense to Mynderse Van Cleef, who in turn delegated the actual work of preparing the case to Professor Oliver L. McCaskill of the Cornell College of Law. Van Cleef explained that Cornell would rest its defense on "the general ground that an educational institution is not liable to a student for injury received on account of the alleged negligence of an instructor engaged in the ordinary work of instruction."[53]

McCaskill filled in the particulars. He assured Van Cleef that there was adequate precedent for the view that eleemosynary institutions, whether privately or publicly funded, "are not liable for the negligent acts of their employees or agents to persons receiving the benefits of such institution. The most numerous cases are those of hospitals, but the doctrine has been applied also to schools, academies and colleges. The school cases are based upon the hospital cases and apply the same line of reasoning." Conceding that the New York State precedents were "not so satisfactory as some from other states on broad doctrines," McCaskill nevertheless thought that they did "point clearly to non liability in our case." Louise Hamburger's complaint, he predicted, "will walk right into a line of cases completely annihilating it." He confidently predicted that his own brief for Cornell "will defeat plaintiff whatever she may allege."[54]

Cornell University v. Louise Hamburger

The filing of the complaint against Cornell led to a legal slugfest lasting nearly a decade. Nash Rockwood, when he agreed to represent Hamburger, was dividing his time between offices in Saratoga Springs and New York City. The forty-seven-year-old attorney had served as Saratoga County Judge from 1900 to 1913. Oliver L. McCaskill, thirty-nine years of age, was a graduate of the University of Chicago Law School who had been in practice with his father for ten years before joining the law faculty at the University of West Virginia and then at Cornell. The case went through two distinct phases: the first, culminating in a trial in the fall of 1921, ended with a decision in favor of Louise Hamburger; the second, however, ended with a resounding victory for Cornell when, in June 1925, the Court of Appeals, in a unanimous opinion by Benjamin Cardozo, reversed the lower court's verdict.

Because he had a practice in Saratoga Springs, Rockwood succeeded in having the dispute transferred to that venue. He failed, however, to persuade the judge who heard the case, Charles C. Van Kirk, to see it his way. In April 1917 Van Kirk sustained McCaskill's point: Cornell qualified as an eleemosynary institution—in the same sense as a hospital, orphanage, or charitable agency—and was therefore not liable to its "beneficiaries" for the negligence of its employees so long as it had exercised reasonable care in selecting them. Rockwood then amended his complaint, but in November 1917 Van Kirk rejected it, too, this time on the grounds that Cornell was acting as a government agent in educating students enrolled in the New York State College of Agriculture and therefore could not be held liable for negligence.

Rockwood then turned to the appellate division of the New York State Supreme Court, which, strangely enough, considered only the second of Van Kirk's rulings, overturning it in September 1918 by a vote of four to one. Justice John Woodward dealt only with Cornell's status as a state agency, not as an eleemosynary institution. The opinion said that a university "devoted to the higher branches of learning, has never been considered as discharging such a duty to the public or the state as to give it immunity from the ordinary rules which govern other corporations." Although incorporated under state law, Woodward reasoned, Cornell University "was not created for the purpose of carrying out any of the governmental functions of the state of New York, and it is not, therefore, freed from the obligations which attach to any other private corporation. It contracted with this plaintiff for the purpose of furnishing her an education in certain lines, and it owed her the duty of exercising reasonable care in the carrying out of that contract."[55]

With this round, at least, settled in his favor, Rockwood thought the time had come to propose a settlement for something less than the $100,000 his client was asking. "Is it your intention to go further with this matter or can we discuss an adjustment?" he asked McCaskill: "Our client was very badly injured and now that the law has been settled by the Appellate Division I think you can conscientiously recommend an adjustment of the case."[56] But Cornell's lawyers wanted no part of any such deal. McCaskill expressed surprise at the ruling but thought it worth challenging, "considering our excellent defense on the facts and opportunity to have the question of law decided on later appeal."[57] Mynderse Van Cleef told Dr. John Kirkendall, who was still trying to collect some of the money owed him, that the university could not pay any of Louise Hamburger's debts until the law was settled.[58]

So Cornell took the matter to the Court of Appeals, only to lose again. On April 22, 1919, the court upheld Judge Woodward's ruling, although without a written opinion.[59] For a second time Rockwood invited McCaskill to make a reasonable offer, now that "the court of last conjecture has decided in our favor."[60] But the law professor rejected the overture. The court's failure to render an opinion, McCaskill said, left things up in the air. Cornell wanted a precedent for future guidance, "but we are at a loss to know what the court has decided other than that some of your allegations state a cause of action." A trial, he added, would allow the issues to be aired and expose the weaknesses in Rockwood's case: "There are some allegations we know you cannot prove unless you are a wizard, for we are certain they do not exist." He also wanted Rockwood to consent to holding the trial in Tompkins County, where Cornell was located, rather than in Saratoga County.[61]

Rockwood naturally refused a change of venue, but his reply to McCaskill artfully combined promises, threats, and appeals. He began by holding out an olive branch, indicating that Hamburger was "willing to make a reasonable and fair settlement" and "would meet you more than half way." He followed with an ultimatum, warning "that to demonstrate before a jury, as would be done in this case, the utter inefficiency and inability of the employees and show that Cornell University instead of rendering to its students the best and highest-class service, was rendering service of an extremely inefficient character, would not redound to the advantage of the University." Then he asked McCaskill whether it would not be best to "approach this in the spirit of liberal and generous treatment, in fact the spirit which animated Ezra Cornell when he founded your institution?" Concluding on a softer note, he made a humorous appeal to a sense of professional solidarity. Rockwood allowed that it was in his own interest, also, to settle the case since Hamburger's "energetic counsel have been waiting a long time for their pay."[62]

None of these varied gambits proved successful. Instead, both sides spent more than two years gearing up for a trial which was finally held in Binghamton, in Broome County, located about fifty miles from Ithaca. Both sides also recruited prominent local attorneys to help in the trial, Rockwood retaining the services of Thomas B. Kattell, and McCaskill those of James T. Rogers. McCaskill told Rogers: "Our chief defense on the law must be that we are an eleemosynary institution and immune from liability to a beneficiary for all acts of subordinate servants." McCaskill added that Cornell "is more interested in the law governing its liability, however, than the question whether there was negligence in this particular case." Nash Rockwood, he warned Rogers, "will bear watching. He is about as tricky as you find them. He is all courtesy and politeness on the surface but he will take advantage of you if he gets the chance. He has desired to settle but we have decline[d] to discuss settlement as this is the case which will afford us opportunity to ascertain our status."[63]

The trial opened at a special term of the Supreme Court on September 27, 1921, before Justice Abraham L. Kellogg. Jury selection was a time-consuming process, with Rockwood preferring working men whose sympathies might be expected to lie with the victim, while McCaskill wanted business and professional types who might be inclined see things from the university's perspective. McCaskill informed Van Cleef, who remained in Ithaca, that the defense team had done the best it could with the available pool, but conceded: "Unfortunately business men were scarce on this panel, and the laboring element preponderated. We have two farmers and one foreman to help out. Mr. Rogers did very well indeed in sifting what we had." The jurors, he thought, were "fair-minded."[64]

The crucial question, however, was never submitted to the jury. Both McCaskill and Rockwood thought the judge should rule as a matter of law on the issue of Cornell's status as an eleemosynary institution, though they naturally urged him to rule in opposing ways. Kellogg agreed it was his responsibility to decide, for otherwise "the jury might get so twisted up with intricate propositions that . . . they would be befogged as to the real issue." McCaskill asked Kellogg for a ruling that Cornell qualified as an eleemosynary institution, that Hamburger, as a student, was a beneficiary and could not sue for negligence. Kellogg reserved judgment until the third day of the trial, when he told McCaskill: "In order that you may have a real question in the Court of Appeals, I will hold as matter of law, that at the time of the accident in question the defendant University was not an eleemosynary institution" and was therefore liable for the negligence of its agents.[65]

The jury, now having to determine only whether the accident on January 12, 1916, had resulted from negligence by university employees, heard first from Louise Hamburger. Forced to take a leave of absence from Cornell after being injured, she had reentered in the fall of 1916 and received her degree in June 1920. Returning to New York City, she had taken a job managing a cafeteria but had resigned in June 1921, partly because she did not like the work but also, she explained, because "I noticed I couldn't do very much clerical work, I mean work that would require intense usage of the eye, for any length of time, without having it ache." During the summer of 1921 she worked as a cashier at a summer camp in the Catskills.[66]

Now, in September, she described the circumstances surrounding the tragic explosion more than five years earlier. She had carefully followed instructions, she maintained, and so the explosion must have occurred because the fifteen-year-old boy working in the stockroom had given her something other than mercuric sulphide. To confirm the seriousness of the injury, Rockwood called a number of other witnesses: two students who had been present in the laboratory, Dr. John Kirkendall, and another physician who had recently examined Hamburger and who reported she had no vision in her left eye. Rockwood explained that he had been unable to locate Edward Feuerstein, the other student whose test tube had exploded.

McCaskill had to walk a fine line in cross-examining Hamburger. He wished to discredit her testimony yet not arouse the jury's instinctive sympathy for her. He first showed that Hamburger had taken a year of high school chemistry and so was not a novice in the laboratory. Hamburger remarked that the high school class had not required experimenting with explosive chemicals but said she could not remember much else about it. To McCaskill's derisive comment that she seemed to be able to remember the events of January 12, 1916, down to the last detail, Hamburger replied, "I had occasion to recall them," having "lived through the whole thing again. It has impressed me, whereas a course in chemistry in high school had nothing in it to impress me at all, particularly."[67] McCaskill next made much of her having copied the results of Experiment 84 from another student, and when she answered that this was customary he snapped: "It was the custom of some students who were a little bit lazy and inclined to slight their work, but was it not in contravention to the express request each student perform his own experiment?" "Probably was," Hamburger replied. Perhaps, McCaskill suggested, she had also violated instructions concerning Experiment 88? "It is not likely since I performed the experiment myself," Hamburger answered: "I don't think the explosion had anything to do with any violation on my part, as far as I can see."[68]

McCaskill's two major thrusts had failed either to rattle the witness or shake her story. But in describing the courtroom drama to Van Cleef, he made it appear, and undoubtedly believed, that he had succeeded in doing both. Referring to the high school chemistry course, he said: "Here we broke into her armor of fairness and candor. Also got her to admit she disobeyed instructions in performing the experiment previous to the one causing her accident, and that she 'cribbed' that experiment from another student." He did not think Hamburger's attorney had presented a strong case: "If she wins it will be on sympathy alone ... We have handled her very carefully and with the utmost deference and politeness so as not to arouse animosities."[69]

McCaskill's case for Cornell was designed chiefly to direct the jury's attention away from fifteen-year-old Max Hagin, who, it transpired, had been hired by the chemistry department and paid $30 a month, and who had dispensed the same substance to Hamburger and Feuerstein from the stockroom immediately before the accident. "She is relying on the 'boy' phase of the case," McCaskill told Van Cleef: "We have a way to tone that down considerably." McCaskill endeavored to show that Max Hagin made no decisions on his own but simply gave out materials prepared by knowledgeable instructors. Calling the Hagins, Andrew and Max, to testify for the defense, McCaskill reported that they made "fair witnesses. The boy was good. I think we are steering things away from the stock room, though it is hard to get any line on our jury."[70]

In his cross-examination, Rockwood aimed to show that neither the father nor the son had any idea of what they were dispensing, a point not contested by the defense, which insisted they dispensed only what they were given. The elder Hagin had no training in chemistry. A farmer most of his life, he had also worked in a gun factory and had been employed in the stockroom for six months. When his son, Max, took the stand, Rockwood asked: "Did you know what you were handing out, as you handed it out?" "No." "It might have been anything?" "Certainly." After the explosion, Max reported, an instructor told him: "There was an accident in the laboratory and not to hand out any more chemicals."[71]

A parade of instructors and professors in the chemistry department, including Louis Munroe Dennis, then marched to the stand. They had taken all reasonable precautions, they said in response to McCaskill's questions, and their tests showed that Hamburger had mistakenly taken the wrong substance from one of the side shelves. Rockwood probed for soft spots in their story. Was it possible, he asked Dyer Lake, that a student might mistakenly have placed the wrong substance in the jar labeled Lime: "I suppose it is possible." Could Dr. Welsh be certain that the material allegedly taken from Hamburger's desk and handed to him after the explosion was actually the material she had been using: "No." Was Professor Chamot sure that the ingredients he was given to analyze came from Hamburger's mortar: "No, sir." Did Professor Dennis test the chemicals that were given out to students to see that they were, indeed, what they were supposed to be: "No."[72]

As the trial progressed, McCaskill removed his boxing gloves in favor of bare knuckles, or at least the legal equivalent thereof. He sought to incite the jurors against Hamburger by mentioning that she was asking damages of $100,000, a figure they would presumably consider exorbitant. Judge Kellogg interjected, "it is for the jury to say what the damages are," but McCaskill kept on punching: "Except as an element of exaggeration in this case which has permeated the entire trial of the case both by counsel and complainant." Rockwood immediately asked the judge to instruct the jury to disregard this "highly erroneous and improper statement," and the judge promptly did so.[73] But McCaskill thought he had "the desired effect" on the jurors. As he told Van Cleef: "I got a rise out of them today on the $100,000 claim, which I commented on in my opening to show the 'modesty' of plaintiff and the tendency to exaggerate. The jury got the point, & showed their disgust. Rockwood was as mad as a wet hen & objected strenuously."[74]

Rockwood was angry not only because of this effort to sway the jury but also, perhaps, because he had twice offered a compromise settlement. The jurors reached a compromise of their own. After a week-long trial, they retired to consider whether, in the words of Judge Kellogg, Cornell had placed "competent and responsible persons, of suitable age, skill and discretion" in charge of the stockroom and had ensured that chemicals "were sufficiently and duly inspected."[75] They then returned a verdict in favor of Louise Hamburger, awarding her $25,000 in damages. From Cornell University's point of view, however, any judgment in her favor was unacceptable, representing, as it did, a rejection of the cardinal principle that universities, as eleemosynary institutions, were not generally liable for negligence. The trial judge's ruling against Cornell on this issue, McCaskill told Mynderse Van Cleef, "is heresy and most startling, if true."[76] McCaskill had endeavored all along to build a record for an appeal to a higher court, where, he was certain, such strange doctrine was sure to be overturned.

"We Do Not Have a Blind Girl"

To carry the case to the appellate division of the Supreme Court, and, if necessary, further, Cornell retained the distinguished Elmira attorney and former judge of the Court of Appeals, seventy-two-year-old Frederick Collin. In July 1922 he conferred in Ithaca with McCaskill and Van Cleef in order to familiarize himself with the university's version of things. Before relinquishing his own role, McCaskill let Collin know just how angry he was at the jury's verdict against Cornell. He conceded that Louise Hamburger was permanently blind in one eye, "but there is little other than this single element to tie damages to. The other eye is normal." She was able to complete her degree, he pointed out, and to find a job although she quit it.

> The normal eye, then, permitted her to do normal work, and her earning capacity was in no way impaired . . . Other than the testimony that she is required to wear glasses of the ordinary type there is not the slightest evidence of disfigurement. The eye is not gone. It is not closed. Shadows can be seen with it. The impairment of sight is caused by a milky lens, but there is not a particle of evidence that the defect is noticeable to any but the expert eye, and upon close inspection . . . We do not have a blind girl, nor one who cannot see well enough to do ordinary work. Her disfigurement is very slight. She has not suffered great pain.

Given all this, McCaskill fumed, the jury's award of $25,000 "takes on a punitive character because of its size. Sentiment and emotions must have entered into it." He suspected that the "inability of plaintiff to secure a husband may have been a factor in the size of the verdict." But in May 1922 she and Edward L. Plass, also a Cornell graduate, class of 1920, were married. Perhaps, McCaskill suggested, it would be "worth while to suggest a change of name of Respondent to get this on the record."[77]

Collin did not follow this advice, and his brief for the appellate division alluded only in passing to the size of the award. After presenting an account of the explosion that exonerated the university of responsibility, Collin came to the heart of his argument: that Judge Kellogg had erred in ruling that Cornell was not an eleemosynary institution. "Judicial decision universally declares that colleges and universities are public and charitable or eleemosynary corporations," Collin stated: "The establishment of an Institution for the dissemination of learning has always been considered a charity." He noted that the university's trustees served without pay and that "there is an entire absence of the element of pecuniary gain in any form inuring to the benefit of the original incorporators, their successors, or the governing body." There were no stockholders, no dividends, and no profits. Any surpluses were ploughed back into the permanent endowment; in 1916 expenditures exceeded income by $35,000.[78]

Unlike Collin, who could cite numerous precedents, Nash Rockwood had to rely chiefly on what he claimed were the facts regarding Cornell's finances. It charged its five thousand students, or the great majority of them, tuition fees; it rented dormitory rooms to students; it had a "large annual income." The university had net assets in excess of $21 million, he declared, but it had given Louise Hamburger nothing: her tuition was paid by a state appropriation to the College of Agriculture, and all other expenses she bore herself. Cornell owed her reasonable care but had failed to meet its obligations, Rockwood concluded, and the verdict was not excessive in view of her pain and loss of vision.[79]

In March 1923, in an opinion truly startling in its scope, the appellate division ruled in Cornell's favor. The decision was written by Justice Harold J. Hinman and joined by Justices Henry T. Kellogg and Michael H. Kiley. Hinman began by declaring that Cornell was a charitable institution. Since it did not seek pecuniary gain but only "the education of those who attend it as students," its goal was "pure benevolence for a public purpose, unstained by personal, private or selfish considerations." Consequently, under current holdings, it was not liable to its beneficiaries for the negligence of its servants so long as due care had been exercised in their selection. Then Hinman took a step Cornell had not even ventured to propose.

Suppose a charitable organization had not selected its servants with due care, but had negligently selected incompetent ones: Would it then be liable? Hinman's answer was unambiguous: "We are unable to conceive of any good reason for a rule which differentiates in the case of a charitable institution between negligence of a servant or agent in carrying out details of work assigned to him and negligence of an agent, although an officer of the corporation, in selecting the servant who causes the injury to a beneficiary of the charity." The issue came down to that of waiver. A beneficiary waived certain rights in accepting benefits, Hinman said, and therefore: "We hold to the doctrine . . . that a charitable corporation is not liable for injury to a beneficiary, for the negligence, either of its managing officers in selecting incompetent servants and employees or of servants and employees selected with care." This interpretation, he thought, was "a manifestly logical development of the law." In a classic instance of understatement, Hinman wrote: "This rule precludes a recovery by the plaintiff against Cornell University."[80]

Justice Gilbert D. R. Hasbrouck's dissenting opinion was equally startling, although for entirely different reasons. Where Hinman cited case law, Hasbrouck questioned the value of precedents drawn from an "archaic and mediaeval" past: "The reasons that existed in the early days of this country for encouraging the efforts of philanthropy in building and equipping hospitals and institutions of education should no longer be so controlling, for such efforts have resulted in the erection and maintenance of such institutions enjoying endowments and revenues beyond the imaginations of the early lawmakers." Where Hinman spoke in the abstract about the purposes of universities, Hasbrouck pointed specifically to the Cornell chemistry laboratory: "The plaintiff appealed for an education to charity and it plucked out her eye; she asked for bread and it gave her a stone. This is not the charity of the book of books describing charity for 'charity suffereth long and is kind.'"

And where Hinman saw a logical unfolding of the law, Hasbrouck saw only loose thinking. With respect to the rule of waiver, Hasbrouck wrote: "How an agreement to waive away a claim for damages for one's life, one's arm, one's leg or one's eye can be implied where there is utter ignorance on the part of the recipient of charity that such an unconscionable deprivation of human right follows the acceptance of charity, I cannot fathom. And this waiver is generally implied and a contract thus made for children under the age of twenty-one seeking an education and incapable of making a contract." Why should eleemosynary institutions be immune from suits for negligence by their beneficiaries, he asked, who were typically "the indigent and poverty-stricken," and not from suits by strangers? "The better reason and the exercise of a broader and sounder justice would be to apply the doctrine of non-immunity to the needy seeker of charity rather than to the stranger."

A model of sociological jurisprudence, Hasbrouck's opinion sought to bring the law into conformity with existing realities. Now that charitable institutions had grown "great and powerful" and no longer needed "the further fostering care of the State," it was time to adopt "a more liberal rule of liability as to these institutions." Was there a danger that exposing such institutions to lawsuits would destroy them? "If the wrong is of such magnitude that the imposition of damages for its commission would destroy the charity, then it seems to me that it ought to be destroyed." Having stated these powerful objections to the court's ruling, Hasbrouck nevertheless concluded that the trial judge had incorrectly charged the jury, and so he would not vote to affirm the verdict but only to order a new trial (which, since he was in the minority, would not be held).[81]

Even as Nash Rockwood prepared to petition the Court of Appeals, that court handed down a decision in another case that appeared to settle conclusively the issue of Cornell University's eleemosynary status. In May 1923 the court ruled in a case involving the will of Benno Loewy. He had divided his estate into two parts: a valuable library which he left to Cornell University on the condition that it be maintained intact, and his other property which was to go for the support of his wife, Isabella. But Section 17 of the Decedent Estate Law prohibited anyone with a surviving spouse "devising or bequeathing to any benevolent, charitable, literary, scientific, religious or missionary society, association of corporation more than one-half part of his or her estate." Loewy's widow challenged the will, arguing that Cornell fell within Section 17. Cornell contended, to the contrary, that it did not.[82]

The university, therefore, was arguing in Loewy that it was not a charitable organization and in Hamburger that it was. The irony was not lost on the lawyer who was handling the Loewy case for Cornell, Henry W. Sackett of New York City. He informed Mynderse Van Cleef that he would do his best "to keep clear of any conflict between your contentions in the *Hamburger* case and ours in this will case." This, of course, was no easy task. But Sackett had no trouble reading the bottom line. As he told Van Cleef, "We must all recognize that that negligence case involves questions of much greater importance to the University than the will case." He also knew that a ruling against Cornell in Loewy virtually guaranteed a favorable ruling in Hamburger. So the university's lawyers were not particularly unhappy when the court ruled unanimously that Cornell fell within the provisions of Section 17 and could not inherit more than half of Loewy's estate.[83]

The brief Nash Rockwood submitted to the Court of Appeals on behalf of Louise Hamburger reflected all the recent legal developments. He reiterated his earlier arguments, of course, but now made much of a point which Justice Hasbrouck had mentioned briefly in his dissent: that Hamburger, as a student in the New York State College of Agriculture, a separate entity which Cornell administered but did not own, was not a "beneficiary" of the university but rather a "stranger." If this was true, then Cornell's status as an eleemosynary institution was beside the point, for Hamburger would be entitled to sue for negligence. According to Rockwood, his client took a chemistry course offered by Cornell because the College of Agriculture was not equipped to give it. Her relation to Cornell "was that of a stranger, or an invitee asked or permitted to come upon defendant's premises upon condition that defendant would instruct her in a certain subject." So Cornell was "bound to use reasonable care to see that there were no pit-falls upon said premises, into which plaintiff might fall while there."

Rockwood had one more blast to level in this, his final effort on Hamburger's behalf. He insisted that Cornell had violated the state's child labor statute by employing a fifteen-year-old to handle explosive materials. Perhaps the violation did not itself constitute negligence, he conceded, but the boy's lack of training certainly created "a dangerous, death-dealing situation, or a trap, for the innocent students who resorted to the laboratory for instruction in chemistry." Cornell had evidenced "a flagrant disregard of the rights of the students." Since the university could well afford to hire competent people, its behavior was more than negligent. "It was wilful. It was criminal. It is impossible to understand how an institution of the character and standing of Cornell University could so disregard its plain duty to its students as to put explosive chemicals in charge of a farmer and of a 15 year old boy, neither one of whom knew either the character or explosive possibilities of the chemicals they were handling."[84]

If Rockwood's brief was long on rhetoric, Collin's reply was equally long on citations. The most important of them was the Benno Loewy case, which, Collin said, made further argument unnecessary. He similarly dismissed the relatively new claim that Hamburger was not a beneficiary of Cornell, arguing that her case from the start had been based on her indeed being a student. As an eleemosynary institution, Cornell was exempt from liability to its beneficiaries, but, he continued, it had not been negligent. All the chemistry instructors and professors were concededly competent, and the two Hagins had performed the routine task of dispensing what the reagent committee gave them "harmlessly and with complete correctness."[85]

But aside from his arguments about what had happened in the Morse Hall chemistry laboratory on that day in January 1916, Collin's chief advantage in May 1925 was that besides *Loewy* he could cite three recent decisions to support his position: *Schloendorff* v. *The Society of the New York Hospital* (1914), *Butterworth* v. *Keeler* (1916), and *Matter of Bernstein* v. *Beth Israel Hospital* (1923). All were decisions of the New York State Court of Appeals, and all were written by Benjamin Cardozo, the judge to whom the case of *Hamburger* v. *Cornell* was now assigned. As it turned out, Cardozo's ruling in *Schloendorff* was of decisive importance in the case of Louise Hamburger.

Mary E. Schloendorff and the New York Hospital

The medical experiences of Mary E. Gamble—she later married one Henry G. Schloendorff—could have provided the raw material for a tale worthy of the combined talents of Poe and Kafka. Born in Oregon in 1854, she had lived most of her life in San Francisco, working as a physical training and voice teacher. The great earthquake of April 1906 so frightened her that she moved to New York City, where her son, Evan, resided. On January 10, 1907, having suffered for a time from indigestion and dyspepsia, she followed the advice of her physician and entered the New York Hospital. Her son saw to her admission and agreed to pay the weekly charge of seven dollars. She was treated by Dr. Frederick H. Bartlett who pumped her stomach and prescribed a diet of milk and raw eggs. After two weeks he pronounced her cured, but with his permission she decided to remain for a third week to gain strength.[86]

Mary Gamble told in chilling detail what happened next. During the course of his physical examination, Bartlett detected a lump in her abdomen. So did two other physicians, George F. Cottle and Lewis A. Stimson. In fact, she had noticed the lump herself, on and off, for about five years, but it had never bothered her. Explaining that they were having difficulty locating the lump because she was so tense, the physicians recommended she undergo an examination under ether so that her muscles would be relaxed. Afterward, they said, she would have the comfort of knowing whether or not surgery was indicated. She consented on condition that no operation be performed. On January 30 she informed her landlady she would be home in a few days; on the thirty-first she packed most of her things and said her good-byes to the staff. Expecting to leave the hospital on February 2, she arranged for her son to help her home.

But at nine o'clock in the evening on January 31, a nurse awakened her, took her to another ward, and told her she was to be examined but would be able to leave the hospital as scheduled. At midnight she was moved again and prepared for surgery. "I am not going to be operated on," she protested, but the nurse assured her that preparation for an operation and an ether examination were the same. Then, she said, "my body was swathed in antiseptic cloths; I was tied up like a mummy and placed back on the bed." About eleven o'clock the next morning, she was put on a cart and wheeled into a room where a doctor said he was going to give her gas, in preparation for the ether examination. She objected: "I want to see somebody—show me somebody. I want to tell them that I am not to be operated on." He assured her she would not be. "But I was frightened and tried to get up; I tried to get off the litter and get away. And he pushed me—I could only raise my hand; all this time I was frightened and so nervous. He had some apparatus there with a rubber tube and mouthpiece, and he took his hand and pushed against my forehead and pushed me back, and put the mouthpiece to my mouth and said, 'Take a deep breath?' I was frightened at the gas and tried to get up, took a deep breath, I guess, and did not know any more."[87]

When she regained consciousness about twelve hours later, she could not get a straight story from anyone about what had been done to her. In fact, Stimson had operated, found four fibroid tumors in her uterus, and performed a hysterectomy. She knew only that she had a large incision in her abdomen which, although dressed daily, failed to heal properly. "I was cut across the stomach from hip to hip," she related: "I suffered a great deal, more than tongue can tell." She also began to experience painful symptoms, first a terrible soreness in her mouth which made it impossible to swallow, and soon pain and numbness in her left arm and hand. When she informed Cottle—a twenty-eight-year-old intern—that "my hand was cold and the nails were blue, and the hand looked as if it was shriveling," he pooh-poohed her fears. Gamble recalled: "My hand grew worse so that I could not sleep; I screamed night and day. I could not eat, I could not sleep for days. Weeks went by, and I was worn to a skeleton." She requested that her own physician be brought to see her, only to be informed that such a consultation was against hospital policy.[88]

One of Stimson's bedside visits, about two weeks after the surgery, was forever imprinted on Mary Gamble's mind: "He playfully punched me with his fist in the abdomen; in a playful way he said, 'How are you, how do you feel, old girl?' I screamed in agony by the pain he gave me. He said, 'What is the matter, did I hurt you?' I told him it almost killed me, and he said, 'Why?' I said, 'You struck me right over the wound where the doctor placed a drain deep in me and there are safety pins fastened onto my flesh." Stimson angrily told Cottle that the incision should have healed by then. She never saw the surgeon again, and was told he had left the hospital. Reflecting on her misery, she said: "I tried to do anything that would relieve me. There was only one thing I refused to do while I was in that hospital; I absolutely refused to die."[89]

In mid-April 1907 she finally left the New York Hospital, still suffering excruciating pain, unable to use her left hand, and with her left leg so swollen it "looked like an elephant's foot." Over the next sixteen months she was in and out of six different hospitals for periods lasting from a few weeks to a few months. Part of her thumb and index finger had to be amputated because they had become gangrenous. Eventually she consulted Dr. George Schoeps, who concluded that the hysterectomy had produced a femoral phlebitis which had caused the blockage of circulation in her left arm, hand, and leg. The danger of such complications was one reason why fibroid tumors should not always be removed, he explained: "If there was no pain, and no hemorrhage from it, I say it ought not to have been operated."[90]

By the time her lawsuit against the New York Hospital came to trial in May 1911, Mary Gamble had changed her name to Schloendorff, hence the name of the case. She was, of course, her own best witness, but her story was confirmed by her son, by a friend who had visited her in the hospital, and by Dr. Schoeps. The hospital defended itself in three ways: it demonstrated that it was a charitable institution which made its facilities available to all, whether or not they could afford to pay; it declared that it carefully selected its staff of interns by means of a competitive examination; and it denied that Gamble had ever told anyone she did not wish to undergo surgery. Every physician and nurse associated with the case gave the same testimony: she "never stated to me directly or indirectly that she did not want to have an operation."[91]

The defense produced Dr. Lewis A. Stimson as its key witness. In 1907 he was sixty-two years old and had been associated with the hospital for nearly twenty years. He was also a professor of surgery at the Cornell University Medical College. His examination of Mary Gamble, he claimed, had revealed "a multiple fibroid tumor of the uterus. I told her I would remove it if she wanted it removed. She did not say she was opposed to an operation." Asked whether he had spoken with the patient before performing the surgery, he allowed: "I cannot remember the details of what I said . . . I don't recall speaking to her after that before I put the knife in her." He was a busy man, he explained, often performing three operations a day, occasionally as many as one hundred a month. "I never operate on a person without their consent," he declared.[92]

When all the evidence had been presented, the attorney for the hospital moved for a directed verdict in its favor, which was immediately granted by the presiding judge, Leonard A. Giegerich, on the grounds that "a charitable institution from which no financial benefit accrues to its directors or organizers, is not liable to the recipient of its charity resulting from the negligence of one employed in furtherance of its objects providing due care was exercised in selecting the employee."[93] The appellate division of the Supreme Court upheld the ruling in February 1912. The Court of Appeals heard argument on March 11, 1914.

The fundamental issue was clearly joined. Mary Schloendorff's attorney asked whether redress for her wrongs was to be denied merely because a hospital labeled itself charitable: "If this be so, what assurance has anyone who places himself or herself in the care of such an institution against like treatment, or against the whims or caprices of those to whose care the lives and limbs of many thousands are entrusted, should they decide to cut open the body of such patient in order to ascertain for their own enlightenment the nature of some mysterious disease or hidden affliction."[94] Counsel for the New York Hospital pointed to legal precedent: "It is the policy of the State to protect trust funds held for a charitable purpose from diversion to meet such claims as the present, unless the patient proves by a preponderance of evidence, not merely negligence in a surgeon, or nurse, but that the surgeon, or nurse, was incompetent and that the hospital was negligent in its manner of selecting the surgeon, or nurse, originally."[95]

On April 14, 1914, the Court of Appeals handed down a unanimous decision affirming the lower court rulings in favor of the hospital. *Schloendorff v. The Society of the New York Hospital* was one of the earliest opinions Cardozo wrote for the court, of which he had been a member for only two months. Forcefully written and artfully composed, Cardozo's decision rested, at bottom, on an imaginative reconstruction of events deriving from his view of the accepted, socially prescribed roles of professionals—in this instance, male doctors and female nurses.

Cardozo began by affirming that the hospital was indeed a charitable institution. He then summarized the contrasting versions of Mary Schloendorff's stay in the hospital, but noted that there had been a directed verdict for the defendant and so, for the purpose of the appeal, "her narrative, even if improbable, must be taken as true." Next, he stated the two reasons why charitable hospitals were not generally liable for the negligence of physicians and nurses. First was the doctrine of implied waiver: "It is said that one who accepts the benefit of a charity enters into a relation which exempts one's benefactor from liability for the negligence of his servants in administering the charity." Second was the relation between hospitals and physicians: "It is said that this relation is not one of master and servant, but that the physician occupies the position, so to speak, of an independent contractor, following a separate calling, liable, of course, for his own wrongs to the patient whom he undertakes to serve, but involving the hospital in no liability if due care has been taken in his selection." Hospitals had been held immune from liability on one or both grounds, he explained, but neither was applicable where "strangers" rather than "beneficiaries"— that is, patients—were involved.

The wrong that Mary Schloendorff was complaining of, however, was not merely negligence, Cardozo continued: "It is trespass. Every human being of adult years and sound mind has a right to determine what shall be done with his own body; and a surgeon who performs an operation without his patient's consent commits an assault, for which he is liable in damages." (Except, he quickly added, in an emergency where the patient is unconscious and cannot give consent). The hospital, therefore, could not rest its claim of immunity on an implied waiver: "Relatively to this transaction, the plaintiff was a stranger." She had entered the hospital only for treatment of her stomach ailment, and had not waived any rights since, on her account, she had forbidden the operation.

The hospital's exemption from liability, therefore, had to rest on the relation between it and the doctors who used its facilities. That relation was not one of master and servant, Cardozo declared, citing both American and English precedents, because the hospital did not act through the doctors but only engaged them and allowed them to act on their own responsibility. "The wrong was not that of the hospital; it was that of physicians, who were not the defendant's servants, but were pursuing an independent calling, a profession sanctioned by a solemn oath, and safeguarded by stringent penalties." They alone were responsible for violating her instructions.

But to demonstrate that the hospital had not received notice that the violation was about to ensue, Cardozo had to find a way around Mary Schloendorff's assertion that the nursing staff had readied her for an operation over her protests. He reasoned as follows: nurses, if not exactly in the same position as doctors, were not servants of the hospital, as were order-lies or administrators. Nurses "are employed to carry out the orders of the physicians, to whose authority they are subject." Although they concededly performed administrative tasks, nurses stood in the same relation to a pa-tient as did doctors. In fact, preparing a patient for an operation is "really part of the operation itself." Nurses acted not as the hospital's servants but as the physician's agents.

What, then, of Mary Schloendorff's allegations that she told the nurses she had not consented to surgery and did not want it? Here Cardozo wrote the most crucial and least persuasive sentence in the opinion: "I do not think that anything said by the plaintiff to any of the defendant's nurses fairly gave notice to them that the purpose was to cut open the plaintiff's body without her consent." Knowing that the chief surgeon "was one of the most eminent in the city of New York" and that the attending physicians were men of "tested merit," what was a nurse to make of the patient's pro-testations? "Was she to infer from the plaintiff's words that a distinguished surgeon intended to mutilate the plaintiff's body in defiance of the plaintiff's orders? Was it her duty, as a result of this talk, to report to the superintendent of the hospital that the ward was about to be utilized for the commission of an assault? I think that no such interpretation of the facts would have suggested itself to any reasonable mind."

The nurses surely assumed, Cardozo wrote, that they were preparing the patient for an examination, not an operation. After all, he said: "The prep-aration for an ether examination is to some extent the same as for an op-eration." However carefully qualified, this assertion did not square with the evidence which showed that the preoperative procedure first involved scrubbing and shaving the affected area and then administering an enema. There followed another incorrect claim: "An ether examination *was* in-tended, and how soon the operation was to follow, if at all, the nurse had no means of knowing." All the nurses did was attempt to soothe a "nervous and excited" patient in the middle of the night by telling her what she wanted to hear, assuming that if, in the light of dawn, she still objected to surgery, the "distinguished surgeon in charge of the case" would follow her wishes. No other reaction could be expected of a nurse, who is "drilled to habits of strict obedience. She is accustomed to rely unquestioningly upon the judgment of her superiors."

Cardozo decided that Mary Schloendorff's protests failed to show that the hospital had notice of a contemplated wrong. A patient's "struggles or outcries" might hypothetically provide such notice, but "I do not find in this record the elements necessary to call that principle into play." Consequently, there had been no error in directing a verdict for the hospital. Cardozo ended with a pat on the back for eleemosynary institutions. A charitable hospital welcomed all who needed its services, gathered "a company of skilled physicians and trained nurses," and helped "the afflicted, without scrutiny of the character or the worth of those who appeal to it, looking at nothing and caring for nothing beyond the fact of their affliction. In this beneficent work, it does not subject itself to liability for damages though the ministers of healing whom it has selected have proved unfaithful to their trust."[96]

It is obvious, then, why the lawyers for Cornell University who were battling the claims of Louise Hamburger found Cardozo's opinion so eminently satisfying. Schloendorff's description of her mistreatment had, for the purposes of her appeal, a presumptive validity, while Hamburger's account of her injury did not; Schloendorff's relationship to the New York Hospital was concededly more that of a "stranger" than Hamburger's was to Cornell; Schloendorff had been victimized, at the very least, by doctors who had disregarded her explicit instructions, but Hamburger had not claimed any such maliciousness on the part of the chemistry department. If under these circumstances the hospital was not held liable, the university, it would seem, had little cause for concern.

Hamburger v. Cornell, 1925

In arguing its case before the Court of Appeals, therefore, Cornell University relied heavily on the *Schloendorff* precedent. More than that, it had the services of a counsel, Frederick Collin, who had served on the Court of Appeals from 1910 to 1920, was a friend of many of the judges who were still on the court in 1925, and knew the kinds of arguments they were likely to find persuasive.[97] The university also had close ties with two members of the court, Frank H. Hiscock, the chief judge, and Cuthbert Pound, both of whom were serving on the Board of Trustees, Hiscock, in fact, as chairman. They naturally recused themselves but may have felt free to participate in strategy sessions with the attorneys for Cornell. At least Mynderse Van Cleef imagined so, for at an earlier stage in the litigation he thought that "possibly Judges Hiscock and Pound might sit in with us, in as much as they would not take part in the decision."[98]

But the greatest advantage of all turned out to be Judge Benjamin Cardozo's attitude toward universities, or more properly speaking, toward the professoriat. His opinion started with an assumption that Cornell qualified as a charitable institution, partly because of his ruling in *Butterworth* v. *Keeler*, a 1916 case involving the construction of a will, which defined schools as eleemosynary institutions if their purpose was "the promotion, not of private profit, but of public learning." Education was as much a charitable undertaking as "the relief of the poor, the halt and the blind. Charity ministers to the mind as well as the body."[99] The question, then, was not whether Cornell enjoyed a certain immunity but only its extent.

Cardozo did not accept the appellate division's answer to that question. Justice Hinman's sweeping ruling had held, in Cardozo's words, "that the defendant was immune from liability to its students for the negligence of its administrative servants as well as of its teachers, and this though incompetent servants had been negligently chosen." But Cardozo did not wish to go nearly that far. "We do not follow the Appellate Division in its holding that carelessness in that respect, if proved, could not result in liability." The rule in New York, unlike some other states, was that "a hospital or university owes to patients or to students whatever duty of care and diligence is attached to the relation as reasonably implicit in the nature of the undertaking and the purpose of the charity."

The way to proceed, Cardozo said, was to recognize the similarities between a hospital and a university, between physicians and professors. Hospitals were not liable for the negligence of doctors who had been properly chosen, he said, citing not only *Schloendorff* but also another recent opinion, *Matter of Bernstein* v. *Beth Israel Hospital*, in which he had declared that a hospital did not heal or attempt to heal patients through others "but merely to supply others who will heal or attempt to heal on their own responsibility." The reason had to do with the nature of the enterprise, and the independence accorded the medical profession.

Then came a daring leap, one Cardozo executed effortlessly, as if he were a seasoned aerialist: "We think a hospital's immunity from liability for the errors of surgeons and physicians is matched in the case of a university by a like immunity from liability for the errors of professors or instructors or other members of its staff of teachers." This was not the case because all eleemosynary institutions needed to be safeguarded from potentially devastating lawsuits (the "trust fund" theory), or because all beneficiaries—

students as well as patients—voluntarily gave up certain rights when they accepted charity (the "implied waiver" theory). He proposed a different reason: "The governing body of a university makes no attempt to control its professors and instructors as if they were its servants. By practice and tradition, the members of the faculty are masters, and not servants, in the conduct of the class room. They have the independence appropriate to a company of scholars."

To support this claim, Cardozo postulated three imaginary forms of negligence, none of which, he stated, should be actionable: "A university is not to answer in damages because false or pernicious doctrine is imparted to its students in laboratory or clinic, or because a warning of the danger of some experiment has been inadvertently omitted, or because either in performing the experiment or in supervising it, a teacher has combined the wrong ingredients or allowed them to be combined by others." Equating three such disparate scenarios was a highly effective strategy. If one accepted Cardozo's view of the first instance (which seemingly involved a defense of academic freedom), then one would be more inclined to accept his view of the second and the third, although the issues were progressively less clear-cut.

What Cornell owed Louise Hamburger, according to Cardozo, was reasonable care in selecting professors, instructors, and teaching assistants, and this it had certainly provided, for no one questioned the credentials of the members of the chemistry department. If, in bringing the chemicals from the basement storeroom to the laboratory, any of the teachers had made a mistake, the university could still not be held liable—any more than a hospital could if doctors failed to sterilize their instruments before performing surgery. Doctors could be held personally liable, as could professors, but not the institutions which employed them.

But if Cornell was not responsible for the negligent acts of professors, now perched comfortably on the same legal pedestal as doctors, it remained an "open question," Cardozo thought, whether the university was responsible for the acts of the stockroom attendants, Andrew L. Hagin and his son, Max. Had they been carefully selected? And, if so, had they been negligent? Cardozo answered the second question first. The chemistry department's reagent committee had exercised personal supervision over the supplies, he maintained: "There was thus no opportunity, it would seem, for error or confusion on the part of Hagin or his son in the handling of ingredients. All that the son did was to deliver to the students the slips of paper already prepared by the father under the directions of an instructor. With the work of preparation the boy had nothing to do." They did only "mechanical work," he added, which "did not involve the smallest amount of expert knowledge or discretion."

Having established, to his own satisfaction, that the attendants could not have been negligent, Cardozo then had an answer to the first question: "We find no evidence that the administrative employees were incompetent when their qualifications are measured by the nature of the tasks assigned to them . . . There is nothing to suggest that either of them was lacking in the requisite intelligence for acts so simple and perfunctory." So even if the Hagins lacked the least knowledge of chemistry, as they in fact did, it made no difference. The inference was complete: the Hagins could not have acted negligently because their jobs involved no discretion; because their jobs involved no discretion, they could not have been hired negligently.

Moreover, Cardozo added, this made it unnecessary to decide the abstract question of whether incompetently chosen servants would have exposed the university to liability. What he then added was intended only as dictum: "For present purposes we assume without deciding that the defendant is liable in like degree to students and to strangers for the negligence of servants. No evidence in the record gives support to the conclusion that there was any such default." This was Cardozo's only reference to Hamburger's claim that as a student in the state College of Agriculture she was a stranger at Cornell, not a beneficiary. Under the circumstances, it made no difference. If members of the reagent committee had made a mistake, Cornell was not liable because, as faculty, they were not "servants" of the university; if the Hagins had made a mistake, Cornell was not liable because, although they were "servants" of the university, there had been no negligence in hiring them because they only performed routine tasks. Either way, "only conjecture or suspicion can impute negligence to any one except in circumstances relieving the university of liability for the wrong of the delinquent."[100]

Three law reviews commented on the decision, and all had generally favorable things to say about the middle path Cardozo had taken between the extremes of strict liability and complete immunity. Above all, the authors expressed their satisfaction with the new status accorded university professors. "The decision adds teachers to the class of those following an independent calling, and holds the employing institution not liable for their negligent acts," noted the *Cornell Law Quarterly*.[101] Writing in the *Illinois*

Law Review, Frederic C. Woodward explained: "The analogy between the hospital surgeon and the university professor is compelling, and in the light of the hospital cases the decision must be approved. Incidentally, it may be said that university professors will appreciate the recognition, in such unequivocal terms and by such an enlightened jurist of their independent status."[102]

Such an unequivocal recognition had been a hallmark of Benjamin Cardozo's career for many years, certainly since 1921 when he gave the Storrs Lectures at Yale. His decision in the Hamburger case came at a time when faculty members around the country were engaged in a struggle to achieve something like the status he now conferred upon them. In 1915 the American Association of University Professors, in advancing claims for academic freedom and tenure, stated that "the professorial office should be one both of dignity and independence" and that everything possible should be done to "enhance the dignity of the scholar's profession."[103] It was in the context of this broad movement for faculty autonomy that Cardozo's decision was especially welcome.

The rules Cardozo laid down regarding the immunity of universities and hospitals remained binding in New York State until 1957. Then, in *Bing* v. *Thunig,* the Court of Appeals explicitly overturned *Schloendorff,* and by implication *Hamburger,* largely on the grounds that liability should be the rule and immunity the exception: "It is not alone good morals but sound law that individuals and organizations should be just before they are generous, and there is no reason why that should not apply to charitable hospitals." Cardozo's view that a hospital did not treat patients but simply procured doctors to treat them on their own responsibility "no longer reflects the fact . . . The rule of nonliability is out of tune with the life about us, at variance with modern-day needs and with concepts of justice and fair dealing. It should be discarded."[104]

The rule of nonliability was out of tune with life even in the era in which Louise Hamburger was injured, sued for negligence, and finally lost, as at least one jurist, Gilbert D. R. Hasbrouck of the state Supreme Court's appellate division, recognized. Cardozo's vision of a university as comprising a company of scholars fearlessly pursuing the truth wherever it might lead was, at best, overly idealized. At worst, it distorted reality beyond recognition. Cardozo could not possibly have known, from the record before him, that Professor Louis Munroe Dennis ruled Cornell's chemistry department as if it were a feudal kingdom, that the chemicals he purchased on his European junkets were stored haphazardly in a dingy basement, or that the Cornell law professor who handled the trial boasted that he had provoked the jury by inserting prejudicial remarks. Had he known, one can only wonder whether he would have thought that concepts of justice and fair dealing required him to decide otherwise.

4

Gender and Sexuality

Chief Judge

From a professional standpoint, Benjamin Cardozo's years on the Court of Appeals—from 1914 to 1932—were the most satisfying of his life. In January 1917, after having served for three years on an interim basis, he accepted an appointment to an unexpired term as an associate judge. This meant he had to relinquish the state Supreme Court judgeship to which he had been elected in 1913 and which he still formally held. Ironically, considering his newly elevated status, he had to accept a reduction in salary from $17,500 to $10,000. He also had to run for the Court of Appeals in his own right in the November 1917 election. At the time, he reported, he was "very reluctant to accept the new appointment. I did not gain enough to compensate for resigning the office which I held, and taking the chance and the bother of re-election. But requests from the bar and from my associates made it impossible to refuse; and now that the choice has been made, I am giving myself no concern about it."[1] Reelection, however, involved little bother and even less chance. Since there were two vacancies, it was arranged that Cardozo, a Democrat, and Chester McLaughlin, a Republican, would receive bipartisan endorsements.

Cardozo enjoyed warm personal relations with his fellow judges. When court was in session most of them resided at the Ten Eyck, a downtown Albany hotel which offered its guests "complete and luxurious comfort, the final word in satisfying appointments and the intelligent service that antic-ipates every need."² The judges usually dined together at the hotel, and often accompanied one another on the short walk to the courthouse. Cardozo's closest friends on the court were Cuthbert Pound, appointed in 1915, and Irving Lehman, elected in 1923. Cardozo said of the first chief judge under whom he served, Willard Bartlett, that he could not "have been kindlier or more generous and thoughtful."³ He appeared to hold Bartlett's successor, Frank H. Hiscock, in similarly high regard. In 1926, when His-cock reached the mandatory retirement age of seventy, Cardozo was elected chief judge with the endorsement of both the Democratic and Republican parties.

That bipartisan support, however, came about only after a fierce strug-gle extending over many months. Democratic party leaders had tried to persuade Governor Alfred E. Smith to bypass Cardozo, who, although nominally a Democrat, had run in 1913 on the anti-Tammany Fusion ticket. They instead supported Cuthbert Pound, a Republican, for the chief judge-ship, hoping thereby to win Republican backing for a Democrat to replace Pound as associate judge. Their favored candidate, Justice John V. McAvoy, was a Catholic. At the time the court consisted of five Protestants and two Jews, and, according to those in the know, "it has been strongly urged from Church quarters that a Catholic be nominated for one position on the Court of Appeals bench, no one now occupying a seat who is of that faith."⁴ As late as September 1926, Cardozo's Jewish allies thought the issue of re-ligious balance would deny him the position. "The hierarchy has set its foot down and all hands bow to its edict," Judge Abram I. Elkus told Rabbi Stephen Wise, "I fear it's a hopeless task as the Catholics feel that they ought to have one judge on th Ct as the J's have two."⁵

If Democrats were prepared to endorse a Republican, some Republicans, in the Byzantine world of state politics, were favorably disposed to Car-dozo. One of their leading gubernatorial candidates, William J. Donovan, came from one of the westernmost counties in the state, and so did Pound: both names on the ballot would produce an unacceptable geographical im-balance. (As it turned out, Ogden Mills, not Donovan, would receive the nomination and would be defeated by Al Smith). Moreover, Republicans thought Cardozo's elevation would give them the better claim to the vacant associate judgeship, and they, too, had a highly eligible candidate: Henry T. Kellogg of Plattsburg, a justice of the appellate division.

In September 1926, after months of hesitation, Smith finally decided to support Cardozo. He did so, it appears, largely at the urging of prominent Jewish judges, lawyers, and religious leaders, including Joseph M. Proskauer, Abram I. Elkus, Louis Marshall, and Rabbi Wise. Never one to underestimate his own influence, Wise recounted: "I made a fiery written protest to Smith; and then we had four hours together during which I hammered and hammered and hammered, inspired, if I may say so, by what I know was the rightness of my case, until Smith finally succumbed and named Cardozo."[6] These same men helped place an editorial in the *New York Times* which declared that the governor "could not excuse himself to his own conscience" if he failed to back Cardozo.[7] On September 22 Smith and Republican leaders agreed on a joint ticket of Cardozo as chief judge and Kellogg as associate judge.

Cardozo and Pound probably knew about some, if not all, of these backroom maneuvers. Though each of them wanted the position, neither wanted it badly enough to lobby for it. To the contrary, each candidate made it clear to supporters that he would refuse to accept the nomination if acceptance would mean an openly partisan contest. In letters to friends they expressed their regard for one other, Pound somewhat more effusively than Cardozo. "Pound is a splendid man—really better in many ways than I am, though I am glad you don't think so," Cardozo wrote to one of his backers, Learned Hand.[8] For his part, Pound explained: "The whole thing has been very trying for me. My consolation comes from the facts that Judge Cardozo in the end has not been slighted or humiliated and that the court has been strengthened or rather not weakened by the choice of Judge Kellogg, who is a learned judge. Cardozo was very sweet about it when it looked as if I would be the nominee. I think he knew little of what was being done, both for and against him. *Magna est veritas,*—and it prevails,—in this instance at least."[9]

Nothing reveals the cordial working relationships among the judges more clearly than the informal reports they circulated before taking action. In each case, the judges had to decide whether to issue an opinion (or opinions when unanimity was lacking), to render an unsigned *per curiam* opinion, or, as often happened, to affirm a lower-court ruling without an opinion. To facilitate the process, one judge would prepare a confidential report outlining the important issues, raising the relevant points of law, and offering a recommendation. These internal reports served as a basis for the court's actions, although the judge who drafted the preliminary report would not necessarily write the published opinion. In eighteen years on the Court of Appeals, Cardozo wrote 653 such reports, many (although not all) of which have survived. Some of them offer remarkably candid insights into his manner of dealing with his colleagues.

Cardozo's memoranda reveal a judge aware of the complexity of issues, of his own limitations, and of the law's uncertainties. Once, in a matter involving complicated financial dealings, he reported: "This case is one that calls for nothing more than an analysis of the facts, but an analysis that should be made by an accountant rather than a judge, particularly a judge who has little understanding of accounts."[10] On another occasion he admitted: "I am not satisfied with this opinion either in form or in substance. I am sending it around as a basis for discussion. I am not as confident as I should like to be that I am right. I hope that those who have a different view will put their thoughts into dissenting opinions, so as to help us to a sound conclusion."[11] In yet a third case he explained to one of his associates: "I am not sure that you will agree with these suggestions, or that after further consideration I shall agree with them myself; but in any event, I should like your thought about them."[12]

In *The Nature of the Judicial Process,* Cardozo had defended a judge's use of the method of "sociology" when precedent and philosophy provided no clear basis for decision. His reports sometimes sounded as if he were translating his theory into practice. In 1923 a case arose involving a conflict over the title to lakefront property: the United States Gypsum Company, which owned land on the east side of Cayuga Lake, claimed that hunters who were shooting ducks along the shore were trespassing. Recommending that the court rule in favor of the hunters, Cardozo wrote: "This case is close and difficult. The question it presents, is an open one in this state. The authorities leave it uncertain . . . We could decide either way with some support in precedent and in reason. Viewing the situation as still open, I am reporting in accordance with what seems to me to be the larger public policy."[13]

In other situations, where Cardozo felt more certain, he said so with a directness that would have been inappropriate in a published opinion. One case, for example, involved a negligence suit in which an insurance company had paid a claimant secretly so that she would not have to pay the legal fees on which she and her attorney had agreed. The insurance company was asking the Court of Appeals to overturn a lower court ruling which required it to pay the lawyer what he rightfully had coming to him. Urging that the motion be denied, Cardozo told his colleagues: "The insurance company acted very shabbily and with wanton indifference to the lawyer's rights. Even now, its opposing affidavits are disingenuous and unsatisfactory as to what the true agreement was."[14]

Rape and Resistance: Carey and Burnhardt

When, in 1918, the court overturned the rape conviction of a man named David Raymond Carey, one of Cardozo's preliminary reports served as the basis for granting the appeal. Cardozo's stance in *Carey* was unusual because he nearly always voted to affirm convictions in cases of sexual assault. In this instance, however, doubts about the woman's character led him to a different conclusion. Those doubts reflected an inclination, evident all his life, to place women in two distinct categories: the many who were innocent, virtuous, and pure, and the few who were corrupt, depraved, and sluttish. The "virgin/whore" polarity usually led Cardozo to empathize with victims of sexual assault, but it could also make him severely censorious.[15]

That certainly was his reaction to the case involving Lillian Tate, a resident of Watertown, who was assaulted by David Raymond Carey on July 12, 1912. He was nineteen years old, she was twenty-five. Carey, who worked in his father's blacksmith shop, and Tate, a paper-mill worker, had known each other for a few years. She was at home that afternoon recuperating from surgery. She admitted Carey to her apartment, they spoke for a while, and he then attacked her. The issue before the Court of Appeals was how much resistance Tate had offered, and whether the exclusion of evidence pertaining to her lack of chastity was relevant to such a determination. The court's *per curiam* opinion, drafted by Cardozo, noted that a conviction for rape in New York State required that the woman "oppose the man to the utmost limit of her power. A feigned or passive or perfunctory resistance is not enough. It must be genuine and active and proportioned to the outrage. The record discloses a situation where conflicting inferences may be drawn whether resistance in that sense was offered."[16]

Lillian Tate's testimony, however, allowed the drawing of only one inference. At the trial in county court, held in February 1913, she related that she and Carey were sitting on a couch and talking. Then, she said, he put his hands "under my clothing, and I told him to leave me alone; he said he wouldn't do it." She tried to get away, "and I got just as far as the door, into the hall and he caught me and he locked the door and put the key in his pocket; then he made the remark in the hall he was going to get what he was after." She tried to escape to the bathroom, but "he let out an awful oath and said, 'If you don't stop hollering I will choke you' and he put his hand on my throat like that [indicating]." He carried her back to the sitting room "and threw me there on the couch and made an awful remark; I can't speak it." He dragged her to the bedroom and threw her on the bed, she went on: "Then he started taking off my clothes . . . I was crying all the while and I was begging for him to leave me alone." Tate reported slapping and kicking him and pulling his hair, but he ripped off her clothing, including the bandage covering her surgical incision, and then took off his own clothes. "I was fighting him all I could," she explained. She ran to the window and threatened to jump, but he grabbed her and again threw her on the bed. "He got over on the bed and pushed me over on my back and he got on top of me," she related: "He had intercourse there." All the while she continued "kicking him, slapping his face and pulling his hair until he took my hands and held them down . . . I couldn't do anything when he had me held down." Afterward, as he was leaving, he stole her watch.[17]

Taking the witness stand, Carey confirmed many of these details although not all of them. He admitted that, while sitting on the couch, "I commenced fooling with her there; she told me to stop, she didn't want to do anything; . . . she kept telling me to stop, she didn't want to do anything, she wasn't feeling good, she just got over an operation; so I kept on fooling with her." He denied forcing her into the bedroom, adding: "She got on the bed; she didn't want to do anything and commenced to pull my hair and slap my face saying she didn't want to do anything; I got on top of her; she commenced to pull and resist a little bit at first, but in the last she took part in the intercourse." He admitted saying "I would get what I was after" but denied using an oath; he admitted stealing her watch but denied she had threatened to jump out the window. Asked if "she continued to slap your face and pull your hair up to the moment of penetration?" he answered: "Yes, sir." Asked "When did she stop slapping you and pulling your hair?" Carey replied: "About half way through with the intercourse, I guess."[18]

The trial judge, George W. Reeves, permitted the defense to introduce evidence regarding a prior sexual encounter between Carey and Tate. In May, two months before the rape, he had made advances while giving her a ride in his coach and buggy: Tate claimed he had stopped when she protested, but Carey said they had sexual intercourse. The judge, however, did not allow medical testimony concerning the possibility that Tate had gonorrhoea. After the attack in her apartment, her underpants were subjected to medical analysis. The defense attorney, Thomas Burns, attempted to ask the physician whether his inspection of the garment had turned up any evidence of disease. The judge sustained the defense's objection to the query. When Burns queried Lillian Tate as to whether she had gonorrhoea, she denied it. Burns persisted: "Would you know it by the name of clap? You have heard that name, haven't you?" Tate replied indignantly: "Tom Burns! Lord!"[19]

In his charge to the jury, Judge Reeves explained that rape required an act of sexual intercourse "against [a woman's] will or without her consent; or when her resistance is forcibly overcome; or when resistance is prevented by fear of immediate and great bodily harm." If a woman consents, "however reluctantly," either by words or acts which "infer consent," then the jury cannot convict. "It also follows that if the woman does not resist, consent will be implied, and there is no rape." He added that there must be resistance to the "utmost," although the meaning of that word would depend on the woman's strength, ability, and willpower. The judge explained that the law also required corroboration of the victim's account. It was provided by the janitor of Tate's apartment house who said he heard screams coming from her room; by a policeman who found her bedsheets bloodstained and in disarray; and by Tate's sister, who first informed the police of the rape. Whether their testimony was sufficiently weighty, the judge explained, was for the jury to decide.[20] Carey was found guilty and sentenced to one year, five months to three years, two months in state prison.

Given the care with which the judge explained the law, it seems peculiar that the Court of Appeals should have ordered a new trial. Aside from mentioning the "conflicting inferences" which could be drawn about Tate's resistance, the judges rested their reversal on an error in Reeves's charge. "The law requires corroboration of the complainant's testimony. The trial judge told the jury that for that purpose they might consider her complaint to the police. The complaint was not corroboration 'by other evidence' within the meaning of the statute." In fact, the trial judge had mentioned a number of corroborating witnesses, leaving the jury free to assess the value of their testimony. Then came the most revealing sentences in the court's *per curiam* opinion: "Some of the members of the court desire to place their concurrence upon the additional ground that error was committed in rejecting testimony tending to prove that the complainant was unchaste. They think that the exclusion of such testimony may work a denial of justice. But that view has not commanded the assent of a majority."[21] This was, in truth, Cardozo's view, as expressed in his internal memorandum.

What disturbed Cardozo was the trial judge's decision to exclude testimony concerning whether "the marks of gonorrhoea" were present on "part of the complainant's clothing." "The testimony, if received, would have justified the inference, in the absence of explanation, that the complainant was unchaste. We must say whether testimony of particular acts of misconduct was admissible to rebut the inference of resistance." It was a difficult question, he went on, because "even an unchaste woman may be ravished. Unchastity diminishes, however, the likelihood of resistance." Consequently, evidence of a woman's "acts of misconduct" with men other than the alleged rapist should be admitted because such evidence was not offered "to impeach her credibility as a witness." Rather, "unchastity is in such cases a fact which is deemed to tend to disprove a constituent element of the crime." Cardozo continued: "There is, of course, a difference in weight between evidence of particular acts and evidence of habitual prostitution. But it is a difference in weight only. The truth remains that chastity has once been yielded, that honor has been lost, and that the great motive which inspired resistance even unto death, has gone. To deny this is to ignore a truth which all history and all literature and all experience proclaim."

Cardozo conceded that the protection of virginity was not the only motive for resisting rape. A married woman would have a different motive: "the protection of wifely honor." He also thought that there was a difference between the kinds of evidence that should be admissible in rape cases and murder cases: while a single prior act of sexual intercourse destroyed a woman's virginity (and therefore in some measure her will to resist), a single prior act of violence "may or may not evidence a violent disposition." Cases involving rape were therefore unique: "We are dealing now with a single element of character which has had a meaning and importance all its own in the status of womankind and in the civilization of the race. Almost invariably, its loss tends to weaken, at least in some degree, the motive for resistance."

Without mentioning Lillian Tate's uncontroverted allegations that she had kept on kicking her assailant, slapping him, and pulling his hair, Cardozo maintained that if she had gonorrhea she must have had prior sexual experience, which in itself "would give new verisimilitude to the defendant's story of consent." Fear of wounding "the complainant's sensibilities," Cardozo said, was not sufficient reason to reject such testimony. The exclusion of evidence pertaining to even a single prior "lapse" was no more justifiable than its exclusion regarding "repeated acts of prostitution." Unable to persuade the rest of the court on this point, Cardozo came up with another reason—the trial judge's presumably flawed instructions regarding corroboration—that produced a decision to reverse.[22]

Cardozo felt strongly enough about the case to discuss it at length three years later in his Yale Law School lectures. He used it to make the point that while judges should generally adhere to precedent, they should make an exception when an existing rule derived from outmoded conditions or institutions, or when it "may not reasonably be supposed to have determined the conduct of the litigants." "Let me take an illustration from the law of evidence," he said: "A man is prosecuted for rape. His defense is that the woman consented. He may show that her reputation for chastity is bad. He may not show specific, even though repeated, acts of unchastity with another man or other men."[23] Here Cardozo cited *People* v. *Carey*, although his summation was not entirely accurate. Carey's defense was only that Tate had "consented" in the technical sense of having ceased resisting to the utmost some time after he had forced her to have sexual intercourse. Moreover, "repeated" acts of unchastity would not have been shown even had the medical evidence been admitted and shown that Tate had a venereal disease.

Cardozo continued:

> The one thing that any sensible trier of the facts would wish to know above all others in estimating the truth of his defense is held by an inflexible rule to be something that must be excluded from the consideration of the jury. Even though the woman takes the stand herself, the defendant is not greatly helped, for though he may then cross-examine her about other acts, he is concluded by her answer. Undoubtedly a judge should exercise a certain discretion in the admission of such evidence, should exclude it if too remote, and should be prompt by granting a continuance or otherwise to obviate any hardship resulting from surprise.

But the present rule, he added, which excluded such evidence "altogether and always," placed "an exaggerated reliance upon general reputation as a test for the ascertainment of the character of litigants or witnesses. Such a faith is a survival of more simple times. It was justified in days when men lived in small communities. Perhaps it has some justification even now in rural districts. In the life of great cities, it has made evidence of character a farce."

Cardozo's argument that "a spirit of realism should bring about a harmony between present rules and present needs" is sensible enough—although hardly substantiated by the circumstances of the Carey case. With a population of 27,000, Watertown retained a sense of itself as a small town in which people took an avid interest in local goings-on and felt little of the anonymity characteristic of the metropolis. The same editions of the *Watertown Daily Times* that described the trial and the overflow crowds attending it, also carried stories, for example, about sixty persons who attended a fundraising event for the Northern Frontier Chapter, Daughters of 1812, played cards, chiefly auction bridge, for two and a half hours, and raised $20 for a battlefield monument; and about jury selection (during a lull in the Carey proceedings) in a case involving a man "charged with poisoning a heifer belonging to his neighbor . . . by placing a dish containing feed and paris green in a lot which the calf entered."[24]

In such a community, one's general reputation might well have served as a reasonable basis for ascertaining character. The trial record indicates that Carey was widely regarded as a disreputable fellow, with other convictions for public drunkenness and petit larceny. His father had twice returned items he had stolen (including Tate's watch) to their rightful owners, and had warned Tate that "if the boy came up to her rooms drunk or sober to have him arrested or send for me." Lillian Tate, on the other hand, was "a respectable young woman," too modest to describe the sexual acts Carey had demanded of her ("it was something I couldn't tell"), and initially hesitant to report the rape because when she entered the police station "I told my sister I couldn't tell that awful thing before these men."[25]

Cardozo's view of the Carey case contrasted sharply with his reaction to other rape cases in which he took the side of the victim. *People* v. *George Burnhardt,* decided in May 1929, is particularly revealing because, as in *Carey,* Cardozo submitted an internal report. He recommended that the judges uphold a conviction for second-degree statutory rape, and they accepted his advice, affirming a lower court ruling without opinion. Since the case involved statutory rape, issues of force, consent, and resistance were irrelevant: under New York State law, the act of sexual intercourse with a woman (not the man's wife) who was under the age of eighteen was a crime.

On the afternoon of January 19, 1928, fourteen-and-a-half-year-old Edna Stokes and two of her friends, both fifteen, ran away from the New York State Training School for Girls in Hudson, where they had been committed about a year earlier. They headed for the railroad station where they found a taxi, driven, they claimed, by George Burnhardt. He asked if they wanted a ride and they said they wanted to go to Great Barrington, Massachusetts, a distance of about forty miles. He offered to take them but at some point along the way he instead propositioned them. Edna, who was in the back seat, at first refused, but he threatened to leave the girls in Chatham, New York, and not give Edna any money. "So I consented, and he got in the back seat with me and we intercoursed."[26]

Asked to describe exactly what happened, she explained: "I took my bloomers off and I raised my dress up and I laid down on the back seat . . . and spread my legs apart and he put his private in mine and we had intercourse."[27] Her friends confirmed her account, although they were sitting in the front seat at the time and could only hear, not actually see, what was happening in the back. The cab driver then took the three girls to the railroad station at Chatham so they could catch a train to Pittsfield, Massachusetts. There they were quickly apprehended and returned to the School for Girls. After relating their tale to the superintendent, they accompanied her and a police officer to the Hudson train depot where they spotted Burnhardt and identified him as the man who had picked them up.

George Burnhardt, who was married and had a three-year-old daughter, denied all the allegations. He had the perfect alibi—if it was believed: the date in question, January 19, happened to be the birthday of both his younger brother and his thirteen-year-old niece. He had been at a birthday party from six that evening until midnight. Four witnesses corroborated his story: his sister and brother-in-law, who had given the party; a sister-in-law (who said he had driven her to and from the affair), and another guest.

At the conclusion of the trial on May 25, 1928, the judge informed the jurors that in cases of second-degree, statutory rape, "any sexual penetration, however slight, is sufficient to complete the crime." Since Edna Stokes was under eighteen, "force is not necessary and it does not make any difference whether the woman consented or not." The judge then added a crucial admonition: the jury might take into account the failure of the defense to produce testimony from either Burnhardt's niece or brother for whom the joint birthday party had allegedly been thrown.[28] The jury returned the next day with a guilty verdict. Burnhardt was sentenced to four to ten years at hard labor.

On January 23, 1929, the appellate division of the Supreme Court upheld the decision by a vote of four to one. The majority did not submit an opinion; Gilbert D. R. Hasbrouck, however, wrote an urgent dissent. He reasoned that Burnhardt had been deprived of his rights when the judge told the jury that it might consider the failure to call Burnhardt's niece and brother as witnesses. Since four witnesses had testified to his presence at the party, the defense may well have thought that two more would be merely cumulative, and therefore had no duty to explain their absence in order to avoid an unfavorable inference. "Here we see the very patent vice of the charge," Hasbrouck said: "It gives to the people the benefit of testimony not produced in saying: 'You may consider the significance of the evidence not produced and the witnesses that have not been produced.'"[29]

The Court of Appeals, however, rejected Hasbrouck's reasoning, adopting instead Cardozo's recommendation to uphold the conviction. Cardozo's memorandum began by noting that Burnhardt, a man "apparently of good repute," denied the allegations. On the other hand, all three girls had claimed that "he had intercourse with the Stokes girl on the rear seat of the sedan." Cardozo admitted: "The three girls are not very trustworthy witnesses, and I am not unmindful of the danger of sending a man to prison on the basis of their testimony. Even so, they may be telling the truth." He found no basis for saying the jury had insufficient evidence to support the verdict. Cardozo added: "No one can read the testimony of Edna Stokes and doubt that there was evidence sufficient to establish penetration if what she said was believed." He denied the trial judge had erred in charging the jury, and simply ignored the issue that had so troubled Hasbrouck.[30]

Cardozo brought to cases involving all aspects of sexuality a set of moral convictions shared by many people raised in genteel circumstances in the Victorian era. The prevailing concept held that women were more virtuous than men, were better suited to be caretakers and nurturers, and were supposed to be "sexually pure and abstinent" except when trying to conceive children with their husbands. As one writer said at the time: "For purity of thought and heart, for patient courage, for recklessly unselfish devotion, for the love that rests, strengthens and inspires, we look to women."[31] Conversely, men were viewed as wild and unruly, even animalistic, subject to "untamed life forces." Cardozo was, in fact, inclined to regard men as sexual aggressors whom the law had to restrain, and women (unless their behavior made them unworthy of respect) as in need of the law's protection.

"Mark the Cynical Bachelor!"

On May 24, 1912, when Benjamin Cardozo turned forty-two, friends and relatives presented him with a homemade birthday card. It contained a flattering pen-and-ink sketch of Cardozo emphasizing his steady gaze, finely chiseled features, and firm jaw, with the whimsical caption, "brilliant young member of the New York Bar." At the top of the card was perhaps a more revealing inscription: "Bachelor-Barrister." But another drawing on the card is missing, either purposely destroyed or accidentally lost. All that remains are the hand and wrist of what may possibly have been a cherub.[32] If so, the figure would have been appropriate. Those who knew Cardozo best viewed him, even when he was well along in years, as childlike and innocent, as, in the words of his adoring housekeeper, Kate Tracy, "more angel than mortal."[33]

When Cardozo alluded to his single status, he generally used the terms "bachelor" and "celibate" interchangeably. Once, as if for added emphasis, he described himself as "a lone bachelor."[34] On another occasion he recounted to a friend the "wisdom" of the ancient sage who was asked the fitting age for marriage: "To the young man he answered 'not yet,' and to the old man 'not at all.' But I don't really believe that—or rather the first part of it—in spite of my celibate existence."[35] Cardozo adopted the same playful tone, but with a hint of sarcasm, in referring to the recent wedding of one of his associates, remarking to a mutual friend: "He is a splendid man, and deserves a good wife and happiness, if marriage is the road to the goal. Mark the cynical bachelor!"[36]

Cardozo professed to be puzzled by women, referring to them as unpredictable if not downright unfathomable beings. Writing to his cousin Maud Nathan about the difficulty of finding his way to her Connecticut summer home, he joked: "I don't know much about the man-made roads of Connecticut. Those of New Jersey I know so well that they no longer have any secrets from me, which shows that they are not feminine in their make-up or constitution."[37] Another time he reassured Nathan, who had complained in passing about writer's block, that she should not be concerned about the silence of the Muse: "She'll have enough to say when she is good and ready. She's a capricious being. I suppose that is why the wise old Greeks understood her to be a woman. List the voice of the cynical old bachelor."[38]

As bachelorhood became a settled pattern, Cardozo confessed to feelings of loneliness which at times grew overwhelming. Those feelings were intensified by the death of his sisters, Elizabeth in 1919, Emily in 1922, and especially Ellen in November 1929. That summer Ellen had been transported by ambulance to the cottage at Allenhurst, New Jersey, and Cardozo seemed to know that it was the last such trip she would ever make. In July he was in an unusually introspective mood, telling his cousin Annie Nathan Meyer that he envied her because she did not know "the meaning of the word loneliness. To me it is a very vivid thing. The sense of being an atom in all this vast universe without any other atom traveling the same daily orbit is annihilating. It doesn't help me much to know that atoms more or less akin are traveling orbits not very distant with feelings of atomic friendship. Even a little separation is a big one when only atoms are involved."[39]

If single life was a lonely life, lacking emotional intensity, it was nevertheless conducive to stability and order. Cardozo, who was once described as being "as utterly dedicated to routine as a baby," recognized that he felt most comfortable doing familiar things in familiar places, and recognized, too, that he paid a price for his preference.[40] When, in his mid-sixties, he read Bruce Lockhart's *Retreat from Glory,* an absorbing account of the British diplomat and banker's adventures in central Europe and the Balkans, Cardozo mused that it "makes me wish to begin life over again. I have missed so much, all the movement and the color and the swift and varied action. But, of course, there have been compensating—partially compensating—gains. 'Cultivate your garden' is a precept not to be despised, though there is little glamor in its homely outlook."[41] Cardozo often referred to himself as "a fearful old 'stick in the mud.'"[42] To a friend, Rupert Joseph, who spent much of his time traveling the globe and whose life was filled with "diversity and excitement," Cardozo allowed that his own was marked by "uniformity and calmness."[43]

A handsome, distinctive-looking man, Cardozo was nevertheless insecure about his looks. He was a finicky dresser who took great pains with his appearance. A barber came to cut his hair every Saturday morning, and if his cousin Adeline Cardozo wished to tease him she had only to remark that "there's a hair out of place."[44] He was vain enough to remove his eyeglasses or replace them with pince-nez when a visitor arrived or when he was having his photograph taken. Yet Cardozo invariably complained about photographs, portraits, etchings, and other likenesses. "The artist says that it is good, but the victim as usual is dissatisfied,"[45] he would say, or else he would want to know: "why in the world didn't he get me better?"[46] Of one portrait, he commented, "Oh yes, that's the one that makes me look like a horse,"[47] and of an etching: "I look as cross as a bear, and my amiability is about the only virtue of which I feel reasonably sure."[48]

Fastidious about his own appearance, Cardozo admitted to being repelled by scruffiness in others. A relative, Aline Goldstone, once evidently made an approving comment about the great unwashed, and to support her point cited Will Rogers's statement to the effect that he had never met a man he didn't like. Cardozo quickly offered a correction. Rogers, he claimed, had actually said "that he had met many prominent men and had never met one he didn't like. That is not quite so magnificent, is it? Your tramp with the unshaven chin could hardly come in the category. Well, I'm willing to go pretty far in my love for humankind, but I can't have stubby chins around me. Fix me up, if you please, an epitaph to suit those sentiments."[49]

So far as is known Cardozo never had a love affair or sexual relationship with anyone. Friends and relatives, who claimed to be baffled by "the riddle of Cardozo's bachelorhood,"[50] offered several explanations: his single-minded dedication to his work, which precluded an active social life; his difficulty in meeting an eligible woman in the relatively small New York City Sephardic Jewish community; his devotion to his sister Ellen, his attentiveness during her protracted illness, and her own fierce possessiveness. All of these are reasonable suggestions, although, given the prejudices of the day, they may have been advanced to discourage speculation that would have reflected less favorably on Cardozo: that he was sexually dsyfunctional, or had an unusually low sexual drive, or was homosexual.

There is no record of contemporaries mentioning this last possibility, although in describing Cardozo they used words such as "beautiful," "exquisite," "sensitive," or "delicate" that suggested a lack of masculinity. Most of these comments seem devoid of any sexual connotations, as when Oliver Wendell Holmes Jr., after meeting Cardozo in 1926, "thought his face beautiful with intellect and character"[51] or when another acquaintance spoke of "that exquisite refinement of his nature."[52] Occasionally, people took care lest they seem to imply more than they intended. Oswald Garrison Villard, for example, editor of the *Nation,* wrote of Cardozo: "'Exquisite' is an adjective which invariably suggests itself yet is so rarely applied to men as to be rather dangerous."[53] Only in private correspondence did Learned Hand, commenting on Cardozo's disinclination to engage in controversy, speak of his "lack of ruggedness, of 'tough mindedness,'" or note, "Dialectic is distasteful to his somewhat feminine nature."[54]

Whether out of simple modesty, a strong sense of reserve, or feelings of actual aversion, Cardozo avoided situations involving physical intimacy with women. Anecdotal evidence suggests a certain primness, even prudishness, on his part. One of his law clerks, who was at his side during his final illness, commented: "BNC didn't like women to handle him. After he was stricken, Harry [his chauffeur] slept at the house and helped in taking care of BNC."[55] He felt uncomfortable even when the topic of sex was treated coarsely. Associates assumed he would be offended by off-color jokes and did not tell them in his presence. One acquaintance described how, at a dinner held in Cardozo's honor in 1932, all of the speakers avoided risque stories. "Even if anyone had desired to tell one, all knew Cardozo's dislike for indecent humor."[56]

Cardozo so rarely discussed the subject of sexuality in his surviving correspondence that one letter, written in December 1924, takes on unusual significance. He wrote it to Annie Nathan Meyer about her play, *Black Souls,* which she had just completed (it would be staged in 1932 in Greenwich Village's Provincetown Playhouse). Meyer was Cardozo's first cousin: her father and his mother were brother and sister. Three years older than Benjamin, Annie was married to Dr. Alfred Meyer, a prominent physician. She was best known for her role in the founding of Barnard College in 1889 and as a writer of magazine articles on politics, art, and literature. But she also wrote a number of books and plays. One of them, *Black Souls,* set somewhere in the deep south in 1919 or 1920, dealt with the tragic results of a love affair between a white woman and a black man. Cardozo's response to a draft of the play suggests that he was troubled not only by the theme of miscegenation but also by the sexual aggressiveness displayed by a young white woman, a character named Luella Verne.

Described as "a pretty girl of seventeen," she is the daughter of state Senator Verne, a financial patron of "Magnolia, a School for Colored People in the Black Belt." The chief black protagonists are Andrew Morgan, the principal of the school; his wife, Phyllis; and her brother, David Lewis, "a poet. Professor of Belles Lettres." Senator Verne, planning to make a major gift to Magnolia, is visiting the school with his daughter. The political angle revolves around the conflict between Andrew Morgan, who has always sought accommodation with powerful whites to ensure their continued support for industrial education for blacks, and his racially militant brother-in-law, David Lewis, a World War I veteran, who tells him "the South says it is afraid of Negro dishonesty and ignorance, but it's more afraid of Negro knowledge and efficiency." The sexual plot is more convoluted. The lascivious Senator Verne had seduced Phyllis when she was only sixteen, and uses the visit to make further unwanted advances. Unbeknownst to him, his daughter had fallen in love with David Lewis during the war, when she was a student in France and his regiment was stationed there.

Luella now resumes her pursuit of David, ignoring his warning that the romance they had known in France could not be rekindled in the American south. But his resistance weakens: at one point, he exclaims "God! You are beautiful!" and she replies, "Ah, now you're more like your old self." She persuades him to accompany her to a deserted shack in the woods around Magnolia:

> *David:* Miss Verne, I begged you not to come here. Really, you must go back at once. I had no right to weaken . . .
> *Luella:* Brrr! You can't frighten me with all the bogies you're trying to stir up . . . I don't want to be safe. Why do you treat me like a child? . . . I want to know everything. *(Rises, stretching out her arms passionately)* To feel everything, to experience everything!
> *David:* Greedy children are always punished.
> *Luella:* I am a woman—with the feelings of a woman.

But just then David notices a white man at the window and to save Luella's honor pretends to be attacking her. Meyer explains: "He would rather be killed for the usual cause than have her encounter the scorn and possible violence that would be aimed against her if white men suspected her of actually inviting him to bring her to this lonely place in the woods."

David's act of chivalry has predictably awful consequences. He is tracked with bloodhounds, captured, tortured, and ghoulishly burned alive. While all this is happening offstage, Andrew Morgan discovers the truth about Senator Verne's earlier seduction of his wife. "You scoundrel!" he shouts: "You damned cur!" Rather than kill a white man and risk sparking a race riot, he subjects the senator to the worst punishment he can imagine: he tells him the truth about Luella and David, who was "guilty of being too complaisant to your daughter's wooing." Verne denies it: "No child of mine could so disgrace her white womanhood." When Luella asserts her love for David, her father denounces her: "You slut!" "Nigger-lover!" Phyllis scornfully says: "*You* dare call her that! . . . How dare you think you can take us black women into your arms without your lusts getting into the blood of your children? If you want your women to stay clean, you've got to stay clean yourselves." White men, she adds, fear above all that white women desire black men: "You're afraid your saintly white women will be known for what they are!"[57]

In December 1924 Meyer sent Cardozo a draft of her play. He responded with characteristic generosity, praising its "literary craftsmanship" as "admirable—vivid, moving, eloquent." Then he offered a more critical evaluation:

I find it hard to believe that an American audience will be in sympathy with the theme. The love of a white woman for a black man has in it something so revolting that many—I fear most—will not wish to hear of it. I know you will say that such things exist in life. So do many sex perversions that it is unpleasant to think of, and still more to discuss. Then too, the average listener will think of the play as an attack upon womanhood generally and an attempt to prove that the black man is merely the pursued. I appreciate your answer that this is a foolish misconception. I know that the literary artist in selecting one phase of life as the subject of his drama does not commit himself to the universality of the truth which it embodies. I am thinking of the crowd, not of the judgment of the elect; and I fear that I do not misread the reaction of the multitude.

Concluding in a softer vein, Cardozo added that "those who care for art must not let themselves bother too much about such repulses and disappointments" for "they have had at least the joy and uplift of creation."[58]

Although Cardozo expressed his reservations diplomatically, alluding only to what the public might think, his choice of language—"revolting," "sex perversions," "attack upon womanhood"—suggests that he was in some measure also expressing his own reaction. And what he objected to most strongly was the portrayal of a woman as the predator and a man as the "pursued." By contrast, he did not comment on Senator Verne's stalking of Phyllis Morgan, a similarly miscegenetic relationship in which, however, the man was the aggressor and the woman the victim. When the play was later produced (and quickly closed after the critics blasted it as "unfortunately inept," "declaratory and halting") Cardozo again tried to account for its unfavorable reception: "I am at a loss to understand why the critics were so hostile. Perhaps there is something repellent and unpleasant in the theme of black and white loves which prevents such a play from being popular."[59]

"Give It to Him, Mama": Dean v. Dean, 1925

Less than a year after reading *Black Souls,* Cardozo was confronted with a case that elicited from him an equally strong reaction. Robert and Amelia Frieda Dean, residents of Ontario, Canada, had been married for seven years, when, in 1919, Robert left his wife and three children. He moved to Erie, Pennsylvania, and obtained a divorce decree, claiming Frieda had deserted him and he did not know her whereabouts. He remarried and moved to Buffalo with his new wife. Then Frieda showed up. She asked the New York courts to negate the Pennsylvania decree (and Robert's subsequent remarriage), and to grant her a divorce with alimony and child support. *Dean v. Dean* presented an intriguing question: Could a man divorce his wife and be free to remarry while, at the same time, the wife remained legally married to him and unable to remarry? Put more starkly, could a wife "be said to have a living husband, while the husband has no living wife?"[60]

The Court of Appeals decided the case in November 1925. Judges Frederick E. Crane and Cardozo wrote opinions for the majority upholding Frieda Dean's claim; Judge Irving Lehman was the only dissenter. None of the judges believed that New York was obligated to recognize the Pennsylvania decree because of the provision in the United States Constitution that "Full Faith and Credit shall be given in each State to the public Acts, Records, and judicial Proceedings of every other State." Cardozo cited *Haddock* v. *Haddock* (1906), in which the United States Supreme Court had ruled, by a vote of five to four, that New York State could award alimony to a woman whose husband had left her, moved to Connecticut, established residence, and obtained a divorce. Connecticut's divorce decree was valid within its own borders, the court held, but not necessarily anywhere else. The constitutional issue disposed of, the question in the Dean case, as Cardozo saw it, was whether "conceptions of public policy and justice" favored the husband's claim or the wife's.[61] The answer depended on whose story one believed, for the Deans gave sharply conflicting accounts of how their marriage had fallen apart.

According to Robert, it was all the fault of "too much mother-in-law." When he married Frieda in November 1912, she asked if they could live with her parents in Kitchener during the winter, and move into their own place in the spring. He agreed, Dean remarked, adding ruefully, "that spring never came." For more than six years—during which time three children were born to the Deans—he pleaded with his wife to leave her parents' home, but she adamantly refused. Finally, in February 1919, Robert continued, he offered to set up house nearby, in Kitchener, and provide Frieda with a telephone so she could speak with her mother as often as she liked. When she again refused, he left, unable to tolerate his mother-in-law's domineering ways. His lawyers wrote to Frieda stating that Robert could not live with her parents any longer, that he was prepared to make a separate home for her and the children, and that he wished her to join him.[62]

Over the next few years, Robert added, he visited Kitchener on numerous occasions in an effort to persuade his wife to go with him. He even asked the minister who had married them to help in smoothing over their differences. But it was a lost cause. On one occasion, he berated his father-in-law: "If you had been half the man you should have been, and let Frieda alone, this trouble wouldn't have occurred." At that point, his mother-in-law "said 'how dare you talk to my husband that way.' She picked up a big jardiniere, and I have the proof on my head yet. She hit me on the head with the jardiniere. My wife stood by and said, 'give it to him mama.'"[63]

Robert moved first to Buffalo, then to Pennsylvania, settling finally in Erie, where he worked as an electrician for Westinghouse. In the summer of 1923 he filed for divorce, informing the Court of Common Pleas that Frieda had left him and he did not know where she was: "the last I have heard of her being two years ago she was somewhere about the thousand islands, but I have been unable to locate her ever since."[64] So Frieda was not personally notified of the divorce proceedings or served with a summons. Instead, a legal notice was published in the local Pennsylvania newspapers asking her to appear to show cause why the divorce should not be granted, a notice which she naturally never saw. In November 1923 the divorce was granted on the grounds that she had deserted Robert. Soon thereafter he remarried and moved to Buffalo.

In March 1924 Frieda left Canada and moved there, too, and as soon as she had established residence, asked the New York courts to grant her a divorce on the basis of Robert's "adultery." She also asked for alimony and child support. A trial was held in state Supreme Court in October at which Frieda (and her mother, who denied the jardiniere incident) disputed Robert's version of events. She depicted him as a cruel husband and a heartless father. Frieda recalled that in May 1919, shortly after Robert had left Kitchener, she asked him to return because their infant daughter had fallen gravely ill. He arrived, tragically, just before she died, and, Frieda related: "When he came home from the funeral he didn't come in the house with me at all. There wasn't a tear in his eye; you couldn't soften him at all. He stayed outside; he was whistling some popular air and shining his ring. He didn't come near me that night when we came to go to bed . . . He said, 'Well, Frieda, I am going to tell you something, there is no use of deceiving you, I would rather have intercourse with any other woman than you.'"[65]

He left the next day, she added, and on subsequent visits, "He told me he didn't want me, he didn't want my God Damn kids . . . He threatened to kill me on different occasions. He said, 'You God Damn son-of-a-bitch, you wake your kids again.' He said, 'I will skin you alive and throw you out of the window.' I would be afraid to cry." To add to her humiliation, "he said he had a pretty brunette which puts me far in the shade, and she has given her consent, she is willing to wait for him; she was willing to wait for him to marry her."[66]

Whatever the truth of the matter, both parties to the dispute had prevaricated: Robert, when he denied knowing Frieda's whereabouts in order to obtain a quick divorce; Frieda, when she claimed she did not know of the divorce and subsequent remarriage until after she moved to Buffalo. In fact, her cousin, a resident of Buffalo, had already run into Robert who proudly—if, in the event, unwisely—introduced his new wife. But Justice Charles A. Pooley's decision, handed down in December 1924, sided with the "wronged wife," not the "offending husband." New York State, he declared, was not bound to honor a divorce fraudulently acquired in Pennsylvania. Pooley found that Robert had "abandoned his wife because he did not want to live with her and had no affection for his children"; that he had "never acquired a separate home in which he could request his wife to live with him"; and that in going to Pennsylvania to obtain a divorce he had committed fraud "because he knew that his wife and children were living with her parents in Canada." He ruled that Frieda was entitled to a divorce and to $12.50 a week, half of Robert's salary, for child support. Were his earnings to increase, Frieda could apply for a larger amount.[67]

In March 1925 the appellate division of the Supreme Court upheld Pooley's decision by a three-to-two margin. The compelling considerations were Robert's fraudulent statement to the Pennsylvania court regarding Frieda's whereabouts, and Canada's policy of not recognizing a divorce where there was no personal notice to the spouse and such notice could have been given. Since the Pennsylvania decree was fraudulently obtained and was not binding in Canada, New York was not bound to recognize it. The minority saw things differently. The validity of divorces granted elsewhere should be upheld unless "justice and morality" dictated otherwise. Had Frieda been a state resident at the time of the divorce, then New York would refuse to recognize a Pennsylvania decree granted without personal notice. But she had come to New York "solely for the purpose of bringing the action." Granting her request would mean "that New York may become a Mecca for certain types of divorce pilgrims."[68]

The prospect of such a caravan of disgruntled spouses did not concern Judge Irving Lehman, who wrote the dissenting opinion when the case reached the Court of Appeals. The key issue, he observed, was Robert's marital status. Since Frieda was not a resident of New York, the question is whether "our policy impels us to hold that after she became a resident here we should disregard the judgment of the Pennsylvania courts which dissolved the marriage of its own citizen." New York was entitled to protect the marital status of its own residents, but "is not called upon to protect the citizens of another State." No citizen of New York was wronged by the Pennsylvania divorce, Lehman continued, and no public policy was contravened: "Our public policy places no obstacle to giving force to a decree of divorce of a sister State which purports to dissolve a marriage of one of its own residents when we have at no time had any jurisdiction over that marriage." To decide otherwise would mean that Frieda, by the simple expedient of changing her residence, could effectively dissolve Robert's marriage to his second wife.[69]

Lehman's opinion is remarkably free of moral judgments; Cardozo's, by contrast, contains little else. In the space of five paragraphs, it describes Frieda as "abandoned" (or variants thereof) no fewer than eight times and as "deserted" twice. It portrays Robert as "the erring husband" who "wrongfully" left his wife and committed "fraud" to gain his freedom. Cardozo summed up his understanding of the issues in two terse sentences: "An abandoned and defrauded wife asks us to maintain her status as it was fixed by the law of her domicile at the date of the fraudulent decree. We cannot say that conceptions of public policy and justice require us to change it."

Conceding that the evidence regarding abandonment was controvertible, and conceding, too, that the trial judge "did not find the fact of abandonment in so many words" but only inferred it from the testimony, Cardozo nevertheless proceeded on the assumption that the husband had indeed abandoned his wife, for "if the husband had not abandoned her, her domicile would have followed his." Further, Cardozo maintained, Robert had lied in order to obtain the Pennsylvania divorce, and Frieda had known nothing of his remarriage until "she took up her home in Buffalo. She found her husband living with another woman." Refusal to recognize the Pennsylvania decree did not depend merely on a wish to protect the residents of New York but rather on broad public policy considerations. Those considerations, Cardozo believed, dictated that New York should grant Frieda Dean the same status she would be accorded in Canada. He reasoned: "The conception of justice prevalent at home will override an opposing conception prevalent abroad, but the conception prevalent at home may exact justice to the stranger as well as justice to the resident. So we think it does. The wife domiciled in Canada and there abandoned by her husband, became by her marriage a party to a relation which the courts of Pennsylvania have attempted to destroy . . . according to the standards of justice prevalent among us, injustice would be done if that attempt were to prevail." To clinch the case, Cardozo pointed to "the husband's fraud" and his "false suggestion that the wife's whereabouts were unknown."[70]

There were good reasons to decide the case as Cardozo did. As one scholar noted in the late 1950s, the vindication of a wife's right to support was "years ahead of its time and coincides with the result which would be reached today by a quite different route."[71] Yet Cardozo's rendition of the Dean case transformed a messy, complicated domestic conflict into a tidy morality play. Cardozo either wanted or needed to view the situation as one in which a bad husband sought to take advantage of a good wife. This led him to ignore Frieda's longstanding unwillingness to leave her parents' home, to overlook the evidence suggesting she approved of her mother's crowning Robert with a jardiniere, and to treat her calculated decision to move to Buffalo as if it were accidental. One of his most revealing statements came in the course of defending Frieda's behavior: "She has never consented that her husband acquire a home apart from her, nor barred herself by misconduct from objecting to his doing so."[72] Women who avoided such misconduct could usually expect Cardozo to give them a sympathetic hearing.

"Satiety of the Body": Hoadley v. Hoadley 1927

He surely could not have been more sympathetic to Elsie Hoadley, whose husband, Leon, wanted their marriage annulled after she had been committed to a mental hospital. The case offers unusual insight into Cardozo's view of sexuality, because he construed it as involving the possible exploitation of a mentally incompetent woman. That possibility, although in no way suggested by the evidence submitted to the Court of Appeals, shaped his reading of the applicability of common law precedents as well as his interpretation of the statute under which the annulment proceedings had been brought.

Leon D. Hoadley and Elsie Rebecca Hawk were married in Binghamton on September 12, 1912. He was twenty-one years old, a postal clerk, and she was nineteen. They had two children, a daughter, Leora, born in September 1915, and a son, Cleveland Ernest, born in January 1918. Elsie was a devoted mother, her daughter recalled many years later, but also compulsive, delusional, and fanatically religious. She feared that the Devil was looking through her window. She believed God was punishing her for having had a second child. Leora was later told that, as a sacrifice, her mother had attempted to drown her infant son in the kitchen sink.[73] On June 20, 1922, the Onondaga County court judged Elsie Hoadley incompetent by reason of lunacy and committed her to the Binghamton State Hospital. Three and a half years later, in December 1925, her husband served her with a summons for an annulment.

The case was heard before Judge Leon C. Rhodes the following February. Leon Hoadley based his request for an annulment on the grounds that, at the time of their marriage, Elsie was a lunatic and he was unaware of her condition. He asked to be awarded custody of their children. In March the trial judge dismissed Leon's complaint without submitting any opinion, and his lawyer took the case to the appellate division of the Supreme Court. In July the five judges unanimously affirmed the trial judge's ruling, simply citing several precedents. The case then moved to the Court of Appeals, which heard argument in January 1927 and rendered its decision in February.

Lawyers for both sides focused on a crucial ambiguity in the state's Civil Practice Act. Section 1137, which dealt with annulment on the grounds that one spouse was a "lunatic," provided that action to annul might be brought "by any relative of the lunatic who has an interest to avoid the marriage." The unresolved question was: Did that include the sane spouse? Leon's lawyer argued that, at common law, the sane spouse had a right to sue for annulment; had the legislature meant to exclude the sane spouse, it would have said so—as it did in cases of marriage involving a person not of legal age, when it explicitly provided that the spouse of legal age might not bring action for annulment. Elsie's attorney—appointed by the court to serve as guardian *ad litem*—claimed that common law precedents had been super-seded by the Civil Practice Act; since the sane spouse had not specifically been given a right to sue, the legislature must have intended to preclude such action.

Rulings in prior cases offered no clear means of resolving the dispute. Leon's attorney cited several precedents, notably *Whitney* v. *Whitney* (1923), to the effect that the authors of the Civil Practice Act must have assumed that the courts retained the power to annul a marriage on the grounds of lu-nacy. "The rule is unthinkable that the person who is deceived in effect, who is placed in this terrible position without fault, should be without relief," Supreme Court Justice Walter Lloyd Smith explained: "The legislature never intended such an absurdity as that an action to annul a marriage in its very essence void could be maintained by one party to it and not by the other; that . . . the main sufferer could not get relief."[74] For her part, Elsie Hoadley could point to *Reed* v. *Reed* (1921), a Supreme Court appellate divi-sion ruling in which Justice H. T. Kellogg declared: "We think that the leg-islature in expressly naming the particular parties who might bring suit for annulment intended thereby to exclude all other persons from rights of action."[75]

Justice Kellogg explained briefly why, in his view, "it is clearly for the public good that this should be the law. Otherwise a man knowingly mar-rying an insane woman might, after cohabitation, discard her at will."[76] Al-though the Hoadley case did not raise that possibility—since Leon alleged that he had been ignorant of Elsie's condition at the time of their mar-riage—it raised, for Cardozo at least, the possibility of other, equally seri-ous forms of sexual exploitation. Before considering those possibilities, however, Cardozo first had to explain why the common law tradition was not applicable. That tradition, Cardozo conceded, held that "a marriage with a lunatic was not merely voidable, but void." On such a view, "there was no room for a holding that the sane spouse and the insane one were on planes of inequality as suitors for relief."

That view, Cardozo continued, still prevailed in England and in some states. It had once prevailed in New York, as indicated by *Wightman* v. *Wightman,* a famous ruling by Chancellor Kent in 1820. But in 1830 New York had revised the statutes governing domestic relations, including the annulment of marriages. The new laws created two distinct categories: mar-riages which were "absolutely void" (those which were incestuous or big-amous); and marriages which were "voidable" by the courts (those in which consent was obtained by force or fraud, or in which one of the parties was an idiot or a lunatic). Having created these categories, Cardozo continued, the legislature had also defined which parties were entitled to bring suit for annulment of a voidable marriage. The provisions of the revised statutes had been carried forward "with little change" into the Civil Practice Act, "where they remain today." The only changes, indeed, were "changes in verbiage . . . The substance is still the same." In effect, Cardozo declared, the law regarding annulment should not be based on a court decision of 1820; rather, it should be based on statutory revisions adopted in 1830.

If statutory law, not the common law, governed annulment in New York, Cardozo then had to explain why, under the statute, "the right of avoidance has been limited to the lunatic and those privileged to act in the lunatic's behalf." He justified his reading of the statute on the grounds that the legislature, in enumerating the parties who might bring suit for annulment, had not included the sane spouse. "If the list was not exclusive," he argued, "there was no occasion for its making." Even though the Act did not specifically exclude the sane spouse, one should assume that "the privilege unless granted is to be taken as denied." When all was said and done, however, Cardozo conceded "that in such a tangle of statutes the quest for certitude is futile. We are to weigh the competing considerations in such scales as are available."

On the scales Cardozo employed, fears of male concupiscence weighed more heavily than competing considerations. To permit the sane spouse to bring suit for annulment could legitimize improper, not to say immoral, behavior. "If a sane husband may avoid a marriage for the insanity of his wife, the question will come up whether he may put his wife aside though her insanity was known to him when the marriage was contracted." Again, suppose the husband, "though ignorant at the beginning, cohabits with the wife after her insanity is known. There is instinctive revolt against the notion that infirmity of the mind shall be used as a pretense for relief against satiety of the body." Or yet again, suppose that a woman, insane at the time of marriage, subsequently regains her reason: "If the wife, becoming sane, confirms the marriage, as she may, will judgment go for the husband to the effect that it is void?" The list of possible "embarrassments and complications," if not endless, was at least uncomfortably long.[77]

All of Cardozo's hypothetical cases involved a sane husband taking advantage of an insane wife. To be sure, his decision in the Hoadley case would also affect situations in which a sane wife brought action for annulment against an insane husband. Yet it is impossible to imagine similar language being used, or similar arguments being advanced, in such a case by Benjamin Cardozo or any other contemporary jurist. One wonders what his reaction would have been had *Whitney* v. *Whitney* reached the Court of Appeals. One of the few cases involving annulment on the grounds of spousal insanity in which the wife was the plaintiff and the husband the defendant, it was decided, as we have seen, in favor of the wife. To Supreme Court Justice Smith, the views expressed by Chancellor Kent more than a century before still made good sense. In *Wightman* v. *Wightman,* the chancellor had defended judicial nullification of marriages involving an insane spouse as "equally conducive to good order and decorum, and to the peace and conscience of the party."[78]

One comment in the Hoadley ruling—"There is instinctive revolt against the notion that infirmity of the mind shall be used as a pretense for relief against satiety of the body"—was particularly revealing because, in Cardozo's view, it actually described Leon's behavior toward Elsie, as the sentences immediately following indicated: "In this very case, plaintiff and defendant lived together for ten years. The insanity is alleged to have existed from the beginning, yet as late as six years after the marriage a child was born of the union. One must suppose that the cases must be rare indeed in which insanity so acute as to vitiate a marriage could remain so long concealed." Putting two and two together—the certainty that Leon was having sexual relations with Elsie at least five years into their marriage, and the likelihood that Elsie's illness would have become apparent by then— Cardozo concluded that the husband might well have taken unfair advantage of the wife. He voiced that fear in the form of a hypothetical question: "If a marriage so contracted is voidable in its inception at the instance of the husband, shall later cohabitation with his wife after her insanity is known be taken as ratification or affirmance or inequitable conduct that will defeat the right of action?"[79]

Yet nothing in the record warranted such an insinuation. Elsie Hoadley had not been judged insane until four and a half years after the birth of her second child; Leon Hoadley had not sought an annulment until three and a half years after her commitment, by which time, presumably, it was apparent that she would never leave the asylum. Meanwhile, unable to remarry, Leon had found it necessary to have his children cared for by relatives, his daughter by Elsie's sister and his son by his sister. The real issue was not that Leon was using Elsie's infirmity of mind as an excuse to annul the marriage because he had tired of her sexually, but rather that the continuation of the marriage subjected him and his family to severe hardship.

Cardozo was by no means insensitive to such difficulties. Of the hardship facing the sane spouse, he wrote: "Not all of it is of such a nature as to be heeded by the law. The theory of annulment on the ground of insanity is not that the sane spouse has made a bad bargain in getting an insane partner. The theory is that the insane partner to the union has manifested a consent that is unreal for lack of a contracting mind." The hardship, he added, would be equally great if insanity developed after the marriage, or if the disease were one of the body not the mind. "The law turns a deaf ear to these and like regrets." Even so, Cardozo recognized that in cases of insanity there remains "a residuum of hardship that may be thought to be special and peculiar." For the sane spouse, the continued marriage remains "a foe to peace of mind, a disquieting reminder of an anomalous position. Considerations such as these may suggest an amendment of the statute that will extend the right of action. Good faith can be assured by coupling the extension with appropriate conditions."[80]

Just a year after the Hoadley decision, the state legislature rewrote the law so as to allow Leon Hoadley (and others similarly situated) to obtain an annulment. On February 17, 1928, Section 1137 of the Civil Practice Act was amended to read: "Where one of the parties to a marriage was a lunatic at the time of the marriage, an action may also be maintained by the other party at any time during the continuance of the lunacy, provided the plaintiff did not know of the lunacy at the time of the marriage." (In 1978 the terms "mentally ill person" and "mental illness" were substituted for "lunatic" and "lunacy.") Leon Hoadley was remarried in 1932, and lived with his second wife until his death in 1975. Elsie Hoadley spent the rest of her life in a mental institution, although on Sundays and holidays she was allowed to spend the night at her sister's. She died in the late 1950s. At her funeral, her daughter, Leora, recalled, Elsie was beautifully attired. It was, thought Leora, "so sad that she never had such a pretty dress when she was alive."[81]

"The Concessions to be Expected of Gentleness and Honor": Mirizio v. Mirizio, 1928

Late in January 1926 Benjamin Cardozo was taken to the hospital, suffering from a urinary tract infection which, he reported, "pretty nearly laid me low."[82] "Look out for the wicked germ staphylococcus pyogenes ureous," he told a friend: "He's a bad one."[83] By February 7 he was allowed to return home "after quite a siege with a reputation as something of a prodigy for being alive."[84] Following his doctor's orders, Cardozo went to a hotel in Atlantic City, New Jersey, for further recuperation. "The tyranny of my physician has banished me to this wild and rugged coast," he wrote on February 16, again affecting the wryly humorous tone he nearly always used when discussing his ailments or poor health.[85] A week later he had recovered sufficiently to return to Albany for the start of the new court session. During his illness the court handed down its decision in *Mirizio* v. *Mirizio,* a case involving marital discord of a rather unusual nature. Although he did not cast a vote, Cardozo may have expressed his views in a portion of Irving Lehman's dissenting opinion. Two years later, when the case came up again, it elicited Cardozo's most basic views regarding sexuality.

Cosmo Mirizio and Fannie Mucci were married on September 3, 1921, in a civil ceremony at the Bronx Borough Hall. Within days, possibly even hours, of their marriage, they had a dreadful falling-out, and they never lived together as man and wife. The legal actions they instituted against each other—Cosmo suing for annulment on the grounds of abandonment, and Fannie suing for separation and alimony on the grounds of nonsupport—dragged on for nearly seven years. The dispute centered on an informal prenuptial agreement that the civil ceremony would be followed, shortly after Christmas, by a religious ceremony, and that they would not have sexual relations until their union had been blessed by the church. Cosmo admitted he had made such a promise but had changed his mind. Without a church wedding, Fannie refused to live with him.

Cosmo Mirizio was born in Italy in 1902. His father emigrated to the United States in 1910, and his mother followed two years later with Cosmo and his three sisters. The Mirizios settled in the Bronx, on East 213th Street, in a working-class Italian neighborhood. Cosmo attended public school and, as a teenager, went to work as an automobile mechanic for a garage on White Plains Road, earning seventy cents an hour. At school he had met Fannie Mucci, whose family lived just around the corner, on Barnes Avenue. She was two years younger than Cosmo. The families worshiped at the nearby Immaculate Conception Church. Cosmo and Fannie became engaged in March 1921, when he was nineteen and she was seventeen.[86]

Why they decided to have a civil ceremony in the first place remains a mystery. When Cosmo's lawyer asked Fannie: "How did you happen to get married in City Hall if you are so staunch a Catholic?" her reply was tantalizingly vague: "Because he came to me, wants to get married, so that we were going to wait until we found rooms to be husband and wife."[87] The trial record provides a few possible clues to another mystery: why Cosmo broke his promise and refused to have a religious ceremony. Cosmo's lawyer offered one suggestion: a day or two after the marriage, Cosmo got into a fight with Fannie's brothers, she took their side, "and the result is that my client would not go thru a religious ceremony."[88] Fannie's lawyer offered another: Cosmo's mother opposed the marriage "because she had a daughter who is 23 years old, and she did not think that her son should marry before his sister had been married."[89] In any event, when Fannie continued to express the hope that Cosmo would allow a priest to sanctify their union, he told her: "'Oh, I don't care to live with you, I don't love you any more. I am going to ask for an annulment' . . . He said, just like that, 'I don't like you any more.'"[90]

That was in January 1922. When Fannie tried to telephone Cosmo, he hung up on her; when they saw each other on the street, she recalled, "he always put his head down as if he did not know me, just looked far away."[91] By May Cosmo had brought his first suit for annulment on the grounds that Fannie had refused to cohabit with him, thereby denying him the rights of a husband. In September he brought a second action which he lost. He filed yet another suit in September 1923 only to withdraw it. By then Fannie was preparing a counter-suit. In November 1923 she asked for a separation and alimony on the grounds that Cosmo had failed to support her. The case went to trial before Supreme Court Justice Richard H. Mitchell in February 1924. Fannie's lawyer claimed that the prenuptial agreement was binding, while Cosmo's asserted that it had no legal standing. In April 1924 Justice Mitchell found in favor of Cosmo, declaring: "The legal status and obligations of the parties have been fixed by the civil ceremony."[92]

After this ruling was upheld by the appellate division (by a four-to-one vote) in April 1925, Fannie took her case to the Court of Appeals. It heard argument in October and handed down its decision on January 22, 1926, when, as we have seen, Cardozo was incapacitated. In effect, the case came down to the issue of when a wife could justifiably refuse to have sexual intercourse with her husband, or, rather, to consummate the marriage. The varying attitudes the judges brought to this issue emerge clearly in the majority opinion, written by Chief Judge Frank H. Hiscock; in the private correspondence of Cuthbert Pound, who concurred with Hiscock; and in the dissenting opinion of Irving Lehman, the final portion of which may have been drafted by Cardozo before he was rushed to the hospital.

To Hiscock, writing for himself and three other judges, Fannie's contention that Cosmo was obliged to support her had no merit because she had refused to be a wife to him. Since marriage is a civil contract, he argued, its obligations could not be modified by any prior arrangements between Cosmo and Fannie. Otherwise, parties "by private agreement may permanently annul or indefinitely postpone the obligations which they assume when they enter into the marriage contract and defeat the policy of the State and the views which have so long and definitely prevailed in a right-minded society." The Civil Practice Act required a husband to support his wife, but Section 1163 also provided that a wife's "misconduct" justified a refusal to provide such support. Although Fannie had been "governed by conscientious and religious scruples" in refusing marital relations, she had nevertheless failed to fulfill her obligations and was "reaping the natural results of her conduct." To accept her claim, Hiscock feared, would establish a principle which the court would have to apply even in cases of misconduct involving less worthy considerations. Hiscock did not rest his argument entirely on the state's domestic relations statute. He also stated: "Public policy in such a vital matter as the marriage contract should not be made to yield to subversive private agreements and personal considerations."[93]

Cuthbert Pound, who concurred with Hiscock, defended his position in a letter to Felix Frankfurter, then a law professor at Harvard. He did not agree with all that Hiscock had said about Fannie's obligations, Pound explained, but still: "I think she is at fault for she refuses to live with her husband as the law requires. The promise was of a religious ceremonial marriage. It might have been a promise to live on Riverside Drive in New York City, buy her an automobile, settle property on her, &c., &c." The question of whether Fannie's refusal to engage in marital relations constituted grounds for her husband to obtain an annulment did not arise, Pound thought, because the court was deciding the merits only of her claim for support, which was barred by the provision regarding "misconduct" in the Civil Practice Act.[94] None of this persuaded Frankfurter, who insisted that the court could easily have construed that Act differently. Since "there is nothing in the formal material of the law to compel the conclusion," Frankfurter insisted, the court should have spelled out "the considerations of policy" which moved it, and not buried them "beneath neutral statutory language."[95]

Cardozo in the late 1920s or early 1930s.

Anna Aumuller.

Hans Schmidt.

Professor Oliver LeRoy
McCaskill.

Louise M. Hamburger.

Cardozo and Chief Justice Charles Evans Hughes at the American Law Institute meeting in Washington, D.C., May 6, 1937.

Louis D. Brandeis and Stephen S. Wise around 1920. In the original photograph, Nathan Straus is standing next to Brandeis and James Waterman Wise is standing next to his father.

Cardozo in the fall of 1937.

Frank Palka and his mother in January 1936, at the time of his first trial.

The jury in the first Palka trial.

BENJAMIN N CARDOZO   CHIEF JUDGE
COURT OF APPEALS   STATE OF NEW YORK

ASSOCIATE JUSTICE
SUPREME COURT
USA 1932 1938

Portrait of Cardozo by Augustus Vincent Tack.

Pound's reply to Frankfurter was as remarkable for its candor as for its clarity:

> The lady desires a ceremonial marriage, or, as its equivalent, separate maintenance and support. Let us concede that she need not live with him and that he cannot obtain a decree against her for abandonment. Shall she be permitted to stick the poor chap? They are both to blame. He because he lied; she because she sets too high a value on the ceremony. If she thought it so important why did she consent to a civil ceremony? The civil ceremony made them man and wife and so long as they are wrangling about the religious ceremony 'the law' should leave them where it finds them and not undertake to help either as against the other. Let him have the ceremony or let her waive it without pestering the courts over a religious row. I don't know 'why.' It seems sensible, that is all.⁹⁶

The down-to-earth quality of Pound's response contrasted vividly with Hiscock's legalistic opinion and Irving Lehman's moralistic dissent.

That dissent began, reasonably enough, by pointing out that a decision in Cosmo's favor could be justified "solely upon grounds of public policy"— on the grounds, that is, that parties to a marriage may not vary its obligations by private agreement—and not "according to any possible standards of honesty or good faith." Yet, by repudiating his promise, Cosmo had placed Fannie in "the hideous position of being legally bound to a man with whom she may not live as wife without being guilty of what in her own conscience . . . would constitute a sin." Lehman then asked a question which he thought answered itself: "Does any rule of public policy dictate such result?" Turning next to the issue of whether Fannie was guilty of "misconduct" under Section 1163, Lehman explained: "I have pointed out that [Fannie's] conduct which it is claimed deprives her of the right to support is the result of [Cosmo's] wrong; . . . that in effect [Cosmo] is permitted by his own wrong to evade his own obligation." To decide in Fannie's favor, Lehman added, would not impair the legal effect of a civil marriage.⁹⁷

Having reached a logical stopping point, the dissenting opinion did not stop but took an unusual turn. In the final three pages, ground already covered was covered all over again. The use of the first-person singular—a form Lehman favored but Cardozo always avoided—abruptly disappeared. The language suddenly began to sound very much like Benjamin Cardozo. If Cardozo indeed wrote (or drafted) these concluding pages, it would not have been unprecedented, for Lehman has recounted that in another instance most of an opinion handed down under his name was actually writ-ten by Cardozo.[98] The last pages of the dissent also closely resemble the opinion Cardozo would write, under his own name, two years later when the case again came before the court.

These pages reiterate many of the same themes found earlier, but the lan-guage carries a higher emotional charge. Fannie had not repudiated her ob-ligation to consummate the marriage, the author explained; she only wished to postpone it until Cosmo complied with his promise "to perform those preliminary rites which will change sexual intercourse from an act which according to her view is morally illicit, to one which is sanctioned by the guardians of her conscience." The opinion continued: "Is her refusal to submit her body to him until that time a wrong to him in his marriage re-lation when that relation was entered with understanding by both that such submission would be a sin which he would not require of her?" Marriage is a bond, the author conceded, but "rigid rules of law which decree that religious, moral and other psychological factors which determine human conduct must be disregarded in the measurement of the performance of marital obligation will tend to make the marriage contract not a bond but a chain."

The disapproval of Cosmo's behavior is now stated even more forcefully than it was earlier. He has committed a "willful wrong," for he

> seeks to evade his obligation to support his wife; he finds the way for such evasion in the unwillingness of his wife to cohabit with him, although such unwillingness is based upon a ground which he could remove and which in good conscience he is bound to remove even though his prom-ise to do so is not enforcible in law. By repudiating his moral obligation to place the plaintiff in a position where in good conscience and accord-ing to the tenets of her religion she could become his wife in fact, he is permitted to escape his obligation to support her.

The law, the opinion went on, ought not to be hostile to religion or to con-strue marital obligations in a way that would cause the parties to violate their religious sensibilities.

If such tell-tale phrases as "guardians of her conscience," "submit her body to him," and "repudiating his moral obligation" were not sufficient indication that Cardozo had written the opinion's concluding paragraphs, the cadence of the final sentence—not to mention its assumption of male immorality and female virtue—was a dead giveaway: "A sense of sin is poor foundation for permanent marriage relation and a husband who demands consummation of marriage at the price of his wife's sense of virtue, and at the same time invites refusal of his demand by willful failure to carry out conditions which induced the wife to enter into the marriage, should not be permitted to urge that refusal as justification for his own failure to support his wife."[99]

On the day after the Court of Appeals handed down its decision Fannie took steps to reassert her claim for support. She wrote to Cosmo declaring that she was "ready to come and live with you as soon as you will have a place ready for me."[100] Cosmo replied that Fannie had spread malicious rumors about him, had tried to get him fired from his job, and in general had done everything she could to make him miserable. "Any love that I had for you at the time we were married you have driven out," he added; after five and a half years, no court would insist that he take her back.[101] To protect her legal status, Fannie pointed out that she had refused to live with him because of her religious principles, but now that the court had spoken, "I must bow to its dictation." She was ready to move in without a religious ceremony, she declared: "You are still my husband and I am your wife and I request and demand that you live up to your marriage obligation . . . I want a home and I want you."[102]

Unable to have either, she decided to settle for financial support. In March 1926 Fannie filed a second suit for separation and alimony. In November a trial was held before Supreme Court Justice John M. Tierney, at which the estranged pair testified. The judge asked Cosmo about an allegation in his letter to Fannie that he had kept her "secret" to protect her name but would no longer do so if she proceeded with a lawsuit; Cosmo, however, was either unable or unwilling to explain what he meant.[103] For her part, Fannie claimed she had refused to live with Cosmo without a religious ceremony only because of her lawyer's advice. "I was willing to live with him, but my lawyer had stopped me . . . He said 'You should not go live with your husband, the children you have, you could not baptize them.' . . . I was told to say that. It is against my will. I was always willing to go live with my husband."[104] In December Tierney ruled in Fannie's favor, ignoring this most recent assertion and holding that her earlier refusal to live with Cosmo had not been willful but had been based on legal advice and religious conviction. Her abandonment had been temporary, pending a legal determination of her rights. Cosmo was ordered to pay $15 a week, about half his earnings, in alimony.

Cosmo naturally appealed Tierney's ruling, and it was subsequently overturned. In January 1928 the appellate division of the Supreme Court ruled that Fannie could not erase five and a half years of abandonment by the simple expedient of writing a letter offering to live with her husband, offering, that is, to do what she should have done in the first place. Justice John V. McAvoy declared: "We do not see that this cause differs at all from that of any wife's who abandons her husband for any other legal reason and who is judicially declared to be separated from him on such grounds as may be legally alleged."[105] The vote in the appellate division was four to one, but the dissenting justice did not submit an opinion. The stage was now set for Fannie's second appeal to the Court of Appeals, and for Chief Judge Benjamin Cardozo to express his view of the Mirizio marriage.

On May 1, 1928, the Court of Appeals reversed the ruling of the Appellate Division by a vote of five to two. Cardozo wrote the majority opinion, which was joined by Irving Lehman and Frederick E. Crane (who had, like Lehman, dissented from Hiscock's 1926 ruling), and by Cuthbert Pound and William S. Andrews (both of whom had concurred with Hiscock). Two judges who had joined the court since 1926, Henry J. Kellogg and John F. O'Brien, dissented but without filing an opinion. Cardozo reasoned as follows: the marital breakup was Cosmo's fault because he had reneged on his promise to have a religious ceremony; Fannie had reasonable grounds to believe that, under the circumstances, the court would find that she was not obligated to cohabit with Cosmo; but once the court had ruled against her, she immediately agreed to abide by its edict. Granted, attempting to rehabilitate such a marriage (by this time, six and a half years of acrimony had elapsed) presented difficulties, but they were entirely of Cosmo's making. Now that Fannie was willing to be his wife he had an obligation to support her. The decision, therefore, reinstated the alimony awarded earlier.

The language Cardozo used in making this argument betrayed the powerful feelings the case aroused in him. He turned Cosmo into the prototypical male—brutal, unfeeling, and sexually aggressive. By refusing to have a religious ceremony, Cosmo had "shamelessly repudiated a promise." His behavior was "ruthless," a form of "provocation and oppression." He must have been "scheming" all along to be rid of his wife, for he had treated Fannie "with indifference to her feelings and in wanton disregard of his solemn word of honor." Failing to conduct himself as "a man of honor and a gentleman," Cosmo had never considered making "the concessions to be expected of gentleness and honor."

By contrast, Cardozo portrayed Fannie as the innocent victim—compliant, dutiful, and submissive. When, on advice of counsel, she refused to cohabit with Cosmo, she had ample reason to believe that "she was not recreant to her duty as a wife." He added: "She invoked the law to aid her. The moment it condemned her, she bowed to its command." Having lost her case in 1926, "she gave notice to the defendant that she would yield submission to the law." Although she "was the victim of mistake," she maintained her "wifely station" in the face of countless "affronts." Her earlier refusal to cohabit did not constitute an abandonment "so definitive as to be unaffected by repentance." Cardozo was more than willing to grant her absolution.

Cardozo also alluded to another issue that had arisen at various stages of the litigation: whether Fannie had ever agreed to reside with Cosmo without a religious ceremony—but not have sexual relations with him. Cardozo commented: "There was some question upon the first record whether the plaintiff had refused to live with the defendant, or only to have intercourse with him. Upon the record before us, that question is no longer open." Fannie now claimed that without the religious ceremony she would not live with him at all. Cardozo said: "She makes no pretense that she offered to live with him as a virgin. For people in their social station, dwelling in one or two rooms, such an offer, if made, would have the aspect of a subterfuge. She resorts to no such evasion, at least in her complaint." In her testimony "she hints at something of the kind, but the court paid no heed to it, and held her to her pleading." The clear implication of Cardozo's comment is that abstinence might well be an option for people of a higher social station—wealthier, better educated, more refined—dwelling in a more spacious home, better able to control their passions.

Cardozo's decision construed sexual intercourse as an act in which a man controls a woman, indeed, possesses, or even owns, her. More than literary convention seems to have been involved, given the frequency and repetitiveness of the comments. Cardozo said, for example, that Cosmo could "have had her for the asking," that he could have "had the plaintiff as his own" if only he had kept his promise, a promise which "would have made her his." Instead, he demanded that "she must yield her body to him anyhow, however ruthless his refusal to have it on her terms."[106]

One might well ask: If Fannie had such strong moral objections to cohabitation without benefit of clergy, how could she so easily have brushed them aside in response to the first Court of Appeals decision? Such a question did not interest Cardozo. The Mirizio case provided him with an opportunity to express deeply held views concerning the ways in which men and women should behave toward each other. Unlike Lillian Tate, the rape victim, or Luella Verne, the fictional heroine of *Black Souls,* both of whom Cardozo regarded as fallen women, Fannie Mirizio seemed to be a worthy wife, as deserving of a protective legal mantle as Frieda Dean and Elsie Hoadley. In *Mirizio,* Cardozo said he wished to apply a standard of "right dealing and humanity." Yet that standard, as he understood it, naturally reflected his underlying view of gender and sexuality.

5

Religion and the State

Jerome Frank and Legal Realism

On a May evening in 1931 Benjamin Cardozo attended a dinner party at the home of Judge Julian W. Mack. A prominent figure in the Jewish community and an ardent Zionist, Mack had served for twenty years as a federal Circuit Court judge. He had originally been assigned to the Commerce Court in Washington, D.C., but Congress abolished that Court in 1913 and Mack thereafter spent most of his time in New York City where he was eligible to sit as a district judge and also with the Second Circuit Court of Appeals. He and his wife maintained a penthouse apartment at the Fifth Avenue Hotel, located on 23rd Street. Mack had "the most discriminating taste in food and drink," a friend recalled, "with a knowledgeable zest unusual even in a gourmet."[1] On that particular May evening, however, it was probably not the meal that lingered longest in the guests' memory but the after-dinner talk.

An intense, exhilarating conversation it surely was, for besides Cardozo the guests included Felix Frankfurter and his Harvard Law School colleague Thomas Reed Powell; Charles C. Burlingham, the New York attorney and civic reformer who had played such a large role in Cardozo's first election to judicial office; Harold Laski, the British socialist who was nearing the end of a four-month lecture tour, and was teaching at both Yale and the New School for Social Research; Morris R. Cohen, the City College philosophy professor whose *Reason and Nature* had just appeared; and Jerome Frank, a brilliant forty-two-year-old New York attorney whose *Law and the Modern Mind,* published a year earlier, had instantly placed him in the front ranks of the legal realist movement.

At some point the talk turned to Cohen's belief that propositions were objectively verifiable, that their truth or falsity was not affected by the psychological makeup or motivation of the person asserting them. Put another way, Cohen denied that "a psychological description of reasoning as a mental event can determine whether the resulting conclusion is true."[2] Frank maintained, just as surely, that the facts an individual used to reach a conclusion were always selective, were, indeed, chosen to support the conclusion the individual wished to reach. By understanding an individual's mind-set, therefore, one could explain why certain facts were heavily weighted and others were not. The debate thus joined that evening would rage for many months, as Cohen and Frank exchanged some thirty letters, often ten to fifteen pages in length, "each blaming the other for straying from the point, being obtuse, and resorting to 'inexcusable abuses of the privileges of friendly correspondence.'"[3]

His disagreement with Cohen went to the heart of Jerome Frank's legal philosophy. *Law and the Modern Mind* rejected the classical view that judges were "living oracles" whose task was essentially passive, finding a preexisting law and applying it to the case before them. Frank claimed that judges "make and change law" on the basis of their life experiences, or, more exactly, the biases resulting from those experiences. To Frank, the facts used to support a judicial ruling would vary with the fact-finder, for a judge would emphasize those elements which supported a predetermined result. By concealing the subjectivity of all judicial decisionmaking, Frank thought, Cohen perpetuated dangerous myths about what judges actually did.

In arguing that judges made law as they went along, Frank expressed a view common to all legal realists, including such prominent law professors as Karl Llewellyn and Robert Lee Hale of Columbia and Walter Wheeler Cook and Arthur L. Corbin of Yale. What put teeth into *Law and the Modern Mind* was its psychological explanation of why most people—including most judges—clung to the myth that law was objective and predictable. "Why this obstinate denial of the juristic realities?" Frank asked, and provided an answer as daring as it was simplistic: "Back of this illusion is the childish desire to have a fixed father-controlled universe, free of chance and error due to human fallibility." The myth "is a direct outgrowth of a subjective need for believing in a stable, approximately unalterable legal world—in effect, a child's world." Frank then ranked judges and legal theorists on a scale ranging from childish to mature, their rank depending on the degree to which they had outgrown legal illusions.[4]

By this reckoning, only Oliver Wendell Holmes Jr. qualified as a "Completely Adult Jurist." But Benjamin Cardozo came in a close second. In a short chapter entitled "The Candor of Cardozo," Frank wrote: "One of the greatest American judges, he is in the forefront of those who realistically face the unavoidable uncertainties in law, the actualities of judicial lawmaking." He quoted approvingly from Cardozo's writings on judge-made law, on the uncertainties inherent in the legal process, and on the necessity of subordinating precedent to social justice. "Cardozo, it would seem, has reached adult emotional stature," Frank said, adding quickly, and sadly, that something still held him back. "Surprisingly, he is not ready to abandon entirely the ancient dream," Frank wrote. Cardozo still cast too many "backward glances," still confessed to "a yearning for an absolute and eternal legal system." The result was paradoxical: Cardozo, who had explicitly stated that judges must be satisfied with "a makeshift compromise, with many a truth that is approximate and relative," nevertheless insisted that law might some day overcome "the curse of 'fluidity.'"[5]

On September 30, 1930, Frank sent Cardozo a copy of his book, following a luncheon (also arranged by Judge Mack) at which it had been a topic of discussion. In acknowledging receipt, Cardozo commented slyly: "Being as yet not wholly adult, but in truth a hopeless juvenile, I did what any juvenile would do; I looked at the index to see the references to myself. I have consulted these with hope and trepidation, and am now strutting about the house, convinced that I am no hobbledehoy, but in truth a grown man." He had not yet read the entire book, Cardozo added, but he had read enough to think it "a notable piece of work." "Perhaps you will succeed in dispelling the wearisome complaint that when a judge moves a little step forward on the path to justice he is unsettling the law and undermining the fabric of society. But is the flux quite as bad as you picture it—are we really so utterly adrift? Perhaps."[6] Cardozo thereby managed to convey his sympathy with Frank's view, while, at the same time, distancing himself from its more radical implications.

Early in 1931 the two men carried on a polite correspondence on fairly mundane matters. So by May, when they appeared at Judge Mack's dinner party, they had established at least a casual acquaintanceship. Just what, if anything, Cardozo contributed to the dinner-table debate between Frank and Morris R. Cohen is not known, but it would have been in character for him to have played the mediator, seeking to meet each man halfway and reconcile their differences. Harold Laski, in describing the evening to Oliver Wendell Holmes Jr., reported: "I much enjoyed Morris' defiant dogmatism and the gentleness of Cardozo's footnotes of dubiety."[7] Frank himself later recalled Cardozo's comment on another of Cohen's famous formulations in *Reason and Nature,* the "principle of polarity": "Ah, Professor Cohen dignifies wobbling."[8]

As late as December 17, 1931, Frank praised Cardozo effusively for a speech he gave at a dinner of the New York County Lawyers Association held in his honor.[9] Frank, who was in attendance, would have been taken by the substance of Cardozo's remarks as well as by their good-natured humor. Cardozo used the occasion to confess, again, his doubts about the judicial process. It was, he conceded, "a heart-breaking sort of a game . . . that we play . . . I have tried hard to learn it, but then I have tried also to learn golf, and sometimes I wonder whether I know much more about the one than I know about the other, which is saying a good deal, as credible witnesses present in this room would be able to testify if they were mean enough to do it." Cardozo went on to say that "a changing civilization" required "a new philosophy of law, a new juristic method, to bring order out of chaos." While pointing out that Americans were developing their own legal philosophy, quite different from England's, Cardozo seconded the view of an English barrister, Claud Mullins: "It was the boast of Augustus that he found Rome of brick and left it of marble. But how much nobler will be our sovereign's boast, when he shall have it to say that he found law dear and left it cheap; found it a sealed book, left it a living letter; found it the patrimony of the rich, left it the inheritance of the poor; found it the two-edged sword of craft and oppression, left it the staff of honesty and the shield of innocence."[10]

Yet even as Frank was complimenting Cardozo on this speech, he had gotten wind of another talk Cardozo planned to give to the New York State Bar Association in which he was going to criticize legal realism in general and Frank in particular. Notoriously thin-skinned about any kind of adverse comment, Frank endeavored to get Cardozo to temper his remarks. He enlisted the help of Oscar Cox, a mutual friend, asking him to forward two recent articles to Cardozo to make sure he could read them before making the speech.[11] Cox informed Cardozo that Frank "is suffering some qualms that you may render public comment upon his book without having read his articles in the November and December issues of the *University of Pennsylvania Law Review*."¹² Cardozo replied that his address was scheduled for January, 22, 1932, adding: "I don't expect to refer by name to the book by Jerome Frank, though I will deal to some extent with its theme."¹³

It is unlikely that the members of the state bar association, assembled at the Hotel Astor, ever sat through a more densely scholastic speech. At the outset, Cardozo announced that he wanted to bring up to date the views he had expressed a decade earlier in *The Nature of the Judicial Process*. His address, filling forty closely printed pages, was twice as long as any of the lectures he had given at Yale in 1921. Replete with references to current work in law, philosophy, anthropology, and history, it could not have been delivered in much less than two hours. Among the writers Cardozo cited were John Dewey and Alfred North Whitehead, Roscoe Pound and Karl Llewellyn, Jeremy Bentham and William Blackstone, Oliver Wendell Holmes Jr. and Henry Adams, Louis D. Brandeis and Frederick Pollock, Benedetto Croce and Bertrand Russell, a Professor Renard of the University of Nancy and a Professor Lambert of the University of Lyons. He also found time to discuss the civil code recently adopted by the Republic of Poland, as well as the commentary on it by a Professor Lyskowski.

But no authors were cited more frequently than Morris R. Cohen and Jerome Frank. Cardozo alluded not only to their recent books but also to their articles and reviews. He referred to Cohen by name several times, usually when agreeing with what he had to say, but never once mentioned Frank. Only when the talk was published some months later, with the actual citations, was it apparent that the writer whom Cardozo termed "the most thorough-going of the realists" and with whom he expressed the sharpest disagreement was, in fact, Jerome Frank. The section of the address entitled "Reason Versus Emotion; What Judges Really Do," represented, in a way, Cardozo's belated entry into the debate at Judge Mack's dinner party.

"The most distinctive product of the last decade in the field of jurisprudence is the rise of a group of scholars styling themselves realists," Cardozo began, "and content with nothing less than revision to its very roots of the method of judicial decision which is part of the classical tradition." He then subjected realism to a searching analysis, arguing that it was anything but new since many of its ideas derived from Holmes and Roscoe Pound as well as continental theorists. Cardozo preferred, therefore, to use the term "neo-realist." Moreover, he noted, many of its adherents differed substantially among themselves; they did not constitute a "school" but rather represented "a movement, an outlook, a tendency, avowing fundamental differences of emphasis and dogma."

Cardozo paraphrased Jerome Frank's version of realism, not unfairly, as follows: "Order in the legal system (so runs the argument) is an illusion, a mirage. The quest for it is a childish dream, the craving of the adolescent for the steadiness that came to him from the guidance of a parent." Much of this argument, Cardozo reasoned, especially its indiscriminate rejection of order, certainty, and coherence, should be rejected "as ill-advised and exaggerated, though said with incisiveness and force and the arresting charm of novelty." What Cardozo found valuable in legal realism was that it loosened the "petrifying rigidity" of precedent and reminded judges that principles had to be reformulated or even abandoned "when they stand condemned as mischievous in the social consciousness of the hour, the social consciousness which it is our business as judges to interpret as best we can."

As usual, Cardozo sought the middle course, the establishment of "an entente between the neo-realists and others." He therefore ventured a balanced assessment:

> What is useful in neo-realism is its insistence upon the "margin of error," the "increase of entropy," the "principle of indeterminacy," which condition the generalizations of judge-made law just as they do the laws of physics . . . What is wrong in neo-realism is a tendency manifest at times to exaggerate the indeterminacy, the entropy, the margin of error, to treat the random or chance element as a good in itself and a good exceeding in value the elements of certainty and order and rational coherence— exceeding them in value, not merely at times and in places, but always and everywhere.

Both sides in the controversy, he said, sought "the pass-word that will reconcile the irreconcilable."

Throughout, Cardozo used religious imagery to convey his sense of the realists' overzealousness. They were "the faithful" or "the votaries of the new faith" or "priests of the new gospel of juridical salvation." They preached a "creed" or a "dogma" which they hoped would "point to stumbling sinners the road to salvation." They "suffered at times from this missionary ecstasy." The most extreme among them were adherents of "a false and misleading cult." Cardozo employed similarly pejorative language in his summation. Noting his disagreement with the realists' deprecation of order and certainty, he admitted that symmetry and coherence could exact too high a price: "The high priests of the new movement will have to say whether this confession makes me a realist or not."[14]

On February 12, three weeks after giving the speech, Cardozo wrote to Karl Llewellyn, remarking: "I liked it so little that I have decided not to print it in the Law Review. Perhaps in about a year it will have to come out in the Year Book of the Association, but no one will notice it there. It is so poor that I hate to send it to you." Then, turning to a subject uppermost in the minds of many, the Supreme Court vacancy created by Oliver Wendell Holmes Jr.'s resignation, Cardozo guessed that President Herbert Hoover would "go to the West for the new judge."[15] But on February 15 Hoover named Cardozo. Jerome Frank immediately sent his congratulations, and Cardozo replied: "Your letter makes me proud and happy. You are pointing a way of life for the judges of the coming years; and even though I am too old in years and too fixed in modes of thought to follow you completely, I admire to the full your brilliant and arresting thought. Perhaps there isn't much difference between us except a slightly variant shade of emphasis."[16]

There matters might have rested had Cardozo's speech not found its way into print. But as he anticipated, it eventually appeared in the state bar association's annual report, where it instantly attracted Jerome Frank's notice. On September 9, 1932, Frank sent Cardozo a letter that was extraordinary even by his standards. Noting that he had written it on the train while commuting to work (Frank resided in Croton-on-Hudson) he said that it formed the basis of a book he planned to write in reply to Cardozo's speech. The letter, in fact, was thirty-one typewritten pages. But that was not all. There were two "postscripts": one of twenty pages entitled "Re your definition of law and your exaggeration of the extent of legal certainty," and another of ten pages containing "Pertinent Quotations from My Writings— Re Valuation of Certainty and Rationality." For good measure Frank enclosed four articles and asked for Cardozo's comments.

By turns defensive and derisive, but always sharply polemical, Frank argued that while Cardozo looked at things from the angle of an upper-court (that is, appellate) judge, he himself saw things from the standpoint "of a lawyer in active practice trying to advise a specific client of his specific 'rights' and 'duties' before litigation." Those rights and duties are "not to be measured by the knowability and fixity of the so-called legal rules and principles." A litigant's fate rested on how the judge and jury construed the "facts," precisely the realm in which uncertainty was greatest. Subjectivity was inevitable when the "'facts' are discoverable only from conflicting testimony." Frank posed a crafty question: "Now in 'contested' cases who can say that the facts as found are the actual objective facts?" It was "the verdict of modern psychology," he explained, that the desired conclusion, "often arrived at non-rationally," was crucially important in determining which facts would be believed. So now it was Frank's turn to revisit the argument at Judge Mack's.

Frank accused Cardozo of misstating his views by assuming that when he described the irrationality of the judicial system he was also approving it. He complained that Cardozo failed to realize that he intended no such normative judgment: "Your remarks indicate fairly clearly that it was I in particular you had in mind when you spoke of the 'over-zealous' among the neo-realists who show a 'petulant contempt' for certainty and rationality and consider them not good but 'evil.'" Frank dismissed Cardozo's point about the realists being "neo"-realists. Realism, or, as Frank preferred, skepticism, naturally had many forerunners, he noted: "Indeed, the legal sceptics can take over almost intact Spinoza's criticism of the pseudo-rationalism of Maimonides."[17]

Cardozo's reply to Frank deserves to be quoted in full, so characteristic was it of his inclination to deprecate his own efforts, to assume others would view his situation sympathetically, and to avoid unpleasantness, especially of a personal sort. He backed down from the battle Frank wanted, pleading that his duties on the Supreme Court did not allow him the time even to read all of Frank's letter:

> It has been impossible for me to do more than skim over its pages. They are full of interest and suggestion—that much appears upon the surface—but "the comments and criticisms" that you invite would take more time than I can spare. My most immediate task is to put in order my new apartment, which I am about to occupy after a lifetime in New York, and this will be followed by the new term of the court with its many and engrossing labors. There will be little time for study or reflection as to the nature of law. I am sorry that you have found so much to criticize in my address, but I do not think very highly of it myself, and so I have no reason to complain that it is unsatisfactory to others. I refused to send it to the law reviews, preferring to bury it in the year book of the bar association, a quiet,

though dignified, place of sepulchre. If you write about it, you will be investing it with an importance which I am quite ready to believe that it does not deserve. My work on the Supreme Court is likely to diminish very greatly the output of my extra-judicial writings. Even so, I shall continue to be interested in the problems of judicial methods and in particular in any contributions that you may make to that fascinating but baffling theme. Please keep me on the mailing list, so that I may keep abreast with the latest thought, and pardon my halting steps if I seem to lag behind.[18]

To the pugnacious Frank, spoiling for a fight, this dismissive reply was probably the worst of all possible responses, far worse than a spirited counter-attack. "I trust that you will forgive my rash intrusion on your valuable time," Frank replied, his letter fairly dripping with sarcasm: "Your intimation that your duties will be so arduous that you may be lost to legal philosophy is distressing. I comfort myself by saying that that is a resolution you will find it impossible to adhere to, and by the further thought that, even if, temporarily, you do not directly utter philosophic treatises, your opinions will never cease to reflect your keen and subtle searchings for the deep-lying postulates of your judgments."[19] Frank thus had the last word on the question of whether judicial decisions reflected reason or emotion.

It was, literally, the last word, because the two men appear never again to have spoken or corresponded. Following Franklin D. Roosevelt's election, Frank moved to Washington to become general counsel to the Agricultural Adjustment Administration, and in 1937 he was appointed to the Securities and Exchange Commission. But his exchange with Cardozo continued to rankle, as was evident in August 1938, a month after Cardozo's death, when Frank referred to it as resentfully as if the argument had occurred, not six years earlier, but the day before yesterday. The occasion was the publication of Beryl Harold Levy's *Cardozo and Frontiers of Legal Thinking,* a volume containing a number of representative decisions with a long, appreciative introductory essay.

Cardozo was given to evasiveness, Frank now informed Levy, was timid if not disingenuous, and was certainly not the intellectual equal of Holmes. Cardozo's oblique, indirect style of writing disclosed "something of his reluctance to follow his own vision with adequate directness." Moreover, he unfairly assailed those who disagreed with him: "It would be too harsh to say it flatly, but it might perhaps be suspected that, in his speech on the 'realists' before the New York State Bar Assn., Cardozo was running down the 'extremists' to 'run himself up.'" But the most interesting aspect of

Frank's reaction was that, more explicitly than before, he compared his dispute with Cardozo to that between two other Jewish thinkers: Maimonides and Spinoza.

Cardozo's greatest mistake, Frank held, was to believe he could reconcile classical legal theory with the new realism. Like Maimonides, who had devoted himself to reconciling religion and reason, Cardozo professed a view of the law as absolute even after the legal realists had shown it to be indeterminate. In that sense, both Cardozo and the famous medieval thinker "aimed to furnish a Guide to the Perplexed—by reconciling irreconcilables and thus played Judas to the best wisdom of their respective eras. The way out of intellectual perplexity is hard thinking." By contrast, Frank regarded himself as a latter-day Spinoza, rejecting, in his case, not Maimonides' synthesis of reason and revelation but Cardozo's effort "to save an old theology which was fundamentally at variance with new, verified, observations."[20]

Like Cardozo, Frank was Jewish, and so it is perhaps not surprising that he viewed their dispute in these terms. Cardozo was not devout, but he maintained ties to Jewish communal organizations and remained close to religious leaders. Frank, by contrast, invariably took stands which most Jewish leaders considered insensitive if not actually hostile to Jewish interests. As general counsel to the Agricultural Adjustment Administration, he privately admitted being "very much embarrassed" by the number of able Jewish lawyers who applied for positions on his staff, and he imposed an informal hiring quota.[21] He favored a staunchly isolationist position in foreign policy (until just before Pearl Harbor). He opposed the creation of a Jewish homeland (until well after World War II) on the grounds, he said, that Zionists were "fanatic Jewish nationalists" who were "not American Jews but Jewish sojourners in America."[22] Frank condemned Cardozo's friend Rabbi Stephen S. Wise (who, it should be said, had criticized him first) as someone who "represents the strain in the Jewish tradition which to me is deplorable—although understandable as of its era—the narrow arrogance of Ezra whose intolerance and tribalism Hitler has emulated."[23]

Quite aside from any philosophical differences with Cardozo, therefore, Frank had reason enough to identify with Spinoza: if not actually excommunicated by the Jewish establishment, he had surely come to feel he was an outcast. It was ironic, then, that Frank was denied an appointment to the Circuit Court for the District of Columbia in 1939 because he was Jewish. The irony, however, was lost on Frank: when the reason was later leaked to the press, Frank said he felt "publicly humiliated by that publicity."[24] In the spring of 1941—three years after Cardozo's death—Frank finally received an appointment to the Second Circuit Court of Appeals. He would continue to take potshots at Cardozo's reputation, reverting always to the argument begun at Judge Mack's dinner table and left unresolved in the exchange of letters after Cardozo's appointment to the Supreme Court. That appointment can be attributed to Cardozo's moderate legal philosophy and, perhaps, to his stature in the Jewish community, the very things, that is to say, that differentiated him from Jerome Frank.

The Supreme Court: "The Homesick Exile"

In February 1932 President Herbert Hoover was considering a number of candidates for a Supreme Court vacancy. "Cordoza," he scribbled on a piece of paper, and then added three practical objections: "Jew," "Democrat," "New York."[25] Hoover had misspelled the name of the man he was going to choose, but he had accurately spelled out the sectional, political, and religious obstacles that seemed to stand in the way of the appointment. At the time New York State was represented on the high court by Chief Justice Charles Evans Hughes and Associate Justice Harlan Fiske Stone. The seat being filled had been occupied by Oliver Wendell Holmes Jr., a Republican. Besides, the Court already had one Justice, Louis D. Brandeis, who was Jewish and whose nomination in 1916 had triggered a bitter confirmation battle in which anti-Semitism played an ugly part.

For a variety of reasons, however, the issue of geographical imbalance turned out to be less troublesome than anticipated. Try as they might, Hoover and his advisors could not come up with a top-level candidate from the West, certainly not one who was as qualified to fill Holmes's seat as Cardozo. When Hoover floated the name of William P. James, a federal district judge in California, Republican Senator William E. Borah of Idaho, a Cardozo supporter, countered, "we will fight him on the ground of his obscurity, which means his unfitness to succeed" Holmes.[26] Moreover, Cardozo's friends arranged for the White House to be bombarded with letters and telegrams from judges and lawyers in western states, all indicating a readiness to waive geographical claims in view of Cardozo's credentials. The influential columnist Mark Sullivan added his voice, also, informing Hoover's secretary: "I do not believe that in this one case geography would raise any objection. Cardoza [sic] is in a unique class by himself."[27]

The political hurdle was cleared just as easily. By February 1932 the

Hoover administration, baffled by the problems of the Great Depression, had become increasingly unpopular not only with Democrats but also with progressive Republicans. The last thing the president wanted was a confirmation fight in the Senate, one that would lead insurgents in his own party to ally themselves with the opposition. Just such a coalition had begun to take shape over Court appointments in 1930, first when Hoover proposed Hughes as Chief Justice and then when he nominated John J. Parker as Associate Justice. The Senate had confirmed Hughes, although over spirited opposition from liberals in both parties, and it had actually rejected Parker. By nominating Cardozo, whose appeal crossed party and ideological lines, Hoover was certain to avoid another such divisive battle, and he could at least hope to shore up his waning support among Republicans.

This may have been what Justice Stone (the member of the Court most anxious to see Cardozo appointed) had in mind when he said: "The interesting thing about Judge Cardozo's appointment is that, although there is nothing political in it, it will prove, I believe to be of immense political advantage to the President."[28] It certainly was what New Jersey Representative Franklin W. Fort had in mind when he urged Hoover to make the appointment. An influential Republican, formerly secretary to the party's National Convention, Fort pointed out that liberals viewed Cardozo "as their outstanding Jurist since Justice Holmes retired" while conservatives saw him "as a Judge of the highest distinction and complete sanity."[29]

Fort added another highly relevant point: "The Jews seem to regard him almost as a saint." In truth, Jewish leaders lobbied vigorously on his behalf. Within days of Holmes's resignation, Borah approached Rabbi Stephen S. Wise about the possibility of securing the nomination for Cardozo. Wise quickly touched base with—who else?—Judge Julian W. Mack, and then conveyed his (and Mack's) enthusiasm to the Senator. Jacob Billikopf, the executive director of the Federation of Jewish Charities, also enlisted in the effort. Lacking entrée to the White House, Wise could not approach Hoover personally, as he had once approached Governor Alfred E. Smith in behalf of Cardozo's candidacy for the chief judgeship of the Court of Appeals. But he and Billikopf helped orchestrate expressions of support from their friends in the West—many but not all of them Jewish—in order to allay Hoover's fears regarding sectional imbalance. Wise, who stayed in close touch with Borah, reported the senator's version of a last-minute White House meeting: Hoover said, "There is a great deal of anti-Semitism

in this country, and this appointment would mean two Jews on the Bench";
to which Borah replied, "Such an opportunity may never again come to
you, Mr. President, to strike a blow at anti-Semitism."[30]

Borah's meeting with the president took place a little after nine P.M. on
Sunday, February 14, the day before Hoover announced that he was nom-
inating Cardozo. Borah's account, given to Wise three weeks later, on
March 7, was misleading in crucial respects. Although Borah believed he
had played a major role in dispelling Hoover's doubts, it appears that
Hoover, who had by that hour assuredly made up his mind, simply wanted
Borah to think he had played such a role. As Borah left the White House,
Secretary of War Henry L. Stimson arrived for a nine-thirty appointment.
Stimson, who had earlier made his support for Cardozo known to the president, reported that Hoover "had very skilfully maneuvered Borah into just
the position that we want him on Cardozo, where he has to support Cardozo."[31] Allowing Borah to take credit for the appointment promised real
political dividends: it was likely, as Mark Sullivan told Hoover, to put him
"in a mood to support the administration."[32]

In the past, anti-Semitism had seriously hurt Cardozo's chance to obtain
a Supreme Court nomination. In 1922, when a vacancy occurred, former
Attorney General George W. Wickersham told Chief Justice William Howard Taft that he did not think "it would do to have two Jews in the Supreme Court."[33] When there was another opening in 1924, Nicholas Murray Butler, Cardozo's former professor who had become president of
Columbia University, proposed Cardozo to President Calvin Coolidge but
conceded that his "religious and racial associations" might be felt to constitute "an insuperable objection."[34] By 1932 things had changed, perhaps
because Cardozo's stature had grown with the years or because memories
of the controversy surrounding Brandeis's appointment had dimmed. "I
don't think you could possibly have made a better selection for the Supreme Court than Judge Cardozo,"[35] Wickersham now told Hoover, and
Butler agreed, praising his former student as "the most profound and the
most scholarly legal mind among all our people."[36]

Cardozo's appointment sailed through the Senate without so much as a
ripple of opposition. Nominated on February 15, he was approved unanimously by a Senate subcommittee on the 19th and confirmed by virtual ac-
clamation—there was not even a debate or roll call vote in the Senate—on
the 24th. Meanwhile he carried on his normal duties in Albany, hearing
cases and writing opinions. On March 3 he presided over his last session of

the Court of Appeals. The next day Cuthbert Pound, the newly designated chief judge, reported that Cardozo "has made his plans to break up his well-organized household, live at the Mayflower and cut himself off from all home ties except that he takes his clerk [Joseph M.] Paley with him for a time. He has had two offers of marriage, one from Indiana and one from Georgia."[37] Justice Stone told Cardozo: "I am overjoyed that you are coming. Hope you come soon. We have been saving up some interesting cases for you."[38]

Shortly before noon on March 15, 1932, Chief Justice Charles Evans Hughes administered the oath of office and Cardozo took his seat on the Supreme Court. Rabbi Wise and Senator Borah were present in the courtroom, along with relatives and other friends, but Cardozo had taken pains to avoid the least hint of repaying a political debt. To Wise's suggestion that he invite Borah to the swearing-in ceremony, Cardozo replied:

I am anxious, of course, to express my appreciation of his great and utterly disinterested support—to the best of my recollection I have never met him even casually—but I am not sure about the best way of making this apparent. My understanding is that a new justice takes the oath in open court, being sworn in by the Chief Justice immediately before taking his seat. If I were to ask Senator Borah to be present, I might have to ask Senator Wagner and perhaps others. Any senator is free to be present just as any member of the bar or even the general public, so that an invitation is really uncalled for. I think Senators often do attend from curiousity—or interest. At any rate I hesitate to give to a movement which was professional in its origin an aspect even faintly political.

As an alternative, Cardozo said he was thinking of writing a letter to Borah as "the safer and more fitting way of telling him how I feel."[39]

As he began a new life in Washington, Cardozo voiced regrets that would only grow stronger during his tenure on the Supreme Court. Chief among them was the sense of displacement he felt in unfamiliar surroundings. He referred to himself as "the homesick exile"[40] and to Washington as "my place of exile."[41] Even after leaving the Mayflower Hotel, his residence during his first term on the Court, and moving into his own apartment on Connecticut Avenue in the fall of 1932 (where he was joined by Kate Tracy, his housekeeper, and the maids who had worked for him in New York), he contrasted the dislocation he felt in Washington with his happiness in New York City. "Washington is my legal domicile now, but not the domicile of my spirit," he explained: "If my heart is separately interred . . . it will be in the old city—that it will rest, wherever they put my body."[42] On visits to New York City, he would say, "I am back amid my native sky-scrapers, rejoicing in the dust and din."[43] He once told Charles C. Burlingham, "I wish I were a traffic cop at 42nd St. and 5th Avenue, the old familiar district."[44]

The loneliness affected him all the more because the Supreme Court lacked the camaraderie he had enjoyed on the Court of Appeals. In Albany Cardozo and most of the other judges resided at the same hotel, were constant companions, and trusted one another. In Washington the justices usually worked at home, meeting only when Court was in session and at Saturday conferences. Dissenting opinions were frequent and sometimes had a distinctly nasty ring. Cardozo established friendships, of a sort, with Justices Stone, Owen Roberts, and Louis D. Brandeis, but not to the point where he was ever on a first name basis even with them.[45] He got on well with the chief justice, whose son, Charles Evans Hughes Jr., had served briefly as Cardozo's clerk in 1914 and thought the world of him. His relations with Justices Willis Van Devanter, Pierce Butler, and George Sutherland remained cordial but distant. Justice James Clark McReynolds, a hardened anti-Semite, treated Cardozo as discourteously as he had treated Brandeis. When Cardozo was nominated McReynolds remarked that to become a justice one only had to be a Jew and have a father who was a crook, and at the swearing-in ceremony he conspicuously buried himself in a newspaper.

Apart from McReynolds's rudeness, the day-in, day-out working environment on the Supreme Court could not have been pleasant for a man like Cardozo who instinctively sought to avoid dissension. In November 1933, less than two years after moving to Washington, he made the kind of comment he had never made in eighteen years in Albany. He told Burlingham that he could not afford to take a break from his work: "The minute one turns one['s] back on the other eight judges, one is in danger of falling into an ambush or something of that sort."[46] Before long he was alluding to himself as a "galley slave."[47] Where he had once looked forward to new sessions of the Court of Appeals, he now complained of the short recesses, saying, on one occasion, "the fetters hurt at first: after wearing them a time I grow used to them, and forget that for a time I was free." He dreaded the end of each summer's vacation, now spent in Rye, New York, rather than on the Jersey shore, and the inevitable return to Washington.[48]

Part of Cardozo's dissatisfaction derived from the kinds of cases, mainly involving the interpretation of statutes, that comprised much of the Supreme Court's docket. He wrote ten opinions in his first term. Four dealt with the legality of the government's seizure of automobiles or vessels used to smuggle intoxicating liquors in violation of prohibition, and so involved the forfeiture provisions of the Tariff Acts of 1922 and 1930. One dealt with an injunction against meat packers under the anti-trust laws. Another dealt with the question of a railroad conductor's negligence under the Federal Employer's Liability Act of 1908. Only one of the cases involved a constitutional question: in *Nixon* v. *Condon,* Cardozo, writing for a five-member majority, struck down a Texas statute under which political parties could allow only whites to participate in primary elections. "Delegates of the State's power have discharged their official functions in such a way as to discriminate invidiously between white citizens and black," Cardozo wrote. "The Fourteenth Amendment, adopted as it was with special solicitude for the equal protection of members of the Negro race, lays a duty upon the court to level by its judgment these barriers of color." (McReynolds's dissent stated coldly: "The reasoning advanced by the court to support its conclusion indicates some inadvertence or possibly confusion.")[49]

The three other opinions involved taxation, precisely those cases Cardozo most disliked. Two years before his appointment, he admitted to Learned Hand: "I think the tax cases would drive me crazy. I despise subsections, especially where they are themselves subdivided from a to z, from alpha to omega. Why not say that any citizen who refuses to pay what the government demands is no patriot, and refuse to hear his case till he purges himself of wrong by recantation and release."[50] On the eve of taking up his new duties, he reiterated his complaint but without the humorous afterthought: "Well, I don't know anything about taxes or rate bases or federal jurisdiction or anything except practice in the Court of Appeals."[51] After becoming bogged down in disputes over the filing of consolidated returns, the proper method of computing losses for tax purposes, and the use of past losses as set-offs for current income, he was gloomier still: "Who cares what a tax statute means—except the poor taxpayer who is generally 'broke' anyhow—and why was I taken from my happy home to give my days and nights to these exasperating puerilities?"[52]

"Now I shall find out whether I really love statutes," Cardozo joked at the time of his appointment.[53] Experience quickly confirmed what he had known all along. By February 1933 he was telling Burlingham: "The work here is hard, because there are so many facts to be explored. Congressional debates, historical origins, almost everything but law. I have proposed to

Holmes that we abolish facts, and dwell in the realm of pure ideas, the rarified upper ether where one can soar instead of plodding."[54] For every case that piqued his interest, there were many that did not, especially in his first two years on the Court, before New Deal regulatory legislation came up for review. A lawyer who argued a patent case before the Supreme Court in the spring of 1934 reported that Cardozo wrote an opinion favorable to his client's side, but added: "The fact that he wrote the opinion was a source of great amazement to me because all during the argument he gave me the impression of enjoying, and when I say enjoying I mean enjoying, a sound *sleep.*"[55]

Despite these difficulties, Cardozo surely derived many compensating rewards. Plaudits and honors came his way, as did the opportunity to influence national policy. He took satisfaction from the knowledge that his idol, Oliver Wendell Holmes Jr., approved of him as his successor ("I revere and admire you to the point of adoration," Cardozo had told Holmes in 1928, "I believe in all sincerity that you are the greatest judge that ever lived, though, of course, it may be that in the stone age or beyond there was juridical genius or achievement beyond our ken today").[56] Then too, there was a never-ending stream of social invitations, many of which he declined (one socialite said "she almost preferred to have him refuse an invitation because then she would receive such a beautiful letter of regret"),[57] but others of which he accepted, sometimes in a uniquely charming manner: "I have just been reading a volume of letters in which the writer accepts an invitation as follows: 'Of course I will. Rather. I should think so. Indeed. And very, very glad.' I adopt the form as my own."[58]

There was, finally, the undoubted satisfaction that came from his association with the able young attorneys who clerked for him. During his years in Albany he had had a secretary, Joseph M. Paley, but only on moving to the Supreme Court did he have the assistance of recent law school graduates. To resolve the competing claims of friends at Harvard, Columbia, and Yale, he decided to select his clerks from among graduates of the three schools on a rotating basis.[59] In 1932 his clerk was Melvin H. Siegel (Harvard); in 1933 Ambrose Doskow (Columbia); and in 1934 Allan M. Stroock (Yale). His exchanges with the young lawyers, although never conducted as between equals, helped fill the intellectual and conversational void. Yet as Doskow recognized: "The great thing he missed when he got to Washington was close association with other judges."[60]

His friends had feared just such a development. In March 1932, as Cardozo was preparing to move to Washington, Louise Wise, whose husband, Rabbi Stephen Wise, had lobbied for Cardozo's appointment, took it upon herself to write to Louis D. Brandeis. She reported that Cardozo was "the loneliest of men, having lost everyone in his family who was dear to him." Now he was moving to "a strange environment, where there is no one who understands him or is interested in him as a human being, who I know hungers for sympathy and understanding, although he would be the last to admit it." By writing, she hoped to "break down the usual reserves that social etiquette seems to have put into men's actions which so often conceals the sympathy and understanding which is in their hearts, and we so love Cardozo, we would feel relieved to know you were to be his friend in a very real sense."[61] But although Brandeis termed Cardozo's appointment to the Court an "unexpected joy," the two men never overcame the usual reserves to which Louise Wise referred.[62] Cardozo was sixty-two years old and Brandeis seventy-six, not a stage in life when close friendships are easily formed, and certainly not when the newcomer was a lifelong loner and the older man was notably circumspect in his personal relationships. The two justices shared a religious heritage, but differed too fundamentally in their Jewishness for it to unite them in the kind of friendship for which the rabbi's wife hoped.

Brandeis, Zionism, and Judaism

To appreciate those differences, we may turn first to Louis D. Brandeis. His parents were Jews who had left Prague for the United States in 1849, settling eventually in Louisville, Kentucky. They did not, however, raise Louis (or their other children) as Jews. He did not have religious training or a bar mitzvah. He never belonged to a synagogue or observed the Jewish holy days. He did not have a Jewish wedding. Throughout his life he exchanged Christmas presents with members of his family; once, when his brother, Alfred, sent him a gift of a ham, he exclaimed, "there is great rejoicing."[63] He established a law practice in Boston but remained uninvolved in the city's Jewish community. Not until 1905, when he was nearly fifty, did he give his first speech to one of Boston's Jewish organizations. He used the occasion to advocate the assimilation of all ethnic and religious groups: "Habits of living or of thought which tend to keep alive difference of origin or to classify men according to their religious beliefs are inconsistent with the American ideal of brotherhood, and are disloyal."[64] When in 1907 his name was proposed for membership on the American Jewish Committee, it was rejected because "he has not identified himself with Jewish Affairs, and is rather inclined to side with the Ethical Culturists."[65]

For the first sixty years of his life Brandeis diligently avoided setting foot in a synagogue. When he finally did, in 1916, it was during a Zionist convention in Pittsburgh. Indeed, his involvement in Jewish life came about entirely through his participation in the Zionist movement. He first showed an interest in the idea of a Jewish state in Palestine in 1910, joined the Federation of American Zionists in 1912, and moved into a leadership role in 1914. In 1921 a dispute with Chaim Weizmann led him to resign as honorary president of the Zionist Organization of America (ZOA), but he remained passionately committed to the creation of a Jewish homeland. By persuading Jews that Zionism was compatible with Americanism, Brandeis made the cause both popular and respectable.

In July 1919 Brandeis visited Palestine and was profoundly moved by the experience. Forty-eight hours after reaching Jerusalem, he had succumbed to the city's spell, writing to his wife: "It is a wonderful country, a wonderful city . . . The ages-long longing, the love is all explicable now . . . It is indeed a Holy Land."[66] His biographer Philippa Strum reports: "He went so far as to break a lifelong habit of staying away from synagogues, visiting the synagogue in Rehovot and going twice to the synagogue in Zichron Yaacov . . . praying with the congregation on Saturday morning and giving a speech at the end of the service."[67] On his return he urged Jewish audiences to go and see for themselves: "If you do that you will enjoy the greatest experience of your life."[68]

The intensity of Brandeis's commitment to Zionism contrasts sharply with Benjamin Cardozo's distinctly lukewarm attitude. As late as 1916 Cardozo entertained doubts about Zionism similar to those of other highly assimilated Jews, although he expressed them more epigrammatically. That summer, vacationing in New Jersey, he discussed the subject with a friend, Abraham Tulin, a New York lawyer and a prominent Zionist. Tulin recalled "that I could not make him see how, to use his exact words which I shall never forget, 'it would help me in walking up Fifth Avenue in New York if there were a Jewish state in Palestine.'" Tulin then "pointed out that the existence of Switzerland, Greece, and other small nations, not to speak of the big nations, helps Americans of Swiss, Greek, etc., descent psychologically; although they are not nationals of their former countries. Cardozo, however, could not, at that time, see this argument."[69]

Two years later Cardozo finally accepted Zionism, but not because he came to agree with Tulin or was fired with Brandeis's enthusiasm. In September 1918 Rabbi Wise and Judge Mack were seeking to recruit prominent Jews for the Zionist Organization of America. In a talk with Cardozo they found him, as Wise related, "more sympathetic than we had anticipated." Wise immediately sent him a membership form, because "I want to have the joy of receiving it and forwarding it to our Chief, Justice Brandeis." Cardozo sent a favorable if cool reply: "I have signed the application with some misgiving, for I have confessed to you that I am not yet an enthusiast. But to-day, the line seems to be forming between those who are for the cause and those who are against it, with little room for a third camp. I am not willing to join those who are against, so I go over to the others. If I am charged with inconsistency, I shall say that a great spiritual leader sustained me in my choice."[70]

Wise's reply suggested that Cardozo's sister Nell may have influenced his decision even though she retained doubts of her own: "You think you are not yet an enthusiast, but you will be, I am certain, in good time. We have long wished for your interest in and support of the movement and now, thanks to Nellie's intervention, or rather despite her anti-Semitism, it is here. Reassure the lady that we shall not call upon you for the present to make any addresses in Yiddish seeing that you state English is preferred by you. With cordial greetings and love to Nellie only provided she is ready to join her brother in the great cause."[71] His reference to Yiddish was a way of acknowledging that Zionism appealed primarily to recently arrived Eastern European Jews rather than to the Sephardic elite represented by the Cardozos, or, for that matter, to the assimilated German Jews represented by the Brandeises.

Shifting his campaign into high gear, Wise then informed Cardozo that Judge Mack wished to announce his affiliation and quote his sentence about there being little room for a third camp. The rabbi reported that when he had told Brandeis that Cardozo was considering joining the Zionist Organization of America, but was finding it a little difficult, Brandeis had replied: "I think Cardozo should be pressed to sign now. If it is unpleasant for him he deserves it for his procrastination. His name would help us now." Referring to Cardozo's letter of September 10, Brandeis said: "The letter is right in a way. Jews should understand that those who are not with us are against us, and act accordingly, whatever their doubts. 'Under which flag, Bensonian.'" Impassive to the end, Cardozo replied: "Do what you please with my name and my letter. The sentence which you quote does not sound to me like a bugle-call, but perhaps it will fit the mood of some other laggards like myself."[72]

Cardozo's stance mirrored the emerging receptiveness to Zionism of other well-established Jewish leaders, particularly those associated with the American Jewish Committee. Its president and guiding force, the New York City attorney Louis Marshall, along with other influential figures—Cyrus Adler, Oscar Straus, Felix Warburg, and Irving Lehman—were all beginning to look somewhat more favorably on Zionist aspirations. In April 1918 the AJC adopted a new policy, largely in response to the Balfour Declaration of 1917 in which Great Britain had endorsed, in principle, "the establishment in Palestine of a national home for the Jewish people." While maintaining that the AJC's chief purpose was unchanged—to obtain civil and religious rights for Jews wherever they might reside—the organization now conceded that many Jews "yearn for a home in the Holy Land for the Jewish people. This hope, nurtured for centuries, has our whole-hearted sympathy."[73] Cardozo felt quite comfortable with this position and later served on the AJC's Executive Committee. He was moderately active in the organization from 1927 until February 1932, when, citing his appointment to the Supreme Court, he resigned.

Unlike Brandeis, Cardozo never visited Palestine, although he evidently once planned such a trip. Among his unpublished papers is the draft of an address prepared for the opening of a School of Jurisprudence at Hebrew University in Jerusalem. The manuscript is undated, but it must have been written in November or December 1928, because it makes reference to a case then before the Court of Appeals. Cardozo was a logical choice as a speaker in view of his eminence and his having served, since 1925, on the Board of Governors of the American Friends of Hebrew University. The reason Cardozo decided not to make the journey is not known, although his sister Nell's failing health may have been responsible.

In the address Cardozo attempted to explain the contemporary relevance of ancient Hebrew law, to discover, as he put it, "the great treasures for jurisprudence" that are "buried in the Holy Land." To demonstrate the enduring wisdom of the sages and prophets, he cited the moral precepts found in Exodus, Deuteronomy, and other sources: "Do not heed a popular cry to convict, nor decide a cause either to please the powerful or to favor the poor." "Abhor a false cause and condemn not to death the man once acquitted or the man that is innocent." "Do not oppress a stranger; ye knew a stranger's life; ye were yourselves strangers in the land of Egypt." It was not only Mosaic law that was worth consulting, he asserted, but also the Talmud, because law draws "its sustenance from the roots of morality and custom." "Law, human and divine, has been the craving of the Hebrew spirit," he concluded. Establishment of a School of Jurisprudence in Jerusalem would show that "law is in touch with the Eternities."[74]

It was not the kind of speech that Louis Brandeis, for all his prophetic fervor, would have composed. Envisioning Palestine as a permanently agrarian society, he always regarded the Hebrew University, in his biographer's words, "as no more than a means of turning out sophisticated farmers."[75] The difference between Cardozo and Brandeis, however, went beyond the varying meanings each attached to the Zionist ideal. Neither of the two Jewish justices was religiously observant, but Cardozo had been raised in an Orthodox home and at some point had decisively broken with that tradition, while Brandeis had never held religious beliefs against which he had to rebel.

Cardozo, who frequently described himself as a "heathen," could make casual references to "God or Providence or the First Great Cause or the Whirl of the Atoms or whatever the presiding genius of the universe may be."[76] At times of impending loss, as, for example, toward the end of Nell's life, he was more introspective, writing, as he did to Louise Wise: "I think a good deal these days about religion, wondering what it is and whether I have any. As the human relationships which make life what it is for us begin to break up, we search more and more for others that transcend them."[77] But even then he did not find solace in religious belief. Stephen Wise, who came as close as anyone to being Cardozo's spiritual advisor, wrote that after Nell's death, Cardozo's outlook "was one of hopefulness rather than of definite faith or conviction. He might almost be described as a hopeful, spiritual agnostic."[78]

Cardozo therefore faced a dilemma when, in 1931, Wise invited him to deliver the commencement address at the Jewish Institute of Religion, the Reform seminary Wise had founded. How could he refuse Wise, a friend of twenty-five years' standing, who had delivered the eulogy for his twin sister, Emily, and who had tried to console him after Nell's death? Yet what could he possibly say to earnest young men about to embark on careers in the rabbinate? Deciding on the topic "Values, or the Choice of Tycho Brahe," Cardozo afterward explained his predicament to Charles C. Burlingham, who had attended the exercises at Wise's urging: "Being so much of a heathen, I was reluctant to talk at such a meeting. I wouldn't have done so if I hadn't felt under personal obligation to Dr. Wise for kindness in hours of trouble. I think I managed to put what I said in such a way as to avoid misconception about my own beliefs."[79] Indeed he had, for the address would have been as appropriate for individuals entering the ministry or priesthood as for those being ordained to the rabbinate.

Cardozo began with a disclaimer, or, as he said, "an apology." "I do not know whether I have the right to talk to you today. I have felt that to earn that right I should be able to say to you that your beliefs are wholly mine, that the devastating years have not obliterated youthful faiths, and that in the darkness of the universe I can see with clearness and certainty a consoling shaft of light." He had agreed to speak, he continued, only because Wise had convinced him that a talk about values would be appropriate. He then turned to the story of Tycho Brahe, reciting lengthy passages from Alfred Noyes's "noble and inspiring" poem, "Watchers of the Sky" (1922). Tracking the stars at his lonely observatory, the Danish astronomer refused to listen to those who told him he was wasting his time, but persevered:

> The victors may forget us. What of that?
> Theirs be the palms, the shouting, and the praise,
> Ours be the fathers' glory in the sons.

In this devotion to one's life's work, Cardozo found an uplifting lesson: "The submergence of self in the pursuit of an ideal, the readiness to spend oneself without measure, prodigally, almost ecstatically, for something intuitively apprehended as great and noble, spend oneself one knows not why—some of us like to believe that this is what religion means."

From these generalities Cardozo moved to more personal reflections, speaking of individuals he had known who, in their own lives, had made Tycho Brahe's choice. "They had made it in humbler forms, by love, by gentleness, by sweetness, by devotion, by sacrifice of self within the narrow circle of the home; but, be it said to their undying glory, they had made it, none the less." He continued: "We know it when death takes them if in hours of pride and darkness we have been blind to it before. The life seemed simple while it lasted. We may not always have been conscious of its beauty. The end comes, and behold it is illuminated with the white and piercing light of the divinity within it. We have walked with angels unawares." Although he never said as much, these remarks may have represented a belated eulogy for his sister Nell, who had died a year and half before.

Only in closing did Cardozo allude to Jewish traditions or values, and even then he was determinedly ecumenical. He predicted that the graduates, once embarked on their careers as "preachers of the eternal values," would encounter mockery and temptation. "Sycophants and time-servers and courtiers and all the lovers of the flesh pots will assail you with warnings that you are squandering the happy days under the sun . . . Then will be the time when you will need to bethink yourselves of the values that were chosen by the prophets and saints of Israel, and by the goodly and noble of every race and clime. You will remember in that hour the choice of Tycho Brahe."[80]

There is no way to know exactly what Cardozo meant when he said that "the devastating years" had "obliterated youthful faiths." As Rabbi Wise noted: "Reserved as he was in most things, he was most reserved with respect to his religious convictions."[81] It is possible that his father's death in 1885, when Benjamin was only fifteen, and his older sister Grace's death that same year, produced a crisis of belief. Or perhaps it occurred in reaction to the hostility Orthodox Jews surely exhibited when his twin sister, Emily, married outside the faith. But whether his doubts came on suddenly or developed over a period of months, years, or decades remains unclear. Two speeches that Cardozo gave, however, the first when he was twenty-five and the second when he was twenty-eight, were sufficiently different in tone and outlook as to suggest that a change occurred during these years.

On June 5, 1895, the hereditary "electors" of Shearith Israel—all of them, by definition, male—met to consider liturgical arrangements in the new synagogue then under construction on Central Park West. A small number of congregants wished to modify Orthodox practices, preferring a more Reform-like setting, which, they believed, would increase attendance at services. They proposed the setting aside of family pews, the use of a pipe organ to provide musical accompaniment, and, most controversial of all, the elimination of separate seating for men and women. A motion stating that the sense of the meeting was "that in the new Synagogue the sexes shall sit together" was introduced by Gratz Nathan, Benjamin Cardozo's cousin—the same man whose shady financial dealings, it will be remembered, had contributed to the downfall of Cardozo's father more than twenty years before.[82]

Three congregants spoke in favor of the motion, and three against it: Adolphus S. Solomon; the congregation's religious leader, Rev. Henry Pereira Mendes; and Cardozo. The minutes merely state that Cardozo made "a long address impressive in ability and eloquence,"[83] but he evidently argued that mixed seating would violate the congregation's constitution, and, according to Mendes's successor, Rabbi David de Sola Pool, threatened to appeal an adverse decision in civil court, saying "if you outvote us, there are laws outside."[84] But there was no likelihood he would be outvoted. During the discussion Nathan was asked to withdraw his motion "in the interest of harmony it being manifest that it could not carry."[85] When he refused, his proposal was overwhelmingly rejected by a vote of seventy-three to seven.

By speaking out, Cardozo may have felt, he was defending a position his father would have favored (as well as opposing the relative whose avarice had contributed to his father's downfall), and he surely knew he was supporting Mendes, who had trained him as a youth. More than that, he was doing exactly what his sisters wanted done. During the debate a resolution was entered "on behalf of certain ladies of the Congregation." Signed by nearly one hundred women, "the remnant of the Sephardic Jews in this country, [who] desire to have our Congregation continue our time honored customs, and our ancient form of worship," the resolution opposed the introduction of pews and an organ as well as mixed seating. It denied that such changes "have in any way in any Congregation, increased Sabbath observance, or Synagogue attendance, in any proportionate degree, or respect for the Hebrews in the eyes of the community." The signatories included many of Cardozo's relatives, including his sisters Nell and Emily.[86]

As of June 1895, then, while he had ceased attending weekly services at Shearith Israel, Cardozo felt sufficiently at home in a synagogue setting to speak on behalf of Orthodox practices. Three years later, however, he made another speech, this one on Benjamin Disraeli, in which he distanced himself from religious tradition. Cardozo offered a balanced assessment of the career of the English statesman (who served as prime minister in 1868 and again from 1874 to 1880) with a focus on the significance of his Jewish heritage and his influence on Jewish life. Disraeli's ancestors (like Cardozo's) were Sephardic Jews, members of London's Spanish and Portuguese synagogue. His parents, however, had converted to Christianity in 1817 when Disraeli was thirteen. Cardozo's theme was that although Disraeli "was faithless with his religion, he was faithful to his race."

Disraeli renounced Judaism, championed the tenets of the Church of England, and, as Cardozo pointed out, claimed that Christianity was a more perfect form of Judaism, not "a new faith but . . . a development of the old one." Though Cardozo argued that this was a delusion, he did not condemn Disraeli for his apostasy. To the contrary, he described Disraeli's outlook sympathetically. "It was impossible that a man with a lineage such as his should prove in all respects forgetful of the ties of birth and blood," Cardozo explained. "He had renounced his faith; but he could not renounce the memories or the spirit which had been bequeathed to him by ages of ancestors more loyal than himself." It is unlikely that these comments were meant to be autobiographical, although they could be construed as such, especially if the concept of renouncing one's faith is not taken literally, in the sense of conversion to Christianity, but simply to indicate a rejection of Orthodox practice.

On the whole, Cardozo praised Disraeli because "he never faltered once in his outward devotion to his race." Never denying his heritage, but rather taking pride in it, Disraeli, Cardozo said, "preached to all the world the dignity of his people's past." He created sympathetic Jewish characters in his novels, and he labored tirelessly on behalf of the Bill to Remove Jewish Disabilities, finally enacted in 1858, which enabled Jews to hold political office. Disraeli had a positive impact on Jews, Cardozo argued, because "he taught us to think worthily of ourselves." He served as an illustration "of our resources, of our intellect, of our vigor; of our enthusiasm, of our diplomacy; of our *finesse*."[87]

Even after Cardozo ceased to be religiously observant he maintained a strong Jewish identity. He was a lifelong member of Shearith Israel. When in 1914 the trustees of the congregation congratulated him on his appointment to the Court of Appeals, he replied that brotherhood "is the tie that binds this historic congregation to all the members of our race." He remained in touch with Mendes (presiding in 1927 at a ceremony marking his half-century of association with the Congregation), and with David de Sola Pool. Cardozo would eat food that was not kosher when dining out, but did not allow it to be served in his home. He was willing to officiate at the marriage of a Jew and a Christian, but only if he knew the bride or groom. "I'm a good deal of a heathen," he remarked in reference to intermarriage: "Moreover, one will perform a ceremony for close friends or relatives, even if it makes one a little uncomfortable, when one might be reluctant to do so for comparative strangers."[88]

Rarely a victim of anti-Semitism himself, Cardozo bitterly resented the least manifestation of such prejudice. In 1928 he explained why he was supporting the presidential candidacy of New York's governor, Alfred E. Smith,

a Catholic: "In the opposite camp will be found all the narrow minded big-
ots, all the Jew haters, all those who would make of the United States an exclusively Protestant Government. I do not mean, of course, that only those
will be found there, but I mean that the defeat of Smith will be acclaimed as
a great victory by that narrow minded group, and will hearten them and the
friends of obscurantism generally."[89] In 1930, when the American Jewish
Committee was discussing ways to combat anti-Semitic hiring practices,
Cardozo "expressed the view that while little can be done with private businesses, it may be possible, by suitable legislation, to curb the practice of dis-
crimination in the matter of employment on the part of public service and
utility corporations."[90] He expressed undisguised contempt for Madison
Grant, an implacable nativist, and his "notorious" attitude toward Jews.[91]

The Nazi persecution of Jews outraged Cardozo. As early as March 1933
he asked: "What can be said of a world in which a multitude of men and
women seem to believe in all sincerity that Jews are not wronged if only
physical violence is restrained, no matter how great the contumely and insult and humiliation and dishonor!"[92] Before long he was referring to "the
Frankfurt ruffian" and "the Hitler horrors," and noting, "the crimes of
violence are almost the least of the whole shameful business."[93] As the years
passed and the Nazis intensified their campaign against the Jews, Cardozo
grew even more indignant. In March 1936, after reading an article by
Oswald Garrison Villard in the *Nation* which attacked Hitler's government
for a "persecution which for calculated brutality and fiendishness surpasses
anything in modern history," Cardozo thanked Villard: "Alas, that so few
are fired with a kindred zeal! . . . There is hardly any one but yourself among
the men I have met who is aflame upon the subject and not merely deco-
rously critical."[94]

Although outspoken in private, Cardozo shared with other prominent
Jews a fear of seeming to be motivated by ancestral loyalties. Nothing illustrated this more clearly than his response to an incident arising out of a
demonstration against the *Bremen*, a German passenger liner, in July 1935.
Organized by communists, the demonstration was intended as a protest
against the Nazi authorities who had arrested a German-born American
seaman and were holding him in a Hamburg prison. The liner, flying a German flag with a swastika superimposed on it (the Nazi symbol was not as
yet the official flag), was scheduled to depart from a midtown Manhattan
pier at about midnight on July 27. Some of the communists, having sneaked
aboard to mingle with the visitors, stormed the deck, cut the halyards of the

flag, and dumped it overboard. A wild scuffle with the police and the German crew ensued. Five demonstrators were arrested and charged with unlawful assembly; a sixth was held for assaulting a police officer with brass knuckles.

A decision in the case was rendered in September by Magistrate Louis B. Brodsky. Dismissing the unlawful assembly (but not the assault) charges, he deftly inserted his anti-Nazi views into his opinion. "It well may be," he declared, "that the flying of this emblem in New York Harbor was, rightly or wrongly, regarded by these defendants and others of our citizenry as a gratuitously brazen flaunting of an emblem which symbolized all that is antithetical to American ideals" and was "an atavistic throwback to pre-medieval, if not barbaric, social and political conditions." Moreover, "rightly or wrongly," the demonstrators may have thought the display "even carried with it the same sinister implications as a pirate ship, sailing defiantly into the harbor of a nation, one of whose ships it had just scuttled, with the black flag of piracy proudly flying aloft." Had a criminal conspiracy been proven, Brodsky added, he would have punished the five defendants. But it was not proven and so they were released.[95]

Faced with indignant protests from the German government, Secretary of State Cordell Hull issued an apology, stating that Brodsky had "unfortunately so worded his opinion as to give the reasonable and definite impression that he was going out of his way adversely to criticize the government, which criticism was not a relevant or legitimate part of his judicial decision."[96] Unappeased, the German minister of justice informed a Nazi party convention then meeting in Nuremberg that "in the name of the German bench I have protested against the characteristic Jewish impudence of Magistrate Brodsky of New York. The time is past that the German people can be insulted by Jews." He went on: "Brodsky is the type to remind us in the future of the danger of justice when it is in the hands of the Jews."[97]

Cardozo had no reason to comment publicly on the affair, but privately he expressed his dismay at the Jewish magistrate who, he believed, had misused his judicial office to denounce Naziism. Writing to a great-niece, Aline Goldstone, Cardozo explained that he was disappointed that she and his cousin Maud Nathan "approved of Brodsky and his shameful utterance. What is the use of striving for standards of judicial propriety if you and she condone such lapses! It would have been bad enough if he had been a Gentile; but for a Jew it was unforgivable. Now the traducers will say—and with some right if you and Maud approve—that these are the standards of the race."⁹⁸ The key phrase—"for a Jew it was unforgivable"—expressed Cardozo's fear that Jews would be seen as betraying professional standards because of their religious loyalties.

Three days after Cardozo wrote this letter, his good friend Rabbi Wise returned to the United States from a trip to Europe and Palestine. Greeted by reporters who asked his opinion of Brodsky's ruling, he replied that he would not "insult the flag of pirates by comparing it to the swastika."⁹⁹ Soon thereafter Wise delivered his Rosh Hashanah sermon at the Free Synagogue. "The horrors of the recent Nuremberg Nazi party days are made more full of horror by the act of our own government in apologizing with exaggerated profuseness and abjectness to the Nazi regime for a word of disrespect and contempt for that regime, uttered in the course of a judicial decision," he declared. "Such apology would have come more fitly if our government had ever uttered one brave word in condemnation of the program and the practices of the Nazi regime. The term 'piracy' has been objected to. I have not heard of pirates who rob and maim and slay their own neighbors and countrymen. That is exactly what the Nazi regime did at Nuremberg to Jews who have lived in Germany."¹⁰⁰

If Wise ever discussed Brodsky's statement with Cardozo, no record of that conversation has survived. But it is unlikely that the rabbi would have been surprised by the justice's view. For two years Wise's efforts to organize anti-Nazi campaigns, notably a boycott of German goods, had met with resistance from prominent Jews. The American Jewish Committee, fearing that Wise's efforts would not help German Jews but would only fuel domestic anti-Semitism, branded "such forms of agitation as boycotts, parades, mass-meetings and other similar demonstrations as futile."¹⁰¹ The "Sh-Sh Jews," Wise called them. Despite his admiration for Cardozo, and their long friendship, Wise, when seeking moral support for his anti-Nazi campaign, turned elsewhere. It was Louis D. Brandeis, not Cardozo, who, after the rabbi had organized a huge rally at Madison Square Garden, pressed Wise's hands between his own and said: "You must go on and lead. No one could have done a finer piece of work."¹⁰²

The Claims of Conscience: Hamilton v. Regents, 1934

Wise also differed with Cardozo, if less sharply, on another issue. Late in 1934 the Supreme Court had to decide whether the California Board of Regents could require male students to enroll in military science and tactics courses offered by the Reserve Officer Training Corps. Two students at UCLA, devout Christians who were conscientiously opposed to war, refused to sign up for such courses and were suspended. The Court, in an opinion by Justice Pierce Butler, upheld the Regents' authority. Cardozo filed a concurring opinion which was joined by Justices Brandeis and Stone. When Wise told Cardozo that some of his "anti-militarist friends" were unhappy with the outcome, the justice replied that the Court had not considered "the fairness or wisdom" of the policy but only its constitutionality.[103] His concurrence in *Hamilton et al.* v. *Board of Regents,* which represented his most important statement on freedom of religion, reflected his skepticism regarding all claims of religious certitude.[104]

In the fall of 1933 two UCLA freshmen, Albert W. Hamilton and W. Alonzo Reynolds Jr., refused on conscientious grounds to take the prescribed courses in military science and tactics. Members of the Methodist Episcopal Church, and the sons of ordained ministers, they believed "that war and training for war and military training are immoral and wrong and contrary to the letter and spirit of the teachings of Jesus and the precepts of the Christian religion." Each felt, moreover, that "he may not participate in military training without doing violence to his deepest religious and conscientious convictions."[105]

At the time UCLA required all able-bodied male students (who were American citizens) to take two years of military science and tactics under the direction of the Reserve Officers Training Corps. In the first year students studied the "theory and practice of the care, mechanics and use of the rifle" as well as "scouting and patrolling"; in the second year they learned about "Infantry Weapons and Musketry" and received "theoretical and practical instruction in the care, mechanics and operation of the automatic rifle."[106] Each term about twelve hundred students registered in the courses which met for three hours a week. Protests against compulsory military training were nothing new in California, but in the fall of 1933 both sides in the controversy anxiously awaited a definitive ruling as to the constitutionality of the requirement.

A recent test case in Maryland had left the issue in doubt. In January 1933 a superior court judge in Baltimore, Joseph N. Ulman, had ruled that Ennis H. Coale, a University of Maryland freshman who was a member of the Methodist Episcopal Church, could not be required to take courses which violated his religious conscience. Noting that the university had in the past exempted Quakers from military training, the judge found that Methodists deserved a similar privilege. Ulman declared: "If religious conscientious objectors are excluded from their State-supported university except upon pain of relinquishing their religious beliefs and principles, then a religious test has been imposed as a condition of their enjoyment of its educational privileges."[107] The university appealed and in June won a reversal when the Maryland Court of Appeals held that the Regents had the authority to implement the training requirement. Since the university no longer exempted Quakers, the Court found, it was not unfairly discriminating against Methodists.[108] The Supreme Court refused to hear Coale's appeal, holding that it did not raise a substantial federal question but only the proper construction of a Maryland statute.

The California Board of Regents meanwhile insisted that, as a land-grant college under the Morrill Act of 1862, the university was "obligated by law to require that military training be taken by every male student." The Act provided that public lands were to be donated to the states and territories for the support "of at least one college of Agriculture, where the leading object shall be, without excluding other scientific and classical studies, and including military tactics, to teach such branches of learning as are related to agriculture and the mechanic arts in such manner as the legislature of the states may respectively prescribe." The language was highly ambiguous, however, since it stated only that courses in military tactics had to be offered, not that they had to be required. Wisconsin and Minnesota had already made the courses optional in their land grant colleges, but the California Regents stubbornly clung to their interpretation, hoping the courts would sustain it.

So when Albert Hamilton informed the university authorities that he could not take part in military training "without sacrificing and compromising my religious convictions," he was promptly suspended (as was Alonzo Reynolds) by Ernest Carroll Moore, UCLA's provost.[109] Moore consulted with the students' attorney, John Beardsley, and arranged to phrase the suspensions so as to provide a basis for a Supreme Court appeal. After the meeting Beardsley reported that he and Moore agreed that the students' claim for exemption from military training "presents an issue about which sincere men may honestly differ, and that whatever court proceeding may develop should be conducted in a dignified manner, with mutual respect and without bitterness or unfriendliness."[110]

Moore, however, showed unrelenting hostility to radical students who opposed ROTC on political rather than religious grounds, denouncing it as "the agency for the dissemination of jingoist, imperialist propaganda." In May 1934 he informed the university's president, Robert Gordon Sproul: "I have, as you know, been brooding over what the communists are trying to do to us here in the United States." In October he stopped brooding long enough to suspend the president of the student council and four other undergraduates who were trying to organize a campus referendum on the creation of a student-run forum to discuss political issues. Moore feared they wanted to convert UCLA into "a hotbed of communism." That summer the provost's worst suspicions were confirmed when a state police official told him that the communists "propose to do two things 1) To make a crusade for sex freedom. Convincing the young people that they should live together without marrying if they want to and quite freely. 2) To make heavy war against compulsory military training."[111]

A fear of appearing weak in the face of such protests influenced the Board of Regents' decision to maintain the compulsory system, or so it appears from the discussion at an executive committee meeting in April 1934. After hearing a report from the university's counsel, John U. Calkins Jr., one of the Regents said: "I am in favor of continuing the compulsory requirement. Possibly, after a while the compulsory part might be modified to an extent but I think for now we should continue it. If we stop we are giving in to professional agitators who are trying to make trouble."[112] At the May meeting another Regent suggested that in the future students who objected to combatant service "might be given training in other branches of military work which would not be directly connected with the bearing of arms." But this "might disorganize the work of the military department and the present is probably not the time to make such a change." The Board then voted to reaffirm its long-standing policy.[113]

Even as the Regents considered their options, Albert Hamilton's case was making its way through the courts. In January 1934 the California Supreme Court unanimously denied his plea for readmittance. In a brief opinion the court noted that the Regents "have full power and authority . . . to prescribe the nature and extent of the courses to be given, and to determine the question of what students shall be required to pursue them."[114] Although a victory for the university, this did not provide the unequivocal interpretation of the Morrill Act that Calkins had wanted. As he explained to Moore: "I am a little afraid that our favorable decision is going to be the basis for more trouble. The leaders of the move declare that they have long hoped for a decision which determines that the full responsibility for compulsory military training rests with The Regents, and now that they have it they will not leave any stone unturned to bring about a reversal of The Regents' policy."[115]

In April 1934 the Supreme Court agreed to review the case and in October the justices heard oral argument. Beardsley and Calkins debated at length whether the Morrill Act required compulsory military training at land-grant colleges. A long supporting brief, filed on behalf of the Regents by Sveinbjorn Johnson, a law professor at the University of Illinois, maintained that the Morrill Act must have envisioned compulsory courses since, at the time, the elective system was generally unknown at American colleges. But the justices never settled the matter, deciding it was not centrally involved. Two other questions commanded their attention: had the students been denied their right, under the Fourteenth Amendment, to equal protection of the laws? And had they been deprived of their First Amendment right to freedom of religion (assuming the states were required to observe its provisions)?

Beardsley conceded that one did not have a right to receive an education at a state-supported university. Even so, he contended, the Regents "may not validly impose as a condition upon which the privilege of education will be accorded, the surrender of rights and privileges and immunities which belong to appellants as citizens of the United States." The two students had been suspended "solely because they decline to forswear their consciences and violate their deepest moral and religious conviction," and this amounted to "a denial of their right to the equal protection of the laws" in violation of Fourteenth Amendment.[116] On behalf of the Regents, Calkins responded that the privilege Hamilton and Reynolds enjoyed of attending the University of California derived solely from their standing as state residents. "They have no privilege to attend which attaches by reason of the circumstance that they are citizens of the United States."[117]

As citizens they undeniably had a First Amendment right to freedom of religion. But were First Amendment guarantees binding on the states under the provision of the Fourteenth Amendment which barred them from depriving any person of liberty without due process of law? Beginning in 1925 the Supreme Court had issued a series of rulings which held that First Amendment freedoms of speech and press were "incorporated" by the Fourteenth Amendment, but the justices had never extended similar protection to religious freedom. And if the guarantee of religious freedom was indeed binding on the states, did the Regents' requirement abridge it?

Beardsley at least had the advantage of consistency in urging the Court to answer both questions affirmatively. If the justices agreed that freedom of religion, like freedom of speech, deserved protection against incursion by the states, then, he thought, they would have to find for the two students: "Certainly freedom of religion means something more than the right to worship according to the dictates of one's own conscience . . . The principle must afford protection to outward manifestations of religious belief."[118] For his part, Calkins was willing to concede that there was "some logic" to incorporating religious freedom, but he insisted that the Regents' requirement was still reasonable because "the freedom is not so absolute as to bar legislation which may incidentally intrude upon it."[119]

On December 3, 1934, the Supreme Court unanimously affirmed the constitutionality of the military training requirement. Justice Pierce Butler, who wrote the opinion, granted that each of the students "is a follower of Jesus Christ; each accepts as a guide His teachings and those of the Bible and holds as a part of his religious and conscientious belief that war, training for war, and military training are immoral, wrong, and contrary to the letter and spirit of His teaching and the precepts of the Christian religion." Nevertheless, Butler rejected Hamilton's and Reynolds' claims. Paraphrasing Calkins' argument concerning the Fourteenth Amendment, Butler found that "the 'privilege' of attending the university as a student comes not from federal sources but is given by the State." Butler never mentioned the First Amendment, noting merely that the students were asserting "that the due process clause of the Fourteenth Amendment as a safeguard of 'liberty' confers the right to be students in the state university free from obligation to take military training as one of the conditions of attendance . . . That proposition must at once be put aside as untenable." Just as the government had a duty to maintain order, Butler held, citizens had a reciprocal duty to defend the government against its enemies.[120]

Had the opinion ended there, Cardozo might never have issued his concurrence. But Butler went on to cite two cases which had sharply divided the Court. In *United States* v. *Schwimmer* (1929) the Court had ruled that the government could deny the naturalization petition of a pacifist, Rosika Schwimmer, because she was not willing to take up arms in defense of the country. Justice Butler had written the decision, and Justices Holmes and Brandeis had dissented. (It was here that Holmes said, "If there is any principle of the Constitution that more imperatively calls for attachment than any other it is the principle of free thought—not free thought for those who agree with us but freedom for the thought that we hate.")[121] Two years later the Court decided that Clyde Macintosh, Dwight Professor of Theology at Yale University, could be denied naturalization because, as a religious objector, he would not promise unqualifiedly to support the United States in every war it might ever fight. Justice Sutherland wrote the majority opinion. Chief Justice Charles Evans Hughes submitted a dissent, which was joined by Holmes, Brandeis, and Stone.

Justice Stone, who had dissented in *Macintosh* and was having second thoughts about voting with the majority in *Schwimmer,* tried to persuade Butler to delete the references to those cases, telling him that they had no particular relevance to *Hamilton:* "My only feeling about them is that they unnecessarily rub salt into the wounds of a great many very worthy people who, I am convinced, dwell on a higher spiritual plane than I do, and I am not at all sure that another generation may not conclude that their views about war are a great deal wiser than my own." In dealing with such a "delicate" subject, Stone continued, "I feel that we ought to avoid causing any unnecessary irritations so far as is reasonably possible."[122] Butler replied that he had indeed attempted "to avoid, so far as is reasonably possible, causing any unnecessary irritation," but insisted that the two cases "are plainly applicable for the points there decided include the questions raised by these students . . . I fear failure now to cite them might, because of the differences on other points reflected by the dissenting opinions, be misunderstood to the detriment of the law."[123]

A "monolith," is how Justice Holmes once described Butler: "there are no seams the frost can get through."[124] Cardozo, finding him just as impenetrable, drafted a concurring opinion and sent it to Stone, asking if he should circulate it. "My impression is that if Justice Butler will drop the passages you object to, I will suppress the memorandum; otherwise not, though, maybe, I should file it anyhow," Cardozo said. Brandeis was prepared to support the concurrence, Cardozo added, and continued: "All through the land conscientious and high principled young men—for ethical if not religious reasons—are opposed to military training. I think it oppressive to make them submit to it in these times of peace though I am satisfied the state has the power to be oppressive if it chooses. The opinion of the Court seems to be quite without sympathy for their attitude. But I suppose it is best to keep one's mouth shut when in doubt."[125]

When Justice Butler refused to remove the controversial citations, Cardozo decided it was best not to remain silent. His concurrence is an extraordinarily revealing document. To begin, he boldly accepted the view that the First Amendment protected religion, as well as speech and press, against encroachment by the states. In his words: "I assume for present purposes that the religious liberty protected by the First Amendment against invasion by the nation is protected by the Fourteenth Amendment against invasion by the states." Not until 1940, in *Cantwell* v. *Connecticut,* would the Court adopt the position Cardozo here asserted. And not until 1947, in *Everson* v. *Board of Education,* would the Court add the establishment clause to the free exercise clause as meriting protection against the states. Cardozo was more than willing to go that far in 1934: "The First Amendment, if it be read into the Fourteenth, makes invalid any state law 'respecting an establishment of religion or prohibiting the free exercise thereof.'"

Cardozo rested his concurrence squarely on the doctrine of judicial restraint. While he denied that instruction in military science either deprived individuals of religious freedom (since Hamilton and Reynolds were not being forced to attend UCLA) or amounted to an establishment of religion (since the courses did not constitute "instruction in the practice or tenets of a religion"), he did not seek to justify the Regents' policy. Referring to the compulsory requirement, he said: "This may be condemned by some as unwise or illiberal or unfair when there is violence to conscientious scruples, either religious or merely ethical. In controversies of this order courts do not concern themselves with matters of legislative policy, unrelated to privileges or liberties secured by the organic law."

One crucially important phrase, "or merely ethical," echoed Cardozo's language in his letter to Stone—"for ethical if not religious reasons." The issue of an ethical objection to military training—one grounded, that is, in secular rather than religious belief—was not involved in the Hamilton case. (More than forty years would pass before the Supreme Court, in 1970, decided that ethical or moral convictions, as well as religious belief, qualified an individual for conscientious objector status under Selective Service.) But in view of Cardozo's tendency to equate religion and ethics, his decision to raise the issue is entirely understandable. Only three years earlier, reluctant to address rabbinical students because his youthful faith had been obliterated, he had finally defined religion as "the submergence of self in the pursuit of an ideal."

Cardozo had told Stone that the Court should show its sympathy for the principled young men involved in the case, and Stone, too, wanted to avoid rubbing salt in their wounds. So far, Cardozo's concurring opinion had accomplished that purpose. But his final paragraph contained a more cutting critique of the students' position than any to be found in Butler's opinion. Historically, Cardozo said, whenever conscientious objectors had been exempted from combatant service, Congress had coupled the exemption with collateral obligations. "Manifestly a different doctrine would carry us to lengths that have never yet been dreamed of," he said. "The conscientious objector, if his liberties were to be thus extended, might refuse to contribute taxes in furtherance of a war, whether for attack or for defense, or in furtherance of any other end condemned by his conscience as irreligious or immoral. The right of private judgment has never yet been so exalted above the powers and the compulsion of the agencies of government."[126] This much could be found in the typewritten draft that Cardozo sent to Justice Stone.

Then, in his own distinctive handwriting, Cardozo added a last, devastating sentence: "One who is a martyr to a principle—which may turn out in the end to be a delusion or an error—does not prove by his martyrdom that he has kept within the law."[127] This was surely a peculiar way to conclude an opinion ostensibly designed to placate youthful idealists by letting them know that some of the justices, if unable to rule in their favor, were at least sensitive to their claims. But it makes perfect sense if taken as a statement by a confirmed agnostic—"so much of a heathen," in his own words—once, but no longer, a believer, who had come to distrust all expressions of religious certainty and the self-righteousness that, he believed, sometimes accompanied them.

6

Law and Order

Roosevelt, the Court, and the New Deal

On Saturday afternoon, March 4, 1933, Franklin D. Roosevelt was inaugurated as President. At a little after six that evening, while a thousand guests were making merry in the White House, Roosevelt asked his ten Cabinet members to gather in the second-floor Oval Office for their swearing-in ceremony. Roosevelt had invited Associate Justice Benjamin Cardozo to do the honors. For the first time in the nation's history the entire Cabinet was sworn in at the same time, in the same place, and by the same official. "A little family party," the President called it with obvious delight, looking "as happy as a schoolboy in the recess hour."[1] Cardozo, while considering it "very gracious" of the President to ask him to administer the oaths of office, responded more prosaically, remarking that "it meant I had to sit shivering through the long parade from 2 P.M. to 6. Luckily I didn't get pneumonia nor even a little cold."[2]

The two men had known each other for some time, inasmuch as Cardozo was already chief judge of the Court of Appeals in 1928 when Roosevelt was elected governor. Yet in 1932 Cardozo still had his doubts about Roosevelt, telling his friend Learned Hand in July, "The nomination of F.D.R. leaves me cold, though I like him personally."[3] Cardozo, who had changed his official residence to the District of Columbia, was unable to vote, but this caused him no concern. Writing to Charles C. Burlingham shortly after the election, he said, "It is a glorious thing to be disfranchised as I have been by moving to Washington. I can look Hoover and Franklin D. squarely in the eye and not flinch with the thought that I have betrayed either one of them."[4]

Like most Americans, Cardozo quickly warmed to the President. Within a week of the inauguration, he was saying that Roosevelt had "done magnificently," and he became increasingly impressed by both the man and his program.[5] In January 1934, preparing to dine at the White House, he explained: "The President will be as gay and winning as if he didn't have a care in the world. How I envy him his boyish nature—the boy who has a precious gift of the wisdom appropriate for age. I think he has done a great piece of work. When men complain of his mistakes, I challenge them to show wherein his course could have bettered."[6] By the time the 1936 election rolled around, Cardozo, expressing none of his earlier reservations, clearly preferred Roosevelt to his Republican rival, Alf M. Landon: "Here in the U.S. the 'vested interests' prate mournfully about the aggressions of the Left, all unconscious, it seems, of the moderation of proposed changes as compared with the convulsions that are transforming life abroad. Roosevelt has made mistakes, but one has only to look at Landon's picture to be convinced that he is not the leader for days of stress and strain."[7]

In the first two years of the Roosevelt presidency the Supreme Court had no occasion to pass on the constitutionality of New Deal measures. In 1935 and 1936, however, the justices finally ruled on the most fundamental aspects of the recovery program and frequently found them defective. Four justices—Pierce Butler, James McReynolds, Willis Van Devanter, and George Sutherland—were staunch conservatives (widely known, in fact, as "The Four Horsemen"), and two others—Chief Justice Charles Evans Hughes and Owen Roberts—although more centrist in approach, were still hostile to the New Deal. Cardozo, Louis D. Brandeis, and Harlan Fiske Stone were the most liberal members of the Court, and of the three Cardozo was the most sympathetic to what Roosevelt was trying to accomplish. His affinity for the broad social objectives of the New Deal, conviction that changing times required a flexible reading of the Constitution, and commitment to judicial restraint shaped his outlook.

Judicial restraint, Cardozo believed, was a way of recognizing the provisional, contingent nature of policymaking. Judges must accept a new statutory formulation if it "is one that an enlightened legislature might act upon without affront to justice."[8] Whenever the issue was one on which "men of reason may reasonably differ," he said, "the legislature must have its way."[9] Cardozo expressed this view marvelously well in a dissent in *Steward Dry Goods Co. v. Lewis,* a 1935 case involving a state's right to impose a tax based on a business's gross sales rather than its profits. In enacting the levy, Cardozo asserted, the legislature had not acted arbitrarily. It had engaged in "no act of sheer oppression, no abandonment of reason, no exercise of the general will in a perverse or vengeful spirit. Far from being these or any of them, it is a pursuit of legitimate ends by methods honestly conceived and rationally chosen. More will not be asked by those who have learned from experience and history that government is at best a makeshift, that the attainment of one good may involve the sacrifice of others, and that compromise will be inevitable until the coming of Utopia."[10]

In January 1935 the Supreme Court rejected its first New Deal measure: a provision of the National Industrial Recovery Act which authorized the President to prohibit the interstate shipment of petroleum that had been produced or withdrawn from storage in excess of an amount prescribed by state authority. Congress had granted the executive this power over "hot oil" in order to raise depressed oil prices, and the question was whether or not the delegation was overly broad. The Court's opinion, written by Chief Justice Hughes, held that Congress had failed to furnish the President with clear standards. If so imprecise a delegation were sanctioned, Hughes wrote, "it would be idle to pretend that anything would be left of limitations upon the power of the Congress to delegate its law-making function."[11] Although Hughes wrote the opinion, it was Justice Brandeis who fired the barbed questions at the government's attorneys during oral argument.

Cardozo was the only dissenter. In his view the discretion granted the President was quite limited and made ample good sense. Congress had not given the President "any roving commission to inquire into evils and then, upon discovering them, do anything he pleases." To the contrary, Cardozo contended, his power was restricted to one commodity, oil, and only when it was produced or withdrawn in contravention of state law; besides, Congress had prescribed the means of enforcement. "The statute was framed in the shadow of a national disaster," Cardozo explained, adding that the separation of powers was "not a doctrinaire concept to be made use of with pedantic rigor. There must be sensible approximation, there must be elasticity of adjustment, in response to the practical necessities of government, which cannot foresee today the developments of tomorrow in their nearly infinite variety."[12]

Cardozo hoped that his stance, if unpersuasive to any of his brethren, would at least commend itself to writers in the law reviews, but as he told Karl Llewellyn, "When the vote is 8 to 1, one must expect disagreement outside the citadel as well as within it."[13] To his cousin Annie Nathan Meyer he explained: "The oil case worried me. But I had to speak my mind. Of course the newspapers gave only scraps of my dissent. I care little for praise or blame from the ordinary run of papers, even the better ones. They think only of the result that pleases them. I feel very confident that the law reviews will be back of me . . . But, of course, I may be wrong. One can only do one's best."[14] A number of legal scholars did indeed express warm approval.

In May 1935, in *A. L. A. Schechter Poultry Corp.* v. *U.S.,* the Court invalidated the linchpin of the early New Deal, the National Industrial Recovery Act. The vote this time was unanimous. The case centered on the National Recovery Administration's live poultry code, which, among other things, established a fifty-cent an hour minimum wage and a forty-hour workweek for the industry, prohibited the sale of diseased chickens, and, to prevent retailers from favoring certain buyers, required that they sell chickens by the coop rather than individually. The four Schechter brothers, who owned a kosher slaughterhouse in Brooklyn, were convicted of violating all of these provisions. There was no chance, though, that a Supreme Court which was unwilling to accept a code governing so vital a resource as petroleum would accept the poultry code. The opinion, again written by Hughes, rejected the government's claims, holding instead that the Schechters' intrastate transactions had a "merely indirect" effect on interstate commerce and so were not subject to federal regulation, and that there was an excessive delegation of legislative power to the executive.

Cardozo reached the same conclusion by a significantly different route. His concurrence, joined by Stone, argued that the distinction between businesses having a "direct" and an "indirect" effect on interstate commerce was not, as Hughes imagined, one of kind but rather one of degree. Even so, "the law is not indifferent to considerations of degree," and the Schechter brothers' intrastate transactions could not be brought within any sensible definition of interstate commerce. Cardozo also thought that there was a significant difference between the clear standards written into the delegation of authority in the petroleum code and the vague effort to prescribe "fair" competition in the poultry business. "What is fair, as thus conceived, is not something to be contrasted with what is unfair or fraudulent or tricky," he said. The delegation simply meant that "anything that Congress may do within the limits of the commerce clause for the betterment of business may be done by the President upon the recommendation of a trade association by calling it a code. This is delegation run riot."[15]

In 1936 Cardozo wrote dissenting opinions for the liberal minority in two important cases. The first, *Jones* v. *Securities & Exchange Commission,* involved a challenge to the SEC's investigative authority, not its constitutionality, but a serious challenge nonetheless. A Wall Street promoter named J. Edward Jones had filed a misleading registration statement with the SEC; he withdrew it at the last moment, citing that as grounds for refusing to comply with a subpoena requiring him to produce certain books and papers. The Supreme Court, in a decision by Justice George Sutherland, acted as if Jones were an innocent, unsuspecting man hauled before a high-handed tribunal. Denouncing the SEC's "unreasonable and arbitrary" procedures, Sutherland compared them to the "intolerable abuses of the Star Chamber."[16]

Here was a case tailor-made for Cardozo. "The rule now assailed was widely conceived and lawfully adopted to foil the plans of knaves intent upon obscuring or suppressing the knowledge of their knavery," he wrote, resorting to the descriptive if antiquated vocabulary he typically employed in cases involving ethical lapses in the business world. Conceding the need to guard against official abuses of power, he injected a note of reality into the deliberations: "Timely too is the reminder, as a host of impoverished investors will be ready to attest, that there are dangers in untruths and half truths when certificates masquerading as securities pass current in the market . . . To permit an offending registrant to stifle an inquiry by precipitate retreat on the eve of his exposure is to give immunity to guilt; to encourage falsehood and evasion; to invite the cunning and unscrupulous to gamble with detection." The SEC had no coercive power, could not arrest or imprison anyone (even if a crime was discovered), and acted under judicial supervision, he noted, yet it "is likened with denunciatory fervor to the Star Chamber of the Stuarts. Historians may find hyperbole in the sanguinary simile."[17] Justice Stone said privately what Cardozo only hinted at: that the Court's opinion was supported merely by "platitudinous irrelevancies."[18]

Jones was handed down in April, and the following month Cardozo wrote a dissent in another case more directly affecting the future of the New Deal, *Carter* v. *Carter Coal Co.* The Bituminous Coal Conservation Act of

1935 regulated coal miners' wages and hours. It provided that conditions of labor were to be regulated by a code, and, to ensure compliance, levied a tax on companies which refused to abide by the code's provisions. Carter brought a stockholder's suit against his own company to enjoin it from paying the tax. The majority opinion, written by Justice Sutherland, had far-reaching implications, for it attacked the "discredited" proposition that "the power of the federal government inherently extends to purposes affecting the nation as a whole with which the states severally cannot deal or cannot adequately deal, and the related notion that Congress, entirely apart from those powers delegated by the Constitution, may enact laws to promote the general welfare."[19] Sutherland could hardly have stated the New Deal's central proposition more precisely.

Where Hughes in *Schechter* had distinguished between "direct" and "indirect" effects on interstate commerce, Sutherland, following a precedent set in *U.S. v. E. C. Knight Co.* (1895), now distinguished between "manufacturing" and "commerce." Since bituminous coal mining qualified as manufacturing, it was outside the scope of the interstate commerce clause. Cardozo, writing also for Brandeis and Stone, thought the Court had fallen into a semantic trap. One could not judge the effect a particular enterprise had on interstate commerce by ritually invoking such words as "direct" or "indirect," or even more precise terms such as "intimate" or "remote." Cardozo stated his objection tersely: "A great principle of constitutional law is not susceptible of comprehensive statement in an adjective."

He also defended the proposition which, according to Sutherland, was "discredited." The government's power under the commerce clause, Cardozo wrote, "is as broad as the need that evokes it." Since nearly all the coal the Carter Company produced was shipped out of state, it was meaningless to say that mining operations involved only production and not commerce, for even if they did, "their relation to that commerce may be such that for the protection of the one there is need to regulate the other." Just he had referred to the actual harm caused by unscrupulous stock-jobbers in his SEC dissent, so Cardozo here referred to labor strife in the coal fields and to the resulting "violence and bloodshed and misery and bitter feeling." The coal producers, he added, had no constitutional right "to persist in this anarchic riot."[20]

Writing to Learned Hand, Cardozo presented what seemed to be an obvious truth about how he, Hand, and all federal judges actually decided commerce clause cases. Such adjectives as "direct" and "indirect" were inadequate guides, he reiterated, and substituting "immediate, proximate, or substantial" would not do the trick.

> They leave much to the judgment or intuition of the judge. So does every problem of causation either in the law of torts or elsewhere. You must size up the whole situation and say when you are through, "This consequence is close enough and that one is too distant to be attributed to an event put forward as a cause." I can't see that constitutional law exacts a different method, though of course there must be greater reluctance in holding that the causal tie is lacking if Congress has spoken and has found it to be present. The truth is, my dear philosopher, the law is a hopeless mess, and you will never make it less of a one by a rigid conceptualism. You will only turn the mess into a poison.[21]

Cardozo wrote this letter in the summer of 1936, at the end of a bitterly divisive term in which the justices had become increasingly waspish and short-tempered. In January, for example, when the Court declared the Agricultural Adjustment Administration unconstitutional by a six-to-three vote, Justice Stone's dissent blasted the majority's "tortured construction of the Constitution." In June the Court invalidated New York State's minimum wage law by an even narrower one-vote margin; Stone berated the majority for indulging its "own personal economic predilections." Shortly thereafter, Stone commented that the Court's term was "in many ways one of the most disastrous in its history."[22] Cardozo agreed, informing Stone, "we did indeed have a hard year in the Court. Next year may be bad, but certainly can't be worse."[23]

Cardozo, who had complained about Washington and the nature of the work on the Court ever since he was first appointed, now sank to a deeper level of despair. He no longer referred to the Court merely as a place of exile but rather as "the concentration camp at Washington."[24] He resorted more often to claustrophobic metaphors, as when he spoke of returning from vacation to find that "the walls of the prison house are closing about me rapidly."[25] He admitted, uncharacteristically, that the anxiety was getting to him, explaining to a friend, "I wake up often at night with nerves on edge as the result of worry about cases."[26] The worry may have contributed to a severe heart attack he suffered in June 1935 which left him bedridden for a month, under the daily care of nurses. He appeared to recover fully, however, and that fall resumed his labors on the Court. By the following summer he was able to make light of his condition. "When I speak of my feeble heart, I refer to its spiritual qualities," he told Annie Nathan Meyer in August 1936. "Physically the old heart is as good as senescence has a right to expect."[27]

Cardozo could not have foreseen that the age of Supreme Court justices was about to become the source of heated controversy; otherwise he might not have made such a remark, even in jest. In February 1937 the President announced his plan to increase the size of the Supreme Court, citing, as a justification, the advanced age of its members. Claiming that they were too old to remain open to new ideas or even to keep abreast of their work, he asked for authority to appoint an additional judge for each federal judge who had served for ten years and did not resign or retire within six months after reaching the age of seventy. This would have permitted Roosevelt to appoint up to six additional Supreme Court justices, for a total of fifteen, depending, of course, on how many of the older justices retired. Every member of the Court, Cardozo included, disliked the plan, viewing it as a personal insult and an affront to the independence of the judiciary.

Controversial from the start, the plan eventually was defeated but was in part responsible for a series of events that, in the short space of three months, revolutionized Constitutional law. On March 29 the justices upheld the state of Washington's minimum wage law by a five-to-four vote; Owen Roberts, who had cast the deciding vote against a similar New York statute in 1936, now switched sides. On April 12 Roberts again provided the needed vote by which the Court upheld the National Labor Relations Act. On May 18 one of the Court's crustiest conservatives, Willis Van Devanter, announced his resignation, thereby assuring Roosevelt the chance to consolidate his new-found if tenuous majority. On May 24 the Court handed down decisions which validated both the old age pension and unemployment provisions of the Social Security Act. Cardozo wrote for the majority in both cases.

Those opinions, *Helvering* v. *Davis* and *Steward Machine Co.* v. *Davis*, boldly affirmed three principles underlying the "constitutional revolution of 1937." First: the original intent of the Founding Fathers, even if discernible, was not necessarily binding on the present. Cardozo needed to make this point in the old age pension case because the First Circuit Court of Appeals, in ruling against the statute, had denied that the imposition of a payroll tax "was clearly within the purview of those who adopted the Constitution or the framers thereof, and where the application of a taxing statute is doubtful it should be resolved against the government."[28] Cardozo rejected this static concept of the general welfare: "Needs that were narrow or parochial a century ago may be interwoven in our day with the well-being of the Nation. What is critical or urgent changes with the times."[29] The real test, as he said elsewhere, was whether a statute was consistent with what the founders "would say today, . . . with what today they would believe, if they were called upon to interpret 'in the light of our whole experience' the constitution that they framed for the needs of an expanding future."[30]

Second: Congress had an obligation, in enacting legislation, to look facts squarely in the face. With respect to unemployment compensation: there had been a fearful rise in joblessness; it had crushing consequences for millions of families ("Disaster to the breadwinner meant disaster to dependents"); it was beyond the ability of the states, with severely limited revenues, to combat.[31] With respect to old age pensions, the facts were equally obvious: it was increasingly difficult for the elderly to find work as the nation became more urban; about three of every four elderly persons were, according to the Social Security Board, "probably dependent wholly or partially on others for support"; and human beings deserved a measure of security in their declining years. Here Cardozo's prose was worthy of a Dickens: "The hope behind this statute is to save men and women from the rigors of the poor house as well as from the haunting fear that such a lot awaits them when journey's end is near."[32]

Third: it was not for the Court to determine whether Congress had used its discretion wisely but only whether it had acted constitutionally. In making that determination the Court could not rely on a simple formula but had to allow Congress reasonably wide latitude. Here Cardozo reiterated a theme of his earlier opinions, only now he was writing for the majority: "There is a middle ground or certainly a penumbra in which discretion is at large. The discretion, however, is not confided to the courts. The discretion belongs to Congress, unless the choice is clearly wrong, a display of arbitrary power, not an exercise of judgment."[33] The justices should not try to provide conclusive answers to every question, such as: Where is the outermost limit of the taxing power? "We do not fix the outermost line. Enough for present purposes that wherever the line may be, this statute is within it. Definition more precise must abide the wisdom of the future."[34]

Taken as a whole, Cardozo's opinions support the view of the constitutional historian Richard D. Friedman: "Nobody on the Court was more consistently hospitable to broad assertions of governmental power to regulate economic matters."[35] But a related question then arises: Would Cardozo be equally hospitable to broad assertions of governmental power in dealing with individuals accused of having committed crimes? Conservative critics of the New Deal claimed that a government powerful enough to regulate the economy would inevitably be powerful enough to threaten personal liberty. In fact, in cases involving the rights of the accused Cardozo usually upheld the power of the state. The line between liberals and conservatives, etched so clearly on New Deal issues, was erased in these cases. Cardozo was as likely to be aligned with one or more of the Four Horsemen as with other, more liberal members of the Court.

Crime and Punishment: Defore and Miller

As a Supreme Court justice, Cardozo wrote the decisions in two major criminal justice cases: *Snyder* v. *Commonwealth of Massachusetts* (1934) and *Palko* v. *Connecticut* (1937). Those opinions were consistent with the views he had expressed as a judge on the New York State Court of Appeals. In Albany, where he frequently heard cases involving issues of search and seizure, the privilege against self-incrimination, and due process, he had taken a strong law-and-order stand. Two Court of Appeals cases illustrated his lack of sympathy for criminal defendants: *People* v. *Le Roy J. Miller*, decided in July 1931, just seven months before he was appointed to the Supreme Court; and *People* v. *Defore*, handed down in January 1926, in which Cardozo boldly rejected the applicability to New York State of rights-protective rulings of the Supreme Court.

John Defore was arrested in November 1924. Nineteen years of age and out of work, he had recently moved from Chicago to New York City, where he leased a room for $8 a week from one Mrs. Caldwell, who ran a boarding house on West 89th Street. He was in his third-floor room talking to a friend when Leslie Caldwell, the landlady's son, entered to say his overcoat was missing from his own room down the hall, and to ask if Defore knew anything about it. Defore said he did not, but when he left to go downstairs, Caldwell reentered the room, looked in the closet, and discovered the overcoat. While his mother kept Defore occupied, Caldwell called the police. Officer Edward Fitzgerald and two other policemen soon appeared on the scene. Defore denied having stolen the garment. Fitzgerald, accompanied by Leslie Caldwell, nevertheless went upstairs and searched Defore's room. He found two suitcases which he brought downstairs and opened in Defore's presence. One contained a blackjack, a slingshot, a billy, and a bludgeon, all contraband under the law. Defore was charged with petit larceny for the theft of the overcoat (valued at under $50) and was acquitted.

But in March 1925 he went on trial for possession of the blackjack, which in his case constituted a felony since it was a second offense (he had earlier been convicted of unlawfully possessing a pistol). His lawyer argued, first, that the arrest was itself unlawful, since a policeman could only make an arrest for a misdemeanor if the crime was committed or attempted in his presence, and, second, that the valise had been obtained through an illegal search and so the evidence was inadmissible. The judge overruled these objections. Defore took the stand to claim the bag belonged to a friend and he knew nothing of its contents. The jury found him guilty, however, and the judge sent him to the Elmira Reformatory. In May the appellate division of the New York State Supreme Court upheld the conviction, asserting that "the court should [not] be compelled indiscriminately to free all criminals who are fortunate enough to have competent evidence, which is necessary to establish their guilt, illegally taken from them."[36]

There was, indeed, no question that Defore was the victim of an illegal search. Fitzgerald did not have either a search warrant or Defore's permission, or even a reason to enter the room since the overcoat had already been retrieved. The only question was whether the evidence turned up in the search ought to be excluded. Section 8 of the New York State civil rights law, containing language identical to the Fourth Amendment, protected people from "unreasonable searches and seizures" and provided that warrants "particularly describing the place to be searched and the persons or things to be seized" would only be issued upon "probable cause." Section 6 of the state constitution incorporated the Fifth Amendment guarantee that no person "shall be compelled in any criminal case to be a witness against himself; nor be deprived of life, liberty, or property without due process of law." The district attorney argued that if Defore's rights had been denied, his recourse was to sue Officer Fitzgerald. Defore's lawyer described Fitzgerald's acts as "officious, bureaucratic and modeled after the worst examples of the Czarist and Prussian police and of the Soviet Cheka."[37]

By the mid-1920s a significant body of constitutional doctrine held federal law enforcement officials to a scrupulous observance of Fourth and Fifth Amendment rights. As early as 1886 the Court had rejected the use of evidence a defendant had given to the government under a threat that failure to do so would be taken as an admission of guilt. Justice Joseph Bradley said of this conduct: "It may be that it is the obnoxious thing in its mild-est and least repulsive form; but illegitimate and unconstitutional practices get their first footing in that way, namely, by silent approaches and slight deviations from legal modes of procedure."[38] In 1914, in *Weeks* v. *United States,* the Court had denounced a warrantless search, refusing to sanction the efforts of police "to obtain convictions by means of unlawful seizures and enforced confessions."[39]

Defore reached the New York Court of Appeals on December 1, 1925, just a few weeks after the Supreme Court, in *Agnello et al.* v. *United States,* fur-ther strengthened the *Weeks* standard. Frank Agnello was a member of a gang arrested for trafficking in cocaine in violation of the Harrison Act. Two federal undercover agents, posing as buyers, bought a few packets of cocaine from Agnello and his buddies; the police then barged in and ar-rested them. On the way to the station house the policemen stopped at Ag-nello's apartment and searched it without obtaining a warrant. They found a can of cocaine which was later used at the trial to refute Agnello's claim that he was unaware of the contents of the packets he had delivered and, in fact, had never even seen narcotics. Writing for a unanimous Court, Jus-tice Pierce Butler reversed Agnello's conviction (but not that of the other defendants). "The protection of the Fourth Amendment extends to all equally—to those justly suspected or accused, as well as to the innocent," Butler said. "The search of a private dwelling without a warrant is in itself unreasonable and abhorrent to our laws." Even "probable cause" to believe that an incriminating article was being concealed, he added, did not justify such a search.[40]

So Defore's attorney, James Marshall, armed with the decision in *Ag-nello,* may have felt particularly confident in arguing his client's case before the Court of Appeals. "There can be no difference in principle between the search of Frank Agnello's room, several blocks distant from the place of his arrest," he pointed out, "and the search of John Defore's bedroom, several flights of stairs from the place of his arrest."[41] But Marshall had not reck-oned on Cardozo's readiness and that of his fellow judges to reject the high court's approach. Cardozo was willing to concede that Defore's arrest was unlawful since the policeman had not witnessed the theft, and to concede, also, that the search was unlawful: "There is no rule that homes may be ran-sacked without process to discover the fruits or the implements of crime." Defore could have resisted the officer, or sued him for damages, or even prosecuted him for oppression. But could he insist that "evidence of criminality, procured by an act of trespass, . . . be rejected as incompetent for the misconduct of the trespasser"?

No, Cardozo said, because New York State was not bound to follow the federal rule. He pointed to an earlier Supreme Court decision which took a harder line than the more recent ones. He noted that most states had not accepted the current standard: of the forty-five states (not counting New York) which had considered the matter, only fourteen had adopted the *Weeks* rule and thirty-one had rejected it. He found it significant that commentators in the law reviews were divided. He observed that the state legislature had never changed its view that "the prohibition of the search did not anathematize the evidence yielded through the search." Finally, Cardozo asserted that the federal rule was inconsistent. It was "either too strict or too lax" since it did not permit the government to use evidence procured illegally by federal officials but did admit such evidence if procured by a private citizen, or, for that matter, by state officials.

On one level Cardozo was arguing that New York was not obligated to accept the federal rule. On another he was arguing that the Supreme Court, facing the same situation he did, and interpreting identical statutes, had made the wrong decision. The justices had placed individual rights above the protection of society, he said, and they knew quite well what they had done, for in *Agnello* "there has been no blinking the consequences." Cardozo then laid out those consequences, as he saw them, in a memorable sentence: "The criminal is to go free because the constable has blundered." He thus transformed the issue from one of protecting the innocent from official lawlessness to one of permitting the guilty to escape because a "constable" had "blundered," language suggesting a harmless image, a Keystone Kop, a well-meaning if inept flatfoot.

The Supreme Court's standard, Cardozo continued, could cripple the effort to obtain convictions even for the most heinous crimes. To clinch the argument, he offered up a chamber of hypothetical horrors: "The pettiest police officer would have it in his power through overzeal or indiscretion to confer immunity upon an offender for crimes the most flagitious. A room is searched against the law, and the body of a murdered man is found. If the place of discovery may not be proved, the other circumstances may be insufficient to connect the defendant with the crime. The privacy of the home has been infringed, and the murderer goes free." Cardozo admitted the force of the opposing argument: that his ruling would preserve the form but not the substance of the right against illegal searches, and, as Defore's lawyer pointed out, invite "a tyrannical and bureaucratic officialdom." But Cardozo saw no other way out: "The question is whether protection for the individual would not be gained at a disproportionate loss of protection for society. On the one side is the social need that crime shall be repressed. On the other, the social need that law shall not be flouted by the insolence of office." There were dangers lurking in either choice, he said, but fewer in his than in the other side's.[42]

At the time Cardozo's decision was widely approved, but eventually the scales tipped against him. Finally, in 1961, the Supreme Court ruled in *Mapp* v. *Ohio* that the Fourth Amendment's exclusionary rule would apply to state as well as federal trials. Justice Tom Clark's majority opinion took note of *Defore:* "There are those who say, as did Cardozo, that under our constitutional exclusionary doctrine 'the criminal is to go free because the constable has blundered.' In some cases this will undoubtedly be the result." But, Clark added, the principle of judicial supremacy must be upheld: "The criminal goes free, if he must, but it is the law that sets him free. Nothing can destroy a government more quickly than its failure to observe its own laws, or worse, its disregard of the character of its own existence . . . The ignoble shortcut to conviction left open to the state tends to destroy the entire system of constitutional restraints on which the liberties of the people rest."[43]

In a second case involving the rights of the accused, Cardozo came close to saying that the criminal should not go free because the judge—or, as he might have put it, the magistrate—had blundered. In 1931 the Court of Appeals reviewed the conviction of Le Roy J. Miller for the murder of Gladys Blaich, whom the newspapers called his "clandestine sweetheart."[44] The trial took place in January 1931 in Onondaga County Court before Judge William L. Barnum. It lasted three weeks and attracted hordes of curious onlookers "from the very nature of the case, the alleged killing of a girl by a married man who was her sweetheart, in a room in a country hotel, the nudity of deceased at the time of the commission of said crime, and the free discussion of sexual relations between the parties in said hotel."[45] The judge eventually closed the courtroom to spectators, which, as it turned out, was the least of his mistakes.

Miller, a thirty-seven-year old traveling salesman, had separated from his wife and had been seeing Blaich for about five years. On the evening of June 25, 1930, they drove to Fayetteville, a town five miles east of Syracuse, where they took a room in an inn, registering as husband and wife. The proprietor brought them a meal. Later, shots rang out and Gladys Blaich was found dead, bleeding from wounds in her chest and temple. Miller also ended up with a head wound. The prosecution claimed Miller had murdered Blaich and then somehow injured himself. The defense countered that Miller was sound asleep the whole time, so Blaich must have committed suicide. He remembered nothing, Miller testified, until he came to in the hospital several days later. The jury found Miller guilty, whereupon the judge imposed the death sentence.

Miller's attorney appealed the decision, arguing the trial had been riddled with prosecutorial misconduct and judicial error. He made many points, one of them that the judge's decision to lock the courtroom doors had deprived Miller of his right to a public trial (an objection that the Court of Appeals refused to consider because it had not been raised in a timely fashion but only after the verdict was announced). Two claims, however, had substantial merit. First, during cross-examination the district attorney had referred to the grand jury testimony of three defense witnesses, one of them Miller's mother; yet when the defense asked to see that testimony, the prosecution objected and the judge sustained the objection, holding that grand jury proceedings could be kept confidential. Second, the police had recovered letters from Blaich's room, ten of which were marked for identification. Although they were not offered in evidence, a prosecution witness was permitted to testify they had been written by the same man, obviously Miller. But the defense was denied access to the letters, because, in the district attorney's view: "Miller wanted to read those letters because his story was all made up, and he was afraid that there was something in those letters that might contradict . . . what he intended to tell, and that is why the desperate effort was made here to compel me to produce them."[46]

On July 15, 1931, Cardozo handed down the unanimous decision of the Court of Appeals. He began by saying that an opinion would not have been necessary "if it were not for erroneous rulings of the trial judge which in this case were harmless, but which if repeated in other cases, where guilt is not so clearly proved, might cause justice to be thwarted." Cardozo then addressed the decision to withhold the grand jury testimony. The district attorney could have refrained from asking about it, Cardozo said, but "he was not at liberty, after exhibiting so much of it as was helpful to the People, to deprive the defendant of the privilege of exhibiting the residue." Yet the error, he quickly added, "was not so substantial in its bearing on the fate of the defendant as to call for a reversal of the judgment of conviction."

The grand jury testimony was "too trivial in its significance" to have mattered. There was "no reasonable possibility" that if the defense had been allowed to use the transcript the jury would have reached a different verdict.

Cardozo next took up the problem of the ten letters. Again, Judge Barnum had erred, for he had discretion only over the timing of the letters' production. The judge's ruling, prohibiting inspection at any stage of the trial, "was error whereby the defendant would be aggrieved if there were a reasonable possibility that it had an effect upon the jury." Once again, however, the error was "harmless in its consequences." Cardozo felt confident in saying this because he had himself read the letters: the district attorney had submitted them to the judges of the Court of Appeals. Cardozo concluded: "We may doubt whether they would have been admissible in evidence if the defendant had chosen to offer them with the exception perhaps of one as to which the People may have opened the door by cross-examination." The letters merely documented Miller's feelings about Blaich, "and this was not disputed."

Cardozo's final point conveyed a certain discomfort on his part in upholding a verdict reached at a trial so deeply flawed, a verdict, moreover, which carried with it the death penalty. The judge, Cardozo noted, had committed yet another error when he had instructed the jury to consider the evidence with a presumption that Gladys Blaich had committed suicide; the proper instruction would have been to consider the evidence with a presumption that Miller was innocent. "This ruling is not complained of by the defendant," Cardozo remarked: "It is a ruling in his favor." It was as if to say that a judge who blundered was as likely to help defendants as to hurt them.[47]

Miller and *Defore* were only two of many cases in which Cardozo took a hard line on crime.[48] On the few occasions when he exhibited sympathy for defendants' rights there were usually extenuating circumstances.[49] In general, his outlook reflected his conservative instincts on social issues, but there is the hint of a more specific explanation in a letter Cardozo wrote in July 1923. He had just taken the train from Albany to his summer cottage in Allenhurst, New Jersey, he noted, and had arrived safely, "having encountered no pickpockets, thugs, or other undesirables."[50] Probably this was nothing more than a passing attempt at humor. But given his marked tendency to make light of matters (such as episodes of poor health) which he found threatening, it is possible that he was referring to an actual crime of which he had been the victim or intended victim.

In any event, his outlook was worlds removed from that of James Marshall, the unsuccessful attorney for John Defore, who said: "To lodge in the hands of the police the power to make unwarranted searches and seizures is far more dangerous to the commonwealth than to leave a blackjack in the hands of a thug. The thug, armed with such a weapon, may endanger a few individuals, but an ignorant or malicious official, secure in his power to disregard constitutional immunities, has by this token the same power to overthrow democratic institutions and the republican form of government."[51] Cardozo's perspective more nearly resembled that of John H. Wigmore, the conservative dean of Northwestern University Law School, who complained that the Supreme Court's strict exclusionary rule illustrated only the "misguided sentimentality" of those intent on "coddling the criminal classes of the population."[52]

Snyder v. Commonwealth of Massachusetts, 1934

On April 9, 1931, while the Miller case was making its way to the New York State Court of Appeals, another person was killed—and this time there was no doubt there had been a murder. James M. Kiley was on his second day on the job as a gasoline station attendant in Somerville, Massachusetts, just outside Boston, when, at about 7:45 in the evening, two armed youths entered the office. Brandishing pistols, one of them ordered, "stay where you are!" but Kiley, a thirty-nine-year-old World War I veteran, advanced toward him and grabbed him by the necktie. A shot was then fired from a .32 calibre automatic pistol; the bullet pierced Kiley's chest, exiting his back and shattering a window. The two men fled, jumped into a moving car, and sped off into the night. Other than the bullet and shell, the police had few clues. Only one eyewitness could offer a description of the assailants or the car, and that was not clear. It was the second such murder in Somerville in less than two months. To quiet public fears, the police chief issued pistol permits to gas station attendants and announced the formation of a "flying squadron, fully armed, . . . furnished with high powered cars."[53]

The first break in the case did not come until several weeks later, when a policeman noticed some youths acting suspiciously outside a Boston rooming house and then peering out, guiltily so he thought, from behind drawn curtains. He entered and found three guns (including, as it turned out, the murder weapon), and two blackjacks. The police then arrested the occupants, John A. Donnellon, Edward Consalvi, James T. Garrick,

Gertrude Rogers, and a man named Kearns. Donnellon, Kearns, and Rogers were soon released, but Garrick and Consalvi were indicted for first-degree murder. They remained in jail, awaiting trial, for a year. Meanwhile, a nationwide manhunt began for Herman "Red" Snyder, named as an accomplice.

A popular detective magazine ran his photograph in its September 1931 issue, and on April, 4, 1932, nearly a year after Kiley's slaying, a man residing in the Seamen's Home in Philadelphia happened to buy the back issue, recognized Snyder as a fellow lodger, and went straight to the police. Quickly taken into custody, Snyder was flown back to Boston, where he admitted that he and Donnellon were the two men in the gasoline station but denied that he had fired the fatal shot, and confirmed that Garrick had driven the getaway car. Consalvi, who had been languishing in jail for a year, now saw the indictment against him dropped. Donnellon, whom the police had mistakenly released, was quickly picked up in Los Angeles. Garrick, in consideration for turning state's evidence, evidently worked out some sort of a plea bargain.

The two defendants, Snyder and Donnellon, had spent much of their young lives getting into trouble. Snyder, twenty years old, was the son of Jewish immigrants. His father, Jacob, had come to the United States from Russia; his mother, Esther, from Poland. Since childhood he had suffered from seizures and fainting spells. When he was eleven his father was committed to an insane asylum, where he died four years later. At sixteen Snyder dropped out of school, taking odd jobs in a fish company and a tire shop. Twice he had run-ins with the law: for receiving stolen property (he was put on probation), and for carrying a slingshot (he received a suspended sentence). Donnellon, twenty-three years of age, had an even stormier youth. His father was an alcoholic who abandoned the family; his mother died when he was fifteen. At seventeen Donnellon was convicted of tire theft and spent nearly a year in prison. In all, he had twenty-two past arrests, many for public drunkenness.

The trial of the two men got under way on May 17, 1932. Both testified to entering the gasoline station with loaded pistols, and to abandoning the stolen car they had used after wiping it clean of fingerprints. There, however, agreement ended: each insisted it was the other who had carried the .32 calibre pistol and fired it. According to Garrick, however, when the two men entered the car it was Snyder who shouted, "For Christ's sake get out of here! I have shot the man!"[54] Assistant District Attorney Frank G. Volpe explained to the jury that it hardly mattered who had pulled the trigger: under Massachusetts law, if a murder was committed during an armed robbery, a crime punishable by life imprisonment, then all who took part in the robbery were guilty of murder in the first degree.

Snyder's attorney, Abraham C. Webber, offered several defenses: Snyder was engaged only in an attempted larceny, not an armed robbery; he had cried, "Beat it!" and had run out of the station when he saw Donnellon struggling with Kiley, thereby abandoning the criminal enterprise; he was legally insane, subject to violent mood swings and unable to tell the difference between right and wrong. But when Snyder took the stand he undermined this last plea by saying he knew it was wrong to enter the gas station armed with a pistol. In his closing argument Volpe called the defendants "wolves who kill on the streets and then cry for mercy in the courts." "If you have any sympathy," he told the jury, "give it to the courageous Kiley who was shot down like a dog in his gas station by gunmen who wanted money for women and liquor."[55] After a week-long trial, the jury required only fifty-five minutes to find both men guilty of murder in the first degree, a conviction that carried the mandatory death penalty.

At the opening of the trial Volpe had asked to have the jury "view" the crime scene. Webber immediately objected unless Snyder was allowed to attend, arguing that under both the federal and state constitutions "no evidence can be offered against anybody in a capital crime, in his absence . . . I take it that what the jury sees on a view is evidence and that is evidence against my client."[56] The trial judge, F. T. Hammond, rejected the request. He would allow Webber to be present but not Snyder (Donnellon's lawyer did not make an issue of his client's exclusion). The judge's ruling provided an important basis for Webber's appeal to the Supreme Judicial Court of Massachusetts. On April 7, 1933, that Court upheld the verdict, ruling that the trial judge had broad discretion over a defendant's right to accompany the jury "because the view is not a part of the trial, it being suspended while the view is taken."[57]

Another execution date was set, but on July 1, 1933, Louis D. Brandeis ordered a stay. Webber and three other defense attorneys had visited the justice at his summer home in Chatham, not far away, and had persuaded him that the decision to bar Snyder from the jury's view raised a substantial constitutional issue. A momentarily jubilant Webber informed the press that this was "the first time in 50 years that the highest court in the land had granted such a stay."[58] The Court heard oral argument on November 7, 1933, and handed down its decision on January 8, 1934, rejecting Snyder's appeal by a five-to-four vote. At the time, Brandeis remarked that "there is a story" about the case, but unfortunately he did not provide any details.[59] Part of the story, surely, was the voting alignment on the Supreme Court. Cardozo wrote the majority opinion, supported by Justices Stone, Hughes, McReynolds, and Van Devanter. Justice Owen Roberts wrote the dissent, and he was joined by Justices Butler, Sutherland, and Brandeis.

Roberts's dissent maintained that a view is a part of a trial, a truth accepted by the courts in every state but Massachusetts. In the Snyder case, moreover, the district attorney had called the jurors' attention to matters relating to distance, angles, and the relative position of objects in the Somerville gasoline station which "went beyond a mere showing, and . . . closely approached argument." The trial judge had assumed as much, Roberts noted, in his instructions to the jury: "Now, what have you before you on which to form your judgment and to render your finding and verdict? The view, the testimony given by the witnesses, and the exhibits, comprise the evidence in this case."

So the question before the Supreme Court boiled down to "whether the denial of petitioner's request to be present at the view deprived him of the due process guaranteed by the Fourteenth Amendment." The proper answer, Roberts concluded, was that it did, for the accused's right to be present throughout the trial "is of the very essence of due process." The accused must be permitted personally to "see, hear, and know all that is placed before the tribunal having power by its findings to deprive him of liberty or life." In any such proceeding, "the Fourteenth Amendment commands the observance of that standard of common fairness, the failure to observe which would offend men's sense of the decencies and proprieties of civilized life."

What particularly offended Roberts and the other dissenters' sense of decency and propriety was the assertion that Snyder had not suffered any harm by being excluded from the view because his being there would not have altered the jury's verdict. Even if that were true, Roberts said, "the denial of his constitutional right ought not be condoned. Nor ought this court to convert the inquiry from one as to the denial of the right into one as to the prejudice suffered by the denial. To pivot affirmance on the question of the amount of harm done the accused is to beg the constitutional question involved." When it came to the conduct of a trial, he concluded, "the guarantee of the Fourteenth Amendment is not that a just result shall have been obtained, but that the result, whatever it be, shall be reached in a fair way."[60]

To counter Roberts's argument, Cardozo restated the themes of *Defore* and *Miller*, although now he was speaking to a far broader audience than when he was on the New York State Court of Appeals. The Supreme Court, he said, should not find that the trial procedures adopted by a state violated the Fourteenth Amendment "because another method may seem to our thinking to be fairer or wiser or to give a surer promise of protection to the prisoner at the bar." Rather, a state was entitled to establish its own procedures, "unless in so doing it offends some principle of justice so rooted in the traditions and conscience of our people as to be ranked as fundamental." Some things surely were fundamental, Cardozo admitted, such as the opportunity to be heard in one's own defense. Other things were not, including trial by jury, grand jury indictments, and the privilege against self-incrimination. With respect to a jury view, the Fourteenth Amendment only meant that the accused had a right "to be present in his own person whenever his presence has a relation, reasonably substantial, to the fulness of his opportunity to defend against the charge." There was no such privilege "when presence would be useless, or the benefit but a shadow."

To explain why a defendant's presence at the jurors' view was not essential to "a fair and just hearing," Cardozo began with a hypothetical situation in which the view consisted only of "a bare inspection, and nothing more, a view where nothing is said by any one to direct the attention of the jury to one feature or another." Surely, he said, a defendant's presence would not then be required because its only purpose would be to ensure that the jury was, indeed, taken to the scene of the crime and not someplace else. Putting conjecture aside, Cardozo then pointed out that there was no dispute over whether the jury in the Snyder case had been taken to the right gasoline station. So if a defendant could be barred from a silent view, then Snyder could be barred from a view where counsel was permitted "to point out particular features of the scene and to request the jury to observe them." The difference between the two views "is one of degree, and nothing more."

Cardozo admitted that "one episode in the view must have a word of criticism." During the visit to the Somerville gasoline station, Judge Hammond had told the jury that one of the three pumps they saw had not been there on the evening Kiley was murdered, an unfortunate statement which went "beyond the bounds" of appropriate explanation. But "the blunder" by Judge Hammond "did not harm" Snyder since the pump's presence or absence had no bearing on the jury's verdict. Besides, Cardozo said, on returning to court the district attorney introduced a diagram of the station and told the jury it was agreed that one pump was not there when the crime was committed. Snyder and his counsel thereby "gave assent by acquiescence. In effect, the agreement was thus renewed and confirmed as if then made for the first time. The defendant was not hurt because it had been made once before."

As Cardozo saw it, the facts in the case were "uncontroverted": Snyder was guilty, the jury had found him so, and he deserved to be punished. So Cardozo thought he had succeeded in reconciling individual rights with social needs. On one side: "Privileges so fundamental as to be inherent in every concept of a fair trial that could be acceptable to the thought of reasonable men will be kept inviolate and inviolable, however crushing may be the pressure of incriminating proof." On the other: "But justice, though due to the accused, is due to the accuser also. The concept of fairness must not be strained till it is narrowed to a filament. We are to keep the balance true." The law risked being discredited "if gossamer possibilities of prejudice to a defendant are to nullify a sentence pronounced by a court of competent jurisdiction in obedience to local law, and set the guilty free."

Cardozo's opinion expressed the preeminent value he attached to social order. It also reflected many of the same assumptions that led him to approve New Deal social welfare legislation: an inclination to defer to legislative or judicial bodies unless a statute or procedure was "flagrantly unjust"; a tendency to conceive of differences in terms of degree, not kind; a reluctance to construe constitutional doctrine too rigidly (as he said in *Snyder*: "A fertile source of perversion in constitutional theory is the tyranny of labels"); and a realization that his own conceptions of right and wrong were only his and not necessarily everyone else's. As he put it, "Not all the precepts of conduct precious to the hearts of many of us are immutable principles of justice, acknowledged semper ubique et ab omnibus . . . wherever the good life is a subject of concern."[61]

Legal scholars praised Cardozo's opinion, but Felix Frankfurter voiced mild criticism. Writing from England, where he was teaching at Oxford, Frankfurter complained that the justice's view that the Fourteenth Amendment's due process clause had substantive meaning, even in the limited way he applied it, could be used by conservative justices to strike down state efforts at economic regulation. In his reply Cardozo agreed that "the criminal must have a square deal," adding,

> I tried my best in New York to give effect to that belief when cases of the third degree came before us for decision. I know you were not in sympathy with my view as [to] the effect of an illegal search, but that was probably a less important evil than brutality. Be that as it may, the Snyder case brought before us, not the question of the wisdom of the Mass. rule as to "views," but its validity—under the 14th Amendment—as you have been quick to appreciate. Well, I protest against the idea that I must change my conclusion as a sort of penance for the wrongs of other judges in applying the 14th Amendment too strictly where the statutes had relation to property or contract.

He would not be convinced, Cardozo concluded, "until you can prove me a sinner in cases where economic interests are at stake."[62]

A week before Cardozo wrote this letter, Herman Snyder and James A. Donnellon had gone to the electric chair. After the Supreme Court decision came down in January, Governor Joseph B. Ely had granted them a one-month respite so their lawyers could decide what to do, but, in fact, there was nothing to be done. After meeting with Snyder's mother and Donnellon's sister, and rejecting their tearful entreaties, Ely set the execution for midnight on February 20. That day, however, a winter blizzard hit the east coast, stalling the train which was carrying the executioner from New York City to Boston. So both men were granted one more day of life. They were electrocuted on February 22, 1934, just after midnight.

Cardozo had once reflected on a judge's duty to enforce the law, however harsh. In the summer of 1933 a friend, vacationing in England, had sent him a postcard with a picture of the lodgings of Sir George Jeffreys, England's infamous "hanging judge." Lord Chief Justice during the reign of King James II, Jeffreys had presided at the trials of hundreds of men who, having supported the abortive rebellion led by the Duke of Monmouth in 1685, were executed, many of them drawn and quartered. "I read a biography some years ago that made me feel he had been a good deal maligned," Cardozo wrote, perhaps only half-seriously, of the man known as "bloody Jeffreys." "The laws of his day were cruel and he enforced them. Perhaps posterity will think little better of us. What a reward—if I can't sell the 75th St. house—to have it reserved as a memorial—the home of bloody Cardozo."[63]

The Story of Frank Palka

The last opinion Cardozo ever read from the bench, *Palko* v. *Connecticut,* was an appropriate farewell message, for it encapsulated the major themes of his judicial career. He delivered it on December 6, 1937, and shortly afterward suffered a heart attack, followed by a stroke, which left him incapacitated. The case involved a man convicted by a Connecticut court of second-degree murder. The state, alleging errors by the judge, proceeded to try him again, this time obtaining a verdict of first-degree murder, punishable by death. The Supreme Court had to decide whether this constituted double jeopardy and, if so, whether the Fourteenth Amendment "incorporated" the Fifth Amendment's guarantee against double jeopardy so as to bind the states as well as the federal government. It will come as no surprise that Cardozo ruled against the defendant, whose name, in a twist of fate, was misspelled in a document somewhere along the way. His name was Frank Palka—not Palko—and his story begins late on a cool September evening in 1935.

At a few minutes after midnight on Monday, September 30, two men approached a music store in Bridgeport, Connecticut, owned by Joseph Gilman. One of the men smashed the plate-glass window with the butt of a .32 calibre Colt revolver, snapping its black handle grips, which fell to the ground. Each of the men grabbed a radio, and then they took off in different directions. A woman living nearby, hearing the glass shatter, called the police, who dispatched two patrol cars. Sergeant Thomas J. Kearney and Patrolman Wilfred Walker were in one of them. Spotting one of the thieves, Walker jumped out, reached for the man, and said, "Where are you going with that radio, bud?" while Kearney approached from the other side. Suddenly the man fired at Walker, hitting him, then turned toward Kearney and shot him, too. He had run only a short distance when the second police car arrived. There was an exchange of gunfire but no one was hit. Dropping the stolen radio, the man vanished into a maze of buildings and backyards. Patrolman Walker died two hours later, and Sergeant Kearney the next day.

It was the first time a Bridgeport policeman had been murdered in the line of duty in twenty-five years. And not just one officer, but two, both of them well known and popular—Kearney had been on the force for twenty-two years, Walker for nineteen—had been killed. The city's entire 260-man force launched "the greatest manhunt in the city's history" to avenge their fallen comrades. Detectives scoured the neighborhood for clues, and, hoping to find the murder weapon, "enlisted the aid of dump scavengers, rag pickers and junk men who might uncover information of value to them." The department rounded up "known criminals" and "suspicious characters," but all of them seemed to have airtight alibis. Rewards totaling $2,500 were offered. Police Superintendent Charles A. Wheeler made it known that the second burglar, if he came forward to identify the murderer, would be charged only with robbery and could expect lenient treatment.

There was one eyewitness, Joseph Schwimer, a police reporter for the Bridgeport *Telegram,* who had been riding with the officers in the second car and had gotten a good look at the man. But the only physical evidence the police had to go on were the handle grips, the bullets, and a faint, badly smudged fingerprint on the radio. Seeking the help of the Federal Bureau of Investigation, Wheeler wrote to Director J. Edgar Hoover, describing the print, enclosing contact photographs, and asking the FBI to search its files for a match. Hoover responded by sending a crack forensic expert to Bridgeport, but the fingerprint later turned out to be only that of a careless policeman. Meanwhile Lieutenant James Bray, a Bridgeport detective, took charge of the investigation.

A few weeks passed and then a lead developed: a woman reported overhearing that a young airplane mechanic, who lived in a rooming house, had suddenly quit his job, and that his roommate was acting peculiarly and also preparing to quit. This led the police to arrest one Frank Szryniawski, aged twenty-three, who went by the name of Frank Burke, and who had two roommates, one of them Frank Palka. (Ironically, both Burke and Palka had been awakened and questioned within two hours of the murders but had convinced the police they had been asleep the whole time.) The murderer, Burke said on being apprehended, was Palka, his accomplice in the robbery, who had recently gone to Buffalo. A quick check by the Bridgeport police revealed that Palka, whom the FBI identified as a paroled ex-convict, had failed to report to his parole officer, left his job, closed his bank account, and skipped town.[64]

Bridgeport detectives rushed to Buffalo, where on the afternoon of October 29 they arrested Palka. The newspapers reported that they spotted "the tall, muscular and well dressed young man in the Riverside Park section and leaped from their car to overpower him."[65] He was carrying a loaded .38 calibre pistol, a blackjack, $500 in cash, and a letter to friends in Bridgeport, reading in part, "Hello everyone. Just arrived and safe. Nothing new here. I didn't see anyone yet, but believe me when I passed the old homestead I sure wished I was there."[66] He offered no resistance. Handcuffed and taken to headquarters, he was grilled for five hours by Lieutenant Bray. He confessed orally to the murders of Kearney and Walker, saying he had fired at them because he feared being sent back to New York to face charges of violating his parole if caught burglarizing the store. He refused, however, to sign a written confession. Extradition was arranged, and by November 5 he was back in Bridgeport, "sullen and with a worn look on his face," in solitary confinement.[67]

Frank Palka was twenty-three years old. The oldest of four children of Julia and Andrew Palka, he was described by Bray as "the 'black sheep' of an honest Polish American couple."[68] The family had always resided in Buffalo, where the father worked as a steam shovel operator. Frank had not completed high school but early on had run afoul of the law. In May 1928 he was given three years' probation as a juvenile delinquent. Then he got into more serious trouble. In May 1931 he was convicted of statutory rape and sent to the Elmira Reformatory for a term of eighteen months to ten years. He was paroled in September 1932 on condition that he report to his parole officer every week and be at home by ten o'clock every night. In April 1935 he moved to Bridgeport, where he shared an apartment with his friends Frank Szryniawski and Thomas Iwanicki. While the former called himself Frank Burke, the latter went by the name of Tommy Evans. Palka got a job as a riveter in the wing shop of the Sikorski Aircraft Corporation, in nearby Stratford, where Burke and Evans also worked.

Palka's trial opened on January 14, 1936, in the Criminal Superior Court for Fairfield County. He was charged with first-degree murder in the death of Officer Kearney, presumably because the firing of the second shot presented the issue of premeditation most clearly. The presiding judge was John A. Cornell. To defend Palka, the court appointed David Goldstein, a thirty-seven-year-old graduate of New York University Law School who had represented Bridgeport in the State Senate for six years. He had recently taken on an associate, George A. Saden, only twenty-five, one year out of Harvard Law School. The prosecutor was William H. Comley. Sixty years of age, a graduate of Yale College and Yale Law School, he had formerly served as a city court judge in Bridgeport and was now state attorney. Lorin W. Willis assisted him.

The prosecution's case relied heavily on the testimony of Palka's roommates, Tommy Evans and Frank Burke, and Frank's brother Jack Burke

(Casimir Srzyniawski), who lived with his wife in the apartment below theirs. They sounded a single theme with only slight variations. Jack Burke alleged that Palka had entered the apartment about one o'clock on Monday morning, September 30, and blurted out that he had killed two policemen. Tommy Evans claimed he had returned to the apartment shortly thereafter (he had been visiting a woman friend) and found Palka in the bedroom, holding the gun, with the grips missing. Evans further claimed that Palka had said he killed the policemen, and that he had been stopped just before entering the apartment by two other officers and would have killed them, too, had they attempted to arrest him, but they had driven off. Frank Burke said he had gone with Palka to the music store, had stolen a radio and run home, but had been too drunk to remember anything else. Later that week, however, he had heard Palka admit responsibility for the murders. The three witnesses reported that they had gone to work on Monday morning with Palka, who had disposed of the revolver by throwing it into a creek behind the factory. Later, as he prepared to leave town, Palka had given Tommy Evans a code to use in writing to him, and also had had Evans send him his Certificate of Baptism, on which he had promptly altered his name to Leanard Adamski.

In questioning the three men Goldstein implied that they had concocted their story and rehearsed it down to the last detail in order to frame Palka and protect the real murderer, Frank Burke. When Palka took the stand he told a story consistent with this theory. He and Burke had purchased two quarts of rye whiskey on Sunday afternoon, he said, and spent most of the day polishing them off, although he found the time to stop in two bars, having two beers in each. By nine in the evening, Palka continued, he was so drunk he passed out, and remembered nothing until some time after two in the morning when he was awakened by the police and briefly questioned. In the morning Tommy Evans told him that he and Burke were involved in a break-in and murder. Over the next few days Palka talked to Evans and the Burkes, and, as Palka said: "Well, Jack Burke thought that it was all my fault that his brother Frank got into trouble, and after talking things over I told him to not worry, that I would assume all responsibility for whatever may happen, if anything happened."[69] It was simple enough, Palka said, to fabricate a story based on the newspaper reports.

The whole truth about what happened on that evening will never be known. A considerable amount of evidence pointed to Palka's guilt. First, although the murder weapon was never recovered, the deadly bullets had come from a .32 calibre Colt revolver, the same make as the one Palka had stolen; he did not deny that the black handle grips found at the scene came from that weapon. Second, Palka had shown a consciousness of guilt by closing out his bank accounts, disposing of the gun, altering his baptismal certificate, asking that letters to him be written in code, and leaving town for two days after the killings. Third, neither the owner nor either of two clerks in the drugstore where Palka said he had purchased the two quarts of rye could remember him. Fourth, the newspaper reporter, Joseph Schwimer, made a positive identification.

But none of this necessarily proved guilt beyond a reasonable doubt. When Goldstein asked Schwimer, "Is it possible that you might be wrong in definitely stating that this man was Palko? Is there a possibility, that is all I am going to ask you?" the reply was: "There may be."[70] Since it was illegal to sell liquor on a Sunday, those who worked in the drugstore had plenty of reason to say they could not remember having sold anyone two quarts of rye. The defense not only offered a reasonable explanation for Palka's behavior in the days following the crime but noted that by the middle of the week he had returned to his full-time job at the aircraft plant, hardly the action of a man who had murdered two policemen. Although Palka testified that he kept the gun in a strongbox in his room, he said that the key was readily accessible.

There were also serious inconsistencies in the prosecution's case. Schwimer's published account of the incident stated explicitly that one of the detectives fired first at the gunman, who then shot back, but the detective testified that the gunman had fired first, an important point for the prosecution since it suggested premeditation. The judge directed the jury's attention to an "entirely erroneous" aspect of Tommy Evans's testimony, also relating to the issue of premeditation. According to Evans, Palka told him that he would have shot the policemen who drove by as he approached his apartment if they had tried to stop him. As Judge Cornell pointed out, "That event could not have happened" because there was no squad car in the vicinity at the time.[71]

During the trial Judge Cornell made three crucial rulings, all favorable to the defense. First, he excluded the oral confession Palka had made to Bray while in custody in Buffalo. Bray admitted outside the jury's presence that he had not informed Palka he had a right to refuse to make a statement, and, worse yet, that he had lied to Palka by telling him that the Bridgeport police had arrested Jack Burke, his wife, Helen, and Tommy Evans, and that they had told the whole story. Second, the judge would not permit Evans to testify that Palka had stolen the .32 calibre Colt revolver from a tavern two months before the murders. Persuaded by Goldstein that the testimony would only "inflame the jury," Cornell admonished the prosecution: "You must be very careful here not to bring in evidence of unconnected crimes unless they come in almost of necessity in proving the case."[72] Third, Cornell refused to allow the arresting officer in Buffalo to testify that Palka was carrying a loaded .38 revolver, information which the defense argued was immaterial and prejudicial since he did not attempt to resist arrest.

But it was the charge to the jury which most troubled the prosecution. To prove murder in the first degree, the judge explained, the state had to show beyond a reasonable doubt that the defendant had acted "willfully, premeditatedly, deliberately and with malice aforethought." Defining the terms, Judge Cornell said that premeditation "requires that between the time that the perpetrator forms an intention to kill and the instant when he carries out such intention, there be an interval of time during which he gave thought to and reflected upon his purpose sufficiently to know what he was doing and what the probable effect of his doing it would be upon his victim." How much time had to elapse between intention and action was for the jury to say, "provided that the time between the two be such that opportunity is afforded the perpetrator to give sufficient thought to the purpose in his mind so that he realizes what he is about to do and that his design, if carried out, will probably kill or fatally wound the person against whom his intention is directed." Deliberation, the judge added, meant that the intent to kill "be carried out without haste or inconsiderately, but coolly."[73]

On January 24, 1936, after deliberating for two and a half hours, the jury reached a verdict. Judge Cornell, moved by the distraught appearance of Palka's mother, who had faithfully attended the trial, suggested that "it might be easier for her not to be present," and so she waited in the sheriff's office.[74] The jury then announced that it had found her son guilty of murder in the second degree, which meant mandatory life imprisonment. On January 28 the judge imposed that sentence, recommending that Palka never be pardoned or paroled. But the prosecutor, dismayed at not obtaining a conviction for first-degree murder, obtained the judge's permission to appeal the verdict. Connecticut law permitted such an appeal to the Supreme Court of Errors "upon all questions of law arising on the trial of criminal cases."[75]

In their arguments to that court, Comley and Goldstein presented radically different views of Judge Cornell's exclusion of the oral confession, disallowance of certain testimony, and instructions to the jury; both sides were able to cite Connecticut precedents in support of their claims. The larger issue involved conflicting conceptions of individual rights and social needs. To Goldstein, the mantle of the law protected everyone: "However depraved or vicious a defendant may be, whatever his mental tendency to commit other crimes . . . he is entitled to be tried only for the crime charged against him and upon the issues presented by his plea of not guilty, and only such evidence as is relevant thereto should be admitted."[76] To Comley, however, there was a more pressing concern. The case, he said, involved "the most serious of all crimes," and went beyond "the private injuries that are involved in the taking of a human life to the very foundations of peace and security of life and property in the community."[77]

The Supreme Court of Errors heard argument in June and handed down its decision on July 30, 1936. The five judges agreed that Judge Cornell had committed reversible error and that the state was entitled to a new trial. The judges were unanimous on the issue of jury instructions. Although Cornell's charge was technically correct since premeditation ordinarily required an interval between intention and action, it was a mistake to have told the jurors that "in the case of an armed burglar who is stopped in his efforts to escape with the stolen property, in determining whether or not there was premeditation they are to regard only the incalculable moment between his realization of the threat of arrest and the pulling of the trigger ready to his hand for that very purpose." The judges also agreed that the prosecution should have been allowed to cross-examine Palka concerning his theft of the .32 calibre revolver, since by taking the stand he had waived certain privileges, and burglary went to the issue of moral turpitude.

On two other matters, however, the judges were divided. A three-to-two majority upheld Judge Cornell's decision to exclude testimony that Palka was armed at the time of his arrest. But a three-to-two majority ruled against Cornell on the critical issue of the admissibility of Palka's oral confession. Even though Lieutenant Bray had failed to inform Palka of his right to remain silent, and had purposely misled the defendant, he had not made any threats, and "The test of admissibility is whether the confession was voluntary, and not whether the accused was well advised." Judges George E. Hinman and Christopher L. Avery sided with the defense on both issues, while Chief Judge William M. Maltbie and Judge Allyn L. Brown sided with the prosecution. The swing vote, therefore, was provided by Judge John W. Banks.[78]

These disagreements notwithstanding, state attorney Comley had gotten what he wanted, and Palka's second trial for the murder of Officer Kearney opened on October 8, 1936, in the same court before a new judge, Arthur F. Ells. This time around, however, Lieutenant Bray was permitted to describe Palka's oral confession and, to refresh his memory, refer to the unsigned written version. According to Bray, Palka said: "While I was going along the street a police car came up in back of me and the officer nearest to the curb got out and grabbed me by the shoulders. I don't know whether I had the gun in my hand or in my pocket but I remember the officer going 'Ugh' . . . and I remember another officer coming out of the same side of the car and he got very close to me . . . My mind went blank. I cannot tell what happened." He added, "If it was not for my parole I would never have shot him."[79] When Palka took the stand he testified that one Buffalo policeman had threatened, "I will knock your teeth out," but that the confession "was a story just the way we made up from the newspapers and with the assistance of Frank, Jack, Steve, and Tommy."[80]

On October 15 the jury returned a verdict of murder in the first degree, and Judge Ells imposed the death sentence. Now it was the defense's turn to appeal, and so David Goldstein and public defender Johnson Stoddard petitioned the Supreme Court of Errors. They made a number of arguments, but none so important as the one concerning double jeopardy, which they now raised for the first time on appeal. True, the Supreme Court of Errors had already upheld the statute under which the state had appealed. But protection against double jeopardy was "a doctrine so deeply rooted in the very heart of our legal tradition" and "so fundamental to every conception of English and American justice," they maintained, that its denial violated the Fourteenth Amendment.[81]

Comley offered a double-barreled rebuttal: this kind of retrial did not constitute double jeopardy—but, even if it did, it was permissible. The Connecticut courts had already held that "no double jeopardy is involved in a re-trial" because in such a situation "the accused has never escaped from the first jeopardy in which he stood." Besides, the Fourteenth Amendment did not prohibit states from subjecting their citizens to double jeopardy. The claim that Connecticut was precluded from doing so rested on the "remarkable proposition" that the state "has set up a process of criminal law which so violates our fundamental notions of justice and humanity as to be beyond the pale of 'due process.'" To ramble on about the principles of the English common law tradition was pointless, Comley said, for those principles, "about which so many rhapsodies have been composed, took form in an age when the great objective was to protect the innocent against political persecution and are now almost invariably invoked by the guilty to defeat what most people regard as the proper ends of justice."[82]

On March 4, 1937, the Supreme Court of Errors ruled unanimously against Palka. In a case such as his, where error is committed, "there is but one jeopardy and one trial . . . The second trial is not a new case but is a legal disposal of the same original case tried in the first instance." Moreover, past Supreme Court decisions made it clear that "the privileges and immunities of citizens of the United States do not necessarily include all the rights protected by the first eight amendments to the federal Constitution against the power of the federal government."[83] And so the stage was finally set for the Supreme Court to consider the issue. On November 12, 1937— more than two years after the murders of Kearney and Walker, more than a year after Palka's second conviction, and eight months after the date first scheduled for his execution—Benjamin Cardozo and his fellow justices heard argument in *Palko* v. *Connecticut,* the case involving a man who, for legal purposes, was known by a name other than his own.

"Ordered Liberty": Palko v. Connecticut, 1937

The brief submitted to the Supreme Court by David Goldstein and George A. Saden, but written largely by Saden, did, in fact, point out that the appellant's name "is properly spelled 'Palka.'"[84] This having been said, his attorneys, in a seventy-five-page document, did not mention his name again. The opposing brief, prepared by Lorin W. Willis, by now the state's attorney, and William H. Comley, also used "Palko" only once and thereafter merely referred to the "appellant." Nor would Cardozo's decision mention the man whose life was at stake. In the Supreme Court, issues pertaining to the trial, the testimony, the confession, and the evidence no longer mattered, but only questions relating to double jeopardy and the meaning of the Fourteenth Amendment.

Saden was on solid ground in arguing that the justices had before them a classic example of double jeopardy. The Court had said as much in a 1904 case involving a lawyer, Thomas E. Kepner, charged with embezzlement. Kepner, who practiced in Manila, was acquitted in a trial before a judge;

the United States appealed to the supreme court of the Philippine Islands, which reversed the verdict; a second trial led to a guilty verdict and a jail sentence. Kepner appealed to the United States Supreme Court, citing the Fifth Amendment's double jeopardy clause. The government claimed that Spanish law, which had prevailed before the United States acquired the Islands, ought to govern the proceedings, but the Supreme Court disagreed, holding instead that Congress intended the Constitution, and, of course, the Bill of Rights, to apply to the Philippines. Finding in Kepner's favor, although by a slender five-to-four vote, the Court held that "a person has been in jeopardy when he is regularly charged with a crime before a tribunal properly organized and competent to try him; certainly so after acquittal." The Fifth Amendment offered protection not against "the peril of second punishment, but against being again tried for the same offense."[85]

Saden ventured onto less secure terrain, however, when he argued that the Fourteenth Amendment's "privileges and immunities" and "due process" clauses incorporated this same right against the states, a point *Kepner,* a federal case, had not addressed. Seeking any foothold, however precarious, he turned first to history. He wished, he said, to submit "a scholarly document which, to counsel's knowledge, has not hitherto been called to the court's attention." It was Horace E. Flack's *The Adoption of the Fourteenth Amendment,* published in 1908 by The Johns Hopkins University Press. After combing through the congressional debates of 1866, Flack had reached an "inexorable conclusion": that "the effect and purpose of the Fourteenth Amendment was to incorporate the first eight amendments of the federal constitution under the due process clause of the Fourteenth Amendment so as to make them applicable to the states."[86]

Granted, the Supreme Court had not accepted this doctrine of full incorporation, but—and here Saden took the next tentative step—it had surely recognized that some elements of the Bill of Rights, notably freedom of speech, applied to the states as well as the federal government. In 1932, moreover, in *Powell* v. *Alabama,* a case growing out of the notorious trial and conviction of the "Scottsboro boys," the Court had applied the Sixth Amendment right to benefit of counsel in capital cases (and effective counsel, at that) to the states. Was the rule against double jeopardy any less vital, any less national in scope, indeed any less "sacred"? Not to Saden, who declared: "The right against double jeopardy is a right so fundamental that it ought once and forever to be placed beyond the control of governmental action."[87]

Willis and Comley endeavored on behalf of Connecticut to refute the double jeopardy argument. They contented themselves, however, with citing Justice Oliver Wendell Holmes's dissent in *Kepner*, where he said that "logically and rationally a man cannot be said to be more than once in jeopardy in the same cause, however often he may be tried. The jeopardy is one continuing jeopardy from its beginning to the end of the cause." The prosecutors further contended that the rule against double jeopardy was not "a fundamental principle of justice" and therefore did not deserve the special status the Court had accorded freedom of speech and the right to counsel. The rule, in fact, had lost whatever value it had once had. A long time ago, in England, it had served as a check on Stuart despotism. "But this is another day and another generation; and as in those days the problem was to secure justice against political autocracy, so in this day a very pressing problem is how better to secure decent, law abiding citizens against the growing threat of daring and defiant crime."[88]

This argument would certainly have appealed to Cardozo, especially when presented as a means of liberating the present from the dead hand of the past. Comley and Willis shrewdly claimed that the Connecticut statute permitting a retrial on the state's initiative showed "that the public policy of one generation may not, under changed conditions, be the public policy of another." But it was another phrase in the state's brief that captured Cardozo's attention. The prosecutors noted that the Connecticut courts' prior approval of the statute "contains no disparagement of the spirit of ordered liberty."[89] Striking language, to be sure, although hardly original. Herbert Hoover had mentioned "ordered liberty" in campaign speeches in 1928 and again in 1932. But the symmetry of the phrase, its apparent reconciliation of incongruous concepts, was perfectly suited to Cardozo's outlook, to his lifelong quest for the happy mean.

Cardozo's opinion in favor of Connecticut, which was joined by all the justices save Pierce Butler, who dissented but gave no reason, takes up only slightly more than eight pages in the Supreme Court Reports. It revealed many of Cardozo's strengths as a judge and most of his weaknesses. His admirers maintain that *Palko* preserved the delicate balance between communal values and individual liberties. "Acting his part in the constitutional distribution of authority," John T. Noonan Jr., has written, "Cardozo had let the community vindicate its officers."[90] John Raeburn Green, however, has characterized Cardozo's opinion as a "belletristic essay, which gave the scantiest consideration to profoundly important matters."[91] Whatever the disagreements, for more than thirty years Cardozo's opinion served as a canonical text for judges and legal scholars who favored selective incorporation, the doctrine that under the Fourteenth Amendment's due process clause only some provisions of the Bill of Rights, not all of them, applied to the states.

At the outset, Cardozo summarized the facts of the case and the lower court rulings and then immediately announced the Court's decision: "The execution of the sentence will not deprive appellant of his life without the process of law assured to him by the Fourteenth Amendment of the Federal Constitution." Even before presenting the defense's argument, therefore, he had signaled that it was not going to be found persuasive. That argument, Cardozo continued, was that the retrial, "though under one indictment and only one," constituted double jeopardy and that "whatever is forbidden by the Fifth Amendment is forbidden by the Fourteenth also." This represented only one aspect of Saden's full incorporation theory, but the aspect—concerning double jeopardy—which Cardozo wished to address first. In fact, he wanted to find a way to employ the Court's decision in *Kepner*, which seemed to bolster the defense, to support an opposite result.

He began this way: "We do not find it profitable to mark the precise limits of the prohibition of double jeopardy in federal prosecutions." He noted that the issue had been "much considered" in *Kepner* and decided "by a closely divided court." He then summarized the majority view, which forbade jeopardy in the same case if the new trial was at the instance of the government, and conceded that "all this may be assumed for the purpose of the case at hand." That is, the federal government would not have been able to do to Palka what Connecticut had done to him. Nevertheless, the dissenting opinions in *Kepner* "show how much was to be said in favor of a different ruling. Right-minded men . . . could reasonably, even if mistakenly, believe that a second trial was lawful . . . Even more plainly, right-minded men could reasonably believe that in espousing that conclusion they were not favoring a practice repugnant to the conscience of mankind."

So the lesson to be drawn from *Kepner* was not that the kind of double jeopardy to which the Manila lawyer had been exposed violated the Fifth Amendment; rather, it was that intelligent people could reasonably disagree about what constituted double jeopardy. Cardozo now felt confident in applying this lesson to the Connecticut case: "Is double jeopardy in such circumstances, if double jeopardy it must be called, a denial of due process forbidden to the states?" Not at all, because the consciences of at least four justices, all of them right-minded, found it acceptable. Cardozo had actually reformulated the issue, for the division in *Kepner* was over whether a certain procedure constituted double jeopardy, not over whether the immunity from double jeopardy was repugnant to the conscience of mankind.

Now he was ready to take on the full incorporation argument. The defense contended, he said, that "whatever would be a violation of the original bill of rights (Amendments I to VIII) if done by the federal government is now equally unlawful by force of the Fourteenth Amendment if done by a state. There is no such general rule." To demonstrate this Cardozo recapitulated prior Supreme Court rulings. On the one hand, the Court had refused to apply certain features of the Bill of Rights to the states, such as the Fifth Amendment provisions for a grand jury indictment and protection against self-incrimination and the Sixth Amendment right to trial by jury. On the other hand, the Court had employed the due process clause to protect freedom of speech and the press, the free exercise of religion, the right of peaceable assembly, and the right to benefit of counsel in certain cases. He concluded: "In these and other situations immunities that are valid as against the federal government by force of the specific pledges of particular amendments have been found to be implicit in the concept of ordered liberty, and thus, through the Fourteenth Amendment, become valid as against the states."

Cardozo's classification of prior decisions was technically correct but somewhat misleading. The cases involving the "unincorporated" rights had arisen in the period between the Civil War and World War I, those involving the "incorporated" rights in the decade from 1925 to 1935. True enough, the more recent decisions had affected rights under the First, not the Fifth Amendment, and in that sense the Court was being asked to do something quite novel. Yet the justices had shown a willingness to amplify the individual rights that were protected against state action. The issue before the Court in 1937 was whether the protection against double jeopardy should be added to that list. Cardozo made it appear as if the issue was whether the protection against double jeopardy fell on one side or another of a fixed line.

That line, Cardozo wrote, "may seem to be wavering and broken if there is a hasty catalogue of the cases on the one side and the other. Reflection and analysis will induce a different view. There emerges the perception of a rationalizing principle which gives to discrete instances a proper order and coherence." The incorporated rights, he said, "may have value and importance. Even so, they are not of the very essence of a scheme of ordered liberty." To abolish trial by jury and grand jury indictments would not violate those principles of justice, and here he quoted his own opinion in *Snyder* v. *Massachusetts,* "so deeply rooted in the traditions and conscience of our people as to be ranked as fundamental." A "fair and enlightened system of justice" would still be possible without them. The same was true of the immunity from compulsory self-incrimination. "This too might be lost, and justice still be done." Some even considered the immunity "a mischief rather than a benefit," and would abolish it. "No doubt there would remain the need to give protection against torture, physical or mental," he conceded, adding: "Justice, however, would not perish if the accused were subject to a duty to respond to orderly inquiry." So the line of division between the two sets of rights had been "dictated by a study and appreciation of the meaning, the essential implications, of liberty itself."

Turning to those liberties which the Court had placed under the shield of the Fourteenth Amendment, Cardozo said that "neither liberty nor justice would exist if they were sacrificed." This was true of freedom of speech: "Of that freedom one may say that it is the matrix, the indispensable condition, of nearly every other form of freedom." So, too, the Court had protected "liberty of the mind as well as liberty of action." A rejoinder to this argument, which Cardozo did not address, could be found in George Saden's brief on behalf of Frank Palka. Since the right against double jeopardy "protects life itself as well as liberty," Saden asserted, it should be considered "paramount" to any other: "Free speech, a free press, peaceable assembly, the aid of counsel, and just compensation for property are of little value to a dead man."

Cardozo faced one final hurdle: the Court's position, and his own vote, in *Powell* v. *Alabama.* Why, after all, should the Sixth Amendment's right to benefit of counsel in capital cases apply to the states, but not the Fifth Amendment's immunity from double jeopardy? The nine black youths who had been accused of raping two white women in Scottsboro, Alabama, had been provided with a lawyer who was incapable of mounting an adequate defense. The Supreme Court had held that the failure "to make an effective appointment of counsel" was "a denial of due process within the meaning of the Fourteenth Amendment."[92] Cardozo plausibly maintained that the right to counsel protected in *Powell* did not derive from incorporation of the Sixth Amendment but rather from the phrase "due process" in the Fourteenth Amendment. He offered the following explanation: "The decision did not turn upon the fact that the benefit of counsel would have been guaranteed to the defendants by the provisions of the Sixth Amendment if they had been prosecuted in a federal court. The decision turned upon the fact that in the particular situation laid before us in the evidence the benefit of counsel was essential to the substance of a hearing."

The way was now clear for Cardozo to relate his general argument to the specific case before him. There was a dividing line, he reiterated, which, "if not unfaltering throughout its course, has been true for the most part to a unifying principle." On which side of the line did *Palko* fall? "Is that kind of double jeopardy to which the statute has subjected him a hardship so acute and shocking that our polity will not endure it?" This formulation represented a dramatic verbal escalation: Cardozo had first talked about a practice repugnant to conscience; then about a practice that violated fundamental principles of justice; and now about a practice that created an unendurably acute and shocking hardship. Phrased that way, the question was an easy one: "The answer surely must be 'no.'"

Cardozo conceded that the answer might be different if the state were seeking to retry a person after a trial free from error, but that was not the situation presented to the Court. "The state is not attempting to wear the accused out by a multitude of cases with accumulated trials. It asks no more than this, that the case against him shall go on until there shall be a trial free from the corrosion of substantial legal error . . . This is not cruelty at all, nor even vexation in any immoderate degree." The state merely sought the same right to appeal a verdict based on error that defendants already had. "There is here no seismic innovation. The edifice of justice stands, its symmetry, to many, greater than before."[93] On April 12, 1938, Frank Palka, playing his part in maintaining that edifice, went to the electric chair "without the slightest faltering or tremor or word."[94]

As John Raeburn Green has pointed out, Cardozo was saying in effect that "the rights of the accused guaranteed by the Bill of Rights were nice things to have, no doubt, but luxuries, not necessities."[95] In one way or another he had been saying the same thing in *Defore, Miller,* and *Snyder.* Yet Cardozo presented a more elaborate theoretical justification for his position in *Palko,* which therefore raised thornier problems than the earlier cases. Cardozo was maintaining three related propositions: that there was an agreed-on hierarchy of rights, that there was a rational way of determining where in that hierarchy a given right stood, and that there was a bright line between rights that were and were not "of the very essence of a scheme of ordered liberty." But Cardozo's "vague formulations," as Richard C. Cortner has said, furnished no reliable criteria for making any of those determinations.[96]

Nevertheless, in later years Cardozo's decision became the lodestar for those who supported the doctrine of selective incorporation. *Palko* pointed the way for Justice Felix Frankfurter, the most ardent champion of that doctrine, when he voted against applying the right to counsel and the privilege against self-incrimination to the states.[97] Ironically, Justice Hugo Black, who had voted with Cardozo in 1937, emerged as the harshest critic of *Palko*. By 1942 he was saying that "the Fourteenth Amendment made the Sixth applicable to the states," and citing the same Horace E. Flack whose work Palka's lawyers had first brought to the Court's attention. In 1947 Black proposed a theory of total incorporation, claiming that it provided the only alternative to "the Court's practice of substituting its own concepts of decency and fundamental justice for the language of the Bill of Rights." The original purpose of the Fourteenth Amendment, he declared, was "to extend to all the people of the nation the complete protection of the Bill of Rights."[98]

The Supreme Court never accepted this in theory, but it did what Black would see as the next best thing: it accepted it in practice. The process of incorporating the criminal justice provisions of the Bill of Rights began with *Mapp* v. *Ohio* in 1961 and culminated in *Benton* v. *Maryland* in 1969. In that case the Court expressly rejected the *Palko* doctrine of the inapplicability of double jeopardy to the states. Justice Thurgood Marshall spoke for the majority: "We today find that the double jeopardy prohibition of the Fifth Amendment represents a fundamental ideal in our constitutional heritage, and that it should apply to the States through the Fourteenth Amendment." The Court, as Marshall explained, was rejecting in its entirety *Palko's* "approach to basic constitutional rights." The validity of a defendant's claim could no longer be judged, Marshall said, "by the watered-down standard enunciated in *Palko*."[99]

Justices John Marshall Harlan and Potter Stewart dissented; Harlan, the most notable defender of the Cardozo-Frankfurter approach, complained: "Today *Palko* becomes another casualty in the so far unchecked march toward 'incorporating' much, if not all, of the Federal Bill of Rights into the Due Process Clause." That march, Harlan argued, threatened to destroy the principle of federalism. He had high praise for the decision Thurgood Marshall so brusquely dismissed: "More broadly, that this Court should have apparently become so impervious to the pervasive wisdom of the constitutional philosophy embodied in *Palko*, and that it should have felt itself able to attribute to the perceptive and timeless words of Mr. Justice Cardozo nothing more than a 'watering down' of constitutional rights, are indeed revealing symbols of the extent to which we are weighing anchors from the fundamentals of our constitutional system."[100]

So the Supreme Court eventually expanded the rights of defendants in state criminal trials. But in 1937 it was logical to assume that *Palko* would lead to a further limitation of those rights. Writing in the *Atlantic Monthly*, George W. Alger, a New York City lawyer, praised Cardozo for favoring a system "in which the rights of the law-abiding are preserved and maintained, and crime both punished and repressed." Alger particularly noted Cardozo's comment that immunity from compulsory self-incrimination was not part of a scheme of ordered liberty. That opened the door for states to require such testimony under proper safeguards. The *Palko* decision, Alger said, was "written in that extraordinarily luminous English with which this Rembrandt of judicial statement expressed the logic of justice."[101] An artistic decision, perhaps, but it was a narrow palette Cardozo brought to his rendering of the Fourteenth Amendment. A later generation of jurists would have a keener appreciation of the creative possibilities implicit in its texture and design.

EPILOGUE

A Contested Legacy

One source of Benjamin Cardozo's unhappiness during his years on the Supreme Court was the attention the press paid to the justices' personal lives. He was especially irked by Drew Pearson and Robert W. Allen, authors of the widely syndicated "Washington Merry-Go-Round" column, whose 1932 volume, *More Merry-Go-Round,* contained a chapter entitled "Nine Old Men." It was, Cardozo said, a "Horrid book!"[1] In their highly flattering portrait of Cardozo, the authors noted that he led a restricted social life: "The new Justice eschews formal society, but is a charming, gay and witty companion in a small gathering."[2] Even that innocuous comment left a bitter taste. Four years later, when Pearson and Allen published *The Nine Old Men,* an updated, book-length version of the earlier chapter, Cardozo alluded to the remark, scribbling some rhymes on a card which he sent to his cousin Maud Nathan:

> I have told the secrets of my life
> In a book of many pages,
> I have a wit that never fails
> A charm that never ages.[3]

Publication of *The Nine Old Men* followed by a few months the appearance of a long, and to Cardozo equally painful, essay in the May 1936 issue of *Fortune.* The article contained long biographical sketches of each member of the Court, and once again Cardozo came off looking good. "For sheer lovableness the Justice sets some sort of record," the author said, adding that this trait had led the press to limit any reference to the misconduct of his father, "a once-notorious Tweed Ring judge," to "the merest innuendo." Cardozo's "congenital gentleness and modesty," chivalric attitude toward women, retiring and unworldly nature—all were mentioned.[4] "When I am dead I shall be glad to have some one write of me as 'Fortune' did," Cardozo said: "I think it is not the kind of article that should be written of the living."[5]

The only book published about Cardozo during his lifetime was Joseph P. Pollard's *Mr. Justice Cardozo: A Liberal Mind in Action.* A graduate of Harvard Law School, class of 1923, Pollard practiced law for a few years and then took up a dual career as teacher and writer. His book appeared in September 1935 with a foreword by Roscoe Pound, the dean of Harvard Law School. Based primarily on an analysis of Cardozo's decisions in the New York State Court of Appeals, but containing a brief account of his first three years on the Supreme Court, Pollard's work praised its subject effusively as a jurist whose "humanity and honor and fair play [were] woven into the law through the loom of a prodigious learning, an understanding of modern human needs, and a vivid and striking power of expression."[6]

Cardozo's reaction was, nevertheless, positively bilious. He wrote to Roscoe Pound, asking how he could have agreed to contribute a foreword to such a monstrosity. (Pound answered apologetically that if he had not consented, someone else would have written a worse one.)[7] He told Maud Nathan he was sorry she had bought the book. "It's a fearful piece of work," he told her, a "horrid thing," a "tragedy."[8] Reading a critical review by the Harvard law professor Thomas Reed Powell in the *New York Herald Tribune,* Cardozo hastily assured him he had nothing to do with "Pollard's fearful book." "If an author writes a book of that kind without notice to the victim," Cardozo added, "the law should require a label that composition and publication were without the victim's knowledge or consent."[9]

In the months and years that followed, whenever he thought of Pollard's book, Cardozo became indignant all over again. The language of victimization was soon replaced by the still more powerful imagery of violation. In October 1936, when a copy of Alfred Lief's *Brandeis: The Personal History of an American Idea* came his way, Cardozo told Charles C. Burlingham: "I was once the victim of an unauthorized and impertinent biographer. Whether

Lief was an intruder I am uncertain. Perhaps if not an 'invitee' (horrid word), he was at least a licensee, and not a wicked trespasser."[10]

Given Cardozo's intensely private nature, it was predictable that his final, incapacitating illness would be kept from the public. The details, indeed, were withheld even from some of his best friends. The decline began on December 10, 1937, when Cardozo experienced a heart attack; a second such incident followed on the 19th. He suffered also from an excruciating case of shingles, and his doctors were not sure "whether the pain from the shingles caused the heart condition or the other way around."[11] Despite his weakened state he managed a letter to Burlingham on December 31: "The pain of shingles is 'exquisite.' In my case a wicked old heart brought about some complications, but I am told that the heart muscles are evincing a satisfaction with present conditions which is not shared by their owner."[12] By January 5 he was able to dictate, but not write, a reply to a get-well message from Franklin D. Roosevelt, concluding, "I cannot rest in comfort without telling you, however brokenly, of all my pride and gratitude."[13] On January 8, 1938, there came a crushing setback: a stroke which left Cardozo's left arm and leg partially paralyzed and cost him the vision in his right eye.

The full extent of his disability was known only to Kate Tracy and other members of his household staff, his law clerks, Christopher S. Sargent and Joseph L. Rauh Jr., a few family members, the Lehmans, and, of course, his doctors and nurses. As Sargent told Annie Nathan Meyer: "Needless to say we are keeping the nature of his illness a secret, and have informed the papers that he has the grippe. And now the secret is yours to guard with us."[14] But even Meyer, who received frequent reports on Cardozo's condition, was unprepared for the sight of her beloved cousin on a brief visit in mid-March. Although she had been informed that he had experienced "periods of great weakness and depression," and that for a time, in January, he had been kept "entirely under the influence of morphine" to ensure rest, she had not been told about the stroke until just before she entered his room.[15] "It was a great shock. I was startled to see how strongly he resembled his mother, my aunt, who had been paralyzed for some years before her death."[16]

By the spring of 1938 members of the Supreme Court, who were naturally concerned by Cardozo's absence, tried diplomatically to find out whether he would be able to resume his duties. His best friend on the Court, Harlan Fiske Stone, who was also the most fully informed about his medical status, gently reminded Irving Lehman that should Cardozo be unable to return in the fall, steps had to be taken quickly to secure for him "the privilege of the retirement act."[17] Lehman replied on April 28, two days after Cardozo had been moved from Washington to Lehman's home at Port Chester, New York. (The house was equipped with an elevator convenient to Cardozo's second-floor bedroom and with wheelchair ramps.) Since his arrival, Lehman wrote, "the improvement is so great that I can see little effect of his last set-back." Cardozo was able to sit for a short while on the outdoor porch, "and we have had a talk quite reminiscent of old times. However slender may be the hope of complete recovery, I still cling to it."[18] Again, on June 1, Lehman reported to Stone that Cardozo "has improved noticeably, although the improvement is slower than his friends would wish."[19]

Yet it was surely obvious to Stone and his colleagues that this hopeful prognosis had little basis in fact. In March, when Chief Justice Charles Evans Hughes made a call, he was permitted to stay no more than a minute. And while Cardozo had improved sufficiently for his doctors to consent to the move to Port Chester, and was able to sit up and even be taken for short drives, there was no reason to believe he would ever be able to resume the burdens of judicial office. On May 23, the day before Cardozo's sixty-eighth birthday, Burlingham paid a visit, but no one was permitted to see him after that because, as Rauh explained, "he has become so highly emotional—partly over his birthday—that visitors evoke tears and sadness generally."[20] If Justice Stone had any remaining doubts, they must have been dispelled by a letter he received from Cardozo, dated June 14. The once splendidly assertive handwriting was reduced to a barely legible scrawl. It must have taken a mammoth effort of will for Cardozo to write even the few words he did, and by the end of the letter his exhaustion was painfully evident. It would be the last letter Benjamin Cardozo ever wrote.[21]

On June 25 he suffered a heart attack, followed on July 1 by another one. Placed in an oxygen tent, he was given blood transfusions and intravenous feedings. According to one of his attending physicians, Dr. Curlin C. Craven, "In delirium, as in his conscious moments, Justice Cardozo's whole interest in his life seemed to be to try to recover for his work. In delirious moments he went over and over again old decisions and court cases. Outside the delirium his mind was surprisingly clear. He was never able to express the hopelessness of his plight. Under opiates the severe pain of his condition was alleviated. I believe he died without hurt."[22] Death came at last on Saturday, July 9, at 6:40 in the evening, as the result, Dr. Craven reported, of "a coronary thrombosis, that is, a clot in the blood vessels of the heart." Joseph Rauh's wife notified the press. Irving Lehman was "too broken up" to issue a statement, as, presumably, was Rauh himself.[23]

Funeral services were held early on Monday afternoon at the Lehman estate. Rev. D. A. Jessurun Cardozo, not a relative, the assistant minister of Congregation Shearith Israel, presided (the minister, Dr. David de Sola Pool, was in London, where he had gone for his father's funeral). It was an Orthodox service, lasting about ten minutes, consisting simply of the reading in Hebrew of the Twenty-Third Psalm and passages from the Book of Proverbs. At Cardozo's request there was no eulogy. Among the two hundred guests were Eleanor Roosevelt, Secretary of the Treasury Henry Morgenthau, Associate Justices Pierce Butler, Owen J. Roberts and Stanley J. Reed (appointed in January 1938 when George Sutherland retired), Governor Herbert Lehman, Senator Robert F. Wagner, Rabbi Stephen S. Wise, Professor Felix Frankfurter, Charles C. Burlingham, George H. Engelhard (Cardozo's old law partner), and Annie Nathan Meyer and Maud Nathan. The coffin, covered with roses with one tall candle burning beside it, rested on an improvised altar in the library. The funeral cortege then proceeded to Cypress Hills Cemetery in Queens, where, as a slight drizzle fell, the mourners recited the Kaddish and Cardozo's coffin was lowered to his final resting place, near the gravesites of his mother, his father, his brother, and all his sisters excepting Emily, his twin, who had married a Christian and who, according to Orthodox Jewish law, could not be buried in holy ground.

Some who were present that afternoon were distressed by the nature of the Orthodox service, which, conducted entirely in Hebrew, seemed to them meaningless and inappropriate. It was commonly assumed that Cardozo's decision to follow Orthodox ritual, like so many decisions he had made, was dictated by what he believed his older sister Nell would have wanted. Even so, Irving Lehman, according to Burlingham, thought the service was "awful," and Burlingham also expressed surprise: "I didn't know the Sephardim were, or was, so fundamentalistic."[24] Kate Tracy, too, was disappointed that Stephen S. Wise, a reform rabbi, had not officiated or been assigned any role, as, she believed, Cardozo had wanted.[25]

These murmurings reflected the first stage of what was to become a continuing dispute over Cardozo's legacy: What exactly was that legacy? and who could rightfully claim it? In the immediate aftermath of his death, a disagreement arose between those who believed his contributions to the law were bound up with the fact of his Jewishness and those who thought they were of a universal nature. Thereafter, a more enduring conflict developed between liberals and conservatives over the fundamental meaning of his jurisprudence. And eventually a struggle occurred over who should interpret his life's work for future generations.

American Jews could not be faulted for making the most of Cardozo's Jewishness even if, in so doing, they exaggerated his religiosity. "Justice Cardozo was a devout Jew," the *American Hebrew* declared,[26] and his own congregation, in which he had rarely set foot, noted that more than forty years before, when it moved into its new structure, "he rendered distinguished service in successfully defending the ancient rituals, rites and customs of the Congregation, which were then threatened with invasion."[27] Rabbi Abraham L. Feinberg of Mt. Neboh Temple on West 79th Street delivered a characteristic eulogy over radio station WJZ's weekly "Message of Israel" program. Cardozo, he said, "combined the knowledge of a scholar, the sympathies of a humanitarian, the literary touch of an artist and the hunger of a saint to preserve his highest vision."[28] At Temple Israel on Long Island, Rabbi David I. Golovensky informed his congregants: "The life of Benjamin Cardozo is a picture of what Americanism, harmoniously synthesized with Judaism, can achieve for the welfare of country and humanity."[29] The Brooklyn *Jewish Examiner* rhapsodized: "With him justice was not a legal device. It was a divine quality . . . The name of Cardozo reflects a lustre upon Jewry which cannot be taken away. His greatness of soul, his pure and unsullied life and distinguished contributions to the cause of a nobler humanity are a silent reproach to the impositions which a pagan world heaps upon its people."[30]

Throughout most of his life Cardozo had moved as comfortably in the world of Christians as in the world of Jews. He was as likely to be found, during the 1920s, dining at the Century Club as attending a meeting of the board of the American Jewish Committee. It was therefore not surprising that even so well-intentioned a friend as Charles C. Burlingham, and one so free of anti-Semitic prejudice, would take exception to the claim that Cardozo's significance was somehow inseparable from his Jewishness. After listening to Judge Learned Hand's eulogy to Cardozo, broadcast on

July 19, Burlingham wrote to Justice Stone: "If you didn't hear L. Hand on the air, I hope he will send you a copy of his speech. No, he won't unless you ask him for it. If you have a memorial meeting, wdn't Hand be as good as any one to speak of him? Be sure to exclude the 'Ebrew-Jews. They are justly proud of B.N.C., but we want him praised as a judge and a man, not as Rabbi Wise wd praise him."[31]

Hand's radio address, "A Tribute to Benjamin Nathan Cardozo," never once mentioned the words "Jew," "Jewish," or "Judaism." Where Jewish eulogists emphasized Cardozo's commitment, Hand emphasized his detachment. Cardozo, he claimed, was a great judge because he successfully reconciled the letter with the spirit of the law. The defining quality of that greatness was wisdom, Hand explained, "and like most wisdom, his ran beyond the reasons which he gave for it. And what is wisdom—that gift of God which the great prophets of his race exalted? I do not know; like you, I know it when I see it, but I cannot tell of what it is composed." The major ingredient, Hand ventured, was detachment, for "the wise man is the detached man," free not only from the desire for selfish gain but, more important, free from his own past. "He was wise because his spirit was uncontaminated, because he knew no violence, or hatred, or envy, or jealousy, or ill-will." According to Hand, it was precisely Cardozo's ability to rise above personal predilections that made him admirable.[32]

Though Burlingham had hoped that Hand would be asked to address the Supreme Court's memorial meeting, that duty fell to others. On the morning of November 26, 1938, formal resolutions honoring Cardozo were presented by the Bar and Officers of the Supreme Court. The invited dignitaries, who said all the appropriate things about Cardozo's contributions to jurisprudence and about his "saintly character," included Solicitor General Robert Jackson, Irving Lehman, and Dean G. Acheson.[33] But it was a speech by George Wharton Pepper which triggered a debate over whether liberals or conservatives were Cardozo's rightful heirs.

A former Republican senator from Pennsylvania and current president of the American Law Institute, Pepper was an unflinching conservative who had argued the case against the constitutionality of the Agricultural Adjustment Administration before the Supreme Court. He began his address innocently enough with the comment that Cardozo "belonged to the Nation." Then, warming to his topic, he subtly rebuked liberals who were claiming Cardozo as one of their own:

In our contemporary American speech, which is rich in words not susceptible of exact definition, he was generally styled a Liberal. If this means
that he was conscious of having a certain part to play and that he always
acted up to what was expected of him, I think it unjust to his memory so
to stigmatize him. If, however, it is meant by the term merely to indicate
that he had a passion for liberty and never consciously ranged himself on
the side of tyranny, then we must freely accord him the title—and that at
a moment when to be a liberal ought to mean what every patriotic American aspires to be.[34]

The gauntlet having been thrown down, officials in the Roosevelt administration were only too eager to take it up. Attorney General Homer Cummings was scheduled to deliver his own tribute to Cardozo at the Supreme
Court on December 19. That left about three weeks to prepare a response
to Pepper. By December 9 an aide, Warner W. Gardner, had come up with
a first draft. He informed Cummings: "The concluding portions of the address bear down rather heavily upon his constitutional philosophy. This
may cause some pain to a few members of the Court, but justice could not
otherwise be done to Cardozo. And it has the further purpose, as you suggested, of reclaiming Cardozo's liberalism from George Wharton Pepper."[35] On December 15 Cummings sent a copy of the revised version to
President Roosevelt, suggesting he would be especially interested in those
passages affirming Cardozo's liberalism. Roosevelt replied: "I am glad that
on Pages 12, 13 and 14 you step so heavily on the toes of a few of the gentlemen whom you will address."[36]

Cummings praised Cardozo for his willingness to defer to legislative
judgments, for finding "no constitutional barrier to prevent the enactment
of legislation which was compelled by the urgent needs of an ever changing society." But the Attorney General's sharpest rejoinder to Pepper came
in his account of Cardozo's opinions upholding the Social Security Act:
"The governmental process must have seemed noblest to him when it was
directed to the relief of the aged, the infirm, and the destitute. His words
seem to have sprung from the heart of one who felt with intensity that government succeeds only as it serves the needs of its people." Cummings concluded by praising the deceased justice as a "shy and gentle scholar, whose
heart was so pure and whose mind was so bold."[37]

But conservatives had one, final round to fire, and, in the person of Chief
Justice Charles Evans Hughes, an experienced marksman. Hughes made

the formal "response" to the attorney general's tribute. "He did not seek public office," Hughes said of Cardozo: "He stood aloof from politics. He did not engage in public controversies or aspire to leadership in organized social efforts. He did not crusade for social reforms. His zeal for human betterment took a direction better suited to his temperament and intellectual interests. He shrank from promiscuous contacts, finding a safe refuge in his books." Satisfied that he had scored a direct hit, Hughes ended by quoting Cardozo to the effect that law could not be based solely on "sentiment or benevolence or some vague notion of social welfare."[38]

Listening first to Cummings and then to Hughes, one thoughtful observer noted that "the contrast was so striking that one wondered if the two eulogies referred to the same man."[39] The same could have been said of the eulogies offered in the Jewish press and by Learned Hand. People saw in Cardozo what they wished to see, made of him what they wanted him to be, largely because he was such a protean figure. Commitment and detachment, liberalism and conservatism—all were parts of his many-sided makeup, and all found their way into his writings and his opinions. His was an ambiguous legacy although few were willing to admit as much.

The struggle over defining that legacy entered its final phase when, within weeks of Cardozo's death, George S. Hellman decided he would write a biography—in fact, as he hoped, *the* authorized biography. Sixty years of age, a poet, playwright, and patron of the arts, Hellman was a prolific author with books on Robert Louis Stevenson and Washington Irving to his credit. He had other qualifications as well, for he was a friend of Cardozo's and knew a number of his relatives. He made no effort to hide his sympathies, informing one of Cardozo's associates: "The biography is more than anything else a labor of love with me—a tribute to a beautiful soul to whose fuller understanding the present public and future generations are entitled for their own enrichment and inspiration."[40]

A labor of love it surely was. Hellman wrote to nearly everyone who had ever known Cardozo, including old college classmates, soliciting any information they might have. He interviewed scores of people, taking meticulous notes on their observations. He clipped and catalogued countless newspaper editorials and stories. He contacted dozens of people with whom Cardozo had corresponded, asking for the letters and, when successful, as he often was, making copies for his files. In fact, the first draft of his book contained three chapters consisting essentially of Cardozo's letters to Maud Nathan, another relative, Aline Goldstone, and a friend, Doris Webster. As work proceeded, Hellman toyed with several titles—"The Ideal Judge," "An American Gentleman," "The Rare Life of Justice Cardozo"—before settling on "Benjamin N. Cardozo: American Judge" (to the annoyance of both Maud Nathan and Annie Nathan Meyer, who protested: "Why omit the Nathan? . . . He was always proud of his Nathan blood").[41]

Several of Cardozo's good friends willingly cooperated with Hellman, who promised everyone whose help he sought that he would respect their wishes concerning confidentiality. Justice Harlan Fiske Stone answered all of his questions and provided him with copies of Cardozo's personal letters. Rabbi Stephen S. Wise was equally generous, lending Hellman all of his correspondence with Cardozo, including the statement Cardozo had given him to aid in preparing a eulogy for Emily. Wise added that his wife, Louise, "is still hunting for some precious letters, those that he sent to Nellie. Possibly Miss Tracy can tell you about them. They are of course very, very intimate and personal. It is a problem whether they ought to be published, even if you can lay your hands upon them."[42] Hellman quickly responded: "I hope that she will find some of Ben's letters to Nellie. I quite agree with you that there is a question whether they should be published, but presumably there is material in them that could be used with discretion."[43] Those letters, however, were apparently never located.

Although Hellman received assistance from a great many people, there were a few notable holdouts: George Engelhard and Learned Hand agreed to talk to Hellman but would not allow him access to any correspondence. Felix Frankfurter, Joseph Rauh, and Charles C. Burlingham wanted nothing to do with the enterprise. Burlingham later said it was at Lehman's "request or suggestion" that he withheld his correspondence.[44] By far the most significant holdout was Irving Lehman, who, since he controlled Cardozo's personal papers, was in a position, as Hellman saw it, to make or break his book.

The exchanges between the eager biographer and the over-protective friend continued for the better part of a year. Hellman promised that he would write a book "without the sensationalism" as Cardozo would have wanted, that he would be guided by Lehman's advice, and that his biography of the "finest" Jew in American history would be "a service—in these days a much needed service—to our race." He sent an eight-page handwritten letter pointing out that the question came down to whether Lehman "should prefer to risk the kind of biography which would be offensive to Ben instead of the kind I hope to write."[45] But Hellman could promise, cajole, and drop subtle threats until he was blue in the face. Not only did Lehman insist that no personal biography of Cardozo should be written, but, as we have already seen, he also proceeded to destroy the bulk of Cardozo's papers in an effort to make sure that no such book ever could be written.

Lehman was willing to concede only that a judicial, as opposed to a personal, biography should be written, but such a work would necessarily be based on Cardozo's published opinions and essays, would be aimed at a scholarly rather than a general audience, and, he added pointedly, would be written by a lawyer or legal scholar. He could not forget, Lehman said, "how often Justice Cardozo and I discussed biographies and how unequivocally he expressed his strong distaste of personal biographies intended for the general public."[46] "I should be unable to give cooperation or approval to the writing of a personal biography of my friend," he told Hellman, "though I might approve of a book by some legal scholar on the work of Justice Cardozo."[47]

Lehman's wariness went well beyond the withholding of personal letters. When Professor Karl Llewellyn asked him if there was an unpublished essay of Cardozo's that would be suitable for a planned joint memorial issue of the *Harvard Law Review,* the *Columbia Law Review,* and the *Yale Law Journal,* Lehman replied that he had raised the question with William H. Freese, Cardozo's executor: "Neither Mr. Freese nor I should be willing to authorize the publication of any writing of Justice Cardozo, unless we felt sure that he himself would be willing to give it to the world." There existed, he said, a lengthy unpublished essay on Alexis de Tocqueville, written in 1931 or 1932. Although "the reasons which caused Justice Cardozo to withhold publication during his lifetime are no longer valid," Lehman reported, "I am inclined to think that it is both too long and too important for publication in the proposed number of the law reviews."[48]

Meanwhile Hellman completed his book, which appeared in March 1940. A warmly admiring personal portrait, at its best informative and revealing, it was, at its worst, sonorous and overly sentimental. It received generally favorable notices in the popular press. "A loving memorial to a great American," said the *Saturday Review of Literature.*[49] The *New York Times Book Review* assigned the book to Joseph P. Pollard, whose own efforts Cardozo had once derogated. "Here for the first time is a revealing picture of the human personality, the modest and saintly character," Pollard declared: "It is a notable biography." Cardozo emerged as a lonely but heroic figure whose moral force was "contagious" and who "radiated human warmth and had the power to charm." Pollard especially liked Hellman's discussion of "the interplay between the decisions and the man who made them," remarking: "In case after case we see the imprint of Cardozo's chivalry, his zeal for family solidarity, his abhorrence of crime and of official brutality . . . , his concern for fair play and humanity, his high ethical conceptions of business relations, his concern to achieve a just balance between individual rights and social good."[50]

Reaction from other quarters was considerably less cordial. The biography was "not worthy" of Cardozo, Burlingham thought.[51] Frankfurter did not review the book, but his former student Mark DeWolfe Howe did, in the *New York Herald Tribune*. Howe, who had clerked for Oliver Wendell Holmes Jr., was dean of the University of Buffalo School of Law. (He later joined the faculty of Harvard Law School and was selected by Frankfurter to write Holmes's biography.) Howe objected to the book's "tone of reverent devotion," which he found "unpleasantly cloying," "irritating and tiresome." More was needed, Howe observed, than a recounting of "trivial events which illustrate his subject's gentle, kindly and modest nature."[52]

But it was left to another former Frankfurter student, Joseph Rauh, Cardozo's last clerk, to administer the *coup de grace*. "The lawyer will find little in this book to satisfy his curiosity about Mr. Justice Cardozo, and the layman will find only an artificial personality episodically portrayed," Rauh wrote in the *Harvard Law Review*: "For here is no biography in any proper sense of the word, but simply a hastily compiled collection of anecdotes from the Justice's life, interspersed with excerpts from his writings and from the writings and statements of others about him. What emerges from this compilation is an unreal and unrecognizable saint, for the human qualities of the man, which constituted his true saintliness, are lost." Rauh complained that Hellman had undertaken a hopeless task "in attempting to portray the personality without first seeking an understanding of the work for which and with which his subject lived." Rauh then relented—"it should be generously acknowledged that the author has rendered valuable service in pulling together some of the Justice's writings not otherwise easily available"—but only for a moment: "But his service in this regard does not undo the perpetuation of the artificial picture of a man who was so real and so human."[53]

The hostility to Hellman's book expressed by Howe and Rauh, and shared, undoubtedly, by Frankfurter, Burlingham, and Lehman, was far out of proportion to its shortcomings, real though they were. Their response reflected a conviction that Cardozo's legacy was properly theirs to interpret, and that Hellman was, in effect, poaching on their turf. They surely were correct in pointing out that Hellman lacked scholarly credentials. But many years later, when Frankfurter learned that the distinguished constitutional scholar Alpheus Thomas Mason was thinking of writing a biography of Cardozo, he again became bitterly resentful: not because Mason, author of the magisterial *Harlan Fiske Stone: Pillar of the Law* (1956), was an intellectual lightweight but because his reading of constitutional history was in important respects at variance with Frankfurter's own.

Shortly after Cardozo's death Frankfurter offered his own appraisal of his jurisprudence. In January 1939, the same month Franklin Roosevelt named him to Cardozo's seat on the Court, Frankfurter published "Mr. Justice Cardozo and Public Law" in the joint issue of the Columbia, Harvard, and Yale law reviews. In what little he said about Cardozo's personality he was hardly less effusive than Hellman. Cardozo exuded a "contagious goodness," Frankfurter wrote, and exhibited a "beauty of character." But Frankfurter wished to show, above all, that Cardozo had succeeded in keeping his personal sentiments out of his opinions. Since the art of judging involves "a long ratiocinative process," Frankfurter asserted, the wisest judges "explore to the uttermost the rational foundations of what they affirm and what they reject, in order to avoid confusion between their private universe and the universe." To practice judicial restraint, as Cardozo did, required "extraordinary powers of detachment [so as] not to confound personal disapproval with an enduring constitutional prohibition." Largely because his "most constant companion was reason," Frankfurter concluded, Cardozo "completely satisfied the requirements of a judge wholly adequate for the Supreme Bench."[54]

Another contributor to the joint number of the three law reviews, Warren A. Seavey, a colleague of Frankfurter's at Harvard Law School, made a similar argument regarding Cardozo's detachment. In "Mr. Justice Cardozo and the Law of Torts," Seavey discussed a number of cases, one of which, *Palsgraf* v. *Long Island Railroad Company* (1928), would become Cardozo's single most famous torts opinion. Helen Palsgraf was waiting on a railroad platform with her two daughters; she was injured when station guards, attempting to help a man board a moving train, accidentally dislodged a package which, it turned out, contained fireworks. The resulting explosion (or the stampeding crowd) toppled scales which struck the woman. By a narrow four-to-three vote the Court of Appeals reversed a judgment in her favor, amounting to $6,000, on the grounds that the guards could not have foreseen that she would be endangered by their action. Writing for the majority, Cardozo had said: "The risk reasonably to be perceived defines the risk to be avoided, and risk imports relation; it is risk to another or others within the range of apprehension."

Seavey asserted that Cardozo, while personally solicitous of those who sustained injuries in such circumstances, "did not become the protector of the injured merely because the defendant had ample funds to meet a judgment or had an ability to spread the loss. His scales were those of legal justice, not sentimental justice." In Seavey's view, Cardozo had not reached his conclusion either "from some internal and inexplicable sense of justice" or from "private opinions of policy" but rather from the consideration of "principles deduced from the cases" and the impartial weighing of "competing interests."[55]

But Professor John T. Noonan Jr.'s classic study, "The Passengers of Palsgraf," demonstrates that the decision cannot be understood apart from "Cardozo as a person," from his background and values. As a bachelor, Noonan argues, Cardozo lacked "the experience of conjugality and the experience of fatherhood" that might have produced greater empathy for Mrs. Palsgraf. Moreover, his desire to avoid any hint of the kind of favoritism that had led to his father's disgrace disposed him to view legal contests in highly abstract terms. Faced with the problem in *Palsgraf* of determining the scope of liability and the unintended consequences of certain actions, Cardozo, according to Noonan, "fashioned a statement of clarity, symmetry, simplicity," one that "imposed order and aesthetic design and generality."[56]

The reluctance of Seavey—and, for that matter, of Frankfurter and Hand—to admit that Cardozo, as a judge, often acted on the basis of personal predilection rather than pure reason manifested, according to Noonan, "the hostility of the orthodox teacher of doctrine to information about the play of persons in the process."[57] Yet Cardozo's entire career illustrated the importance of personal values in the judicial process. In cases involving morality, sexuality, religion, and social order, he was guided by a code of conduct firmly rooted in his early experiences. His rulings depended on a selective reading of both the evidence and the precedents, although Cardozo had a genius for making it seem as if the results he reached were logical, inevitable, and legally unassailable.

His opinions sustaining New Deal measures also reflected Cardozo's general view of social circumstances, for his conservatism in matters of morality and criminal justice was quite compatible with a statist approach to economic regulation. His decisions in the 1937 Social Security Act cases upholding old age pensions and unemployment insurance saw a happy convergence of his political convictions and his belief in judicial restraint. Practically speaking, it made good sense for him to emphasize the principle of judicial deference, but he left little doubt that he sympathized in this instance with the legislative action to which he was deferring.

In the years since his death, many of the doctrines that mattered most to Cardozo have been overturned. His views regarding the selective incorporation of the Bill of Rights, the exclusionary rule, the exemption of eleemosynary institutions from most negligence suits, and the admission of testimony regarding the prior sexual history of rape victims have all been rejected. It is not surprising that the law would change significantly over more than half a century. It is rather a mark of Cardozo's stature that modern courts, even when reversing him, have gone out of their way to explain the considerations which led them to adopt different rules.

Had Cardozo not been so private a person from so young an age, it would be tempting to think that he objected to publicity because the more the secrets of his life were revealed, the more his rulings might come to be regarded as reflecting personal idiosyncrasies rather than overarching principles. That fear may have prevented him from accepting the full implications of legal realism. Although prepared to concede the existence of "judge-made law," as he did in his 1921 Storrs Lectures at Yale, he would never admit that, in making—or interpreting—law, judges acted largely on their own inclinations. When legal realists such as Jerome Frank embraced that view, Cardozo drew back, as from a dizzying precipice.

In a commencement address at St. John's Law School, Cardozo defined law as "the medium, the instrument by which society represses conduct which awakens fear of such intensity as to make toleration impossible."[58] As a judge he had played his own part in that process, attempting always to chart a middle course between the extremes of toleration and repression because he was, by nature, a seeker of consensus. So he took a liberal, facilitative approach to issues of economic welfare, accepting the enlightened opinion of the day when it came to old age pensions and unemployment insurance, while taking a conservative, even restrictive, stand in cases involving what he regarded as immoral, harmful, or criminal behavior.

He therefore exhibited no sympathy for so extraordinarily diverse a group of claimants as Hans Schmidt, an evildoer who sought to hide behind an insanity plea; Louise Hamburger, a wronged student who brought a negligence suit against a university; Robert Dean, Leon Hoadley, and Cosmo Mirizio, husbands who attempted to extricate themselves from unhappy marital situations; Albert Hamilton, a conscientious objector who claimed his religious beliefs should exempt him from military training; and Le Roy J. Miller, Herman Snyder, and Frank Palka, murderers, as Cardozo viewed them, who thought to find legal loopholes to escape the punishment they deserved.

Cardozo once remarked that appellate judges should treat individuals' grievances as if they were merely the "algebraic symbols" from which a "formula of justice" would emerge. In deciding all of these cases, however, he was not speaking the language of coefficients and equations, nor even, considering how pervasively his values affected these rulings, the language of precedents and legal maxims. He was more the moralist than the mathematician, and the language he spoke was, in truth, the language of good and evil.

NOTES

Prologue: A Man of Fastidious Reticence

1. This and other quotations are drawn from articles in the Feb. 16, 1932, editions of the *New York Times, New York Herald-Tribune, San Francisco Chronicle,* and *Atlanta Constitution.*

2. Cardozo to George A. Kohut, Jan. 23, 1932, Stephen Wise MSS.

3. Cardozo to Learned Hand, Feb. 17, 1932, Hand MSS.

4. George Hellman, "Notes on Conversation with Judge Learned Hand," Nov. 15, 1938, Benjamin Cardozo MSS. Unless noted, all citations to the Cardozo MSS are to the collection at Columbia University.

5. *New York Herald Tribune,* Feb. 17, 1932.

6. Cardozo to Thomas Reed Powell, Sept. 8, 1935, Powell MSS.

7. Cardozo to David de Sola Pool, Oct. 18, 1937, Congregation Shearith Israel MSS.

8. Hellman, "Notes on Conversation with Judge Learned Hand," Nov. 15, 1938, Cardozo MSS.

9. Speech, Nov. 26, 1938, copy in Cardozo MSS.

10. Irving Lehman to Harlan Fiske Stone, April 28, 1938, Stone MSS, Box 19.

11. *New York Times,* July 29, 1938.

12. Irving Lehman to George S. Hellman, Aug. 31, 1938, Hellman MSS, Box 8.

13. George S. Hellman to Irving Lehman, Sept. 7, 1938, ibid.

14. Irving Lehman to George S. Hellman, Sept. 20, 1938, Cardozo MSS.

15. George S. Hellman to Irving Lehman, April 5, 1939, ibid.

16. Philip M. Hayden to George S. Hellman, Oct. 3, 1939, ibid.

17. Frank D. Fackenthal to Karl N. Llewellyn, April 30, 1940, Llewellyn MSS.

18. Harry Willmer Jones to Karl N. Llewellyn, Jan. 27, 1960, ibid.

19. Stephen Wise to George Hellman, Jan. 16, 1939, Cardozo MSS.

20. Cardozo to Oscar Cox, Nov. 19, 1931, Cox MSS.

1. Such a Delicate Youth

1. 1870 Census, New York City, Roll 1045; 1880 Census, New York City, Roll 895.

2. Certificate of Death, Oct. 28, 1879, New York City Health Department.

3. Annie Nathan Meyer, *It's Been Fun* (New York, 1951), p. 86.

4. Elizabeth C. Cardozo, *Salvage* (Boston, 1912), p. 48.

5. Cardozo to Learned Hand, April 10, 1921, Hand MSS.

6. Paul V. Ragan and Thomas H. McGlashan, "Childhood Parental Death and Adult Psychopathology," *American Journal of Psychiatry*, 143 (Feb. 1986), 155–56. See also Alan Breier and Stacy A. Beller, "Early Parental Loss and Development of Adult Psychopathology," *Archives of General Psychiatry*, 45 (Nov. 1988), 987–92; Christopher Tennant, "Parental Loss in Childhood: Its Effect in Adult Life," ibid., 1045–49; and David W. Krueger, "Childhood Parent Loss: Developmental Impact and Adult Psychopathology," *American Journal of Psychotherapy*, 37 (Oct. 1983), 582–92.

7. Christina Sekaer, "Toward a Definition of 'Childhood Mourning,'" *American Journal of Psychotherapy*, 41 (April 1987), 216. See also Erna Furman, *A Child's Parent Dies: Studies in Childhood Bereavement* (New Haven, 1974).

8. George Hellman, "Notes of Conversation with Miss Kate Tracy," Nov. 15, 1938," Cardozo MSS, Box 9.

9. Aline Lewis Goldstone to George Hellman, April 18, 1939, Cardozo MSS, Box 6.

10. Hellman, "Notes in re Our Conversation" [with Addie Cardozo], Nov. 6, 1938, ibid.

11. Stephen S. Wise, *Challenging Years: The Autobiography of Stephen Wise* (New York, 1949), p. 44.

12. *Brother and Sister: A Memoir and the Letters of Ernest and Henriette Renan* (New York, 1896), trans. Lady Mary Dowd, p. 35.

13. Cardozo to Annie Nathan Meyer, July 3, 1925, Meyer MSS.

14. Cardozo to Learned Hand, Aug. 17, 1926, Hand MSS.

15. Cardozo to Annie Nathan Meyer, Aug. 22, 1928, Meyer MSS.

16. Cardozo to Learned Hand, Nov. 30, 1929, Hand MSS.

17. The poem may be found in Melville Cane, *And Pastures New* (New York, 1956), pp. 34–36.

18. Cardozo to Melville Cane, Dec. 21, 1929, Cane MSS.

19. Cardozo to Charles C. Burlingham, April 15, 1922, Burlingham MSS, Box 22.

20. Cardozo to Harlan Fiske Stone, April 11, 1922, Stone MSS (CU).

21. A copy of the tribute may be found in Box 9 of the Cardozo MSS.

22. Amram Scheinfeld, *Twins and Supertwins* (Philadelphia, 1967), p. 185: "With the typical boy-girl pair, there is apt to be nothing but individuality. They are by all odds the least 'twinny' of twins." See also Jane E. Mitchell et al., "Masculinity and Femininity in Twin Children: Genetic and Environmental Factors," *Child Development*, 60 (1989), 1475–85; and Michael Rutter and Jane Redshaw, "Annotation: Growing Up as a Twin: Twin-Singleton Differences in Psychological Development," *Journal of Child Psychology*, 32 (1991), 885–95.

23. Hellman, "Notes of Conversation with Miss Kate Tracy," Nov. 15, 1938, Cardozo MSS, Box 9.

24. Cited in Stephen Birmingham, *The Grandees: America's Sephardic Elite* (New York, 1971), p. 299.

25. Hellman, "Notes in re Our Conversation" [with Addie Cardozo], Nov. 6, 1938, Cardozo MSS, Box 9.

26. The poem is printed in George C. Hellman, *Benjamin N. Cardozo: American Judge* (New York, 1940), p. 16.

27. Meyer Kayserling, "Sephardim," *Jewish Encyclopedia* (12 vols., New York, 1901), XI, 197. See also Martin A. Cohen and Abraham J. Peck, eds., *Sephardim in the Americas: Studies in Culture and History* (Tuscaloosa, Ala., 1993).

28. N. Taylor Phillips, "Cong. Shearith Israel: Dedication of Its New Synagogue," *Jewish Messenger*, May 21, 1897.

29. "Historical Tableaux at Shearith Israel Synagogue," *American Hebrew*, March 5, 1915.

30. This account is based on David and Tamar de Sola Pool, *An Old Faith in the New World: Portrait of Shearith Israel, 1654–1954* (New York, 1955).

31. Ibid., pp. 57–67.

32. Ibid., pp. 192–201.

33. H. Pereira Mendes to Maud Nathan, July 4, 1926, Nathan MSS.

34. Phillips, "Cong. Shearith Israel."

35. H. Pereira Mendes, *Bar-Mitzvah for Boyhood, Youth and Manhood* (New York, 1938).

36. George Hellman, "Notes on Conversation with Dr. David de Sola Pool," Nov. 9, 1938, Cardozo MSS, Box 8.

37. De Sola Pool, *An Old Faith*, p. 200.

38. Harold F. Wilson, *The Jersey Shore* (3 vols., New York, 1953), I, 502.

39. George W. Childs, *Recollections* (Philadelphia, 1890), p. 103.

40. See Ross L. Muir and Carl J. White, *Over the Long Term: The Story of J. & W. Seligman & Co.* (New York, 1964).

41. Gary Scharnhorst with Jack Bales, *The Lost Life of Horatio Alger, Jr.* (Bloomington, Ind., 1985), p. 64. See also Carol Nackenoff, *The Fictional Republic: Horatio Alger and American Political Discourse* (New York, 1994).

42. The documents pertaining to the incident have been published in Gilbert K. Westgard II, "Following the Trail of Horatio Alger, Jr.," *Newsboy: The Publication of the Horatio Alger Society*, 18 (Dec. 1979), 5–7; and Gary Scharnhorst, "The Brewster Incident: Additional Evidence," ibid., 19 (Dec. 1980), 8–13.

43. Cited in Westgard, "Following the Trail," 6–7.

44. Ibid.

45. Cited in Scharnhorst, "The Brewster Incident," 11.

46. Ibid., 9–12.

47. Gary Scharnhorst, *Horatio Alger, Jr.* (Boston, 1980), p. 31.

48. Scharnhorst and Bales, *The Lost Life*, p. 70.

49. Ibid., p. 66.

50. For *Ragged Dick*, see Scharnhorst and Bales, *The Lost Life*, pp. 81–87.

51. Ibid., p. 86.

52. "Horatio Alger, Jr.," *Golden Argosy*, Oct. 17, 1885, p. 364.

53. Cited in Scharnhorst and Bales, *The Lost Life*, p. 77.

54. George Hellman, "The Story of the Seligmans," p. 235, Seligman Family MSS.

55. Ibid., pp. 85–86, 102.

56. Michael Zuckerman, "The Nursery Tales of Horatio Alger," *American Quarterly*, 24 (May 1972), 207.

57. Horatio Alger, Jr., *Bob Burton* (New York, 1886), pp. 49, 55.

58. Horatio Alger, Jr., *Frank Hunter's Peril* (Philadelphia, 1885 [1896]), p. 287.

59. Ibid., p. 335.

60. Cited in Hellman, *Cardozo*, p. 15.

61. Horatio Alger to E. R. A. Seligman, July 1, 1885, Seligman MSS.

62. Certificate of Death, Feb. 3, 1885, New York City Health Department.

63. New York *Herald Tribune*, Nov. 6, 1885.

64. Ibid.

65. *New York Times*, Nov. 9, 1885.

66. Charles F. Wingate, "An Episode in Municipal Government," *North American Review*, 245 (Oct. 1874), 395–96.

67. Ibid.

68. James G. Wilson, ed., *The Memorial History of the City of New York* (4 vols., New York, 1893), III, 543.

69. *Fisk* v. *Chicago, Rock Island and Pacific Railroad*, New York Special Term, Feb. 3, 1868, pp. 484–85.

70. Cited in Leo Hershkowitz, *Tweed's New York: Another Look* (Garden City, N.Y., 1977), pp. 158–60.

71. *Charges of the Bar Association of the City of New York against . . . Hon. Albert Cardozo, Justice of the Supreme Court, . . . and Testimony thereunder taken before the Judiciary Committee of the Assembly of the State of New York* (4 vols., New York, 1872), I, p. 1.

72. Ibid., pp. 1–14.

73. Ibid., p. 380.

74. Ibid., pp. 13, 43.

75. Ibid., p. 2. See also Kenneth D. Ackerman, *The Gold Ring: Jim Fisk, Jay Gould, and Black Friday, 1869* (New York, 1988).

76. *Charges of the Bar Association*, pp. 122, 132.

77. *New York Times*, April 10, 1872.

78. *Charges of the Bar Association*, p. 298.

79. Charles F. Wingate, "An Episode in Municipal Government," *North American Review*, 253 (Oct. 1876), 404.

80. *New York Times*, April 10, 1872.

81. Wingate, "An Episode," 404, 417.

82. *Argus*, May 2, 1872.

83. Ibid.

84. Wingate, "An Episode," 417.

85. New York *Herald Tribune*, Nov. 6, 1885.

86. *New York Times*, Nov. 12, 1885.

87. Charles C. Burlingham to Felix Frankfurter, July 14, 1938, Frankfurter MSS (LC), Reel 19.

88. Annie Nathan Meyer to Oswald Garrison Villard, July 23, 1938, Villard MSS.

89. Birmingham, *Grandees*, p. 296.

90. Hellman, *Cardozo*, p. 10.

91. Arthur L. Goodhart, *Five Jewish Justices of the Common Law* (Oxford, 1949), p. 52.

92. Cardozo to Arthur Wolff, Oct. 19, 1934, Cardozo MSS.

93. Cardozo to Annie Nathan Meyer, May 9, 1934, Cardozo MSS (HUC).

94. *Charges of the Bar Association*, p. 134.

95. John W. Burgess, *Reminiscences of an American Scholar* (New York, 1934), pp. 180, 168.

96. Cardozo's Lecture Notes on Nicholas Murray Butler's "History of Philosophy," Cardozo MSS, Box 4.

97. Hellman, *Cardozo*, p. 21.

98. All three of the essays may be found in the Cardozo MSS, Box 4. The essay on Arnold has been published in Margaret E. Hall, ed., *Selected Writings of Benjamin Nathan Cardozo* (New York, 1947), pp. 61–76.

99. These comments were made in letters to George Hellman from the following: Remsen Johnson, Oct. 29, 1938; Frank W. Crane, Nov. 15, 1938; Leonard D. White, Nov. 14, 1938; Frank P. Graves, Oct. 24, 1938; Henry M. Powell, Oct. 25, 1938; Douglas F. Cox, Oct. 25, 1938; Sally Nathan, Dec. 28, 1938, all in Cardozo MSS, Box 6.

100. Hellman, *Cardozo*, p. 24.

101. See the above-cited letters to Hellman from Johnson, Cox, and Graves.

102. Cited in Milton Halsey Thomas to Oscar S. Cox, Feb. 11, 1932, Cox MSS.

103. Hellman, *Cardozo*, p. 22.

104. *New York Times*, June 13, 1889.

105. The speech has been published in Hall, ed., *Selected Writings*, pp. 47–51.

106. Hellman, *Cardozo*, p. 25.

107. Cardozo to Ernest Abraham Cardozo, Nov. 21, 1932, Cardozo MSS. See also Hellman, *Cardozo*, p. 37.

108. Julius Goebel Jr., et al., *A History of the School of Law, Columbia University* (New York, 1955), pp. 62, 42, 63.

109. Ibid., pp. 34, 36–37, 39.

110. Ibid., p. 114.

111. Ibid., p. 131.

112. Ibid., p. 138.

113. Cardozo, "The Comradeship of the Bar," in Hall, ed., *Selected Writings*, p. 423.

114. Goebel, *History of the School of Law*, pp. 122, 131.

115. Cardozo, "The Game of the Law and Its Prizes," in Hall, ed., *Selected Writings*, p. 414.

116. *The Writings of George Eliot: Romola* (Boston, 1909), I, 138.

2. The Insanity Defense

1. George Hellman, "Notes of Conversation with Mrs. William Cardozo," [n.d.], Cardozo MSS, Box 9.

2. 1910 Census, New York City, Roll 1302.

3. William Nelson, *The New Jersey Coast in Three Centuries* (3 vols., New York, 1902), II, 57.

4. George C. Hellman, *Benjamin N. Cardozo: American Judge* (New York, 1940), p. 43.

5. The clerk, Charles Evans Hughes Jr., is cited in ibid., pp. 45–46.

6. All quotations are taken from Benjamin N. Cardozo, "Identity and Survivorship," in Allan McLane Hamilton and Lawrence Godkin, eds., *A System of Legal Medicine* (2 vols., New York, 1897), I, 213–242.

7. The brochure may be found in the Cardozo MSS, Box 13.

8. New York *Herald Tribune,* July 10, 1938, cited in Jerome I. Hyman, "Benjamin N. Cardozo: A Preface to His Career at the Bar," *Brooklyn Law Review,* 10 (Oct. 1940), 16.

9. Ibid., 22.

10. *People* v. *Katz,* 209 N.Y. 311 (1913).

11. *People* v. *Hyde,* 131 N.Y. Supp. 56 7 (1911).

12. Cited in Hyman, "Cardozo: A Preface," 23.

13. *Waldorf Astoria Segar Co.* v. *Salomon,* 184 N.Y. 584 (1906); see Hyman, "Cardozo: A Preface," 18–19.

14. Benjamin N. Cardozo, *The Jurisdiction of the Court of Appeals of the State of New York* (Albany, 1903), pp. 11, 76.

15. Cardozo to Felix Frankfurter, March 2, 1934, Frankfurter MSS (LC), Reel 70.

16. *New York Times,* Aug. 15, 1913.

17. Abraham Tulin to George Hellman, Nov. 4, 1938, Cardozo MSS, Box 9.

18. Letter to the Editor, *Jewish Tribune* (May 30, 1930), p. 6.

19. *New York Times,* Aug. 27, 1913.

20. Cited in Hellman, *Cardozo,* p. 55.

21. Ibid., p. 57. For the election of 1913 see Edwin R. Lewinson, *John Purroy Mitchel: The Boy Mayor of New York* (New York, 1965); the 32nd and 34th Assembly Districts are described as chiefly Jewish in Robert F. Wesser, *A Response to Progressivism: The Democratic Party and New York Politics, 1902–1918* (New York, 1986), pp. 240–41.

22. *New York Times,* Jan. 6, 1914.

23. Wise to Martin H. Glynn, Jan. 28, 1914; see also *Jewish Daily News,* Dec. 21, 1913, Glynn MSS, Box 4. For lawyers' approval of Cardozo, see James F. Tracey and A. T. Clearwater to Glynn, Feb. 3, 1914, ibid.

24. *New York Times,* Sept. 7, 1913. For two brief accounts of the case, see T. M. Mc-Dade, "Crime Hunt," *Armchair Detective,* 18 (Fall 1985), 421–24; and Jacques M. Quen, "The Case of Anna Aumuller and Father Hans Schmidt," *Newsletter of the American Academy of Psychiatry and the Law,* 12 (Sept. 1987), 26–27, largely based on McDade.

25. *New York Times,* Sept. 7, 1913.

26. Ibid., Sept. 15, 1913.

27. The People v. Hans Schmidt, Case and Points, 216 N.Y. 324 (1915), p. 355.

28. New York *Tribune,* Sept. 15, 1913; *New York Times,* Sept. 15, 1913.

29. Ibid.

30. Ibid., Sept. 17, 1913.

31. Ibid.

32. Schmidt, Case and Points, pp. 540–546.

33. *New York Times,* Sept. 20, 1913.

34. Schmidt to "My dear brother," March 27, 1913, District Attorney Case Files.

35. *New York Times,* Sept. 16, 1913.

36. Petition of Alphonse G. Koelble to the Court of General Sessions, Nov. 20, 1913, District Attorney Case Files.

37. *New York Times,* Sept. 23, 1913.

38. Cardozo to Archie M. Palmer, Sept. 30, 1925, Cardozo MSS, Box 6.

39. New York *Tribune,* Dec. 9, 1913.

40. Ibid.

41. Ibid., Dec. 13, 1913.

42. Ibid.

43. *New York Times,* Dec. 18, 1913.

44. Schmidt, Case and Points, p. 795.

45. Ibid., p. 754.

46. Ibid., p. 747.

47. Ibid., pp. 765–73.

48. Ibid., pp. 809.

49. Ibid., p. 769, 802.

50. On the defense psychiatrists see John C. Burnham, *Jelliffe: American Psychoanalyst and Physician* (Chicago, 1983); and Arcangelo R. T. D'Amore, ed., *William Alanson White: The Washington Years* (Washington, 1976).

51. Schmidt, Case and Points, p. 725.

52. Ibid., p. 851.

53. Ibid., p. 827.

54. Ibid., pp. 821, 846.

55. Ibid., pp. 828–32.

56. Ibid., p. 841.

57. Ibid., p. 861.

58. Ibid., p. 1156.

59. Ibid., p. 1284.

60. Ibid., p. 1329.

61. Ibid., pp. 969–70.

62. Ibid., pp. 972, 1017.

63. H. Gavin, *On Feigned and Factitious Diseases* (1843), p. 148, cited in Jeffrey L. Geller, et al., "Feigned Insanity in Nineteenth Century America: Experts, Explanations, Evaluations and Exculpations," *Anglo-American Law Review*, 20 (Oct.–Dec. 1991), 463.

64. F. Wharton and M. Stille, *A Treatise on Medical Jurisprudence* (1855), p. 110, cited in ibid., p. 467.

65. George W. Jacoby, *The Unsound Mind and the Law: A Presentation of Forensic Psychiatry* (New York, 1918), pp. 110–11.

66. *New York Times,* Dec. 29, 1913.

67. Ibid., Dec. 30, 1913.

68. New York *Tribune,* Dec. 30, 1913.

69. Ibid., Dec. 31, 1913.

70. *New York Times,* Jan. 22, 1914.

71. Ibid., Feb. 6, 1914.

72. Ibid., Feb. 7, 1914.

73. Schmidt, Case and Points, pp. 118–24.

74. Ibid., "Affidavit of Hans Schmidt," Oct. 30, 1914, pp. 5–18.

75. Ibid., "Affidavit of Alphonse G. Koelble," Dec. 4, 1914, pp. 19–34; "Affidavit of George L. Lewis," Nov. 24, 1914, pp. 46–48.

76. Ibid., "Affidavit of Henry W. Cattell," Nov. 20, 1914, pp. 36–39; "Affidavit of Justin Herold," Nov. 24, 1914, pp. 40–43.

77. Ibid., "Affidavit of Justin Herold."

78. Cyril C. Means, "The Law of New York Concerning Abortion and the Status of the Foetus, 1664–1968: A Case of Cessation of Constitutionality," *New York Law Forum,* 14 (Fall 1968), 476–93.

79. Leslie J. Reagan, "'About to Meet Her Maker': Women, Doctors, Dying Declarations, and the State's Investigation of Abortion, Chicago, 1867–1940," *Journal of American History,* 77 (March 1991), 1251. Vandiver's essay is cited on the same page.

80. Schmidt, Case and Points, "Affidavit of Felix Klugman," Nov. 16, 1914, pp. 59–62.

81. Ibid., "Statement Made by Defendant in Sing Sing Prison," Feb. 15, 1914, pp. 116–17.

82. *New York Times,* April 26, 1914; May 30, 1914.

83. Ibid., "Affidavit of Arnold G. Leo," Nov. 17, 1914, pp. 48–51; "Affidavit of Bertha Zech," Nov. 17, 1914, pp. 52–53; "Affidavit of Arthur Heibing [Ernest Muret]," Nov. 12, 1914, pp. 54–56.

84. Ibid., "Statement Made by Defendant in Sing Sing Prison," Sept. 25, 1914, pp. 291–96.

85. Ibid., "Statement Made by Defendant in Sing Sing Prison," Sept. 28, 1914, pp. 325, 343, 351.

86. H. Snowden Marshall to the Attorney-General, Nov. 9, 1914, Central Files of the Department of Justice (#170339).

87. Frank H. Hiscock, "The Court of Appeals of New York: Some Features of its Organization and Work," *Cornell Law Quarterly,* 14 (Feb. 1920), 131–40.

88. Ibid., "Defendant's Brief," Oct. 1915.

89. Ibid., "Respondent's Brief," Oct. 1915.

90. See Richard Moran, *Knowing Right from Wrong: The Insanity Defense of Daniel McNaughtan* (New York, 1981); and Michael L. Perlin, *The Jurisprudence of the Insanity Defense* (Durham, N.C., 1994), pp. 335–37; Perlin also discusses the fear of shamming on pp. 236–45.

91. *The People of the State of New York* v. *Hans Schmidt,* 216 N.Y. 324 (1915), pp. 324–42. For the context see Robert Allan Carter, *History of the Insanity Defense in New York State* (Albany, 1982).

92. Lord Goddard in *Regina* v. *Windle,* 2 Q.B. 826 (Court of Criminal Appeals, 1952), cited in Robert Lloyd Goldstein and Merrill Rotter, "The Psychiatrist's Guide to Right and Wrong: Judicial Standards of Wrongfulness since McNaughtan," *Bulletin of the American Academy of Psychiatry and Law,* 16 (1988), 361.

93. Schmidt, Case and Points, "Defendant's Answering Brief," Oct. 1915, p. 24.

94. Charles S. Whitman to Walter H. Volckening, Sept. 18, 1913; Whitman to A. Ross Diefendorf, Sept. 27, 1913; Whitman to Ernest Muret, Dec. 2, 1913; Whitman to Anna Huttner, Dec. 3, 1913, District Attorney, Official Correspondence, Rolls 61–62.

95. Charles S. Whitman, "The World's Greatest Prosecuting Office," *American Review of Reviews* (June 1914), p. 711

96. John Temple Graves, "Whitman: Peerless Prosecutor," *Cosmopolitan,* 56 (Feb. 1914), 373.

97. "The Next Mayor of New York City," *Current Literature* (Dec. 1912), p. 636.

98. *The Public Papers of Governor Whitman, 1915* (Albany, 1916), pp. 10–11.

99. *The Public Papers of Governor Whitman, 1916* (Albany, 1917), p. 350.

100. *New York Times,* Jan. 12, 1916.

101. Ibid., Jan. 13, 1916.

102. Ibid., Jan. 8, 1916.

103. The People of the State of New York v. Hans Schmidt, Feb. 9, 1916, Blotters of Governor's Actions and Decisions, Box 31.

104. Ibid.

105. Ibid.

106. Amos O. Squire, *Sing Sing Doctor* (Garden City, N.Y., 1935), p. 156.

107. Ibid., p. 184; *New York Times,* Feb. 18 and 19, 1913.

108. Cardozo to Archie M. Palmer, Sept. 30, 1925, Cardozo MSS, Box 6.

109. Cardozo to Felix Frankfurter, May 14, 1927, Frankfurter MSS (Harvard Law School), III, Reel 24.

110. "What Medicine Can Do for Law," in Margaret E. Hall, ed., *Selected Writings of Benjamin Nathan Cardozo* (New York, 1947), pp. 386–87.

3. Scholars and Universities

1. George G. Bogert to Cardozo, Dec. 3, 1921, Records of the Dean, Cornell Law School, Box 8; Livingston Farrand to Cardozo, June 7, 1922, ibid.; Cuthbert Pound to Bogert, Dec. 14, 1921, ibid.

2. Cardozo to Bogert, Sept. 11, 1922, ibid.

3. Cornell *Daily Sun,* Nov. 14, 1923. It appears that this was an early version of lectures delivered at Yale Law School a year later and published as *The Growth of the Law,* from which some of these quotations are taken.

4. Ithaca *Journal-News,* Nov. 14, 1922.

5. Cardozo to Frank Thilly, Feb. 15, 1923, Thilly MSS.

6. Cardozo to Morris R. Cohen, June 1, 1931, Cohen MSS

7. Cardozo to Cohen, Aug. 25, 1927, ibid.

8. Cardozo to Roscoe Pound, April 2, 1921, Pound MSS, Box 182.

9. Cardozo to Karl Llewellyn [1933], Llewellyn MSS.

10. Cardozo to Bogert, Oct. 7, 1922, Records of the Dean, Cornell Law School, Box 8; Cardozo to Joseph M. Paley, Sept. 23, 1922, Cardozo MSS, Box 1.

11. Cardozo to Roscoe Pound, July 21, 1920, Pound MSS.

12. Cardozo to Annie Nathan Meyer, Aug. 8, 1927, Meyer MSS.

13. Inscription in Frankfurter's copy of *The Paradoxes of Legal Science,* located in the Law Library, Hebrew University of Jerusalem.

14. Cardozo to Roscoe Pound, Aug. 9, 1920, Pound MSS.

15. Cardozo to Annie Nathan Meyer, Nov. 21, 1932, Cardozo MSS (HUC).

16. Pound to Felix Frankfurter, May 26, 1930, Frankfurter MSS, Reel #55 (LC)

17. Cardozo to James M. Landis, Feb. 11, 1931, Landis MSS.

18. Cardozo to George Hellman, March 22, 1938, Cardozo MSS, Box 1; Cardozo to Mrs. E. R. A. Seligman, March 10, 1928, ibid., Box 6.

19. Ibid.

20. Benjamin N. Cardozo, *The Growth of the Law* (New Haven, 1924), p. 14.

21. William H. Manz, "Cardozo's Use of Authority: An Empirical Study," *California Western Law Review,* 32 (1995), 38, 41. See also Richard A. Posner, *Cardozo: A Study in Reputation* (Chicago, 1990), pp. 134–35.

22. Cardozo to James M. Landis, May 27, 1930, Landis MSS.

23. Arthur L. Corbin, "The Judicial Process Revisited: Introduction," *Yale Law Journal,* 71 (Dec. 1961), 195–201.

24. Benjamin N. Cardozo, *The Nature of the Judicial Process* (New Haven, 1921), pp. 10–12. For an astute analysis of this work see Stanley Charles Brubaker, "Benjamin Nathan Cardozo: An Intellectual Biography" (Ph.D. diss., University of Virginia, 1979), ch. 6.

25. Ibid., p. 66.

26. Ibid., pp. 69, 140–41.

27. Ibid., pp. 174–75.

28. Cardozo to Learned Hand, June 25, 1929, Hand MSS.

29. Cardozo to Learned Hand, July 18, 1928, ibid.

30. "A Ministry of Justice," in Margaret E. Hall, ed., *Selected Writings of Benjamin Nathan Cardozo* (New York, 1947), pp. 357–70; Harlan Fiske Stone to Cardozo, Nov. 4, 1921, Stone MSS (CU).

31. N. E. H. Hull, "Restatement and Reform: A New Perspective on the Origins of the American Law Institute," *Law and History Review,* 8 (Spring, 1990), 56.

32. Ibid., p. 73.

33. Ibid., p. 86.

34. Cardozo, *Growth of the Law,* pp. 9–13.

35. Ibid., pp. 54–55.

36. Cardozo to Bogert, Sept. 11, 1922, Records of the Dean, Cornell Law School, Box 8.

37. Cited in Cardozo, *Growth of the Law,* p. 2.

38. The facts regarding the case are drawn from the trial record and other documents found in Louise Hamburger v. Cornell University, Case and Points, 240 N.Y. 328 (1925).

39. Emile M. Chamot and Fred H. Rhodes, "The Development of the Department of Chemistry and the School of Chemical Engineering at Cornell" (Cornell University Archives), pp. 64–70.

40. Ibid. See also A. W. Browne, "American Contemporaries: Louis Munroe Dennis," *Industrial and Engineering Chemistry,* 22 (Nov. 1930), 1–4.

41. Louis M. Dennis and F. W. Clarke, *The Laboratory Manual to Elementary Chemistry* (New York, 1902), p. 164.

42. Hamburger v. Cornell, Case and Points, p. 77.

43. Dennis and Clarke, *Laboratory Manual,* p. 170

44. Hamburger v. Cornell, Case and Points, pp. 78–83.

45. Ibid., pp. 84–85.

46. Ibid., pp. 209–18.

47. Ibid., pp. 61–70.

48. Ibid., p. 90.

49. Ibid., p. 70.

50. Louis M. Dennis to C. D. Bostwick, July 7, 1916, Mynderse Van Cleef MSS.

51. Cornell *Daily Sun,* Feb. 14, 1916.

52. Louise Hamburger Affidavit, July 7, 1916, Van Cleef MSS.

53. Van Cleef to Carey D. Davie, Aug. 17, 1916, ibid.

54. McCaskill to Van Cleef, July 11 and 14, 1916, ibid.

55. 172 NY Supp., 5–7 (1918).

56. Rockwood to McCaskill, Sept. 13, 1918, Van Cleef MSS.

57. McCaskill to Mynderse Van Cleef, ibid.

58. Van Cleef to Kirkendall, Oct. 18, 1918, ibid.

59. 226 N.Y. 625 (1919).

60. Rockwood to McCaskill, April 23, 1919, Van Cleef MSS.

61. McCaskill to Rockwood, April 25, 1919, ibid.

62. Rockwood to McCaskill, April 28, 1919, ibid.

63. McCaskill to Rogers, March 5, 1920, ibid.

64. McCaskill to Van Cleef, Sept. 27, 1921, ibid.

65. Hamburger v. Cornell, Case and Points, pp. 51, 296.

66. Ibid., p. 92.

67. Ibid., p. 99.

68. Ibid., p. 112.

69. McCaskill to Van Cleef, Sept. 27 and 28, 1921, Van Cleef MSS.

70. McCaskill to Van Cleef, Sept. 27 and 29, 1921, ibid.

71. Hamburger v. Cornell, Case and Points, pp. 334–41.

72. Ibid., pp. 368, 492, 506, 533.

73. Ibid., p. 298.

74. McCaskill to Van Cleef, Sept. 29, 1921, Van Cleef MSS.

75. Hamburger v. Cornell, Case and Points, pp. 560–78.

76. McCaskill to Van Cleef, Sept. 29, 1921, Van Cleef MSS.

77. McCaskill to Collin, Oct. 10, 1922, ibid.

78. Collin, "Brief for Cornell University," ibid.

79. Rockwood, "Brief for Respondent," ibid.

80. 204 N.Y. Supp, 664–73.

81. Ibid., 674–77.

82. *Unger* v. *Loewy*, 236 N.Y. 73 (1923).

83. Henry W. Sackett to Van Cleef, Oct. 5, 1921, July 19, 1922, June 4, 1923, Van Cleef MSS.

84. Rockwood, "Brief for Appellant," Nov. 18, 1924, ibid.

85. Collin, "Brief for Cornell University, Respondent" [n.d.], ibid.

86. The facts regarding the case are drawn from the trial record and other documents in Mary E. Schloendorff v. The Society of the New York Hospital, Case and Points.

87. Schloendorff v. New York Hospital, Case and Points, 211 N.Y. 125 (1914), pp. 21–24.

88. Ibid., pp. 25–28.

89. Ibid., pp. 195–96.

90. Ibid., pp. 32, 62.

91. Ibid., p. 94.

92. Ibid., pp. 108–29.

93. Ibid., p. 200.

94. Augustus Van Wyck, "Appellant's Brief," Schloendorff v. New York Hospital, Case and Points.

95. Austen G. Fox and Wilson M. Powell Jr., "Respondent's Points," ibid.

96. *Mary E. Schloendorff* v. *the Society of the New York Hospital*, 211 N.Y. 125, pp. 125–35.

97. In fact, Collin had been one of the concurring judges in Cardozo's *Schloendorff* opinion.

98. Van Cleef to Henry W. Sackett, Oct. 6, 1921, Van Cleef MSS.

99. *George F. Butterworth* v. *William H. Keeler,* 219 N.Y. 446, pp. 449–50.

100. *Louise Hamburger* v. *Cornell University,* 240 N.Y. 328, pp. 331–41. For another case which also reveals Cardozo's sympathy for institutions of higher learning, see *Allegheny College* v. *National Chautauqua County Bank*, 246 N.Y. 369 (1927); and the discussion in Alfred S. Konefsky, "How To Read, Or at Least Not Misread, Cardozo in the Allegheny College Case," *Buffalo Law Review*, 36 (1987), 645–99.

101. G. B. Rice, "Charitable Corporations: Liability of for Various Types of Negligence," *Cornell Law Quarterly*, 11 (Dec. 1925), 63.

102. Frederic C. Woodward, "Charitable Institutions—Liability for Torts of Ser-vants—Status of University Professors," *Illinois Law Review,* 20 (Dec. 1925), 376. See also "Charities—Liabilities for Torts," *Michigan Law Review,* 24 (Feb. 1926), 408–10.

103. Cited in Matthew W. Finkin, "'A Higher Order of Liberty in the Workplace': Academic Freedom and Tenure in the Vortex of Employment Practices and Law," *Law and Contemporary Problems,* 53 (Summer 1990), 378.

104. *Isabel Bing* v. *Louis A. Thunig,* 2 N.Y. 2d 656 (1957), pp. 666–67. The opinion was written by Judge Stanley Fuld. For the current status of a university's liability for acci-dents in chemistry laboratories, see the two-part article by J. Ric Gass, "Chemistry, Courtrooms, and Common Sense," in *Journal of Chemical Education,* 67 (Jan. 1990), 51–55; (Feb. 1990), 132–34.

4. Gender and Sexuality

1. Cardozo to Learned Hand, Jan. 27, 1917, Hand MSS.

2. *Albany Directory* (Albany, 1926), p. 190.

3. Cardozo to Mrs. Willard Bartlett, Jan. 18, 1925, Willard Bartlett MSS.

4. *New York Times,* Sept. 17, 1926.

5. Elkus to Stephen Wise, Sept. 19, 1926, Wise MSS.

6. Wise to Richard W. Montague, June 2, 1927, in Carl Hermann Voss, ed., *Stephen S. Wise: Servant of the People, Selected Letters* (Philadelphia, 1969), p. 150.

7. *New York Times,* Sept. 15, 1926.

8. Cardozo to Learned Hand, Aug. 17, 1926, Hand MSS.

9. Pound to Felix Frankfurter, Oct. 8, 1926, Frankfurter MSS (LC), Reel 55.

10. *Parascandola* v. *Hammond,* Feb. 11, 1930, Internal Records of the Court of Ap-peals, Box 4 (4666).

11. Cardozo to Associates, July 9, 1928, re: *Sorentino* v. *Sorentino,* ibid. (3833).

12. Cardozo to William S. Andrews, Nov. 7, 1917, ibid., Box 1 (1067).

13. Stewart v. Turney, Sept. 5, 1923, ibid., Box 2 (1652).

14. *In re Stone* v. *Wiebke* (June 8, 1928), ibid., Box 4 (4668).

15. See Audrey T. Rodgers, *Virgin and Whore: The Image of Women in the Poetry of William Carlos Williams* (Jefferson, N.C., 1987), pp. 11–12.

16. *People* v. *Raymond Carey,* 233 N.Y. 519 (1918).

17. People v. Raymond Carey, Case and Points, pp. 23–28, 34–36.

18. Ibid., pp. 163–64, 209–10.

19. Ibid., p. 111.

20. Ibid., pp. 307–21.

21. *People* v. *Carey,* 233 N.Y. 519.

22. *People* v. *Carey,* Internal Records of the Court of Appeals, Box 1 (1060).

23. Cardozo, *Nature of the Judicial Process,* pp. 156–58.

24. *Watertown Daily Times,* Feb. 21–22, 1913.

25. People v. Carey, Case and Points, pp. 244, 69, 42.

26. People v. George Burnhardt, Case and Points, 251 N.Y. 521 (1929), p. 24.

27. Ibid., p. 27.

28. Ibid., pp. 166–75.

29. Dissenting Opinion of Justice Hasbrouck, ibid., pp. 188–92.

30. People v. Burnhardt, May 28, 1929, Internal Records of the Court of Appeals, Box 4 (4350).

31. Dean Briggs (1900) cited in Sheila M. Rothman, *Woman's Proper Place* (New York, 1978), p. 23.

32. Birthday card [May 24, 1912], Maud Nathan MSS, Reel 2.

33. Kate Tracy to George S. Hellman [Sept. 1938], Hellman MSS.

34. Cardozo to Learned Hand, Sept. 21, 1922, Hand MSS.

35. Cardozo to Charles C. Burlingham, March 6, 1933, Burlingham MSS, Box 22.

36. Cardozo to G. Herbert Cone, Aug. 11, 1918, Cardozo MSS (HLS).

37. Cardozo to Maud Nathan, July 9, 1927, Hellman MSS.

38. Cardozo to Maud Nathan, Aug. 14, 1928, ibid.

39. Cardozo to Annie Nathan Meyer, July 20, 1929, Meyer MSS.

40. Babbette Deutsch, "Benjamin Cardozo—Idol of Bench and Bar," *New Yorker* (March 22, 1930), p. 27.

41. Cardozo to Annie Nathan Meyer, June 16, 1935, Meyer MSS.

42. Cardozo to Annie Nathan Meyer, July 27, 1931, ibid.

43. Cardozo to Rupert L. Joseph, Aug. 7, 1933, Cardozo MSS (HUC).

44. George Hellman, "Notes in re our conversation with Addie Cardozo," Nov. 6, 1938, Cardozo MSS.

45. Cardozo to Harlan Fiske Stone, June 1, 1929, Stone MSS, Box 8.

46. Cardozo to Annie Nathan Meyer, March 9, 1932, Cardozo MSS (HUC).

47. George Hellman, "Notes on conversation with Moses Hadas," Feb. 1, 1939, Cardozo MSS.

48. Cardozo to Annie Nathan Meyer, Nov. 3, 1932, Cardozo MSS (HUC).

49. Cardozo to Aline Goldstone [summer 1935], Hellman MSS.

50. George S. Hellman, *Benjamin N. Cardozo* (New York, 1940), p. 49.

51. Holmes to Harold Laski, May 13, 1926, Mark De Wolfe Howe, ed., *Holmes-Laski Letters,* (New York, 1963), II, 84.

52. Jonathan M. Wainwright to Irving Lehman, July 11, 1938, Wainwright MSS, Box 3a.

53. Oswald Garrison Villard, "Issues and Men," *Nation,* 147 (July 16, 1938), 69.

54. Hand to Felix Frankfurter, May 4, 1932, Frankfurter MSS (HLS), Reel 26.

55. George S. Hellman, "Interview with Christopher S. Sargent" [n.d.], Cardozo MSS.

56. George Hellman, "Notes on Conversation with Augustus Vincent Tack," Feb. 10, 1939, ibid.

57. Annie Nathan Meyer, *Black Souls: A Play in Six Acts* (New Bedford, Mass., 1934)

58. Cardozo to Annie Nathan Meyer, Dec. 29, 1924, Meyer MSS and Cardozo MSS (HUC): each collection contains a portion of this letter.

59. Cardozo to Annie Nathan Meyer, Aug. 26, 1932, Cardozo MSS (HUC).

60. *Amelia F. Dean* v. *Robert J. Dean,* 241 N.Y. 240; dissenting opinion of Irving Lehman.

61. 241 N.Y. 240, 245. See William H. Rodgers Jr. and Linda A. Rodgers, "The Disparity between Due Process and Full Faith and Credit: The Problem of the Somewhere Wife," *Columbia Law Review,* 67 (1967), 1363–1403.

62. Dean v. Dean, Case and Points, pp. 43–45.

63. Ibid., p. 46.

64. Ibid., pp. 73–74.

65. Ibid., p. 15.

66. Ibid., pp. 55–56.

67. Ibid., pp. 118–22.

68. Ibid., pp. 130–42.

69. 241 N.Y. 240, 246–51.

70. Ibid., 242–46.

71. Brainerd Lurrie, "Married Women's Contracts: A Study in Conflict of Law Method," *University of Chicago Law Review,* 25 (1958), 257.

72. 241 N.Y. 240, 244.

73. Allison Binder, "In Sickness and in Health," Seminar paper, Cornell University (1992), citing interview with Leora Hoadley, Dec. 4, 1992.

74. *Whitney* v. *Whitney,* 121 Misc. 485 (1923), 493.

75. *Reed* v. *Reed,* 195 App. Div. 531 (1921), 533.

76. Ibid.

77. *Leon D. Hoadley* v. *Elsie R. Hoadley,* 244 N.Y. 424.

78. Cited in 121 Misc. 485, 489.

79. 244 N.Y. 424, 435.

80. Ibid., 437.

81. Allison Binder interview with Leora Hoadley, Dec. 4, 1992.

82. Cardozo to Melville Cane, Jan. 28, 1926, Cane MSS.

83. Cardozo to Learned Hand, Feb. 7, 1926, Hand MSS.

84. Ibid.

85. Cardozo to Mrs. E. R. A. Seligman, Feb. 16, 1926, Seligman MSS.

86. Information on both families may be found in 1920 Census, New York City, Roll 1139.

87. Mirizio v. Mirizio, Case and Points, Supreme Court, Bronx County, p. 46.

88. Ibid., p. 36. Fannie had a brother four years older than she was, and two younger brothers.

89. Ibid., p. 21. Cosmo had an older sister and two younger sisters.

90. Ibid., Supreme Court, Appellate Division, p. 28

91. Ibid., p. 30.

92. Ibid., Supreme Court, Bronx County, p. 46.

93. *Fannie Mirizio* v. *Cosmo Mirizio,* 242 N.Y. 74 (1926), 76–84.

94. Cuthbert Pound to Felix Frankfurter, April 16, 1926, Frankfurter MSS (LC), Reel 55.

95. Frankfurter to Pound, April 30, 1926, ibid.

96. Pound to Frankfurter, April 26, 1926, ibid.

97. 242 N.Y. 74, 88–93.

98. In *The Influence of Judge Cardozo on the Common Law* (Garden City, 1942), pp. 18–20, Lehman explains that most of his opinion in *People* v. *Mummiani,* 258 N.Y. 394 (1931), a case involving allegations of a coerced confession, was written by Cardozo.

99. 242 N.Y. 74, 93–97.

100. Mirizio v. Mirizio, Case and Points, Supreme Court, Appellate Division, p. 47.

101. Ibid., pp. 48–49.

102. Ibid., pp. 49–50.

103. Ibid., p. 45.

104. Ibid., pp. 29–33.

105. Ibid., p. 77.

106. *Fannie Mirizio* v. *Cosmo Mirizio,* 248 N.Y. 175 (1928), 177–81.

5. Religion and the State

1. Horace M. Kallen, "Julian William Mack," in Harry Barnard, *The Forging of an American Jew: The Life and Times of Judge Julian W. Mack* (New York, 1974), p. xxi.

2. Morris R. Cohen, *Reason and Nature* (New York, 1931), p. 11.

3. Robert Jerome Glennon, *The Iconoclast as Reformer: Jerome Frank's Impact on American Law* (Ithaca, 1985), p. 23. See also David A. Hollinger, *Morris R. Cohen and the Scientific Ideal* (Cambridge, 1975), pp. 85–89.

4. Jerome N. Frank, *Law and the Modern Mind* (New York, 1930), chs. 4, 8. See also Neil Duxbury, "Jerome Frank and the Legacy of Legal Realism," *Journal of Law and Society,* 18 (1991), 175–205.

5. Frank, *Law and the Modern Mind,* ch. 6.

6. Cardozo to Jerome N. Frank, Oct. 5, 1930, Frank MSS, Box 4.

7. Laski to Holmes, May 11, 1931, in Mark DeWolfe Howe, ed., *Holmes-Laski Letters* (New York, 1963), II, 364–65.

8. "The Speech of Judges: A Dissenting Opinion," *Virginia Law Review,* 29 (1943), 631. This article, written by Frank, was signed "Anon Y. Mous." To mask his identity, Frank wrote of Cardozo's comment on Cohen: "I am told that one evening . . ." In the original version he had written, "I recall an evening, some ten years ago . . ." Frank MSS, Box 157.

9. Frank to Cardozo, Dec. 18, 1931, Frank MSS, Box 2.

10. Cardozo, "Faith and a Doubting World," in Margaret E. Hall, ed., *Selected Writings of Benjamin Nathan Cardozo* (New York, 1947), pp. 99–106.

11. Frank to Oscar Cox, Dec. 7, 1931, Cox MSS, Box 135.

12. Cox to Cardozo, Dec. 7, 1931, ibid.

13. Cardozo to Cox, Dec. 8, 1931, ibid.

14. Cardozo, "Jurisprudence," in Hall, ed., *Selected Writings,* pp. 7–46.

15. Cardozo to Karl Llewellyn, Feb. 12, 1932, Llewellyn MSS.

16. Cardozo to Frank, Feb. 19, 1932, Frank MSS, Box 2.

17. Frank to Cardozo, Sept. 9, 1932, ibid.

18. Cardozo to Frank, Sept. 16, 1932, ibid.

19. Frank to Cardozo, Sept. 19, 1932, ibid.

20. Frank to Levy, Aug. 1, Aug. 30, 1938, Frank MSS, Box 4.

21. Cited in Peter H. Irons, *The New Deal Lawyers* (Princeton, 1982), p. 127.

22. Cited in Glennon, *Iconoclast as Reformer,* p. 31.

23. Frank to Felix Frankfurter, Dec. 8, 1941, Frankfurter MSS (LC), Reel 34.

24. Cited in Glennon, *Iconoclast as Reformer,* p. 80.

25. Memorandum [Feb. 1932], Herbert Hoover MSS, Presidential Subject—Judiciary. Two excellent accounts of Cardozo's nomination are Andrew L. Kaufman, "Cardozo's Appointment to the Supreme Court," *Cardozo Law Review,* 1 (1969), 23–53; and Ira H. Carmen, "The President, Politics and the Power of Appointment: Hoover's Nomination of Mr. Justice Cardozo," *Virginia Law Review,* 55 (1969), 616–59.

26. Stephen S. Wise to Felix Frankfurter and Julian W. Mack, March 8, 1932, Wise MSS.

27. Mark Sullivan to Lawrence Richey, Jan. 18, 1932, Herbert Hoover MSS.

28. Harlan Fiske Stone to Hoover, Feb. 10, 1932, ibid.

29. Franklin W. Fort to Hoover, Jan. 26, 1932, ibid.

30. Wise to Frankfurter and Mack, March 8, 1932, Wise MSS; see also Wise to Frankfurter, Jan. 19, 1932, ibid.

31. Henry L. Stimson Diary, Feb. 14, 1932, Stimson MSS.

32. Sullivan to Richey, Jan. 18, 1932, Hoover MSS.

33. George W. Wickersham to William Howard Taft, Sept. 25, 1922, Taft MSS, Reel 245.

34. Nicholas Murray Butler to Calvin Coolidge, Dec. 9, 1924, Coolidge MSS.

35. George W. Wickersham to Hoover, Feb. 15, 1932, Hoover MSS.

36. *New York Times,* Feb. 16, 1932.

37. Cuthbert Pound to Felix Frankfurter, March 4, 1932, Frankfurter MSS (LC), Reel 55.

38. Harlan Fiske Stone to Cardozo, Feb. 15, 1932, Stone MSS, Box 74.

39. Cardozo to Stephen S. Wise, Feb. 20, 1932, Wise MSS.

40. Cardozo to Louise Wise, April 28, 1932, ibid.

41. Cardozo to Morris R. Cohen, Dec. 27, 1932, Cohen MSS.

42. Cardozo to Rupert L. Joseph, May 19, 1933, Cardozo MSS (HUC).

43. Cardozo to Morris R. Cohen, June 11, 1932, Cohen MSS.

44. Cardozo to Charles C. Burlingham, Nov. 14, 1933, Burlingham MSS.

45. Cardozo eventually signed his letters to Brandeis with the informal "BNC" instead of his full name, but always addressed them to "Justice Brandeis."

46. Cardozo to Charles C. Burlingham, Nov. 14, 1933, Burlingham MSS.

47. Cardozo to Rupert L. Joseph, Jan. 24, 1934, Cardozo MSS (HUC).

48. Cardozo to Rupert L. Joseph, Oct. 8, 1933, ibid.

49. *Nixon* v. *Condon,* 286 U.S. 73 (1932).

50. Cardozo to Learned Hand, March 22, 1930, Hand MSS.

51. Cardozo to Hand, Feb. 17, 1932, ibid.

52. Cardozo to Charles C. Burlingham, Sept. 21, 1933, Burlingham MSS.

53. Cardozo to James M. Landis, Feb. 18, 1932, Landis MSS.

54. Cardozo to Charles C. Burlingham, Feb. 16, 1933, Burlingham MSS.

55. Ed Darby to Lee de Forest, May 23, 1934. I am indebted to James Hijiya for this letter from the Lee de Forest Memorial Archive (Los Altos, California).

56. Cardozo to Oliver Wendell Holmes, Dec. 14, 1928, Holmes MSS, Reel 28.

57. George S. Hellman, "Conversation with Christopher S. Sargent [n.d.], Cardozo MSS.

58. Cardozo to Mrs. Max J. Rossbach, Sept. 11, 1934, Herbert Lehman MSS.

59. Herbert Wechsler to Karl Llewellyn, Feb. 4, 1955, Llewellyn MSS.

60. George S. Hellman, "Conversation with Ambrose Doskow," June 1939, Cardozo MSS.

61. Louise W. Wise to Louis D. Brandeis, March 8, 1932, Brandeis MSS, Reel 50.

62. Louis D. Brandeis to Julian W. Mack, Feb. 16, 1932, Mack MSS.

63. Jonathan D. Sarna, "'The Greatest Jew in the World since Jesus Christ': The Jewish Legacy of Louis D. Brandeis," *American Jewish History,* 81 (Spring-Summer 1994), 348.

64. Lewis J. Paper, *Brandeis* (Englewood Cliffs, N.J., 1983), p. 200.

65. Sarna, "Greatest Jew," 348.

66. Philippa Strum, *Louis D. Brandeis: Justice for the People* (Cambridge, Mass., 1984), p. 244.

67. Ibid., pp. 244–45.

68. Ibid., p. 279. In *Rabbis and Lawyers: The Journey from Torah to Constitution*

(Bloomington, Ind., 1990), p. 143, Jerold S. Auerbach argues that Brandeis "developed a rationale for Zionism that expanded its appeal by contracting, indeed all but eliminating, its Jewish content."

69. Abraham Tulin to George Hellman, Nov. 4, 1938, Cardozo MSS, Box 9.

70. Stephen S. Wise, *Challenging Years: The Autobiography of Stephen Wise* (New York, 1949), pp. 157–58.

71. Stephen S. Wise to Cardozo, Sept. 12, 1918, Wise MSS.

72. Wise, *Challenging Years*, pp. 158–59.

73. Naomi W. Cohen, *Not Free to Desist: The American Jewish Committee, 1906–1966* (Philadelphia, 1972), p. 109.

74. Cardozo, "Reflections upon a School of Jurisprudence at the Hebrew University" [1928], Cardozo MSS, Box 13.

75. Strum, *Brandeis*, p. 274.

76. Cardozo to Morris R. Cohen, Aug. 13, 1935, Cohen MSS.

77. Cardozo to Louise Wise, Sept. 21, 1929, Stephen S. Wise MSS.

78. Wise to George H. Farnum, Aug. 8, 1938, ibid.

79. Cardozo to Charles C. Burlingham, May 25, 1931, Burlingham MSS.

80. Cardozo, "Values: or The Choice of Tycho Brahe," in Hall, ed., *Selected Writings*, pp. 1–6.

81. Stephen S. Wise to George H. Farnum, Aug. 8, 1938, Wise MSS.

82. Elector's Minutes, June 5, 1895, Congregation Shearith Israel MSS.

83. Ibid.

84. George Hellman, "Notes on Conversation with Dr. David de Sola Pool," Nov. 9, 1938, Cardozo MSS, Box 8.

85. Elector's Minutes, June 5, 1895, Congregation Shearith Israel MSS.

86. Ibid.

87. This essay (and another on Disraeli by Emma Lazarus) has recently been published: Michael Selzer, ed., *Disraeli, the Jew* (Great Barrington, Mass., 1993), pp. 41–66.

88. Cardozo to Frances N. Wolff, March 26, 1935, Cardozo MSS, Box 1.

89. Cardozo to Aline Goldstone, Aug. 20, 1928, George Hellman MSS.

90. Minutes of the Executive Committee, May 11, 1930, American Jewish Committee MSS.

91. Cardozo to Annie Nathan Meyer, June 8, 1935, Cardozo MSS (HUC).

92. Cardozo to Rabbi Jacob Weinstein, March 28, 1933, ibid.

93. Cardozo to Stephen Wise, April 29, 1933, Oct. 31, 1933, Cardozo MSS, Box 9.

94. Cardozo to Oswald Garrison Villard, March 12, 1936, Villard MSS.

95. *New York Times*, Sept. 7, 1935.

96. Ibid., Sept. 15, 1935.

97. Ibid.

98. Cardozo to Aline Goldstone, Sept. 14, 1935, George Hellman MSS. See also the general discussion in Andrew Kaufman, "Benjamin N. Cardozo, Sephardic Jew,' in *The Jewish Justices of the Supreme Court Revisited: Brandeis to Fortas, The Journal of Supreme Court History* (1994), pp. 35–59.

99. *New York Times*, Sept. 18, 1935.

100. Ibid., Sept. 28, 1935.

101. Cohen, *Not Free to Desist*, p. 164.

102. Melvin I. Urofsky, *A Voice That Spoke for Justice: The Life and Times of Stephen S. Wise* (Albany, 1982), p. 269.

103. Cardozo to Stephen S. Wise, Dec. 8, 1934, Wise MSS.

104. Cardozo had touched briefly on the topic in lectures given at Columbia University and published as *The Paradoxes of Legal Science* (New York, 1928), pp. 98, 102–15, but had done little more than offer some broad generalizations.

105. *Brief* for Hamilton and Reynolds, pp. 5, 15.

106. "Program of Instruction for Senior Division Units of the ROTC," March 22, 1932, Files of the Chancellor's Office, UCLA.

107. The decision in *Coale* v. *Pearson,* Superior Court of Baltimore County, Jan. 24, 1933, may be found in *Friends Intelligencer,* 90 (Second Month 18, 1933), ibid.

108. *University of Maryland* v. *Coale,* 165 Md. 224 (1933).

109. Albert Hamilton to Ernest C. Moore, Sept. 21, 1933, Files of the Chancellor's Office, UCLA.

110. John Beardsley to Rev. Frank Toothaker, Oct. 31, 1933, ibid.

111. Robert Cohen, *When the Old Left Was Young: Student Radicals and America's First Mass Student Movement, 1929–1941* (New York, 1993), pp. 29, 118–20.

112. Minutes, Board of Regents, Executive Session, April 13, 1934.

113. Ibid., May 18, 1934.

114. *Hamilton* v. *Regents,* 29 P. (2nd) Cal. 355 (1934).

115. John U. Calkins to Ernest C. Moore, Jan. 29, 1934, Files of the Chancellor's Office, UCLA.

116. *Brief* for Hamilton and Reynolds.

117. *Brief* for Appellees, p. 10.

118. *Brief* for Hamilton and Reynolds, pp. 23–24.

119. *Brief* for Appellees, p. 14.

120. *Hamilton et al.* v. *Regents of the University of California et al.* 293 U.S. 245 (1934).

121. *United States* v. *Schwimmer* 279 U.S. 644, 653–54 (1929).

122. Harlan Fiske Stone to Butler, Nov. 28, 1934, Stone MSS, Box 61.

123. Butler to Stone, Nov. 30, 1934, ibid.

124. David Danelski, "Pierce Butler," in Melvin I. Urofsky, *The Supreme Court Justices* (New York, 1994), p. 82.

125. Cardozo to Harlan Fiske Stone, Nov. 30, 1934, Stone MSS, Box 61.

126. 293 U.S. 245, 265–268 (1934).

127. Draft of concurring opinion with handwritten addition, Stone MSS, Box 61.

6. Law and Order

1. *New York Times,* March 5, 1933.

2. Cardozo to Annie Nathan Meyer, March 11, 1933, Cardozo MSS (HUC).

3. Cardozo to Learned Hand, July 6, 1932, Hand MSS.

4. Cardozo to Charles C. Burlingham, Nov. 17, 1932, Burlingham MSS.

5. Cardozo to Annie Nathan Meyer, March 11, 1933, Cardozo MSS (HUC).

6. Cardozo to Felix Frankfurter, Jan. 24, 1934, Frankfurter MSS (LC), Reel 70.

7. Cardozo to Rupert L. Joseph, Aug. 11, 1936, Cardozo MSS, Box 1.

8. *Burnet* v. *Wells,* 289 U.S. 670, 679 (1933), cited in Henry M. Holland Jr., "Mr. Justice Cardozo and the New Deal Court," *Journal of Public Law,* 12 (1963), p. 395.

9. *Williams* v. *Baltimore,* 288 U.S. 36, 101 (1933), cited in ibid., p. 396.

10. 294 U.S. 550, 576 (1935).

11. *Panama Refining Co. et al.* v. *Ryan et al.,* 293 U.S. 388, 430 (1935).

12. Ibid., 433–48. For an excellent discussion of the case see Peter H. Irons, *The New Deal Lawyers* (Princeton, 1982), ch. 3.

13. Cardozo to Karl Llewellyn, Jan. 15, 1935, Llewellyn MSS.

14. Cardozo to Annie Nathan Meyer, Jan. 14, 1935, Meyer MSS.

15. *Schechter Poultry Corp.* v. *United States,* 295 U.S. 495, 551–53 (1935).

16. 298 U.S. 1, 28 (1935).

17. Ibid., 29–33.

18. Cited in Alpheus Thomas Mason, *Harlan Fiske Stone: Pillar of the Law* (New York, 1956), p. 421.

19. 298 U.S. 238 (1936).

20. Ibid., 331–37.

21. Cardozo to Learned Hand, July 31, 1936, Hand MSS.

22. Cited in Mason, *Stone*, pp. 410, 422, 425.

23. Cardozo to Harlan Fiske Stone, July 2, 1936, Stone MSS, Box 74.

24. Cardozo to Jane Perry Clark, Sept. 14, 1937, Clark MSS.

25. Cardozo to Annie Nathan Meyer, Sept. 13, 1936, Cardozo MSS (HUC).

26. Cardozo to Jane Perry Clark, Nov. 7, 1935, Clark MSS.

27. Cardozo to Annie Nathan Meyer, Aug. 28, 1936, Meyer MSS.

28. "Brief for Petitioner," *Helvering* v. *Davis,* 301 U.S. 619 (1937), p. 30.

29. 301 U.S. 619, 641 (1937).

30. Unpublished concurrence, *Home Building and Loan Association* v. *Blaisdell,* 290 U.S. 398 (1934), in Stone MSS.

31. *Steward Machine Co.* v. *Davis,* 301 U.S. 548 (1937).

32. 301 U.S. 619, 641 (1937).

33. Ibid., 640.

34. 301 U.S. 548 (1937).

35. Richard D. Friedman, "On Cardozo and Reputation: Legendary Judge, Underrated Justice?" *Cardozo Law Review,* 12 (1991), 1939.

36. *People* v. *Defore,* 213 App. Div. 643 (1925).

37. People v. Defore, Case and Points, 242 N.Y. 13, "Appellant's Brief," p. 5.

38. *Boyd* v. *United States,* 116 U.S. 616, 635 (1886).

39. *Weeks* v. *United States,* 232 U.S. 383, 392 (1914).

40. *Agnello* v. *United States,* 269 U.S. 19, 32 (1925).

41. People v. Defore, Case and Points, "Appellant's Reply Brief," p. 4.

42. *People* v. *John Defore,* 242 N.Y. 13, 17–28.

43. *Mapp* v. *Ohio,* 367 U.S. 643, 653 (1961).

44. Syracuse *American,* Jan. 11, 1931.

45. People v. Miller, Case and Points, 257 N.Y. 54, "Respondent's Brief," pp. 63–64.

46. Ibid., "Trial Record," p. 1615.

47. *People* v. *Le Roy J. Miller,* 257 N.Y. 54, 56–61.

48. See also *People* v. *Nick Chiagles,* 237 N.Y., 193 (1923), and *People* v. *Kendall Lytton,* 257 N.Y. 310 (1931).

49. See *People* v. *Joseph Zackowitz,* 254 N.Y. 192 (1930).

50. Cardozo to Joseph M. Paley, July 14, 1923, Cardozo MSS, Box 1.

51. People v. Defore, Case and Points, "Appellant's Brief," p. 60.

52. John H. Wigmore, "Evidence Obtained by Illegal Search and Seizure," *Journal of the American Bar Association,* 8 (Aug. 1922), 480–82.

53. Boston *Globe,* April 11, 14, 1931.

54. *Commonwealth* v. *Snyder et al.*, 185 N.E. 376, 378 (1933).

55. Boston *Globe,* May 25, 1932.

56. Snyder v. Commonwealth of Massachusetts, Case and Points, "Transcript of Evidence," Appendix I, pp. 35–37.

57. *Commonwealth* v. *Snyder et al.*, 185 N.E. 376, 380 (1933).

58. Boston *Globe,* July 5, 1933.

59. Brandeis to Felix Frankfurter, Jan. 11, 1934, in Melvin I. Urofsky and David W. Levy, eds., *"Half Brother, Half Son": The Letters of Louis D. Brandeis to Felix Frankfurter* (Norman, Okla., 1991), p. 537.

60. *Snyder* v. *Commonwealth of Massachusetts,* 291 U.S. 97, 123–38 (1934).

61. Ibid., 97, 102–22.

62. Felix Frankfurter to Cardozo, Feb. 19, 1934; Cardozo to Frankfurter, March 2, 1934, Frankfurter MSS (LC), Reel 70.

63. Cardozo to Aline Goldstone [summer 1933], George Hellman MSS.

64. The murders and investigation were fully covered in the *Bridgeport Post,* the *Hartford Daily Courant,* and the *Waterbury Republican,* Sept. 30–Oct. 3, 1935.

65. *Hartford Daily Courant,* Oct. 30, 1935.

66. State of Connecticut v. Frank Palko, 121 Conn. 669, Case and Points, Trial Transcript, p. 323.

67. *Waterbury Republican,* Nov. 6, 1935.

68. *Bridgeport Post,* Oct. 30, 1935.

69. State of Connecticut v. Frank Palko, Case and Points, Trial transcript, p. 355. This testimony comes from the second trial but undoubtedly was the same as that given at the first.

70. Ibid., p. 305.

71. Ibid., "Plaintiff's Appeal," pp. 37–38.

72. Ibid., pp. 66–67.

73. Ibid., pp. 33–34.

74. *Hartford Daily Courant,* Jan. 24, 1936.

75. General Statutes, Connecticut, Sec. 6494, Rev. 1930.

76. State of Connecticut v. Frank Palko, Case and Points, "Brief for Appellee," p. 39.

77. Ibid., "Brief for the State (Appellant)," p. 25.

78. *State of Connecticut* v. *Frank Palko,* 121 Conn. 669, 670–82 (1936).

79. State of Connecticut v. Frank Palko, Case and Points, Trial Transcript, p. 284.

80. Ibid., pp. 281, 355–56. Steve Burke was the third brother.

81. Ibid., "Brief for Appellant (Accused)," pp. 11–12.

82. Ibid., "Brief for the State of Connecticut," pp. 6–11.

83. *State of Connecticut* v. *Frank Palko,* 122 Conn. 529 (1937), 530–42.

84. *Palko* v. *Connecticut,* "Brief for the Appellant," p. 3.

85. *Thomas E. Kepner* v. *United States,* 195 U.S. 100 (1904).

86. "Brief for the Appellant," pp. 31, 40.

87. Ibid., p. 69.

88. "Brief for the State of Connecticut," pp. 6–7, 35.

89. Ibid., pp. 22–23, 35.

90. John T. Noonan Jr., "Ordered Liberty: Cardozo and the Constitution," *Cardozo Law Review,* 1 (1979), 282.

91. John Raeburn Green, "The Bill of Rights, the Fourteenth Amendment and the Supreme Court," *Michigan Law Review,* 46 (1948); rpt. in Robert G. McCloskey, ed., *Es-*

says in Constitutional Law (New York, 1957), p. 392. See also Jay A. Sigler, *Double Jeopardy: The Development of a Legal and Social Policy* (Ithaca, N.Y., 1969).

92. *Powell* v. *Alabama* 287 U.S. 45 (1932). See William E. Leuchtenburg, "The Birth of America's Second Bill of Rights," in *The Supreme Court Reborn: The Constitutional Revolution in the Age of Roosevelt* (New York, 1995), p. 248.

93. *Palko* v. *Connecticut,* 302 U.S. 319 (1937).

94. *Bridgeport Post,* April 13, 1938.

95. Green, "The Bill of Rights," p. 392.

96. Richard C. Cortner, *The Supreme Court and the Second Bill of Rights: The Fourteenth Amendment and the Nationalization of Civil Liberties* (Madison, Wis., 1981), p. 131.

97. The cases were *Betts* v. *Brady* 316 U.S. 455 (1942) and *Adamson* v. *California* 332 U.S. 46 (1947).

98. Cortner, *The Supreme Court and the Second Bill of Rights,* pp. 138ff.

99. *Benton* v. *Maryland,* 395 U.S. 784, 793–96.

100. Ibid., 808–09.

101. George W. Alger, "The Passing of the Alibi," *Atlantic Monthly,* 164 (July 1939), 105–10.

Epilogue: A Contested Legacy

1. Cardozo to Charles C. Burlingham, Sept. 3, 1932, Burlingham MSS, Box 22.

2. Drew Pearson and Robert S. Allen, *More Merry-Go-Round* (New York, 1932), p. 100.

3. Cardozo to Maud Nathan, Aug. 5, 1936, Nathan MSS.

4. "The Honorable Supreme Court," *Fortune,* 13 (May 1936), 80–82.

5. Cardozo to Maud Nathan, May 16, 1936, George Hellman MSS.

6. Joseph P. Pollard, *Mr. Justice Cardozo: A Liberal Mind in Action* (New York, 1935), p. 7.

7. Roscoe Pound to Cardozo, May 3, 1935 (replying to Cardozo to Pound, May 1, 1935, a letter that I could not locate), Pound MSS, Box 9.

8. Cardozo to Nathan, May 24, 1935, George Hellman MSS.

9. Cardozo to Thomas Reed Powell, Sept. 8, 1935, Powell MSS, Box 2. Powell's review appeared in *New York Herald Tribune Books,* Sept. 8, 1935.

10. Cardozo to Charles C. Burlingham, Oct. 15, 1935, Burlingham MSS, Box 22.

11. Joseph Rauh to Annie Nathan Meyer, Jan. 4, 1938, Meyer MSS.

12. Cardozo to Charles C. Burlingham, Dec. 31, 1937, Burlingham MSS, Box 22.

13. Cardozo to Roosevelt, Jan. 5, 1938, Franklin D. Roosevelt MSS, President's Secretary's File, 186.

14. Christopher S. Sargent to Annie Nathan Meyer, Dec. 14, 1938, Meyer MSS.

15. Joseph Rauh to Meyer, Jan. 10, 1938, ibid.

16. Annie Nathan Meyer, *It's Been Fun* (New York, 1951), p. 92.

17. Harlan Fiske Stone to Lehman, April 26, Stone MSS, Box 19.

18. Lehman to Stone, April 28, 1938, ibid.

19. Lehman to Stone, June 1, 1938, ibid., Box 74.

20. Joseph Rauh to Learned Hand, May 30, 1938, Hand MSS.

21. Cardozo to Stone and Mrs. Stone, June 14, 1938, Stone MSS, Box 74.

22. *New York Times,* July 10, 1938.

23. Ibid.

24. Burlingham to Felix Frankfurter, July 19, 1938, Frankfurter MSS (LC), Reel 19,

25. See Jacob Billikopf to Stephen S. Wise, Aug. 9, 1938, Wise MSS, Box 105.

26. Arthur T. Weil, "Cardozo, Philosopher-Jurist, Passes, *American Hebrew* (July 15, 1938), p. 4.

27. Death notice, Congregation Shearith Israel MSS, Box 15.

28. *New York Herald Tribune,* July 17, 1938.

29. Ibid.

30. Clipping, Benjamin N. Cardozo MSS (CU), Box 6.

31. Burlingham to Harlan Fiske Stone, July 31, 1938, Stone MSS, Box 7.

32. "A Tribute to Benjamin Nathan Cardozo," July 19, 1938, Oscar Cox MSS, Box 135.

33. *Proceedings of the Bar and Officers of the Supreme Court of the United States in Memory of Benjamin Nathan Cardozo* (Washington, 1938), p. 37. The phrase "saintly character" was used by Acheson.

34. Ibid., pp. 23–26.

35. Warner W. Gardner to Homer Cummings, Dec. 9, 1938, Cummings MSS, Box 85.

36. Roosevelt to Cummings, Dec. 15, 1938, ibid.

37. *Proceedings,* pp. 81–94.

38. Ibid., 95–101.

39. John T. Moutoux, "In Washington," *Knoxville News Sentinel,* Dec. 26, 1938, clipping in Cummings MSS, Box 85.

40. Hellman to George Engelhard, Oct. 26, 1938, Cardozo MSS (CU).

41. "Working titles," Hellman MSS, Box 39; Meyer to Hellman, March 22, 1940, ibid., Box 8; Nathan to Hellman, March 25, 1940, ibid.

42. Stephen S. Wise to Hellman, Jan. 16, 1939, Wise MSS.

43. Hellman to Wise, Jan. 18, 1939, Cardozo MSS.

44. Charles C. Burlingham to Edgar J. Nathan, Nov. 18, 1955, Burlingham MSS, Box 2.

45. George S. Hellman to Lehman, Sept. 7, 1938, Hellman MSS, Box 8.

46. Lehman to Hellman, April 13, 1939, ibid.

47. Lehman to Hellman, Sept. 20, 1938, Cardozo MSS, Box 8.

48. Lehman to Karl Llewellyn, Dec. 19, 1938, Llewellyn MSS.

49. Review by James Reid Parker, *Saturday Review of Literature,* April 15, 1940, p. 3.

50. *New York Times Book Review,* April 14, 1938.

51. Charles C. Burlingham to Edgar J. Nathan, Nov. 18, 1955, Burlingham MSS, Box 2.

52. *New York Herald Tribune Books,* March 21, 1940.

53. *Harvard Law Review,* 53 (1940), 1404–06.

54. Felix Frankfurter, "Mr. Justice Cardozo and Public Law," *Columbia Law Review,* 39 (1939), 88–118.

55. Warren A. Seavey, "Negligence—Subjective or Objective?" *Harvard Law Review,* 41 (1928), 6. *Palsgraf v. Long Island Railroad Co.,* 248 N.Y. 339 (1928).

56. John T. Noonan, "The Passengers of *Palsgraf,*" in *Persons and Masks of the Law: Cardozo, Holmes, Jefferson, and Wythe as Makers of the Masks* (New York, 1976), ch. 4. See also Walter Otto Weyrauch, "Law as Mask—Legal Ritual and Relevance," *California Law Review,* 66 (1978), 699–711.

57. Noonan, *Persons and Masks of the Law,* p. 149.

58. "Our Lady of the Common Law," in Margaret E. Hall, ed., *Selected Writings of Benjamin Nathan Cardozo* (New York, 1947), p. 94.

MANUSCRIPT SOURCES

Library of Congress: Hugo Black MSS; Calvin Coolidge MSS; Felix Frankfurter MSS; Warren G. Harding MSS; Charles Evans Hughes MSS; James Landis MSS; Joseph Rauh MSS; Theodore Roosevelt MSS; Harlan Fiske Stone MSS; William Howard Taft MSS; Willis Van Devanter MSS; Woodrow Wilson MSS

Columbia University: Mrs. Julius Adler MSS; Willard Bartlett MSS; Nicholas Murray Butler MSS; Melville Cane MSS; Benjamin N. Cardozo MSS; Charles Evans Hughes MSS; Joseph M. Price MSS; E. R. A. Seligman MSS; Harlan Fiske Stone MSS

School of International Affairs, Columbia University: Herbert H. Lehman MSS

Barnard College Archives: Annie Nathan Meyer MSS

New York Historical Society: Loren Reich MSS; Seligman Family MSS; Jonathan Mayhew Wainwright MSS

New York City Municipal Archives: District Attorney (Charles S. Whitman) Official Correspondence; District Attorney Case Files

Congregation Shearith Israel: Congregation Shearith Israel MSS; David de Sola Pool MSS

Stephen S. Wise Free Synagogue: Stephen S. Wise MSS

American Jewish Committee Archives: American Jewish Committee MSS

Rare Books and Manuscripts Division, The New York Public Library, Astor, Lenox and Tilden Foundations: Rupert L. Joseph MSS; George S. Hellman MSS; Miscellaneous Collection; Gilbert H. Montague Collection

New York State Archives: Martin H. Glynn MSS; Charles S. Whitman MSS; Blotters of Governor's Actions; Internal Records of the Court of Appeals

American Jewish Historical Society, Brandeis University: Stephen S. Wise MSS

American Jewish Archives, Cincinnati: Benjamin N. Cardozo MSS; Louis Marshall MSS

Central Zionist Archives, Jerusalem: Julian W. Mack MSS

Harvard University: Oswald Garrison Villard MSS

Harvard Law School Library: Louis D. Brandeis MSS; Charles C. Burlingham MSS; Benjamin N. Cardozo MSS; Zechariah Chafee MSS; Felix Frankfurter MSS; Sheldon Glueck MSS; Erwin Griswold MSS; Learned Hand MSS; Oliver Wendell Holmes MSS; Manley Ottmer Hudson MSS; Roscoe Pound MSS; Thomas Reed Powell MSS

Radcliffe College: Maud Nathan MSS

Yale University: Edwin W. Borchard MSS; Charles E. Clark MSS; Jane Perry Clark MSS; Jerome Frank MSS; Charles Nagel MSS; Henry L. Stimson MSS

Division of Rare and Manuscript Collections, Kroch Library, Cornell University: Livingston Farrand MSS; Jacob Gould Schurman MSS; Frank Thilly MSS; Mynderse Van Cleef MSS; Records of the Dean of the Law School

Department of Special Collections, The University of Chicago Library: Morris R. Cohen MSS

University of Chicago Law School: Karl Llewellyn MSS

University of Louisville Law School: Louis D. Brandeis MSS

Franklin D. Roosevelt Library: Franklin D. Roosevelt MSS; Oscar Cox MSS

Herbert C. Hoover Library: Herbert Hoover MSS

Indiana University: Lewis Browne MSS

Syracuse University: Paul Shipman Andrews MSS

University of Michigan: Henry M. Bates MSS

Special Collections Department, University of Virginia Library: Homer Cummings MSS

UCLA: Ernest Carroll Moore MSS; Chancellor's Office Records

University of California: Minutes of the Board of Regents

Freedom of Information Act: Records of the FBI

Privately held: Lambert Family MSS

National Archives: Central Files of the Department of Justice

SELECTED BIBLIOGRAPHY

Ackerman, Kenneth D. *The Gold Ring: Jim Fisk, Jay Gould, and Black Friday, 1869.* New York, 1988.

Alger, George W. "The Passing of the Alibi," *Atlantic Monthly,* 164 (July 1939).

Atkinson, David N. "Mr. Justice Cardozo: A Common Law Judge on a Public Law Court," *California Western Law Review,* 28 (1980).

Auerbach, Jerold S. *Rabbis and Lawyers: The Journey from Torah to Constitution.* Bloomington, Ind., 1990.

Barnard, Harry. *The Forging of an American Jew: The Life and Times of Judge Julian W. Mack.* New York, 1974.

Baskerville, Stephen W. *Of Laws and Limitations: An Intellectual Portrait of Louis Dembitz Brandeis.* Rutherford, N.J., 1994.

Birmingham, Stephen. *The Grandees: America's Sephardic Elite.* New York, 1971.

Breier, Alan, and Stacy A. Beller. "Early Parental Loss and Development of Adult Psychopathology," *Archives of General Psychiatry,* 45 (1988).

Bricker, Paul. "Justice Benjamin N. Cardozo: A Fresh Look at a Great Judge," *Ohio Northern University Law Review,* 11 (1984).

Bodenheimer, Edgar. "Cardozo's Views on Law and Adjudication Revisited," *University of California at Davis Law Review,* 22 (1989).

Brubaker, Stanley Charles. "Benjamin Nathan Cardozo: An Intellectual Biography." Ph.D. diss., University of Virginia, 1979.

Burgess, John W. *Reminiscences of an American Scholar.* New York, 1934.

Cardozo, Benjamin N. "The Earl of Beaconsfield: A Jew as Prime Minister" In Michael Selzer, ed. *Disraeli, the Jew.* Great Barrington, Mass., 1993.

———*The Growth of the Law.* New Haven, 1924.

——— "Identity and Survivorship." In Allan McLane Hamilton and Lawrence Godkin, eds., *A System of Legal Medicine.* 2 vols. New York, 1897.

———*The Jurisdiction of the Court of Appeals of the State of New York.* Albany, 1903.

———*The Nature of the Judicial Process.* New Haven, 1921.

———*The Paradoxes of Legal Science.* New York, 1928.

Carmen, Ira H. "The President, Politics and the Power of Appointment: Hoover's Nomination of Mr. Justice Cardozo," *Virginia Law Review,* 55 (1969).

Carter, Robert Allan. *History of the Insanity Defense in New York State.* Albany, 1982.

Charges of the Bar Association of the City of New York against . . . Hon. Albert Cardozo, Justice of the Supreme Court . . . and Testimony thereunder taken before the Judiciary Committee of the Assembly of the State of New York. 4 vols. New York, 1872.

Cohen, Martin A., and Abraham J. Peck, eds. *Sephardim in the Americas: Studies in Culture and History.* Tuscaloosa, Ala., 1993.

Cohen, Naomi W. *Not Free to Desist: The American Jewish Committee, 1906–1966.* Philadelphia, 1972.

Cohen, Robert. *When the Old Left was Young: Student Radicals and America's First Mass Student Movement, 1929–1941.* New York, 1993.

Corbin, Arthur L. "The Judicial Process Revisited: Introduction," *Yale Law Journal,* 71 (Dec. 1961).

Cortner, Richard C. *The Supreme Court and the Second Bill of Rights: The Fourteenth Amendment and the Nationalization of Civil Liberties.* Madison, Wis., 1981.

de Sola Pool, David and Tamar. *An Old Faith in the New World: Portrait of Shearith Israel, 1654–1954.* New York, 1955.

Deutsch, Babbette. "Benjamin Cardozo—Idol of Bench and Bar," *New Yorker* (March 22, 1930).

Duxbury, Neil. "Jerome Frank and the Legacy of Legal Realism," *Journal of Law and Society,* 18 (1991).

Finkin, Matthew W. "'A Higher Order of Liberty in the Workplace': Academic Freedom and Tenure in the Vortex of Employment Practices and Law," *Law and Contemporary Problems,* 53 (Summer 1990).

Frank, Jerome N. *Law and the Modern Mind.* New York, 1930.

——— "The Speech of Judges: A Dissenting Opinion," *Virginia Law Review,* 29 (1943).

Frankfurter, Felix. "Mr. Justice Cardozo and Public Law," *Columbia Law Review,* 39 (1939).

Friedman, Richard D. "On Cardozo and Reputation: Legendary Judge, Underrated Justice?" *Cardozo Law Review,* 12 (1991).

Furman, Erna. *A Child's Parent Dies: Studies in Childhood Bereavement.* New Haven, 1974.

Gass, J. Ric. "Chemistry, Courtrooms, and Common Sense," *Journal of Chemical Education,* 67 (Jan.–Feb. 1990).

Geller, Jeffrey L., et al. "Feigned Insanity in Nineteenth Century America: Experts, Explanations, Evaluations and Exculpations," *Anglo-American Law Review,* 20 (Oct.–Dec. 1991).

Glennon, Robert Jerome. *The Iconoclast as Reformer: Jerome Frank's Impact on American Law.* Ithaca, 1985.

Goebel, Julius, Jr., et al. *A History of the School of Law, Columbia University.* New York, 1955.

Goldberg, John C. P. "Community and the Common Law Judge: Reconstructing Cardozo's Theoretical Writings," *New York University Law Review* 65 (Nov. 1990).

Goldstein, Robert Lloyd, and Merrill Rotter. "The Psychiatrist's Guide to Right and Wrong: Judicial Standards of Wrongfulness since McNaughtan," *Bulletin of the American Academy of Psychiatry and Law,* 16 (1988).

Goodhart, Arthur L. *Five Jewish Justices of the Common Law.* Oxford, 1949.

Green, John Raeburn. "The Bill of Rights, the Fourteenth Amendment and the Supreme Court," *Michigan Law Review,* 46 (1948). Rpt. in Robert G. McCloskey, ed. *Essays in Constitutional Law.* New York, 1957.

Hall, Margaret E., ed. *Selected Writings of Benjamin Nathan Cardozo.* New York, 1947.

Hellman, George C. *Benjamin N. Cardozo: American Judge.* New York, 1940.

Hershkowitz, Leo. *Tweed's New York: Another Look.* (Garden City, N.Y., 1977).

Hiscock, Frank H. "The Court of Appeals of New York: Some Features of Its Organization and Work," *Cornell Law Quarterly,* 14 (1920).

Holland, Henry M., Jr. "Cardozo on Legal Method: A Reconsideration," *Journal of Public Law,* 15 (1966).

——— "Mr. Justice Cardozo and the New Deal Court," *Journal of Public Law,* 12 (1963).

Hollinger, David A. *Morris R. Cohen and the Scientific Ideal.* Cambridge, Mass., 1975.

Howe, Mark DeWolfe, ed. *Holmes-Laski Letters.* 2 vols., New York, 1963.

Hull, N. E. H. "Restatement and Reform: A New Perspective on the Origins of the American Law Institute," *Law and History Review,* 8 (1990).

Hyman, Jerome I. "Benjamin N. Cardozo: A Preface to his Career at the Bar," *Brooklyn Law Review,* 10 (Oct. 1940).

Irons, Peter H. *The New Deal Lawyers.* Princeton, 1982.

Kaufman, Andrew L. "Benjamin N. Cardozo, Sephardic Jew." In *The Jewish Justices of the Supreme Court Revisited: Brandeis to Fortas, The Journal of Supreme Court History* (1994).

——— "Cardozo's Appointment to the Supreme Court," *Cardozo Law Review,* 1 (1979).

——— "The First Judge Cardozo: Albert, Father of Benjamin," *Journal of Law and Religion,* 11 (1994–95).

Konefsky, Alfred S. "How To Read, Or at Least Not Misread, Cardozo in the Allegheny College Case," *Buffalo Law Review,* 36 (1987).

Krueger, David W. "Childhood Parent Loss: Developmental Impact and Adult Psychopathology," *American Journal of Psychotherapy,* 37 (1983).

Lehman, Irving. *The Influence of Judge Cardozo on the Common Law.* Garden City, N.Y., 1942.

Leuchtenburg, William E. "The Birth of America's Second Bill of Rights." In *The Supreme Court Reborn: The Constitutional Revolution in the Age of Roosevelt.* New York, 1995.

Levy, Beryl Harold, ed. *Cardozo and Frontiers of Legal Thinking.* New York, 1938, rev. ed., 1969.

Lewinson, Edwin R. *John Purroy Mitchel: The Boy Mayor of New York.* New York, 1965.

Lurrie, Brainerd. "Married Women's Contracts: A Study in Conflict of Law Method," *University of Chicago Law Review,* 25 (1958).

Manz, William H. "Cardozo's use of Authority: An Empirical Study," *California Western Law Review,* 32 (1995).

Mason, Alpheus Thomas. *Harlan Fiske Stone: Pillar of the Law.* New York, 1956.

McDade, T. M. "Crime Hunt," *Armchair Detective,* 18 (Fall 1985).

Means, Cyril C. "The Law of New York Concerning Abortion and the Status of the Foetus, 1664–1968: A Case of Cessation of Constitutionality," *New York Law Forum,* 14 (1968).

Meyer, Annie Nathan. *Black Souls: A Play in Six Acts.* New Bedford, Mass., 1934.

———*It's Been Fun.* New York, 1951.

Mitchell, Jane E., et al. "Masculinity and Femininity in Twin Children: Genetic and Environmental Factors," *Child Development*, 60 (1989).

Moran, Richard. *Knowing Right from Wrong: The Insanity Defense of Daniel McNaughtan*. New York, 1981.

Mushkat, Jerome. *The Reconstruction of the New York Democracy, 1861–1874*. Rutherford, N.J., 1981.

Nackenoff, Carol. *The Fictional Republic: Horatio Alger and American Political Discourse*. New York, 1994.

Noonan, John T., Jr. "Ordered Liberty: Cardozo and the Constitution," *Cardozo Law Review*, 1 (1979).

———— "The Passengers of Palsgraf," in *Persons and Masks of the Law*. New York, 1976.

Odem, Mary E. *Delinquent Daughters: Protecting and Policing Adolescent Female Sexuality in the United States, 1885–1920*. Chapel Hill, N.C., 1995.

Ormond, Carol J., and John Denver. "Justice Cardozo: A Mediator of Jurisprudential Thought in the 1920s and 1930s," *Cooley Law Review*, 2 (1984).

Paper, Lewis J. *Brandeis*. Englewood Cliffs, N.J., 1983.

Pearson, Drew, and Robert S. Allen. *More Merry-Go-Round*. New York, 1932.

Peck, David W. *Decision at Law*. New York, 1961.

Perlin, Michael L. *The Jurisprudence of the Insanity Defense*. Durham, N.C., 1994.

Pollard, Joseph P. *Mr. Justice Cardozo: A Liberal Mind in Action*. New York, 1935.

Posner, Richard A. *Cardozo: A Study in Reputation*. Chicago, 1990.

Probert, Walter. "Applied Jurisprudence: A Case Study of Interpretive Reasoning in *MacPherson* v. *Buick* and Its Precedents," *University of California at Davis Law Review* (1988).

Proceedings of the Bar and Officers of the Supreme Court of the United States in Memory of Benjamin Nathan Cardozo. Washington, 1938.

Quen, Jacques M. "The Case of Anna Aumuller and Father Hans Schmidt," *Newsletter of the American Academy of Psychiatry and the Law*, 12 (Sept. 1987).

Ragan, Paul V., and Thomas H. McGlashan. "Childhood Parental Death and Adult Psychopathology," *American Journal of Psychiatry*, 143 (1986).

Reagan, Leslie J. "'About to Meet Her Maker': Women, Doctors, Dying Declarations, and the State's Investigation of Abortion, Chicago, 1867–1940," *Journal of American History*, 77 (1991).

Rodgers, Audrey T. *Virgin and Whore: The Image of Women in the Poetry of William Carlos Williams*. Jefferson, N.C., 1987.

Rodgers, William H., Jr., and Linda A. Rodgers. "The Disparity between Due Process and Full Faith and Credit: The Problem of the Somewhere Wife," *Columbia Law Review*, 67 (1967).

Ross, Charles Stanley. "Cardozo and the Place of Tradition in Creating Law," *Legal Studies Forum*, 17 (1993).

Rothman, Sheila M. *Woman's Proper Place*. New York, 1978.

Rutter, Michael, and Jane Redshaw. "Annotation: Growing Up as a Twin: Twin-Singleton Differences in Psychological Development," *Journal of Child Psychology*, 32 (1991).

Sanier, A. L., ed. *Law Is Justice: Notable Opinions of Mr. Justice Cardozo*. New York, 1938.

Sarna, Jonathan D. "'The Greatest Jew in the World since Jesus Christ': The Jewish Legacy of Louis D. Brandeis," *American Jewish History*, 81 (1994).

Scharnhorst, Gary. "The Brewster Incident: Additional Evidence," *Newsboy: The Publication of the Horatio Alger Society,* 19 (1980).
———*Horatio Alger, Jr.* Boston, 1980.
Scharnhorst, Gary, with Jack Bales. *The Lost Life of Horatio Alger, Jr.* Bloomington, Ind., 1985.
Scheinfeld, Amram. *Twins and Supertwins.* Philadelphia, 1967.
Sekaer, Christina. "Toward a Definition of `Childhood Mourning,'" *American Journal of Psychotherapy,* 41 (April 1987), 216.
Sigler, Jay A. *Double Jeopardy: The Development of a Legal and Social Policy.* Ithaca, 1969.
Strum, Philippa. *Louis D. Brandeis: Justice for the People.* Cambridge, Mass., 1984.
Tennant, Christopher. "Parental Loss in Childhood: Its Effect in Adult Life," *Archives of General Psychiatry,* 45 (Nov. 1988).
Urofsky, Melvin I. *A Voice That Spoke for Justice: The Life and Times of Stephen S. Wise.* Albany, 1982.
Urofsky, Melvin I., and David W. Levy, eds. *"Half Brother, Half Son": The Letters of Louis D. Brandeis to Felix Frankfurter.* Norman, Okla., 1991.
Voss, Carl Hermann, ed. *Stephen S. Wise: Servant of the People, Selected Letters.* Philadelphia, 1969.
Weisberg, Richard H. "Law, Literature and Cardozo's Judicial Poetics," *Cardozo Law Review,* 1 (1979).
Wesser, Robert F. *A Response to Progressivism: The Democratic Party and New York Politics, 1902–1918.* New York, 1986.
Westgard, Gilbert K., II. "Following the Trail of Horatio Alger, Jr.," *Newsboy: The Publication of the Horatio Alger Society,* 18 (1979).
Weyrauch, Walter Otto. "Law as Mask—Legal Ritual and Relevance," *California Law Review,* 66 (1978).
White, G. Edward. *The American Judicial Tradition: Profiles of Leading American Judges.* New York, 2nd ed., 1988.
Wigmore, John H. "Evidence Obtained by Illegal Search and Seizure," *Journal of the American Bar Association,* 8 (1922).
Wise, Stephen S. *Challenging Years: The Autobiography of Stephen Wise.* New York, 1949.
Zuckerman, Michael. "The Nursery Tales of Horatio Alger," *American Quarterly,* 24 (May 1972).

INDEX